D0571980

Well Advised

Your Guide for Making Smart Health Decisions

Well Advised

Your Guide for Making Smart
Health Decisions

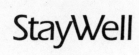

Park Nicollet

Park Nicollet Institute

StayWell®

Executive Editor: Pam Garfield
Project Editor: Janet Davis
Production Manager: Michele Schumaker-Trottier
Designer: Renée Duenow
Illustrator: Jeanne Robertson
Cover Designer: Jeanne Wolfgeher

Park Nicollet

Park Nicollet Institute

Editor: Paul E. Terry, PhD
Managing Editor: Lisa Harvey, MPH
Senior Writer: Lori Asplund, BS
Writers: Lisa Bartels-Rabb, MSJ;
Jeanne Mettner, MA; Linda Picone, BS
Publications Coordinator: Sheila Buffie

SECOND EDITION

Text copyright © 2003 by Park Nicollet Institute, Park Nicollet Health Services.
Illustrations copyright © 2003 The StayWell Company.
Previous edition copyrighted 1999, 1995.

All rights reserved. No part of this publication may be reproduced, stored in a retrieval system, or transmitted, in any form or by any means, electronic, mechanical, photocopying, recording, or otherwise, without written permission of the publisher.

The material in this publication is for general information only and is not intended to provide specific advice or recommendations for any individual. Your doctor or other health-care professional must be consulted for advice with regard to your individual situation.

The StayWell Company
780 Township Line Road
Yardley, PA 19067

Composition by Graphic World, Inc.
Printing/binding by Banta

ISBN: 1-4111-0000-X

03 04 05 / 10 9 8 7 6 5 4 3 2 1

Senior Medical Editors

Allan Kind, MD; Kenneth Olson, MD;
Jeremy Springer, MD

Reviewers/Contributors

Allergy: David Graft, MD;
William Schoenwetter, MD; Richard Sveum, MD

Cardiology: Steve Benton, MD;
J. Mark Haugland, MD;
Richard Madlon-Kay, MD; Jackson Thatcher, MD

Dermatology: Spencer Holmes, MD;
Louis Rusin, MD

ENT: Gerard O'Halloran, MD

Endocrinology: Marion Franz, RD

Family Practice: Donald Abrams, MD;
Barbara Benjamin, MD; Michael Dukinfield, MD;
Janet Frost, RN; John Haugen, MD;
Mark Hench, MD; Jeanne Hesse, MD;
Douglas Lowin, MD; Joseph Lukaska, MD;
Donald Lynch, MD; Rosa Marroquin, MD;
Charles McCoy, MD; David VonWeiss, MD

Gastroenterology: Ann Kools, MD;
Michael Levy, MD

Infectious Diseases: Leslie Baken, MD

Internal Medicine: David Abelson, MD;
Avis Baumann, RN; Nancy Jarvis, MD;
Jane Oh, MD; Jennifer Olson, MD;
Barbara Steigauf, RN; Anthony Woolley, MD

Mental Health: Susan Czapiewski, MD;
Joseph Nelson

Neurology: Daniel Freking, MD;
Sandra Hanson, MD; Eric Schenk, MD

OB/GYN: Kathy Baer, RN; Janet Claxton, NP;
Barbara Davenport, NP; Robert Junnila, MD;
Laura Mueller, MD; Leslie Pratt, MD;
Lois Satterberg, NP; Deborah Thorp, MD

Occupational Medicine: David Parker, MD;
Robert Gorman, MD

Oncology: Steven Duane, MD

Ophthalmology: Timothy Diegel, MD;
Richard Freeman, MD; Anton Willerscheidt, MD

Orthopedics: Matthew Putnam, MD;
Gregg Strathy, MD

Pediatrics: Renner Anderson, MD;
Jayne Boche, MD; David Griffin, MD;
Rebecca Kajander, CPNP, MPH;
Robert Karasov, MD; Douglas Martin, MD

Pharmacy: Richard Bleck, RPh;
Scott Bryngelson, RPh; Roger Mickelson, RPh

Podiatry: Anthony Pojman, MD

Preventive Services: Joan Bissen, RD;
Susan Deno, RD; Mark DePaolis, MD;
Christine Follett, MPH; Jinnet Fowles, PhD;
Susan Hanson, RD; Larry Kitzman;
Mary Kruse, MA; Linda Leimer, RN;
Penny Marsala, MA, MLIS; Deborah Meade, RN;
Jane Norstrom, MA; Laura Olevitch, MS

Pulmonary Medicine: Joan Fox, MD;
Kevin Komadina, MD; A. Stuart Hanson, MD

Rehabilitation Medicine: Ann Brutlag, MD;
  Daniel Kurtti, MD

Rheumatology: Scott Glickstein, MD;
  Eric Schned, MD

Urgent Care: Paul Bearmon, MD; Gary Coon, MD;
  Thomas Haas, MD; John Kaintz, MD;
  Carol Manning, MD; Mary Ratz, MD;
  Suzanne Schaefer, MD

Urology: William Borkon, MD;
  William Sharer, MD; Erol Uke, MD

INTRODUCTION

Well *Advised* was written to give you the information you need for a lifetime of good health. Your knowledge, actions, and beliefs have more to do with your future health than anything the medical system has to offer. And the more you know, the better your health care experiences will be.

Well Advised answers your questions about common health problems and offers clear, simple advice. It also includes information on how to handle medical emergencies, how to be an active health care consumer, and how to take charge of your health through lifestyle choices and good health decisions. The advice in this book is based on proven, scientific evidence and has been reviewed by doctors, nurses, and other health care professionals.

Rely on *Well Advised* to care for minor problems and make informed health care decisions. However, like any book of its kind, *Well Advised* should not be considered a substitute for quality medical care from your doctor or other health care provider. Also, consider your own health history and medical condition when reading the advice presented here, and check with your own

doctor if you are not sure if the self-care tips apply to you.

The term *doctor* is used throughout this book, but the person you see may not always be a doctor. It is likely that many other health care professionals will be involved in your care, including physician's assistants and nurse practitioners. A physician's assistant or nurse practitioner may even be your primary care provider. In some cases, you may also receive treatment from specialists—doctors who have extensive training in specific areas of medicine.

How to Use the "What to do about . . ." Guides

The "What to do about . . ." guides found throughout this book can help you make decisions about the best course of treatment when you are ill or injured. If you still have doubts after using these guides, call your doctor. *These guides are not for infants under 3 months old.* Always call your doctor if you are concerned that your infant is seriously sick.

In each "What to do about . . ." guide, possible Symptoms/Signs are accompanied by a recommended Action.

Following are explanations of the Actions recommended in the "What to do about . . ." guides:

- *First Aid/Self-care*: Symptoms can usually be treated at home. If symptoms persist, you should call your doctor for advice.

- *Continue self-care*: You may continue to follow the recommended self-care steps if they are working and your symptoms are getting better.

- *Call doctor*: Symptoms may be treated at home or they may require a visit to your doctor. Usually, you and your doctor need to share additional information about your condition to decide what is best for you.

- *See doctor*: Symptoms need to be evaluated by a doctor. When you call to make an appointment, your doctor will help you determine how soon you need to be seen.

- *Go to hospital*: Symptoms in this category are serious and should usually be seen within two hours. Depending on your health insurance, you may choose to call your doctor to determine if you should be seen in the doctor's office, in an urgent care center, or in an emergency room.

- *Call 911*: Symptoms in this category are life threatening and require immediate medical treatment.

CONTENTS

SECTION 1:
FIRST AID AND URGENT CARE, 1

First Aid and Urgent Care, 3
Using the Emergency Room, 3
Allergic Shock, 4
Bites: Human and Animal, 6
Bites and Stings: Insect and Spider, 7
Bites: Snake, 10
Bites: Tick, 12
   Lyme Disease, 14
Burns, 15
Burns: Chemical, 17
Carbon Monoxide Poisoning, 19
Choking, 21
Cuts and Scrapes, 22
Dehydration, 25
Dislocations, 27
Dizziness, 28
Drowning/Near-Drowning, 31
Ear Emergencies, 33
Electrical Shock, 34
Fishhook Wounds, 36
Fractures, 37
Frostbite, 39
Head Injuries, 41
Heart Attack, 43
Heat-Related Problems, 44
Hyperventilation, 46
Hypothermia, 47
Marine-Life Stings, 49

Poisoning, 51
Seizure, 53
Shock, 55
Slivers/Splinters, 57
Smashed Finger or Toe, 58
Stroke, 59
Tooth Knocked Out or Broken, 60

SECTION 2:
COMMON PROBLEMS, 61

Skin, Hair, and Nail Problems, 63
Acne, 63
Athlete's Foot, 65
Blisters, 66
Boils, 37
Bruises, 69
Corns, 69
Dandruff, 70
Hair Loss, 71
Hives, 73
Ingrown Toenail, 75
Jock Itch, 76
Lice, 77
Mouth Sores, 79
   Cold Sores, 80
   Canker Sores, 81
Poison Ivy/Oak/Sumac, 82
Rashes, 85
Ringworm, 87
Rosacea, 88

Contents

Scabies, 90
Skin Cancer, 92
Sunburn, 94
Warts, 97

Head and Neck and Nerve Problems, 99

Encephalitis, 99
Headaches, 101
Meningitis, 104
Neck Pain, 106
Numbness and Tingling, 109

Eye Problems, 111

Burning Eyes, 111
Foreign Object in the Eye, 113
Pinkeye, 116
Styes, 118
Vision Problems, 119

Ear, Nose, and Throat Problems, 123

Bad Breath, 123
Earaches, 125
    Middle Ear Infections, 125
    Swimmer's Ear/Earwax Buildup, 127
    Ear Stuffiness/Airplane Ears, 128
Hoarseness/Laryngitis, 129
Nosebleed, 131
Sinusitis, 132
Sore Throats, 134
Swollen Glands, 136
Tinnitus, 138

Stomach And Bowel Problems, 141

Abdominal Pain, 141
Black or Bloody Stools, 146
Colorectal Cancer, 147
Constipation, 150
Diarrhea, 152
Foodborne Illness, 154
Gastroesophageal Reflux Disease, 156
Heartburn, 158
Hemorrhoids, 160
Hernia, 161

Inguinal Hernia, 161
    Hiatal Hernia, 162
Rectal Pain or Itching, 163
Viral Hepatitis, 165
Vomiting, 168

Kidney and Bladder Problems, 171

Kidney Stones, 172
Urinary Incontinence, 174
Urinary Tract Infections, 177

Heart and Circulation Problems, 181

Chest Pain, 181
Coronary Artery Disease, 183
High Blood Cholesterol, 189
High Blood Pressure (Hypertension), 195
Palpitations, 197
Stroke, 198

Lung Problems, 201

Allergies, 201
Asthma, 205
Bronchitis (Acute), 209
Colds (Viral Upper-Respiratory
    Infections), 211
COPD, 213
Cough, 215
Fever in Adults, 217
Flu (Influenza), 219
Lung Cancer, 222
Pneumonia, 225
Shortness of Breath, 227
Wheezing, 229

Muscle and Joint Problems, 231

Ankle Pain, 231
Back Pain, 234
Body Aches, 241
    Arthritis, 241
    Fibromyalgia, 242
    Joint Pain, 243
    Muscle Cramps, 243
    Muscle Imbalance, 244

Muscle Tightness, 244
Referred Pain, 244
Repetitive Motion Injuries, 244
Elbow Pain, 246
Foot Pain, 248
Hip and Thigh Pain, 253
Knee Pain, 257
Lower-Leg Pain, 262
Osteoporosis, 265
The RICE Method: Rest, Ice, Compression,
    Elevation, 267
Shoulder Pain, 268
Wrist and Hand Pain, 270

Health Concerns for Men, 273
Prostate Problems, 273
Testicular Problems, 277
    Testicular Cancer, 277
    Testicular Pain, 279

Health Concerns for Women, 281
Bleeding Between Periods, 281
Breast Cancer, 283
Cervical Cancer, 287
Endometriosis, 288
Menopause, 290
Menstrual Pain, 294
Missed Periods, 295
Pelvic Inflammatory Disease, 297
Premenstrual Syndrome, 299
Toxic Shock Syndrome, 302
Vaginal Discharge and Irritation, 303

Sexual Issues, 307
Birth Control, 307
Erection Problems, 312
Loss of Sexual Desire, 314
Sexual Concerns, 316

Sexually Transmitted Diseases, 319
Common Sexually Transmitted Diseases, 319
    Chlamydia, 320
    Genital Herpes, 321

Genital Warts, 321
Gonorrhea, 322
Hepatitis B Virus, 323
Human Immunodeficiency Virus, 324
Syphilis, 325
Trichomoniasis, 326

Mind-Body Problems, 329
Alcohol and Drug Abuse, 329
Anxiety, 332
Depression, 334
Stress, 336
Suicide, 339
Violent Behavior, 340

Sleep Problems, 343
Fatigue, 343
    Chronic Fatigue Syndrome, 345
Insomnia, 346
Sleep Apnea, 349

Endocrine Problems, 351
Diabetes, 351
Hyperthyroidism, 354
Hypothyroidism, 356

Special Concerns for Children, 359
Attention Deficit/Hyperactivity Disorder, 359
Chicken Pox, 361
Colic, 364
Cradle Cap, 366
Croup, 367
Diarrhea, 369
Fever, 371
Fifth Disease, 373
Growing Pains, 374
Hand-Foot-and-Mouth Disease, 374
Impetigo, 376
Lead Poisoning, 377
Pinworms, 379
Children's Rashes, 381
Tonsillitis, 382
Vomiting, 384

SECTION 3:
HEALTHY LIVING, 387

Health Care at Home, 389
Equipping Your Home for Self-Care, 389
Managing Your Medicine, 390

Lifestyle Choices, 399
Activity, 399
Healthy Eating, 403
Maintaining a Healthy Weight, 407
Smoking, 413

Preventing Health Problems, 417
Immunizations, 418
Recommendations for Routine Preventive
    Care, 420
    Birth to 24 Months, 420
    2 to 6 Years, 420
    7 to 11 Years, 420
    12 to 18 Years, 420
    Ages 19 to 39, 421
    Ages 40 to 64, 422
    Ages 65 and Older, 422

SECTION 4:
YOUR ROLE AS A HEALTH CARE CONSUMER, 425

Your Role as a Health Care Consumer, 427
Choosing a Doctor, 427
Deciding About Surgery, 428
Family and Personal Medical History, 432
Finding Quality Health Information
    on the Web, 438
If Your Doctor Recommends
    Hospitalization, 439
Complementary and Alternative
    Medicine, 440
Preparing for an Office Visit, 443
Reviewing Medical Fees and Bills, 444
Seeking Quality Health Care, 445

Resource List, 449

INDEX, 455

Well Advised

Your Guide for Making Smart Health Decisions

1 FIRST AID AND URGENT CARE

Many accidents, injuries, and serious medical symptoms require immediate attention. This section explains how to handle these situations—whether they require first aid, emergency medical care, or both. Review this information before an accident occurs, so you are prepared to make the best decisions when faced with an emergency. ∷

First Aid and Urgent Care

Using the Emergency Room

When you or someone you love is sick, it isn't easy to wait for relief. People often rush to a hospital emergency room with things like the flu, earaches, and sore throats. Although an emergency room can treat almost anything, some visits may not be covered by your insurance company.

An emergency room visit is always covered by insurance if the condition is life threatening. It's a good idea to know which hospitals are covered by your plan, so you don't have to worry about it when you actually have an emergency. If your condition is so serious that traveling to a plan hospital might put your health in danger, go to the nearest hospital or call an ambulance. In a life-threatening situation, insurance plans will usually cover a visit to any emergency room, not just those of their member hospitals.

If your condition is not life threatening, you should go to your clinic or urgent care center instead of the emergency room. Even minor broken bones and wounds requiring stitches can be treated in a clinic. When the clinic and urgent care centers are closed, go to an emergency room.

Co-payments for emergency room care—if your insurance plan requires them—are usually much higher than co-payments for urgent care center services and clinic visits. If you have a condition that's not life threatening, it's up to you to decide if the cost of an emergency room visit is worth it to you.

Allergic Shock

An allergy is your body's reaction to things in the environment. You can be allergic to certain animals or foods, to chemicals, to insect stings, or to pollen in the air. The substances that cause allergies are called allergens. Some allergies are so mild that you may not even know that you have one. But some allergic reactions can be so severe that they put your life in danger. When you go into allergic shock, or anaphylaxis, your whole body reacts to the allergen that affects you.

Causes

You are most likely to go into allergic shock after taking a drug or eating something you are allergic to, or after an insect sting. Allergic shock also can happen after skin contact with an allergen, such as latex. Under certain conditions, you can develop allergic shock while exercising.

Symptoms

Mild allergic reactions can include sniffling, sneezing, and watery eyes, almost like the symptoms of a cold. You may also have a mild rash. When you go into allergic shock, your whole body can be involved. Allergic shock can happen within 15 minutes of exposure to an allergen, so quick action is needed. Signs of allergic shock include:

- Choking or gasping for air
- Difficulty swallowing/lump in throat
- Extensive facial swelling
- Swelling of lips, tongue, or throat
- Dusky, bluish color of lips or nails
- Tight feeling in throat that persists or progresses
- Trouble speaking or husky voice
- Persistent coughing and difficulty breathing
- Cool, clammy, pale skin
- Significant weakness or dizziness
- Drowsiness, confusion, or loss of consciousness
- Seizures

First Aid

- Some people with severe allergies carry an EPIPEN, a syringe that injects a medication that makes the reaction less severe. If the person shows symptoms of a severe allergic reaction, use the EPIPEN immediately.
- A double dose of Benadryl can be given to help control the reaction if no EPIPEN is available.
- Call 911.

What to do about Allergic Shock

Symptom/Sign	Action
Mild allergic reaction that resembles a cold	Self-care
Rash accompanying the allergy	Self-care and call doctor
Runny nose, watery eyes, and sneezing that last longer than 10 to 14 days	Call doctor
Rapid pulse, flushed face or skin, bluish color around lips*	Go to hospital
Severe gastrointestinal symptoms, such as vomiting or diarrhea*	Go to hospital
Insect sting causing a widespread rash* (see Bites and Stings: Insect and Spider, p. 7)	Go to hospital
Allergic reaction including chest tightness, wheezing, and a hivelike rash	Call 911
Choking or difficulty swallowing or breathing*	Call 911
Swelling of lips, tongue, or throat*	Call 911

*If these symptoms occur within 1 to 15 minutes after exposure to allergen, remember: Allergic reactions are potentially emergency conditions; if you are concerned, call your doctor immediately or go to an urgent care center or an emergency room.

Prevention

- Avoid foods, chemicals, drugs, and other substances that have caused allergic reactions.

- Wear a medical alert bracelet that warns of your allergy and tells what to do in an emergency. Inform your friends and co-workers of your allergies.

- Tell your doctor and dentist about any medication allergies you have. This includes prescription and over-the-counter medications.

- Check labels before taking over-the-counter medication or eating foods if you have medication or food allergies.

Bites: Human and Animal

Human bites happen more often than you think. The "biters" usually are children playing or fighting with each other. The bite can become infected because of the amount and type of bacteria in the human mouth.

Animal bites raise three concerns: bleeding, the possibility of viral infections such as rabies, and the possibility of bacterial infections such as tetanus. Animal bites that break the skin often cause infections. A cat bite is more likely to get infected than a dog bite.

First Aid

- If you have a human bite that is bleeding, apply pressure directly to the bitten area and try to raise the wound above heart level. Using a washcloth and mild soap, wash the bitten area vigorously under running water for at least 5 minutes.

- Watch the wound site closely for signs of increased redness, swelling, or pain.

- Wash all animal bites vigorously with soap for 15 minutes and then rinse under running water for 10 minutes, even if the bite has not bled. Apply an antibacterial ointment (such as bacitracin) to shallow puncture wounds, and watch for signs of infection. Deep puncture wounds and cat bites (shallow or deep) should be treated immediately by a doctor.

- If a pet has bitten you, take it to the veterinarian.

- The main carriers of rabies are wild animals, especially skunks, raccoons, bats, and foxes. If a wild animal has bitten you, avoid contact with it. Report the injury to local police, so that they can locate the animal for observation and confine it if necessary. For more information on wild-animal bites, call your local health department.

- With any kind of bite, check to be sure your tetanus booster is up to date.

When You Need a Tetanus Booster

- Wound, cut, or scrape is deep or caused by a dirty object or your skin was dirty and your last tetanus shot was more than 5 years ago.
- Wound, cut, or scrape is clean and minor, but your last tetanus shot was more than 10 years ago.
- You never had the initial tetanus vaccination.

HIV Transmission and Bites

The possibility of the human immunodeficiency virus (HIV) being spread through the bite of an HIV-infected person is considered extremely unlikely. To date there have been no documented examples of HIV transmission through biting.

Bites and Stings: Insect and Spider

B ees, wasps, hornets, yellow jackets, mosquitoes, flies, spiders, chiggers, ticks, gnats, and other insects can all produce painful stings or bites. Most insect bites are harmless, but some can be very dangerous, even fatal.

What to do about Bites

Symptom/Sign	Action
Bite does not penetrate skin	First aid
Animal has up-to-date vaccination records and bite is not serious	First aid
Any strange-animal bite	Call doctor
Tetanus booster needed (see p. 6)	Call doctor
Any sign of infection (such as increased redness and swelling around bite)	Call doctor
Bite on feet, neck, genitals, or over a joint or bone	See doctor
Cat bite or deep cat scratch	See doctor
Bleeding that cannot be controlled; bite on face or hands	Go to hospital

Symptoms

It may be difficult to determine if you have been bitten or stung—and by what. The reaction to minor bites is usually confined to the area around the bite. It may be red or have slight swelling. It may itch. Pain and swelling usually improve in 24 hours.

Swelling can vary from a small dot to half an inch in size. A large swelled area doesn't mean you are allergic to insect bites. The size of the swelling doesn't necessarily mean the bite is serious.

Mosquito and gnat bites near the eye or ear can become very swollen. It also is not unusual for glands to become swollen as a reaction to insect bites.

Dangerous, life-threatening reactions to insect bites occur throughout the body usually within 20 minutes following the bite. The reaction appears on a part of the body separate from the sting site. Dangerous reactions include:

- Hives, intense itching, or swelling all over the body
- Shortness of breath
- Wheezing
- Swelling of the throat that causes difficulty swallowing
- Nausea
- Stomach cramping
- Vomiting
- Loss of bowel and bladder control
- Weakness
- Dizziness or fainting
- Drop in blood pressure
- Shock or unconsciousness

First Aid

- Remove the stinger when stung by a bee, wasp, hornet, or yellow jacket. Scrape over the stinger (which looks like a splinter) with a credit card, fingernail, knife blade, or other rigid object. Don't try to pull it out with your fingers or a tweezers; you might end up squeezing more venom into the skin.
- Wash the site of the bite and the surrounding area thoroughly with soap and water.

- Apply cold quickly. Cool compresses or ice packs will help ease the pain and prevent swelling from most insect bites. The longer you wait to apply a cold treatment, the less benefit it will have. Apply cold packs for no more than 20 minutes at a time to avoid frostbite.
- Don't scratch that itch. Apply calamine lotion, hydrocortisone cream, or baking soda and water. Take Benadryl (an antihistamine) if itching or more local swelling occurs. Benadryl will help reduce late-appearing symptoms but is not an effective emergency treatment. It can also cause sleepiness or hyperactivity in children.

Special Care for Children with Insect Bites

- Trim child's nails to prevent trauma from scratching.
- Protect babies from insects, especially those under 1 year, because they can't swat them away.
- Note that bites on young children and babies will be more swollen in general, and may form hard lumps that last for several months.

What to do about Insect and Spider Bites and Stings

Symptom/Sign	Action
Throbbing pain	First aid
Burning, redness, itching	First aid
Significant swelling and pain that doesn't get better within 48 hours	Call doctor
Unusual rash	Call doctor
Signs of infection (increasing pain, redness, swelling) or fever over 101° F	Call doctor
Bite by a brown house spider or black widow spider (most common in the South)	See doctor
Sting in nose or mouth	Go to hospital
Nausea, vomiting, abdominal pain, loss of bowel or bladder control	Go to hospital
Dizziness or fainting; shortness of breath; swelling of throat, face, or tongue; difficulty swallowing	Call 911
Hives, intense itching, or swelling all over the body	Call 911
History of severe allergic reaction	Call 911

Prevention

Don't use perfumes, aftershave, scented hairsprays, or scented deodorants. Wear insect repellent, light-colored clothing, long-sleeved tops, long pants, socks, and shoes. Floral patterns attract bees, as do food, beverages, and garbage cans. If a bee comes near you, avoid sudden movements. Stay still or move away slowly.

Using Insect Repellents

DEET is the most effective insect repellent, offering protection for about 3 hours.

- Be careful when using DEET on children. Use low concentrations (no more than 10 percent) and apply lightly no more than twice a day. Follow manufacturer's instructions.

- Don't get insect repellent with DEET on your mouth or eyes, and wash it off your hands after applying.

- Other repellents, such as Skintastic and Skin-So-Soft, may be safer but less effective.

- Citronella comes in lotions, sprays, and candles and offers limited protection against some mosquitos.

- Repellents are less effective in higher temperatures because they evaporate.

Prevention for People with Serious Reactions to Bee Stings

People who have had a serious reaction to a bee sting can take the following steps to prevent a serious reaction in the future:

- Carry a bee-sting kit at all times. A doctor can prescribe one and show you how to use it. These kits contain injectable adrenaline, also called epinephrine, which can be lifesaving.

- Carry a card or wear a bracelet that alerts others to the condition.

- Ask your doctor if venom desensitization injections will help. (Desensitization is a process of making you less sensitive to venom.)

Bites: Snake

Most snakes are harmless, but don't risk a snakebite by approaching or handling one. Learn to identify snakes in your area, and find out if any are poisonous.

How to Identify Poisonous Snakes

There are two families of poisonous snakes in North America. They are known as *pit vipers* and *coral snakes*.

Pit vipers include the copperhead, cottonmouth (also called water moccasin), and rattlesnake. Pit vipers have long, moveable fangs, triangular heads, slit-like eyes, and a poison sac located behind the eyes. Cottonmouth and copperhead snakes live mainly in the southeast and south central United States. Rattlesnakes can be found throughout the country.

Coral snakes are brightly colored with red, yellow, and black stripes. Some nonpoisonous snakes also look like coral snakes. Remember the verse, "Red against black does venom lack, red against yellow kills a fellow." Coral snakes are found mainly in the southeastern United States.

Symptoms

The signs of a bite vary with the type of snake. A bite from a pit viper looks like a puncture mark. Immediate pain, burning, redness, and swelling occur within a few minutes. Nausea and vomiting, weakness, increased saliva, and possible seizures may also occur.

Symptoms from a coral snake bite may not appear until up to 12 hours after the bite. The bites appear like tiny scratches in a semicircle. Blurred vision, drowsiness, slurred speech, weakness, increased saliva, and sometimes seizures occur after a bite from a coral snake.

Snakebites from poisonous snakes are rarely fatal when medical assistance is quickly provided. However, anyone bitten by a poisonous snake needs immediate medical attention. Remember what the snake looked like so you can describe it to the doctors who treat you.

First Aid

- Don't panic! Venom will spread more rapidly through the body if the person runs or becomes excited. Before giving first aid, identify the snake. Do not use ice on the bite; it can cause serious tissue damage.

- If the bite involves a coral snake, raise the bitten area and don't move it, then go to the nearest emergency facility.

- If the bite involves a poisonous snake that is not a coral snake, within 30 minutes place a light tourniquet (tight band of any sort) 3 to 4 inches above the bite, between the bite and torso (middle of the body). Do not cut off the circulation. You should be able to slip a finger beneath the band.

- Avoid moving the bitten area and don't consume alcohol or stimulants.

- For a nonpoisonous snakebite, keep the bite below the level of the heart. Clean the area thoroughly with soap and water, and place a bandage over the wound. Seek medical help promptly.

- Seek medical attention for snake antivenom.

- Get tetanus booster (see p. 6).

What to do about Snakebites

Symptom/Sign	Action
All snakebites	Go to hospital
Known poisonous snakebite	Call 911

Prevention

Snakes strike only when frightened or trapped. You can take the following steps to prevent snakebites:

- Be cautious when in snake territory. Be especially careful around water.

- When hiking, wear long pants and boots to protect your feet and ankles.

- Hike with a companion.

- Walk on clear paths and carry a walking stick.

- Use a flashlight and wear boots at night. Snakes are more active in the cool of the evening.

- Never reach into an area such as a hole or cave without first looking into it. Be cautious when looking.

- Stop walking if you see a snake. Quickly move away, at least 20 feet back along the path you just walked. Watch for other snakes in the same area.

Bites: Tick

Ticks probably spread a larger variety of diseases to humans and domestic animals than all other pests. The tick's bite is relatively painless; the real dangers are the viruses, bacteria, and other organisms the tick may have. Some types of ticks carry diseases such as Rocky Mountain spotted fever, Colorado tick fever, and Lyme disease.

Causes

People usually pick up ticks from woody underbrush, tall grass or weeds, and the fur of outdoor pets. Once on a host, the tick bites the skin, embeds its head, and taps into a blood source—a small vein or capillary.

Symptoms

Unless you see the tick while it is attached to you, you may not know you've had a tick bite—and you may have no reaction to it. Symptoms of a reaction to a tick bite, or to illness carried by a tick, are:

- Red ring or "bull's-eye" rash that quickly expands, usually occurring 3 to 30 days after a bite. The rash can be a few inches or very large and can last up to 3 weeks.

- Increased pain, redness, swelling, and fever can indicate an infection from the bite.
- A general feeling of not being well about 2 weeks after a tick bite can signal a tick-borne illness.

First Aid

- If you discover a tick on your skin or clothing, remove it immediately. The sooner you remove it, the less your chance of picking up infectious organisms.
- Don't use nail polish, solvents, or alcohol to remove a tick. They can cause the tick to release harmful secretions under the skin. Use tweezers to grasp the tick as close to the skin as possible. Slowly and gently pull the tick up from the skin until it releases its grip.
- Avoid twisting or jerking to prevent breaking off the head or mouth. Do not crush the tick. If tweezers are not available, pull off the tick using your fingers or a loop of thread around the jaws.
- If the tick's head stays in the skin, use a sterile needle to remove it.
- Dispose of the tick after it has been removed by burning or flushing it.
- Clean the skin thoroughly with soap and water after the tick has been removed.

What to do about Tick Bites

Symptom/Sign	Action
Tick easily removed	First aid
Entire tick can't be removed	See doctor
Red ring or "bulls-eye" rash (rapidly expanding border, typically occurs 3 to 30 days after bite; rash can be a few inches or very large and last up to 3 weeks)	See doctor
Symptoms of infection: increased pain, redness, swelling, fever	See doctor
Fever, rash, headache, muscle or joint pain about 2 weeks after tick bite	See doctor

The wood tick is the size of an apple seed with a white mark near its head. The deer tick is the size of a poppy seed with an orange-brown spot near the head.

Prevention

- The best way to prevent ticks from attaching to your skin is to find them before they attach. Do regular "tick checks" when you are in the woods. Twice daily, inspect your skin, scalp, and clothing for ticks.

- Avoid being a target for ticks. Wear long pants, long-sleeved shirts, a hat, socks, and shoes. Tuck your shirt into your pants and your pants into your socks to help prevent ticks from attaching themselves to your skin.

- Apply insect repellent containing no more than 30 percent DEET to your pants, socks, and shoes. Higher concentrations of DEET are not recommended, especially for young children and those with sensitive skin.

- Apply permethrin insecticide for treatment of clothing.

Lyme Disease

One of the diseases often spread by deer ticks is Lyme disease. It is an infection that can affect the skin, joints, brain, and heart, as well as other organs. It was identified in 1975 in the woodlands around Lyme, Connecticut. The disease is caused by a previously unknown bacteria. Lyme disease is spread only by deer ticks, not the common dog tick or wood tick. Deer ticks are smaller—about the size of a poppy seed—and have different markings than those of wood ticks (see illustration, p. 13).

Symptoms

Lyme disease symptoms can vary greatly from person to person; however, three phases have been identified.

Phase one: Between 3 and 30 days after being bitten by an infected tick, a small red bump may appear at the site. The bump is surrounded by a ring of red, or bull's-eye, rash that slowly expands for several days before fading. Flulike symptoms—fatigue, headache, chills, joint and muscle aches, and a low fever—may occur during this period. However, a third of those who get Lyme disease never get a rash.

Phase two: Weeks or months after the bite, about 20 percent of untreated people have neurological or cardiac disorders, ranging from poor coordination to facial paralysis to abnormal heart rhythm. Skin lesions develop in about half of those who are untreated. These symptoms also disappear, usually within a few weeks.

Phase three: Up to 60 percent of untreated people may develop recurring or chronic arthritis after a period of up to 2 years. The arthritis mainly affects large joints, most often the knees.

Treatment

Lyme disease can be treated and nearly always cured, especially in its early stages. The bacteria that cause Lyme disease are sensitive to antibiotics such as tetracycline, penicillin, and erythromycin. If you see or have had the bull's-eye rash, see your doctor right away.

Prevention

Follow the measures for tick-bite prevention and:

• Shower after being in a wooded area and check for ticks.

• Keep in mind that you can prevent the disease by using good protective measures (see p. 14).

Burns

A burn is damage to the skin from contact with heat. The longer the skin touches something hot, the worse a burn may be.

Causes

Touching a hot surface can cause burns. Steam, hot liquids, flame, and some chemicals (see Burns: Chemical, p. 17) also can cause burns.

Symptoms

Doctors grade burns as being first, second, or third degree. The higher the number, the more serious the damage to the skin's layers.

First-degree burns affect only the top, or first, layer of skin. The skin can be red, dry, or swollen. These burns may peel and are usually painful. A mild sunburn or a slight scalding usually results in first-degree burns. You don't need to see a doctor for a first-degree burn unless a large area of skin is damaged. First-degree burns usually heal in 5 to 6 days without leaving scars.

Second-degree burns affect the two top layers of skin. Symptoms include redness, swelling, and some blisters. Second-degree burns are painful, and the pain may be severe. Healing takes 3 to

4 weeks and may leave scars. Second-degree burns can be fatal if more than half the body is damaged. You can treat most second-degree burns at home if only a small amount of skin is burned. But you should see the doctor if:

- The burn covers more than 1 square inch of skin.

- The burn causes a lot of blistering.

- The burn is on the hand, face, or groin.

Third-degree burns damage all three layers of skin. They may even harm tissue, muscle, nerves, bones, or fat underneath the skin. With a third-degree burn, skin may be red, white, waxy, or charred black. These burns can be very painful or, if the nerves are destroyed, painless. The burned area may "weep," or ooze large amounts of clear liquid. You must see a doctor right away for all third-degree burns. Treatment by a burn specialist and skin grafts are needed for third-degree burns. There may be permanent scars from the burn.

First Aid

- Soak small burns in cold water or apply cold, wet compresses. Do not use ice water or snow, unless that is the only source of cold available. The wet, cooling action helps stop any more burning below the skin.

- Cover the burn with a clean, dry, preferably nonstick dressing or cloth that covers the entire burn area. You can use an over-the-counter product with aloe vera in it to help ease pain. Don't put butter or any other greasy substance on the burn. Don't break blisters that form on the burn.

- Call your doctor if you see any signs of infection on the burned area.

- Burned skin can itch for weeks and is sensitive to the sun for up to a year after it has healed. Remember to use sunscreen to prevent further damage.

- Check to see whether a tetanus shot is needed (see p. 6).

Severe Burns

- If a person's clothes are on fire, put out the fire with a blanket, towel, rug, or coat. Wrap it over the flames. Press down to keep air from reaching the fire. The person may struggle or try to run. Make the person lie still on the floor.

- Pull away bits of clothing that may be smoldering. Leave alone cloth that sticks to the skin but is not burning. Emergency-room workers can take off these stuck pieces of cloth safely.

- Call 911, or take the person to a doctor right away if the area of the burn is not too large. Don't let the burned person drive.

- If you can't get the burned person to a hospital right away, treat for shock (see Shock, p. 55)

- If the burned person is conscious and is not vomiting, try to get him or her to drink warm water. The water will help replace fluids lost from the burn.

- Check to see whether a tetanus shot is needed (see p. 6).

What to do about Burns

Symptom/Sign	Action
Burn affecting only the outer layer of skin (may be some pain and tenderness)	First aid
First- and second-degree burns greater than 2 inches in diameter	See doctor
Burns involving groin or buttocks	See doctor
First- and second-degree burns that cover more than 10 percent of the body	Go to hospital
Third-degree burns or burns caused by an explosion	Call 911
Burns with smoke inhalation	Call 911
Significant burns to face and neck	Call 911
First- and second-degree burns that cover more than 30 percent of the body	Call 911

Burns: Chemical

Chemical burns are caused by being doused or splashed with a harsh acid or alkaline chemical. These chemicals can burn the skin just like a fire or hot surface. Chemical burns are especially dangerous to your eyes.

First Aid

- React quickly to chemical burns. Flush the affected area right away, even before calling your doctor. Flush the burned area with a gentle, constant spray of cool water for at least 10 to 30 minutes using a hose, bucket, or shower. Do not rub the area while rinsing. Remove all clothing on the burned area. Keep flushing until you are certain all the chemical has been washed away.

- After flushing, call the local poison control center or your doctor for more instructions.

- Dry the wound site and cover with a clean cloth or dressing.

- Do not put first-aid ointments, antiseptics, or home remedies on chemical burns. Cool, wet dressings work best to relieve pain.

Eye Burns

If you get chemicals in your eye, you need to flush the eye right away, before doing anything else. If you wear contact lenses, take them out. Flush the eye with a constant stream of cool, clean water for at least 20 to 30 minutes. A stream of water can't harm the eye. Thorough washing can reduce the risk of permanent eye damage. If there is no water handy, use milk to wash your eye. Do not bandage the eye before seeing a doctor.

To flush the eye, hold your head under a faucet or use a pitcher of water, plastic squirt bottle, drinking fountain, or shower spray. Hold your eyelids open for proper flushing. Make sure the water runs from the inside corner of the eye (near the nose) outward, so the contaminated water doesn't flow into the unaffected eye.

If both eyes are affected, let water flow over both or quickly alternate flushing each eye. Make sure water gets to all parts of the eye by lifting and separating the eyelids. You can also put the top half of your face in a large bowl or sink filled with water. Open both eyes and move the eyelids up and down. Don't do this with people (especially young children) who are upset or who can't hold their breath.

Don't rub your eyes. After rinsing the eye, immediately go to the nearest hospital emergency room. Bring the chemical container with you for analysis.

What to do about Chemical Burns

Symptom/Sign	Action
Small or mild skin burn	First aid
Skin burn with blistering, swelling, or discharge	See doctor
Chemical burn to eyes	Go to hospital

Prevention

- Read labels of all household products and follow any precautions. Buy potentially dangerous substances in safety containers.

- Wear protective clothing, gloves, and goggles when handling chemicals.

- Never store household products in food or drink containers.

- Safely store chemicals immediately after use, and keep out of the reach of children.

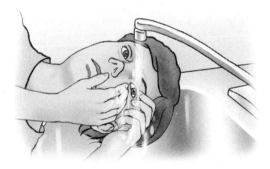

Flush eye with cold, clean water for at least 20–30 minutes.

Carbon Monoxide Poisoning

Carbon monoxide is a gas you can't see or smell. It's made when carbon or materials that contain carbon (such as gasoline, kerosene, natural gas, or wood) are burned. When you breathe in carbon monoxide, your blood can't get the oxygen it needs. If you don't get away from the carbon monoxide, its effects can kill you. Unborn babies, infants, elderly people, and people with a history of heart or respiratory disease are especially susceptible.

Causes

Carbon monoxide poisoning can come from exposure to improperly vented gas appliances (such as a furnace, hot-water heater, or oven), automobile exhaust, or smoke inhalation from a fire. Carbon monoxide poisoning should be suspected in any situation where gas cannot escape, such as a car with a running engine or fires in poorly ventilated areas. It's possible to get carbon monoxide poisoning even inside a tent, where it may seem like there's plenty of ventilation.

Symptoms

Because carbon monoxide has no smell, you may not know you are being exposed to it until you start to feel ill. The first symptoms of carbon monoxide poisoning are mild. You may have a headache, dizziness, or fatigue that goes away when you get fresh air.

Carbon monoxide poisoning can have the same symptoms as the "stomach flu." If everyone in your household has these symptoms at the same time, it could be carbon monoxide poisoning.

Symptoms of carbon monoxide poisoning include:

• Severe headache

• Confusion

• Agitation

• Nausea or vomiting

• Skin rash

• Fatigue

• Stupor/sleepiness

• Coma

First Aid

• If you feel tired or have headaches, open a window. If that makes you feel better, you should check your home for carbon monoxide.

- Don't stay in the room if you think carbon monoxide poisoning is possible. Get everyone, including pets, into fresh air before starting first aid.

- Call 911 if the person is unconscious. Check for breathing and pulse. If the person is not breathing, start cardiopulmonary resuscitation (see Why You Should Learn CPR, p. 43) if you have been trained. Continue until the person with carbon monoxide poisoning has started to breathe again or medical assistance arrives.

What to do about Carbon Monoxide Poisoning

Symptom/Sign	Action
Known exposure to carbon monoxide with headache, confusion, nausea, and fatigue	Go to hospital
Person is found unconscious or not breathing	Call 911

Prevention

- Get a carbon monoxide detector. These work the way smoke detectors do, to give you an early warning that there is carbon monoxide in your home. If you only have one, put it in or near your bedroom. If the alarm goes off, leave your home.

- If members of the household are experiencing headache, nausea, confusion, and fatigue, get out of the house and call to have it checked for carbon monoxide poisoning.

- Have your fuel-burning appliances, such as gas and oil furnaces, gas and wood fireplaces, space heaters, hot-water heaters, dryers, and pool heaters, inspected at least once every 2 years.

- Don't leave a car running in the garage, even with the door open. Don't drive with the trunk or tailgate of your car open. Check the car's exhaust system regularly.

- Don't use a gas oven to heat your home, even for a short time.

- Don't ever use a charcoal grill indoors.

Choking

Choking occurs when a piece of food or other object becomes lodged in the throat, blocking air flow.

Causes

Choking can be caused by food or by small household items. Some foods are more likely to cause choking than others, including:

- Hot dogs
- Nuts
- Chunks of meat, cheese, or peanut butter
- Whole grapes
- Hard candy
- Popcorn
- Raw carrots

Symptoms

People who are choking may cough hard to try to get rid of whatever is stuck in the throat. Someone whose airway is completely blocked can't speak, breathe, or cough at all. He or she may clutch at the throat.

First Aid

Choking is life threatening and needs immediate action. If the person can speak, cough, or breathe, this means air is still passing through the airway.

- Let the person try to expel the object. Reassure the person, and advise him or her to breathe deeply and slowly. This will help relax the muscles surrounding the windpipe.

- If the person is unable to breathe or make sounds, have someone call 911. If you have been trained in how to use the Heimlich maneuver, you may use it.

- Watch for coughing, difficulty breathing, or wheezing that continues after a choking incident. These may be signs of a partial obstruction, which could move and totally block breathing again. If this occurs, seek immediate help.

What to do about Choking

Symptom/Sign	Action
Choking person can speak, cough, or breathe	First aid
Choking person unable to breathe or make sounds	Call 911
Wheezing, coughing, difficulty breathing, or pain when swallowing after choking incident	Call 911

Prevention

- Chew food thoroughly.

- Don't eat too fast.

- Avoid talking and laughing while eating.

- Don't walk or run with food or objects in your mouth.

- Keep small toys and household items away from infants and children.

Cuts and Scrapes

You can get an infection whenever your skin is broken, whether it's a scraped knee or a gunshot wound.

Scrapes or abrasions occur when one or more layers of skin are torn or scraped off. They happen so often they may seem unimportant, but they should be treated to reduce the chance of infection or scarring.

Cuts

Minor cuts damage only the skin and the fatty tissue beneath it. They usually heal without permanent damage. More serious cuts may damage muscles, tendons, blood vessels, ligaments, or nerves. These cuts should be examined by a doctor.

A puncture wound is a small but deep hole produced by a sharp object such as a pin, nail, tack, needle, tooth, or fang.

Are Stitches Needed?

Sometimes it is difficult to tell if stitches are needed. Signs that stitches may be necessary are:

- The wound is deep, gapes, is very dirty or irregular, or can't be held together with a bandage.

- A deep cut is located on an elbow, knee, finger, or other area that bends.

- The cut is on the finger or thumb joint, palm of the hand, face, or other area on which you would like to minimize scars.
- The cut occurs on a young child who is likely to pull off the bandage.

First Aid

The next time you get a cut from a nail, a knife, or even a piece of paper, follow these steps.

Stop the Bleeding
- Clean area well. Use crushed ice to apply pressure for 20 minutes or cover the wound with a gauze pad or a thick, clean piece of cloth. Use your hand if nothing else is available.
- Press on the wound hard enough to stop the bleeding. Don't let up on the pressure even to change cloths. Just add a clean cloth over the original one.
- Raise the wound above heart level, unless this would be painful.
- Get medical help immediately if blood spurts from a wound or bleeding does not stop after several minutes of pressure.

Clean the Wound
- Wash the cut with soap and water. Avoid hydrogen peroxide, alcohol, mercurochrome, Merthiolate, or io-

dine. They are not necessary and can be very painful and delay healing.
- Make sure no dirt, glass, or foreign material remains in the wound.
- Call your doctor if the cut or wound does not heal in 10 to 14 days.

Bandage the Wound
- Bandage a cut (rather than seeing a doctor for stitches) when its edges tend to fall together and when the cut is not very deep.
- Use "butterfly bandages," strips of sterile paper tape, or adhesive strip bandages to keep edges together.
- Apply the bandage crosswise, not lengthwise. This will bring the edges of the wound into firm contact and promote healing.
- Moist wounds heal faster and with less scar tissue than dry wounds. The scab that is formed by dry healing interferes with the movement of epidermal cells. Apply bacitracin to keep the wound moist and soft.

Scrapes

Scrapes are usually caused by falls onto the hands, knees, or elbows. This exposes nerve endings, all of which carry pain impulses to the brain. Because scrapes can affect so many nerve endings, they are usually much more painful than cuts.

Although most abrasions and scrapes can be treated at home, you should call your doctor if they become infected.

First Aid

- It is important to carefully clean scrapes to help prevent infection. Wash your hands before washing wounds, then carefully remove all dirt and debris. Use soap and warm water to thoroughly scrub the scrape for at least 5 minutes. Liquid soap provides better cleansing penetration. Use Vaseline to remove tar from wounds and wet gauze to "tease" gravel or dirt from the abrasion. Avoid antiseptic agents such as alcohol, Merthiolate, iodine, mercurochrome, or hydrogen peroxide. They do little good and cause stinging.

- Next, apply direct pressure to the scrape, using nonstick gauze or a clean cloth to hold on the scrape and stop the flow of blood. If the gauze or cloth becomes soaked with blood, do not remove it. Instead, place another clean layer of cloth or gauze directly on top and reapply pressure. Because blood takes time to clot, you may have to apply pressure for 5 to 10 minutes. Raising the scrape above the level of the heart will also help reduce the blood flow. If you cannot control the bleeding, see your doctor.

- On the scalp or a fingertip, you may apply an ice pack wrapped in a towel to constrict the blood vessels and stop the bleeding. Apply the ice pack for no more than 15 minutes or until the wound begins to feel numb. After a 10-minute rest, the ice pack may be reapplied. This procedure can be repeated several times.

- Within 24 hours, remove the bandage and wash the area with mild soap and running water. The wound should be washed daily with plain tap water and soap. Use antibiotic ointment to keep the skin flexible and prevent the formation of a scab, which can slow healing. Change bandages two to three times daily. Watch for signs of infection.

What to do about Cuts and Scrapes

Symptom/Sign	Action
Bleeding that stops within 10 minutes with direct pressure	First aid
Shallow cut or scrape that is minor and not on face	First aid
Bleeding that cannot be controlled after applying pressure for 20 minutes	See doctor
Cut caused by an obviously dirty object, such as a rusty nail or shovel point; foreign object embedded in the wound; or debris in the wound	See doctor
Tetanus booster needed (see p. 6)	See doctor
Deep or irregular cut; cut more than half an inch long; edges of the wound are separated or gaping and cannot easily be held together with a bandage	See doctor
Large scrape, scrape that causes severe pain, scrape on face, or puncture wound in hand	See doctor
Signs of infection— increased redness or swelling around wound	See doctor
Numbness or weakness	See doctor
Uncontrollable bleeding	Go to hospital
Unable to move fingers or toes normally	Go to hospital
Signs of shock	Call 911
Puncture wound or cut on head, chest, abdomen, or over a joint	Call 911

Dehydration

Dehydration is the result of not having enough body fluids for your body to function well.

Causes

Dehydration can be caused by loss of fluids from sweating too much, vomiting, diarrhea, or heavy urine output. You can also become dehydrated if you are not taking in enough liquid, which is sometimes the result of a loss of appetite or of nausea.

Symptoms

Don't use thirst as a measure of whether you are becoming dehydrated. By the time you feel thirsty, you are already low on fluids. The color and amount of your urine is a good indicator of the level of dehydration. If there isn't very much urine and it is dark yellow, this means your body is low on fluids.

Early signs of dehydration include:

• Decreased urine output

• Dry mouth

• Dark circles under the eyes

• Decreased activity in children

• Fatigue in adults

FIRST AID AND URGENT CARE

Late signs of dehydration include:

- Confusion
- Weakness
- Fainting
- Skin lacking its normal elasticity and sagging back into position slowly when pinched into a fold

First Aid

- Mild dehydration can be treated by drinking water or other decaffeinated fluids, such as sports drinks. Begin by drinking small amounts frequently until you are urinating normally. Rest is also important.

- If you are experiencing any of the signs of late dehydration, you need to see your doctor. You may need to receive fluids through your veins, or intravenously (IV). Severe dehydration can result in cardiovascular collapse and death, and should be treated immediately.

- Infants and young children may benefit from specific electrolyte solutions such as Pedialyte. Infants with frequent vomiting and diarrhea are at the greatest risk for dehydration and need immediate medical attention.

What to do about Dehydration

Symptom/Sign	Action
Excessive sweating due to fever or exercise	First aid
Decreased urine output, increased thirst, or dry mouth	First aid
Infant or child with vomiting and diarrhea	Call doctor
Fainting, confusion, or anxiety related to excessive sweating or illness	See doctor

Prevention

Dehydration is easier to prevent than it is to treat. To prevent dehydration:

- Drink adequate fluids throughout the day no matter how active or inactive you are, or whether you are ill. Those most at risk are the very young and the very old, especially if they are ill with fever, vomiting, or diarrhea.

- Monitor fluid intake and drink more than normal if you are ill.

- Children have a lower tolerance for high temperatures than adults and should be monitored to make sure they are drinking at least 5 ounces of water every 20 minutes during exercise in warm or humid climates.

- Drink at least a quart of water or other electrolyte-replenishing fluid every hour when you are sweating or doing exercise.

Dislocations

A dislocation is when the ends of two bones at a joint move out of their normal positions. You can have a dislocation at any joint, from fingers and toes to the hips or even the jaw.

Causes

Most dislocations are the result of a sudden blow or a sudden twist, either of which can knock the bones out of their position in the joint. Dislocations often occur during sports activity, especially contact sports such as football or hockey. Falls are also a common cause of dislocations. A blow to the face or yawning can cause a dislocated jaw.

Symptoms

- A dislocation is usually very painful, with swelling in the joint area.

- You may be able to see that the bones are not lined up properly.

- Movement of the joint may be limited.

- There may be considerable pain when a joint, such as the knee, tries to support weight.

First Aid

- Sometimes dislocated bones will "pop" back into position in the joint on their own, but do not try to force them back into place.

- Try to keep the joint immobile. Put a splint on it or use a sling so it will not move while you get to a doctor.

- Use ice packs to ease pain.

What to do about Dislocated Joints

Symptom/Sign	Action
Pain and swelling, misshapen joint, limited movement after a blow or fall	First aid and see doctor

Dizziness

People use the word *dizzy* to describe a variety of sensations. Some people use the word *dizzy* to refer to feeling light-headed or faint. Others use it when they feel imbalance or a spinning sensation (vertigo).

Causes

Problems with your ears, certain medications, and medical conditions can cause dizziness. Upper respiratory allergies affecting your ears and motion sickness may also cause dizziness.

Types of Dizziness

Light-headedness

When you are light-headed, you may feel woozy or as if you are going to pass out. Some people feel light-headed for a moment when they get up from a sitting or lying position too quickly. This dizziness, called *postural* or *orthostatic hypotension*, is caused by a drop in blood pressure to the brain when you change position. It usually passes very quickly. You can take steps to avoid it. Before you get up, sit on the edge of the bed or chair to get your bearings. As you stand up, tighten your leg muscles. This

causes more of your blood to flow toward your brain.

Other possible causes of feeling light-headed include blood pressure and heart problems or anxiety. If you are taking medications for high blood pressure and feel light-headed, tell your doctor.

Balance Problems

When you have balance problems, you may not be able to walk straight. Your feet may feel unsteady, and you may feel like you are going to fall. The risk of injury makes balance problems dangerous.

Poor balance is often related to aging of the inner ear, decreased sensation in the nerves of the leg and foot joints, arthritis, and poor vision. We are able to keep our balance using input from our ears, eyes, and nerves of the joints (especially the leg joints). The brain sorts out this information and enables us to walk straight without falling.

If you have poor balance and your feet feel unsteady, call your doctor. To keep yourself from falling, leave a light on at night and use a cane or walking stick.

Vertigo

Vertigo makes you feel as if objects around you are spinning or moving. It may also cause nausea, vomiting, or blurry vision.

Vertigo is usually temporary and not life threatening. It can have many causes, including labyrinthitis, benign positional vertigo, and Meniere's disease.

Labyrinthitis. Labyrinthitis is an inflammation of the inner ear. It may be caused by a virus and is often accompanied by nausea, vomiting, and involuntary movements of the eyes. A person may have these symptoms suddenly during the day or may wake up with them. Labyrinthitis causes a severe spinning sensation that lasts for several days, usually goes away on its own, and may never return. It usually takes up to several months to disappear. During this time, some people experience a spinning sensation while moving their head in a specific direction or holding it in certain positions. This is called *benign positional vertigo*.

Over-the-counter medicines can reduce dizziness. They are most helpful during the first week, when vertigo is most severe. If used for long periods, these medicines may get in the way of recovery and make you drowsy. Talk to your doctor before taking any medicine for your dizziness.

Benign Positional Vertigo. Benign positional vertigo, usually caused by problems in the inner ear, is the most common cause of dizziness in adults. It occurs when a person is looking up or down or side to side or is rolling over in bed. The spinning sensation usually lasts less than a minute. It can occur anywhere from once a day to every time a person moves his or her head. Benign positional vertigo may follow labyrinthitis, or it can appear alone. It usually goes away on its own in about 4 months. If you have severe spinning sensations, talk to your doctor.

Meniere's Disease. Meniere's disease is a common condition that can affect adults of all ages. It causes recurring episodes of vertigo with fluctuating hearing loss and pressure, fullness, or noise usually in one ear. It may occur with nausea and vomiting. Symptoms usually last for several hours. Episodes can occur as often as every day or as infrequently as every 10 years. Between episodes, most people with Meniere's disease feel normal. If you have dizziness with hearing loss, see your doctor.

Fainting

Dizziness and fainting can be related. People who faint lose consciousness or pass out. Fainting occurs when blood pressure is low and not enough blood can get to the brain. It may be a sign of problems with the heart or blood pressure, or it may simply be a reaction to a stressful event. Some people faint at the sight of blood. No matter what the cause, fainting can be dangerous, because it increases your risk of injury from falling. Fainting is not usually related to vertigo, an imbalance caused by problems of the inner ear. Fainting is common in older adults. Up to 12 percent of people over age 85 faint. If you have fainted, call your doctor.

First Aid

- Take your time getting up if you have dizzy spells when you rise quickly from sitting or lying positions.

- When an episode of dizziness or vertigo strikes, slowly move to a sitting or reclining position. You'll be less likely to fall and injure yourself. If you feel faint or if your vision begins to go dark, sit with your head between your knees.

- Drink more fluids to avoid dehydration and help maintain your blood pressure.

- Avoid caffeine, alcohol, and smoking.

- Avoid driving.

- Use relaxation techniques to combat anxiety. Breathe deeply and slowly.

- If you feel an episode of vertigo coming on, keeping your eyes open and focused on a stationary object may lessen the symptoms.

- If others in your household also have dizziness, headache, or nausea and vomiting, it may be carbon monoxide poisoning (see Carbon Monoxide Poisoning, p. 19). Get out of the house, call your gas company, and go to the hospital.

What to do about Dizziness

Symptom/Sign	Action
Occasional light-headedness or dizziness when first standing or getting out of bed	First aid
Vertigo (room seems to be spinning) that lasts for more than 3 days	See doctor
Vertigo (room seems to be spinning) with nausea and vomiting	See doctor
Dizziness with fever, hearing loss, ringing ears, or ear pain	See doctor
Dizziness with head injury or severe headache	Go to hospital
Dizziness with numbness or weakness of arms or legs or loss of control of bowels or bladder	Call 911
Dizziness with blurred or double vision, loss of hearing, or slurred speech	Call 911
Dizziness with symptoms of shock (rapid pulse; rapid, shallow respirations; cool, clammy, pale skin)	Call 911
Dizziness with chest pain or pressure	Call 911

Drowning/Near Drowning

Drowning is one of the leading causes of accidental death in the United States. When a person drowns, oxygen doesn't get to the brain. Drowning can occur whether or not the lungs fill up with water.

Near drowning happens after a long time under water. Being under water, or submerged, keeps oxygen from reaching the lungs and other vital organs, including the brain, which can lead to brain injury.

Symptoms

The near-drowning person may be awake, semiconscious, or unconscious with little or no breathing or heartbeat. Vomiting, cold skin, and a bluish-white paleness are common signs.

First Aid

- Call 911.

- Rescue the near-drowning person if you are trained in rescue methods and can do it without endangering yourself. Throw a life preserver or use a pole, towel, or boat to reach the person if you can't swim to him or her safely.

- If necessary, immediately open the person's airway and begin artificial respiration (see Why You Should Learn CPR, p. 43) even before the person is taken out of the water. *Hypothermia*—the lowering of body temperature—often afflicts near-drowning persons, especially when incidents involve submersion in icy water. Therefore it is extremely important that cardiopulmonary resuscitation (CPR) be continued until medical help arrives.

Head and Spinal Injuries

- The head and spine are often injured in diving accidents. If the person is floating face down, gently turn the person over, supporting the head and neck to keep them level with the back. Don't take the person out of the water; instead, keep the person floating on his or her back. Basic CPR rules apply to person of head and spinal injuries.

- If possible, wait for professional help. If the person has to be moved, immobilize the head and neck first, using a backboard, table leaf, door, or several people working as a team to support the head and neck and keep them in line with the back. When a board or other flat, rigid surface is used, it should extend from the head to the buttocks.

Near drowning is an upsetting experience. Stay with a recovering near-drowning person to provide support and reassurance. Any near-drowning person should be taken to the nearest hospital for intensive care, even if the person has regained consciousness. Complications or death from heartbeat disturbances can happen as much as 24 to 48 hours after the accident.

Ear Emergencies

Many ear emergencies result from something being put into the ear. It's usually children who put foreign objects in their ears, objects that then get stuck. But adults sometimes use inappropriate objects to clean their ears, causing damage that can be painful or that can result in hearing loss.

There is other sudden ear damage that requires emergency help. Illness and infection also can cause pain and hearing loss (see Ear, Nose and Throat Problems, p. 123).

Causes

It's not clear why children put foreign objects in their ears, but they do. Sometimes they may not be aware, or they may forget, that they have put a small object in the ear until it starts to bother them or cause problems. Some adults attempt to clean their ears using a cotton swab or a thin, sharp instrument. Even a cotton swab can puncture the delicate eardrum. Other causes of a ruptured eardrum include:

- A blow to the ear
- A very loud noise close to the ear

- Rapid change in pressure, as happens while flying, while scuba diving, or even sometimes while driving at high altitudes

Symptoms

- Earache, a partial hearing loss, and discharge or even bleeding from the ear can indicate a perforated eardrum.
- Dizziness, nausea, or a buzzing in the ear can indicate an ear emergency if there has been some kind of trauma to the ear.

First Aid

- If you can see an object in the ear clearly and you can grab the end of it easily with a tweezers, you can remove the object.
- If you can't see what's stuck in the ear, get medical help. Don't try to dig into the ear canal with tweezers or another instrument. You could force the object deeper into the ear or damage the eardrum.
- If the eardrum may have been ruptured, put some sterile cotton in the outer part of the ear to keep it clean while you get a doctor's help.

- Don't flush your ear if you think you may have a ruptured eardrum or an infection.

- If the ear is draining, have the person lie on his or her side with the affected ear down so that it can drain.

- Ease pain by placing a warm cloth on the ear.

What to do about an Object in the Ear

Symptom/Sign	Action
Object stuck in ear not easily visible	See doctor
Trauma to ear that causes pain or hearing loss	See doctor
Discharge of fluids from the ear or any type of severe, constant ear pain	See doctor

Prevention

- Never put anything inside your ear to clean it. A cotton swab can puncture your eardrum. Use a washcloth and your finger to clean your ears.

- Protect your ears at times when there is likely to be loud noise, such as at a live concert, by using earplugs.

Electrical Shock

An electric shock can cause serious injury, including deep burns and internal damage. Burns are serious medical emergencies. Electricity can also cause the heart to stop beating or to beat unevenly.

Causes

You can suffer an electric shock indoors or out, whether it's from accidentally touching a frayed electric cord or being struck by lightning. Even a mild shock can cause burns, and a major shock can be fatal.

First Aid

- Call 911 and report a medical emergency.

- Do not touch or get within 20 yards of someone who is being electrocuted. This electricity can leap across gaps and strike you. Don't try to rescue the person until the current has been shut off. If possible, turn off the electric current by flipping the main breaker or removing the fuse.

- You may approach a person who has been struck by lightning right away.

Unless the person is in immediate danger, do not try to move him or her.

- When the person is no longer touching a live wire, check to see that he or she is breathing and has a heartbeat. If the person has stopped breathing and you have been trained in CPR, begin it immediately.

- Cover the burned area with dry, sterile dressings.

- To prevent shock, lay the person on a flat surface and raise his or her feet 8 to 12 inches. Do not raise the person's feet if you suspect head, neck, back, or leg injuries. Cover the person with a blanket or coat to maintain body temperature. Stay with the person until professional medical assistance arrives.

What to do about Electrical Shock

Symptom/Sign	Action
Small skin burns	Go to hospital
Person struck by lightning	Call 911
Known or suspected significant electrical exposure	Call 911
Person has stopped breathing	Call 911

Prevention

- Use child safety plugs in all outlets.

- Keep electrical cords out of reach.

- Don't use electrical appliances while showering or when wet.

- Don't touch electrical appliances and faucets at the same time.

- Have your home's wiring inspected every 10 years.

- Don't talk on the phone or use electrical appliances during a thunderstorm.

- If you're outdoors during a thunderstorm, seek shelter. Avoid water, high ground, open spaces, light poles, metal fences, trees, and tents.

Fishhook Wounds

A fishhook caught in the body is a common injury. The barb on the fishhook causes the most injury. When only the point of the fishhook has entered the skin, the fishhook can easily be removed. If the fishhook is so deeply embedded that the barb has entered the skin, you may try to remove it if medical care is not close by. No attempt should be made to remove a fishhook embedded in the eye.

First Aid

- If only the point of the fishhook has entered the skin, remove it by simply backing the fishhook out the way it went in.

- If the barb has entered the skin and medical care is nearby, take the person to a doctor to get the hook removed. If medical care is far away, remove the fishhook using either the pliers or fishline method. If you cannot remove it easily, seek medical care.

- After the fishhook has been removed, wash the wound thoroughly with mild soap and water. Cover the wound with an adhesive bandage and watch for signs of infection (increased redness and swelling).

Removing Fishhooks with Pliers or a Fishline

Use the following methods only if you can't get to a doctor within 24 hours.

Pliers method

- Before beginning the pliers method, check to be certain you have pliers with tempered jaws that can cut through the hook. Cut through an extra hook to ensure the pliers work well enough. Use ice, cold water, or hard pressure to temporarily numb the area before beginning.

- Gently push the embedded hook farther into the skin until the point and barb come out through the skin. Using the pliers, cut off the barb and back the hook out the way it entered, or cut off the other end of the hook and pull it through. Although this method can be painful, it works if the proper pliers are available and the barb is not too deeply embedded to be pushed through to the surface of the skin.

Fishline method

- Loop or tie a piece of fishline to the embedded hook near the skin surface. Immobilize the area where the hook is embedded and use ice, cold water, or hard pressure to temporarily numb the skin.

- With one hand, press down about ½ inch on the eye of the hook to disengage the barb. While still pressing the hook down, jerk the line parallel to the skin surface so the hook shaft leads the barb out of the skin.

What to do about Fishhook Wounds

Symptom/Sign	Action
Barb not embedded	First aid
Hook with barb embedded, not easily removed	See doctor
Signs of infection (increased redness and swelling)	See doctor
Tetanus booster needed (see p. 6)	See doctor
Hook embedded in face, neck, or near major artery	Go to hospital
Hook embedded in eye	Call 911

Fractures

A broken or cracked bone is a fracture. There are two types of fractures: open and closed. A closed fracture means the bone has been broken and the skin has not been damaged. An open (or compound) fracture, in which the skin is broken and bone is visible, is more dangerous and may involve severe bleeding. Open fractures also are more likely to get infected.

Symptoms

A fracture may show one or more of the following symptoms:

- Tenderness over the bone
- Shooting pain
- Visible deformity
- Increased pain with movement
- Bone protruding through the skin

First Aid

- Apply ice packs to the injury. For open fractures, use clean, preferably white, wrappings. Immediately applying cold will help decrease swelling and inflammation. If you think there may be a broken bone, protect and rest the injured limb immediately. To rest a bone effectively, immobilize the joint above and below the suspected fracture.

- If you suspect a fracture, immobilize it to prevent further injury until treatment is completed. A fracture can be immobilized by wrapping something around the injured limb or fixing the limb to some other part of the person's body (this is called splinting). It is best to immobilize the joint above and below the injured area. Maga-

zines, cardboard, or rolled newspaper can be used as a splint. Do not wrap too tightly or circulation will be cut off. A limb that cannot be used at all is probably broken and should be seen by a doctor.

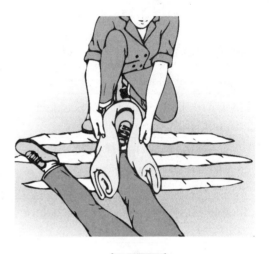

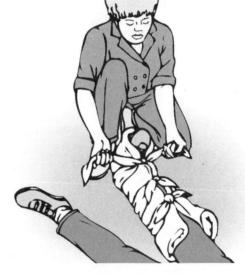

Applying a rigid splint: Use a board or similar object to immobilize a broken limb. Be careful not to cut off circulation by tying too tight. Check for feeling, warmth, and color.

Applying a soft splint: Use a blanket, pillow, or similar soft object to support the injured area. Check for feeling, warmth, and color after tying bandages.

- Minutes and hours are not crucial unless the limb is crooked, arteries or nerves are injured, or the injury is causing great pain. A fractured limb that is protected and rested is likely to mend well, even if casting or splinting is delayed.

What to do about Fractures

Symptom/Sign	Action
Suspected fracture	Call doctor
Crooked limb	See doctor
Unable to use limb or bear weight	See doctor
Cool, blue, or numb limb or portion of limb	Go to hospital
Open fracture (bone breaks through skin) or open skin over fracture	Call 911
Possible hip or pelvic fracture	Call 911

Frostbite

Many of us live in or visit regions where winter brings the threat of frostbite. Frostbite occurs when skin and tissue freeze.

Causes

Frostbite can occur anytime skin is exposed to temperatures below about 28° F. Wind and colder temperatures can increase the risk. Hands, feet, nose, ears, and cheeks are the areas most commonly affected.

Symptoms

- Skin with frostnip, in which only the outermost layers of skin are frozen, may feel numb. It may also appear pale and waxy, and the surface of the skin may feel hard or rubbery.

- With superficial frostbite, all layers of skin are frozen and the skin feels hard all the way through, not just on the top. A frostbitten area is cold, white or grayish-yellow, and hard to the touch. The area may feel very cold and numb, or there may be pain, tingling, or stinging. As the area thaws, it becomes red and painful. Blisters usually form within 24 hours after rewarming.

- With deep frostbite, in which underlying tissue, blood vessels, nerves, muscles, and even bone are frozen, the tissue under the skin also will feel wooden, because it is frozen. Deep frostbite requires prompt medical care.

First Aid

- If you suspect frostnip or frostbite, get out of the cold immediately.

- Warm the affected area by putting the area next to another warm part of your body.

- Warm the affected area by putting it in barely warm, not hot, water (100° F).

- Do not rub the frostbitten area. That can cause further injury to the frozen area.

- Do not use dry heat (such as a heating pad), and do not hold the area near a flame to rewarm. You can burn yourself, especially because you will not have full feeling in the frozen area to warn you when it is getting too hot.

- Drink warm liquids, such as tea, coffee, or hot chocolate.

- Get medical help immediately if the frostbitten area remains numb after you've tried to warm it.

- Do not rewarm a frostbitten area if there is a chance that it will freeze again before you can get to shelter and medical help. If you are in the wilderness or otherwise unable to get to help, keeping the frostbitten area frozen will not cause much additional harm. Further serious injury can occur if the area is warmed and then refrozen. Do cover the area, however, to protect it from freezing any deeper while you are trying to get to shelter and medical help.

- Do not pop blisters. Follow your doctor's treatment plan to prevent infection as the area heals.

- Protect previously frostbitten areas from exposure to cold. Tissue that has been damaged by frostbite will be more sensitive to frostbite in the future.

- Watch for signs of infection as the frostbitten area heals. These include pus or oozing, redness, an odor, or a red line moving away from the injured area.

- You may need a tetanus booster even if frostbite did not involve broken skin. Frostbite may cause skin to slough off later.

What to do about Frostbite

Symptom/Sign	Action
Numbness or tingling	First aid
Pale, white skin	First aid
Numbness continuing after half an hour of first aid	See doctor
Large or multiple blisters or blisters with red fluid	See doctor
Signs of infection (increased redness or swelling)	See doctor
Signs of hypothermia, including slurred speech, confusion, severe shivering, and sleepiness	Call 911

Prevention

- Pay attention to weather conditions and dress accordingly. Wear a hat or ear muffs, mittens, and a scarf.

- Wear warm clothing. Layers are especially effective for protecting against cold.

- Use the "buddy system"—don't go out alone in severe weather.

- Avoid alcohol and nicotine when you will be spending time out in the cold. Both reduce blood circulation to the extremities—your fingers, toes, nose, and ears.

- Be alert to signs of frostnip and frostbite. Get out of the cold as soon as possible to prevent further injury.

Head Injuries

A head injury can make your scalp bleed quite a lot, which can be frightening. Most head injuries are minor, but any head injury is cause for concern.

Symptoms

Bleeding from a scalp wound should stop within 10 minutes after you start applying pressure to it. If it doesn't, the wound may be serious.

You need to watch someone with a head injury for 24 hours. Be alert for any signs of problems, such as headaches, extreme drowsiness, difficulty walking or talking, neck pain, vomiting, fever of more than 101° F, blurred vision, or seizures.

First Aid

- Use an ice bag to ease the swelling of a bump.

- Don't take any medicine before you talk with your doctor.

- Limit activity for 24 hours.

- Wake a child every hour or two to make sure that he or she is responsive.

- Wake an adult every few hours to check breathing and responsiveness. Ask for the person's name, age, and address to make sure he or she is not confused.

- Call 911 right away if the person has bleeding that won't stop, confusion, headache, or vomiting, or if you are unable to wake the person up.

- If the head is bleeding, apply pressure to the wound.

- Clean and bandage the wound.

First Aid for Neck or Back Injury

Call 911 right away, then stay with the person. Don't move anyone with a head, neck, or spine injury, unless you think he or she is in danger. If you can, wait for professional help. If you must move the person to keep him or her safe, use these steps:

- Be careful not to move the head, neck, or back.

- Use a heavy towel or scarf to make a collar around the neck.

- Slide a wide and rigid board under or behind the person. A table leaf or a door will do. Whatever you use should give solid support from the head to the buttocks. If you can, have several people work as a team. They should support the head and neck and keep both level with the back.

- Use broad straps to secure the person to the board. Wide belts or ties will work.

- Treat for shock (see p. 55).

What to do about Head Injuries

Symptom/Sign	Action
A slight bump or knot that causes minor discomfort	Self-care
Bleeding from the scalp that lasts more than 10 minutes, even when pressure is applied	Self-care and see doctor
Bad headache or neck pain	Self-care and go to hospital
Headaches that get worse or vomiting	Go to hospital
Bloody or clear liquid draining from the nose or ears	Go to hospital
Fever rising to about 101° F	Go to hospital
Neck or back injury	Self-care and call 911
Seizures	Call 911
Confusion, dazed look, or difficulty waking	Call 911
Difficulty walking or talking	Call 911
Blurred vision or pupils that are not the same size	Call 911
Difficulty breathing	Call 911
Loss of consciousness	Call 911

Heart Attack

The heart pumps blood and oxygen throughout the body, but it also depends on a supply of blood and oxygen to do its work. A heart attack happens when one of the arteries that brings blood to the heart is blocked. A portion of the heart muscle is damaged or dies due to inadequate blood flow.

Symptoms

The most common warning signals of a heart attack are:

- Uncomfortable pressure, fullness, squeezing, tightness, heaviness, or pain in the center of the chest lasting more than a few minutes
- Pain spreading to the shoulders, neck, arms, or jaw
- Chest discomfort with lightheadedness, fainting, sweating, nausea, or shortness of breath

Less common warning signs of heart attack are:

- Stomach or abdominal pain; indigestion-like discomfort in the chest, especially with activity
- Nausea or dizziness
- Shortness of breath and difficulty breathing
- Unexplained anxiety, weakness, or fatigue
- Palpitations, cold sweat, or paleness

Why You Should Learn CPR

CPR stands for *cardiopulmonary resuscitation*. When you learn CPR, you learn a skill that may save a person's life. You use CPR when someone is not breathing or does not have a heartbeat. With CPR, you can keep oxygen in the person's blood and keep blood moving so oxygen gets to the brain and other organs.

You should not try to learn CPR from a book. You need to take a class to learn the right method and timing

It is not a good idea for you to try to learn CPR from a book. You need to follow certain steps in an exact order for CPR to work. You also need to act quickly and go through the steps at the right pace.

The American Heart Association (AHA) approves classes and teachers for CPR. In these classes, you practice on dummies. A trained teacher will show you how to tell when someone needs CPR. The teacher coaches you to make sure you know how to do the right thing at the right time. Call your local AHA chapter to find out where and when classes are taught in your area. You can also call the American Red Cross.

If you took a class a long time ago, call about a refresher course.

First Aid

If you think you may be having a heart attack, call 911 and get to the hospital as quickly as possible. Do not drive yourself. Take an aspirin (not ibuprofen or acetaminophen [Tylenol]).

Know the Signs of a Heart Attack

- Crushing, squeezing, burning feeling in the chest
- Feeling of pressure in the chest
- Pain that spreads to the jaw, arms, neck, or back
- Pain not relieved by rest or prescribed medication
- Pain lasting longer than 15 minutes
- Nausea, vomiting, shortness of breath, sweating
- Pain while resting or that wakes you from sleep

Heat-Related Problems

Many of us live in or visit regions where sunburn, heat exhaustion, and heat stroke are summer health risks. If you live in a hot region, the heat can affect your health all year round. The three phases of heat-related problems are heat cramps, heat exhaustion, and heat stroke.

Symptoms

Heat cramps can be in the muscles being used while exercising or working in warm temperatures, or there can be abdominal cramps.

Heat exhaustion typically occurs when people work or exercise in hot, humid conditions. But it can also occur during extended periods of hot, humid weather. The symptoms are:

- Cool, pale, and clammy skin
- Heavy sweating
- Dilated pupils
- Headache
- Nausea
- Dizziness
- Faintness
- Rapid pulse and breathing

In heat stroke, body temperature rises rapidly to 104° F or higher. There is a strong, rapid pulse. The person may be confused or unconscious. He or she may also vomit.

First Aid

Heat Cramps

To treat heat cramps:

- Stop the activity.

- Get out of the heat.

- Drink cool water or a sports drink in small amounts—not in big gulps.

- Eat some salty food.

- Massage the cramped muscle, gently stretching it for 20 seconds.

As with all heat illnesses, it is important to treat heat cramps right away. The same conditions that caused the cramps can lead to more serious heat exhaustion or heat stroke.

Heat Exhaustion

If heat exhaustion strikes:

- Get the person to a cool area.

- Loosen or remove the person's clothing.

- Have the person lie on his or her back with the feet slightly raised.

- Give cool water or an electrolyte sports drink.

- Call the doctor's office for advice if you don't notice an improvement within a half hour. Also stay alert to signs of heat stroke.

Heat Stroke

Heat stroke is life threatening. It requires immediate medical attention. Call for an ambulance immediately if someone is suffering from heat stroke. While waiting for help, wrap him or her in wet sheets and fan the body with your hands or an electric fan. Give the person water if he or she is able to drink.

What to do about Heat-Related Problems

Symptom/Sign	Action
Symptoms of heat exhaustion	First aid
Muscle pain or spasms in legs, abdomen, or shoulders	First aid
Symptoms of heat exhaustion—not better after a half hour of self-care	See doctor
Heat exposure with fever or frequent vomiting	See doctor
Dry mouth, increased thirst, severe dizziness, scant or no urinary output	Go to hospital
Hot, red skin; absence of sweat; fever; rapid, shallow breathing	Call 911

Prevention

Heat-related illnesses can be serious. Although certain people (older adults, individuals who are obese, and individuals taking certain medications) may be more susceptible to heat illnesses than others, anyone can be affected. The best advice is to use care.

- Put off strenuous tasks for a cooler day or plan to do them during the coolest parts of the day, such as before dawn or in the early morning. Plan ways to get out of the heat, especially during the hottest part of the day, between 10 a.m. and 6 p.m. If you do not have air conditioning or fans at home, go for at least part of the day to a public air-conditioned place, such as a library, shopping mall, or movie theater, to get out of the heat.

- When outside, wear lightweight and light-colored clothing. Wear a broad-brimmed hat or carry an umbrella for shade. Sponge off with cool water from time to time throughout the day.

- Most important of all, drink lots of water, juices, or sports drinks. (You are drinking enough if your urine is clear, as opposed to yellow.) Avoid caffeine and alcohol.

Hyperventilation

Hyperventilation is breathing faster and more deeply than normal due to anxiety or stress. Breathing too quickly causes the carbon dioxide levels in the blood to fall quickly. The person feels like there is not enough air getting into his or her lungs and may complain of lightheadedness. Feeling the need for more air, the person breathes faster, making the symptoms worse.

Causes

Hyperventilation is usually caused by anxiety, but injury or illness can also be the cause. Hyperventilation may also be linked to emotional problems, such as a panic attack. A panic attack is a brief period of intense fear or discomfort in which symptoms such as dizziness, sweating, or palpitations occur.

Symptoms

The most common symptoms of hyperventilation are:

- Rapid breathing
- Difficulty getting a deep, satisfying breath
- Lightheadedness
- Numbness or tingling in the hands and feet and around the mouth

- Muscle twitching
- Convulsions or fainting

First Aid

Slowing down the breathing will restore the normal balance in the blood, and the symptoms should disappear. If you are unable to calm the person and slow his or her breathing, or if the person faints, bring the person to the nearest hospital or call 911.

Breathing rate can be slowed by following these steps:

- Tell the person to close his or her mouth.

- While the person holds his or her breath, silently count "one-one-thousand, two-one-thousand, three-one-thousand."

- Allow the person to take a shallow breath (mouth still closed).

- Repeat counting and shallow breathing until symptoms disappear. Within several moments, the symptoms should begin to disappear.

What to do about Hyperventilation

Symptom/Sign	Action
Lightheadedness and rapid breathing	First aid
Frequent hyperventilation	First aid
Convulsions or fainting	Call 911

Hypothermia

Hypothermia happens when the body's core temperature drops below the normal 98.6° F. This can occur gradually through exposure to cold weather or suddenly by immersion in cold water.

In cold temperatures (45° F or below), the evaporation of moisture from damp clothing can cause the body to lose heat. Not wearing warm enough clothing can also lead to hypothermia. The gradual drop in body temperature in these conditions is called *exposure*.

The second basic type of hypothermia is *immersion*. When a person is immersed in cold or cool water, the body loses heat rapidly. Depending on the water temperature, hypothermia from immersion can occur in a matter of minutes.

Symptoms

Early symptoms of hypothermia include:

- Uncontrollable shivering
- Cold, pale skin (usually beginning in the hands and feet and moving up toward the body)
- Confusion, irritability, and irrational or erratic behavior
- Slurred speech
- Memory lapses
- Fumbling, stumbling, or staggering

FIRST AID AND URGENT CARE

At first, the heart rate and breathing may be faster than usual, but as the body temperature continues to drop, breathing may become abnormally slow. The person may also become tired or apathetic. The condition becomes grave when shivering stops, muscles become stiff, and skin turns bluish.

First Aid

- To treat hypothermia, get the person out of the cold and remove any damp or wet clothing. Dress the person in warm, dry clothing and wrap in blankets, or put the person in a bath of warm water (unless the person is unconscious). Give warm, nonalcoholic drinks such as coffee, tea, hot cider, or cocoa.

- Do not rub or massage the person. Doing so may cause cold blood from the extremities to flow back toward the heart, making it even more difficult for the body to rewarm.

- If you are out in the wilderness, have someone stay with the person. Don't try to move a person with hypothermia. It is better to wait for help to come to you. If you have blankets or a sleeping bag available, wrap yourself up together with the person. Use your body heat to help warm him or her. Lying naked, or with only underwear

on, will allow more body heat to reach the other person.

- Call the doctor's office for advice if the only symptoms are shivering and cold, pale skin. The doctor or nurse will be able to tell you whether a trip to a clinic or hospital is necessary. If the person develops other symptoms of hypothermia, get medical help as soon as possible, even if the person seems to have warmed up again.

What to do about Hypothermia

Symptom/Sign	Action
Uncontrollable shivering	Call doctor
Rapid pulse and breathing	Go to hospital
Pale, cold, clammy skin or cold, white, or grayish-yellow skin	Call 911
Irritability or lack of coordination	Call 911
Confusion, slurred speech	Call 911
Stiff muscles and bluish skin	Call 911
Slowed breathing or unconsciousness	Call 911

Prevention

Fortunately, hypothermia can be prevented by using good judgment and dressing appropriately. Follow these cold-weather tips to help prevent situations that can lead to hypothermia:

- Protect your body from cold and wet conditions by dressing in layers. Begin with long underwear made from a material (such as silk or polypropylene) that will wick moisture (including sweat) away from the skin. Cotton takes a long time to dry and therefore is not a good fabric for this first layer. Add warm layers of outer clothing. Wool is an especially good insulator. Top it all off with a windproof and waterproof outer shell.

- Wear a hat. By keeping your head covered you can prevent a significant amount of heat loss from your body.

- Be prepared! In winter, always carry an emergency kit in your car. Winter emergency kits should include a blanket, high-calorie food (such as several candy bars), a few candles, matches, and a coffee can (in which to safely place a burning candle). For outdoor sports or other activities, bring along foul-weather gear and any other gear you may need (for instance, if in the wilderness, fire-starting materials and a makeshift shelter).

- During cold-weather activities, keep moving, eat high-calorie foods, and bring along an insulated container of tea or hot chocolate.

Marine-Life Stings

Stings from some types of marine life are poisonous. Jellyfish and Portuguese man-of-war stings are the most common marine-life stings encountered by swimmers, divers, and beachcombers.

Causes

Jellyfish deliver their venom through stinging cells on their tentacles. These stings produce a mild burning and stinging sensation and long, whiplike marks that develop on the skin. In most cases these stings can be treated using first aid. If the reaction is severe, however, call your doctor immediately.

Floating colonies of Portuguese man-of-war are easily spotted, but their transparent tentacles can trail invisibly for up to 60 feet. The pain and burning from these stings can be worse than those of jellyfish stings. They may cause breathlessness, stomach cramps, nausea, and shock.

Symptoms

Symptoms of marine-life stings may include:

- Skin rash

- Muscle cramps

- Severe burning pain
- Nausea or vomiting
- Difficulty in breathing
- Shock due to severe allergic reaction

First Aid

- Do not raise a venomous sting above the level of the person's heart or give the person aspirin, stimulants, or pain medication unless told to do so by your doctor.

- To slow the rate at which the venom spreads in the person's body, keep the person still. If necessary, carry the person to safety. Remove any rings or other tight items in case the injured area swells. If pain continues, call your doctor.

- Be careful with tentacle pieces. A tentacle can sting even after it is removed from the body of the jellyfish. Carefully remove any embedded tentacles using tweezers, pliers, or forceps, or wrap cloth around your hands. Never rub tentacles off! This will activate more stinging cells.

- Try to find out what caused the sting, if you can do so quickly and without endangering yourself.

- If the sting is not bleeding severely, clean the wound and rinse with seawater or saltwater. Marine-life stings need to be thoroughly cleaned to remove sand, spines, bristles, shell fragments, or coral. If the sting is bleeding heavily, cover it with a towel and apply direct pressure.

- After washing, apply a thick (heavy enough to stick on) paste of baking soda or a vinegar solution ($\frac{1}{3}$ cup vinegar to $\frac{2}{3}$ cup water). Scrape off the paste after half an hour and reapply the solution. Don't rub the wound or rinse it with fresh water because this may discharge stinging cells. If a dangerous reaction or signs of shock (see p. 55) occur, call 911.

- Place ice wrapped in cloth or a cold compress on the sting. Be careful not to touch the area with an unprotected hand.

- Call your doctor if pain continues after using self-care.

What to do about Marine-Life Stings

Symptom/Sign	Action
Mild burning and stinging sensation	First aid
All tentacles can't be removed	See doctor
Persistent muscle cramps or spasms	See doctor
Symptoms of infection: increased pain, redness, swelling, and fever	See doctor
Hives, redness and swelling over entire body	Go to hospital
Weakness, faintness, dizziness, difficulty breathing	Call 911

Poisoning

Poison can enter the body in many ways. It can be swallowed, breathed in, or injected. It can also enter the body by coming in contact with the skin. Many substances or combinations of substances can produce fumes that can be especially toxic in a closed area, such as carbon monoxide. Different poisons affect body functions differently. Some interfere with the blood's ability to carry oxygen. Others burn and irritate the digestive tract and respiratory system. If someone suddenly becomes ill for no apparent reason, acts strangely, or is found near a toxic substance, you should suspect poisoning.

Symptoms

Signs and symptoms of poisoning can vary widely, depending on the type of poison involved, the size and general health of the person, and how much time has elapsed. Symptoms can also take time to develop. Do not wait for them to become obvious. Seek immediate medical attention if you suspect poisoning has occurred. Poisoning symptoms include:

- Fever
- Chills
- Loss of appetite

FIRST AID AND URGENT CARE

- Headache or irritability

- Dizziness, weakness, or drowsiness

- Pain in swallowing or increased saliva

- Abdominal pain, vomiting, diarrhea, or nausea

- Skin rash or chemical burns around the nose or mouth

- Seizures, stupor, or unconsciousness

- Double vision or blurred vision

- Muscle twitching

First Aid

Poisoning is a life-threatening situation. If you suspect poisoning, even if there are no symptoms, call a poison control center, 911, hospital emergency room, or your doctor immediately.

When poison has been swallowed, be prepared to provide the following information:

- Information from the label of the substance container

- The person's age

- Name of the poison and how much was swallowed

- When the poison was swallowed

- Whether or not the person has vomited

- How long it will take to get the person to a hospital

If the person is unconscious, keep the airway open. Do not induce vomiting unless told to do so. If you have been told to induce vomiting, use syrup of ipecac, if available. Follow the directions on the label, and do not attempt to give it to a person who is not alert enough to swallow it. Save a sample of vomit and the poison container for analysis. Do not induce vomiting if you are unsure what poison is involved.

First Aid for an Inhaled Poison

If poisonous fumes are suspected, take the following steps:

- Call 911. Ventilate the area before attempting to rescue the person.

- Remove the person from the area before starting treatment. Take a few deep breaths of fresh air, then hold your breath before entering the area. Drag or pull the person to fresh air. If possible, quickly shut off any open source of fumes. Do not flip a switch or light a match; either action could produce a spark or flame and cause an explosion.

- Check breathing and pulse. If the person is not breathing, begin CPR, if you have been trained (see Why You Should Learn CPR, p. 43). If the person is conscious and breathing, cover him or her with a blanket and check on breathing until help arrives.

What to do about Poisoning

Symptom/Sign	Action
Suspected poisoning: person found comatose or stuporous	Call 911
Witnessed poisoning	Call 911
Evidence of possible poisoning: empty container, burns or redness around mouth, chemical smell on breath	Call 911
Suspected poisoning: slurred speech, irritable, uncoordinated	Call 911

Seizures

A seizure occurs when the electrical signals in the brain are disrupted. During a seizure, the brain and nervous system malfunction and the person having the seizure may experience anything from a few minutes of confusion to total unconsciousness. A person who has epilepsy has recurring seizures.

Causes

The cause of some seizures is unknown. Causes can include:

- Brain tumor

- Infection that affects the brain

- Drugs, alcohol, or toxic substances, and sometimes withdrawal from those substances

- Certain chemical disturbances in the body from disease, dehydration, or even lack of sleep

- Scar tissue in the brain from an earlier illness or trauma

- Strokes or other blood system disorders

- Trauma to the brain from an accident or blow to the head

- High fever (in infants)

Symptoms

Partial or focal seizures involve part of the brain. A person suffering a partial seizure does not become unconscious during the seizure. Symptoms of a partial seizure can include:

- Uncontrolled twitching of some part of the body
- Loss of awareness for a couple of minutes
- Compulsive repetitive mannerisms such as picking at things for a few minutes
- Abnormal behaviors or emotions, such as laughing inappropriately

Primary generalized seizures cause loss of unconsciousness. The two kinds of primary generalized seizures are grand mal, in which the body convulses while unconscious, and petit mal, in which it does not.

Symptoms of a grand mal seizure, which can last up to 2 minutes, can include:

- Sudden loss of consciousness
- Rigid body, either straight or arched backward
- Shaking of the arms, legs, and torso
- Biting the tongue
- Loss of bladder control

Symptoms of a petit mal seizure can include:

- Lapse of awareness
- Sudden collapse into unconsciousness, over in just a few seconds
- Sudden jerks of the arms and legs on one or both sides of the body, lasting no more than a few seconds

First Aid

A seizure is not, in itself, usually dangerous, although it may look frightening to others. If someone is having a seizure, take these steps:

- Make sure the person is in a place where he or she is not in danger.
- Move any objects the person might bump into during a seizure.
- Roll the person onto his or her side. Put a pillow or something else soft under the person's head.
- Do not put any object, or your fingers, into the person's mouth.
- Don't try to restrain the person.
- Stay with the person through the seizure.
- Look for a medical alert bracelet that will tell you who to contact in an emergency and what medications the person may use.

- If the person doesn't wake a few minutes after the seizure, call for emergency help.

- If there is another seizure right away, or if the seizure lasts more than 2 minutes, call for emergency help.

Someone with epilepsy, or recurring seizures, doesn't need to see a doctor after each one. But if the person is pregnant, there are signs of illness or injury, or there are changes in the way the person feels during or after seizures, he or she should see the doctor.

What to do about Seizures

Symptom/Sign	Action
Unconscious or disoriented	Self-care
Seizure in an infant with a high fever	Call doctor
Signs of injury or illness	See doctor
Seizure in pregnant woman	See doctor
Seizure lasting more than 2 minutes	Call 911
Failure to wake a couple minutes after seizure	Call 911

Shock

Shock occurs when the heart and blood vessels can't send enough oxygen to every part of the body. Without oxygen, the brain, heart, kidneys, and other organs begin to slow their functions and may stop all activity. Shock is a life-threatening condition that requires immediate medical treatment. Shock does not improve on its own. It typically goes from bad to worse. Without treatment, the person in shock will die.

Causes

Any serious injury or illness, such as blood loss, heart failure, severe infection, burns, or breathing trouble, can result in shock.

Symptoms

Shock may produce these symptoms:

- Shallow breathing

- Rapid and weak pulse

- Lightheadedness

- Nausea and vomiting

- Pale, gray-bluish, clammy skin

- Shivering and coldness in limbs

- Confusion

First Aid

Call 911 and say you have a medical emergency. People in shock need to go to a hospital emergency room as soon as possible. The following suggestions for action are things you can do until the ambulance arrives.

- Try to find the cause of shock and check for a medical alert tag or card. Make sure the person has an open airway and is breathing. If necessary, begin rescue breathing or CPR if you have been trained and certified (see Why You Should Learn CPR, p. 43).

- Stop any bleeding. Lay the person flat and raise the feet 8 to 12 inches, using any available materials for support. Do not raise feet if you think there may be head, neck, back, or leg injuries, or if the person is having trouble breathing. Do not put pillows under the person's head.

- Give first aid for the illness or injury that caused the person to go into shock, if possible. Cover the person with a blanket or coat for warmth. Do not apply direct heat. If the person is drooling or vomits, turn the head to one side so fluids can drain. Check the person's breathing and pulse until trained medical help arrives.

First Aid for Possible Spinal Injury

- Do not move a person who may have a neck or back injury. Keep the person in the same position unless he or she is in immediate danger. Cover the person with a coat or blanket to help keep warm. Do not apply direct heat.

- Try to find the cause of shock and check for a medical alert tag or card. Make sure the person has an open airway and is breathing. If necessary, begin rescue breathing or CPR if you have been trained and certified.

- If the person vomits or is drooling, protect the airway by rolling the person onto one side while carefully supporting the head and neck. Have others help to gently roll the person. Begin CPR if needed. Continue to check the person's breathing and pulse until medical help arrives.

Slivers/Splinters

A sliver is a foreign object that has become embedded in the skin. Most slivers are small wood splinters that do not penetrate deeply. Thorns, glass, or metal fragments can also be slivers. Slivers can be painful if pressure is applied to the affected area.

First Aid

- Wash the affected area with soap and water.

- Sterilize a pair of tweezers with alcohol or in a flame.

- Gently pull the sliver out with the tweezers. If the sliver is deeply embedded in the skin, you will need to fully expose the end of the sliver first. To expose the sliver, slit the skin over the end of the sliver using a sterilized needle or the tip of a razor. Lift up the end of the sliver with the needle or razor, then grasp the sliver firmly with the tweezers. Pull the sliver out at the same angle it went in the skin.

- Seek medical assistance if the sliver does not come out easily or if it is a fishhook or an object with a barb. You should also see your doctor if the sliver was deeply embedded.

What to do about Slivers/Splinters

Symptom/Sign	Action
Foreign object embedded in skin	First aid
Sliver that doesn't come out easily; object is a fishhook or has a barb	See doctor
Tetanus booster needed (see p. 6)	See doctor

Smashed Finger or Toe

A finger or toe smashed in a car door or jammed against a hard object is a common injury, especially among children. When these injuries involve only the end segment of the finger or toe, and not a deep or bad cut, they often can be treated successfully at home.

First Aid

Minor fractures of the bone in the tip of the finger or toe are often left untreated. However, some fractures need to be splinted.

Blood often pools under the nail of the smashed finger or toe, causing severe throbbing pain. A doctor can relieve this pressure by draining the blue-black blood you can see through the nail. If the blood is under more than a third of the nail, see your doctor.

Often the nail is partly pulled off during the accident. Do not pull it off. See your doctor, who may be able to fix it.

There are several steps you can take to relieve pain and speed healing of a smashed finger or toe or torn nail. If symptoms do not improve in 2 to 3 days, call your doctor.

For Smashed Fingers:

- If the person can move the smashed finger or toe easily and the injury does not involve the nailbed, apply an ice pack to reduce swelling and use acetaminophen (Tylenol) or a similar over-the-counter pain reliever.

- If the finger or toe is bleeding, apply pressure on the wound and elevate above the heart until bleeding stops. Wash the wound with soap and water, and watch for any signs of infection.

- If you suspect a possible bone fracture or the smashed finger or toe involves a deep or serious cut, seek medical attention immediately.

For Torn Nails:

- Clip carefully along the line of tear.

- Soak nail for 20 minutes in cold water to reduce swelling.

- Apply antibiotic ointment (such as bacitracin) and cover with nonstick sterile dressing to keep clean.

- On second and third days, cover loosely with an adhesive bandage, use antibiotic ointment, and continue to soak.

- On fourth through sixth day, soak daily in warm salt water ($\frac{1}{4}$ teaspoon in 8 ounces of water) and apply antibiotic ointment. Cover with nonstick sterile dressing to keep clean.

- On seventh day, stop the soaking and dressing; new skin should be formed.

What to do about Smashed Fingers and Toes

Symptom/Sign	Action
Minor discomfort (slight redness, swelling, pain; may have red/brown linear marks)	First aid
Torn nail	First aid
End of nail appears to droop	See doctor
Significant pain and swelling	See doctor
Visible deformity	See doctor
Severe pain and visible blood under nail if blood is under 1/3 of nail	See doctor
Deep cuts or scratches that may need stitches (edges separate or gape more than 1/2 inch in length)	See doctor
Tetanus booster needed (see p. 6)	See doctor
Crushing or wringer type injury, unable to straighten finger or toe	Go to hospital
Nail completely torn off (bring nail to doctor)	Go to hospital
Numbness or tingling in finger or toe, cool to touch	Go to hospital

Stroke

Stroke is a leading cause of impairment in older adults and the third leading cause of death after heart disease and cancer.

Causes

When the blood flow to a part of the brain stops, a stroke occurs. The conditions that contribute to a stroke can be caused by a variety of diseases, including diabetes and coronary artery disease.

Symptoms

Symptoms of stroke include:

- Sudden numbness or weakness of the face, arm, or leg, especially on one side of the body
- Sudden confusion or trouble speaking or understanding
- Sudden trouble seeing in one or both eyes
- Sudden trouble walking, dizziness, loss of balance or coordination
- Sudden, severe headache with no known cause

Treatment

You cannot treat a stroke at home. Emergency room care for a stroke is very important. If you have symptoms of a stroke, call 911. Early care can reduce damage to your brain and limit the effects of the stroke.

Tooth Knocked Out or Broken

Teeth can be cracked or knocked out as a result of sports injuries, falls, vehicle collisions, or other accidents. With quick action, sometimes permanent teeth that have been knocked out can be reimplanted.

First Aid

Knocked-out tooth

If a tooth has been knocked out:

- Don't touch the roots of the tooth; hold it at the top.
- Rinse the tooth gently in a bowl of water. Don't use running water, and don't scrape or rub the tooth to clean it.
- See if you can gently replace the tooth in the socket. If you can, bite down gently on a damp cloth to help keep it in place.
- If you can't replace the tooth, put it in a solution of $\frac{1}{4}$ teaspoon salt and 1 quart warm water, in warm milk, or in your own saliva and get medical attention right away.
- Contact your dentist immediately.

Broken Tooth

For a broken tooth, do the following:

- Rinse your mouth with warm water.
- Use cold compresses to help keep swelling down.
- Contact your dentist immediately.

2 COMMON PROBLEMS

Common problems are the health problems people most often go see the doctor for—everything from colds to back pain to heartburn. Many are conditions that make people wonder if they should go to the doctor, or if they can just take care of the problem at home. This section explains each condition—what causes it, what the symptoms are, and how it can be treated and prevented. Each topic includes a "What to Do About . . ." section that lets you quickly see if you should treat the condition yourself, call or see your doctor, go to the hospital, or call 911. For conditions that can be treated at home, self-care tips are included so you'll know how to best relieve symptoms and speed your recovery.

Skin and Hair Problems

Your skin is the largest organ of your body. It covers and protects your bones, muscles, and other organs and regulates your body temperature. Your skin, hair, and nails often reflect your overall health and are important parts of your appearance.

Many skin, hair, and nail concerns can easily be treated at home. For some conditions, you may need a doctor's help. Dermatologists are doctors who specialize in treating skin concerns. Allergists may also be involved in treating some skin conditions. ::

Acne

Three out of four teenagers have some acne, and some adults continue to have acne into their 20s, 30s, and 40s. Acne occurs when the hair follicles of your skin become plugged with oil and dead skin cells. It usually affects the face, back, chest, and upper arms, though adult acne occurs mainly on the face. Although acne is not life threatening, its effects on self-esteem and self-confidence should not be downplayed.

Causes

Acne is often caused by hormonal activity. An increase in hormones can cause the sebaceous glands to enlarge and produce more sebum (oil), which can lead to plugged pores and outbreaks of pimples. Heredity can play a role in the development of acne. Certain medications may also cause acne. For most people, acne is not caused by food, dirt on the skin, cosmetics, or stress.

Types of Acne

- *Blackheads* are large clogged pores. They are a black or grayish-brown due to chemical changes in the waxy plug in the pore, not because of dirt. Blackheads can sometimes be removed by a doctor.

- *Whiteheads* are clogged pores with only a tiny opening. They are not easily removed without a doctor's assistance.

- *Pustules,* or pimples, are white or yellow bumps that result when the pore's contents leak into the surrounding skin. Squeezing a red pimple can increase the leakage and make the pimple larger.

- *Cysts* are deep, painful, pus-filled lesions that can cause scarring.

Treatment

Most cases of acne can be treated with over-the-counter lotions, creams, or gels. Benzoyl peroxide, resorcinol, salicylic acid, and sulfur are common ingredients used in these medications. Benzoyl peroxide helps kill the bacteria that cause acne. Resorcinol, salicylic acid, and sulfur help break down blackheads and whiteheads.

If over-the-counter medications aren't helpful, your doctor may recommend a prescription medication:

- Lotions, creams, or gels containing tretinoin (commonly called Retin-A) help stop pimples from forming by preventing the pore from clogging.
- Antibiotics work by inhibiting bacteria and reducing inflammation.
- Severe cases of acne can be treated with a capsule containing isotretinoin (Accutane). This medicine does have side effects, however, and cannot be taken by women who are pregnant or planning to get pregnant in the near future.

Regular use of topical acne medications, perhaps combined with medication prescribed by your doctor, can help you avoid outbreaks and potential scarring.

Self-Care

Use these steps to care for acne and prevent further outbreaks.

- Gently wash your face once or twice daily with a mild soap. Avoid excessive or rough face washing.
- Shampoo your hair daily.
- Apply an over-the-counter acne medication to the affected area daily or as directed. If your skin becomes excessively dry, decrease use to every 2 to 3 days.
- Use moisturizers, makeup, and sunscreens that are *noncomedogenic*, which means they won't clog pores.
- Avoid picking or squeezing blemishes.

What to do about Acne

Symptom/Sign	Action
Mild acne	Self-care
No improvement after 6 to 8 weeks of self-care, or acne worsens	Call doctor
Large, red, sore bumps that last longer than 3 days	See doctor
Lowered self-esteem because of appearance	See doctor

Athlete's Foot

A thlete's foot is a fungal infection that thrives in hot, moist conditions and lives on the skin. You don't have to be an athlete to get athlete's foot.

Symptoms

Athlete's foot usually shows up between the toes. Symptoms include redness, scaling, and peeling skin. The affected area may also itch. In some cases the infection spreads to the toenails, causing them to become thick and discolored.

Self-Care

- Wash between the toes and dry thoroughly.

- Use powder to help keep the infected area dry. This adds to comfort and may slow infection.

- After drying, apply an antifungal product such as clotrimazole (Lotrimin) or tolnaftate (Tinactin).

What to do about Athlete's Foot

Symptom/Sign	Action
Athlete's foot responds promptly to self-care	Continue self-care
Increased redness or swelling around the infection	Call doctor
Infection that has not cleared up in 4 to 6 weeks	Call doctor

Blisters

A blister is a thin-walled, fluid-filled bubble on your skin. A blister begins as a "hot spot," an uncomfortable area on your skin that feels like it is being rubbed too much. If ignored, the hot spot will develop into a blister.

Causes

The most common cause of blisters is friction or pressure. Wearing shoes without socks or wearing shoes that are too tight can lead to blisters. You may develop a blister on your palms and fingers if you are doing work that causes rubbing.

Blisters can also be caused by burns, allergic reactions, chemical irritation, or more serious health problems such as shingles or chickenpox. Tiny blisters that appear on the genitals can be herpes simplex virus type 2 (see Genital Herpes, p. 321). Talk with your doctor about any large, unusual blisters that are not caused by friction.

Self-Care

- If the blister breaks open, treat it like an open wound. Wash it with soap and warm water. Apply an antibacterial ointment and cover it with a clean bandage. Watch for signs of infection, such as redness, pain, swelling, or red streaks leading toward the heart.

- Friction blisters are best left unbroken if skin irritation can be avoided until the fluid disappears.

What to do about Blisters

Symptom/Sign	Action
Minor blister	Self-care
Unusual blister appearing without warning or that is not caused by friction	See doctor
Tiny blister on genitals and possible exposure to a sexually transmitted disease	See doctor
Signs of infection (increased redness and swelling around the blister)	See doctor

Prevention

To keep common friction blisters from developing, wear work gloves when doing physical labor. To prevent blisters on your feet:

- Use foot powder.

- Wear a thin sock that wicks away moisture under a thick, moisture-absorbing sock.

- Wear shoes that fit properly.

- Hikers should wear good shoes and thin inner socks and change socks at least once a day. Moist feet get more blisters.

- Use moleskin (a soft material that prevents chafing, which you can purchase from a drugstore) on any hot spots that develop to prevent a blister from forming.

Boils

Boils are painful, pus-filled inflammations of the skin. They can range in size from a pea to a walnut. Although boils may be found anywhere on the body, they most commonly occur in areas where there is hair and friction, such as the neck, armpits, genitals, breasts, face, and buttocks.

Carbuncles are extremely large boils or a series of boils, usually deeper and more painful than regular boils. Always check with a doctor if you suspect a carbuncle, because the infection can get into your bloodstream and you may need antibiotics.

Causes

A boil develops when bacteria invade a hair follicle. Skin tissue swells, and a tender, red, pus-filled lump emerges. The pus contains white blood cells fighting the infection. Until the boil opens and the pus is released, the boil will be painful and tender to the touch.

Self-Care

- Wash hands with antibacterial soap before and after touching a boil with crust or pus around it.

- Wash area gently with antibacterial soap three to four times a day.

- Apply warm compresses three to four times a day for 15 minutes to relieve pain and bring the boil to a head.
- Cover the boil with thick, absorbent gauze and keep dry.
- Avoid scratching the boil because it can spread infection.
- Do not squeeze or lance the boil. If the boil opens, carefully squeeze out the pus.
- Take a pain reliever to reduce pain and inflammation.
- Avoid using over-the-counter antibiotic creams or ointments unless your doctor tells you to.
- Your doctor may lance the boil by making a small incision with a surgical blade so that the pus can drain. Never attempt to lance a boil yourself without approval from your doctor.

What to do about Boils

Symptom/Sign	Action
Mild tenderness, redness, and swelling or itching	Self-care
Boil not forming a head or improving after 3 days of self-care	Call doctor
Extremely painful or pus-filled boil, or pain that interferes with activity	See doctor
Boil on face, spine, or rectal area	See doctor
Fever of 101°F or higher, or red streaks leading away from boil	See doctor
Frequent boils	See doctor

Bruises

Bruises form when blood cells seep from injured veins into surrounding skin tissue. Basically they are sores that don't break the skin. Newer bruises usually appear black and blue. As they heal they may look green and yellow.

Causes

Most bruises are caused by a hard blow to the skin. Some medications, such as anticoagulants and aspirin, can cause people to bruise more easily.

Self-Care

• Apply ice and firm pressure to the bruised area as quickly as possible. This helps veins constrict, reducing the flow of blood into the skin tissue and helping to minimize the bruise.

• Elevate and rest the bruised area.

What to do about Bruises

Symptom/Sign	Action
Sudden increased appearance or multiple bruises, or on anticoagulants or aspirin	Call doctor
New onset of bruising easily with minor injuries	See doctor
Bruising with severe pain and swelling	See doctor

Corns

Corns are yellowish, calluslike growths that develop on the tops of the toes in spots where shoes rub against them. They are usually caused by poor-fitting shoes. If the rubbing continues, corns can become red, inflamed, and painful. Corns are not serious and can usually be treated with self-care.

Self-Care

• Soak feet in warm water and Epsom salts for 15 minutes. Dry carefully and apply a moisturizer. Use a clean nail file or pumice stone in a side-to-side motion to smooth the corn. Repeat daily until the corn is gone. Never try to cut or shave off a corn; this could lead to infection.

• Decrease pressure by changing to a very wide shoe, sandal, or sneaker with a hole cut out for the corn.

• Use a nonmedicated corn pad to relieve pressure on the area. Be careful with medicated corn pads or removers. They can cause skin irritation and infection, especially in people who have diabetes or poor circulation.

What to do about Corns

Symptom/Sign	Action
Corns responding to self-care	Continue self-care
Corns not responding to self-care	See doctor
Recurring corns	See doctor

Prevention

The best way to prevent corns is to wear shoes with a toe box large enough to comfortably surround your toes and the ball of your foot without rubbing.

Dandruff

Dandruff is a common problem, affecting about 20 percent of adults in the United States. Many people are embarrassed by dandruff, but it is not contagious and is fairly easy to control.

Cause

The skin all over your body, including your scalp, sheds dead cells all the time. Dandruff occurs when dead skin cells on the scalp stick together and become visible white flakes.

Self-Care

Although there's no cure for dandruff, there are things you can do to control it.

- Gently brush hair before each washing.

- Wash hair every day. It may be enough to keep mild dandruff under control.

- Use antidandruff shampoos if your scalp is red and flakes are obvious.

- Follow antidandruff shampoo directions. Most say to lather and let it sit for at least 5 minutes before rinsing.

- If a dandruff shampoo seems to lose its effectiveness after several weeks, try another. Coal-tar shampoos may be the most effective.
- Try not to scratch or brush your scalp too hard. Too much scratching may cause more dandruff.

What to do about Dandruff

Symptom/Sign	Action
Responds to self-care	Continue self-care
No improvement after several weeks of self-care	See doctor
Constant irritation or itchiness	See doctor
Thick scales, yellowish crusts, or red patches	See doctor

Hair Loss

Everyone loses between 50 and 100 hairs per day. The average life span of an individual hair is 3 to 7 years. Ninety percent of the hairs on your head are actively growing; the other 10 percent are resting. The resting stage lasts between 2 and 6 months, after which the hairs fall out.

Causes

Losing more than 50 to 100 hairs a day has a variety of causes:

Hereditary balding is the most common cause of hair loss. It can be inherited from either your mother's or father's side. Hereditary balding affects both men and women, although in different ways. Men's hairlines recede and eventually join bald spots on the top and back of the head. Some women notice a slow or occasional thinning on the front of the head. The earlier the thinning starts, the worse it's likely to be.

Medical treatments can cause hair loss in some people. Some blood pressure medicines, anticoagulants, antidepressants, and anti-arthritis and antigout medications can cause reversible hair loss. Radiation and chemotherapy used to treat cancer can cause people to lose up to 90 percent of their hair. Birth control pills can cause increased hair loss while they are taken.

Hormone levels in women can cause hair loss as they rise and fall. Many women lose hair after childbirth, and some have hair loss during menopause or during postmenopausal hormone therapy.

Alopecia areata is a disease that causes hair to fall out, leaving smooth, round patches. The scalp looks normal (no dandruff, scales, or sores).

Other causes of hair loss include:

- Thyroid disease
- Lupus
- Major surgery, infection, or high fever
- Ringworm (a fungal infection)
- Crash diets
- Wearing tight braids or ponytails

Treatment

- Hair transplants can be done to move hair from other parts of your body to your scalp, sometimes a hair at a time. Transplants can cost several thousand dollars and usually aren't covered by health insurance.

- A medication (finasteride) may help men keep their hair. It cannot be used by women.

- Alopecia areata often goes away on its own. If it doesn't, your doctor may prescribe a steroid lotion.

Self-Care

Although there's no cure for hereditary baldness, there are some things that can make hair loss less obvious:

- Minoxidil (Rogaine), an over-the-counter hair restorer, is successful in producing hair in about one-third of the people who try it. The newly grown hair on the crown of the scalp falls out, however, when the drug is no longer applied.

- Use toupees, wigs, or hairpieces to cover thinning or bald areas.

- Do what hairdressers do: color or perm your hair (avoid overbleaching, which causes hair breakage), use a hair dryer for more volume, wash daily with a gentle shampoo, use mousse.

- If you suspect your hairstyle is causing your hair to fall out, avoid curlers, braiding, ponytails, or anything that pulls on your hair.

What to do about Hair Loss

Symptom/Sign	Action
Gradual hair thinning or loss	Self-care
Hair loss occuring 2 to 3 months after surgery, major illness, or childbirth	Self-care
Hair loss that may be associated with medication	Call doctor
Hair loss with pain, soreness or tenderness, scabs, scales, or pus on scalp	See doctor
Sudden occurrence of bald spots, loss of eyebrows or eyelashes, or loss of hair on other body areas	See doctor

Hives

Hives occur when an allergic reaction prompts cells to release histamine, a chemical found in the skin. The histamine causes nearby blood vessels to dilate (open up). Fluid leaks out and collects under the skin in a raised, flushed, itchy bump called a hive.

Extensive outbreaks of hives can be very serious, such as when hives form on the lips and in the throat, interfering with breathing and swallowing. Shock—in which severe swelling, dizziness, and even loss of consciousness occur—can accompany widespread hives.

Causes

Some people know that certain foods or medications give them hives. For others, the causes may not be obvious.

Some foods that occasionally cause hives are nuts, eggs, beans, chocolate, berries, tomatoes, seasonings (mustard, ketchup, mayonnaise, spices) fresh fruits (especially citrus fruits), corn, fish and shellfish, milk, wheat, and cheese.

Medications that have been known to cause hives include penicillin, sulfa antibiotics, and codeine. If you develop hives shortly after you begin taking a new medication, stop taking it immediately and call your doctor.

Symptoms

Some hives look like mosquito bites. They often come in groups, and they may be as small as pencil erasers or as large as 2 or 3 inches across.

Acute hives (hives that are a reaction to something specific, such as a medication) can last for hours or days. Chronic hives (often of unknown cause) can last for weeks or months.

Self-Care

- Try to determine the source of your hives so you can prevent a reaction in the future.

- Take an oral antihistamine, such as Benadryl or Chlor-Trimeton. Read the directions and warnings on the label carefully; these medications may make you drowsy.

- Rub ice directly over the hives or take a cool shower for temporary relief from itching.

- Soak in a lukewarm or cool bath with 1 cup of baking soda or an oatmeal product such as Aveeno.

- If hives develop after a bee sting or other insect bite, call your doctor or the emergency room.

What to do about Hives

Symptom/Sign	Action
Hives responding well to self-care	Continue self-care
Hives of unknown cause	Call doctor
Hives not responding to self-care after 7 days	Call doctor
Hives that develop shortly after you begin taking a new medication	Call doctor
Widespread hives over body	Go to hospital
Extensive hives with swelling around the face and in the throat and mouth; difficulty breathing	Call 911

Ingrown Toenail

Ingrown toenails occur when the sides or corners of a nail grow into the skin. This can cause swelling and redness and can be quite painful. The big toe is most often affected.

Causes

Some people are born with nails that have a tendency to become ingrown, but the most common causes of ingrown toenails are wearing shoes that don't fit well and trimming nails improperly. An injury to a toenail may also cause it to become ingrown.

Treatment

If the problem is mild, you may be able to use self-care. But if the pain is severe or getting worse, see your doctor.

Doctors usually treat ingrown toenails with a minor surgical procedure. After numbing your toe, your doctor will cut the nail and remove the part that's grown into the skin. In some cases, doctors use a laser or chemical on the area to prevent that part of the nail from growing back.

Self-Care

- Soak your foot in warm water for 15 to 20 minutes several times a day. After soaking, put a small piece of sterile cotton under the edge of the nail that's ingrown. This can help the nail start to grow above the skin, rather than into it.
- Use an antibiotic ointment on the area.
- Wear wide or open-toed shoes until your toe feels better.

What to do about Ingrown Toenails

Symptom/Sign	Action
Mild ingrown toenail	Self-care
Ingrown toenail that is severe or getting worse despite self-care	See doctor
Ingrown toenail and you have diabetes	See doctor

Prevention

- Trim your nails straight across, and don't trim or round the corners. Be careful not to trim them too short.

- Wear shoes that fit well. Avoid high heels and other shoes that pinch or put pressure on your toes.

- If your nails are difficult to cut, soak them in warm water for 5 to 10 minutes before trimming.

Jock Itch

Jock itch is a fungal skin infection in the groin that appears as a red, ring-shaped patch with a clear center. It may be itchy and scaly. Jock itch is more common in men but can also occur in women.

Causes

Jock itch is caused by a fungus that lives on the outer layer of the skin. Heat and moisture contribute to the development of jock itch, so it is more common in the summer.

Self-Care

Jock itch usually clears up in 4 to 6 weeks with self-care.

- Wash the groin daily with a mild soap; rinse and dry thoroughly.

- Apply an over-the-counter antifungal cream (such as Lotrimin or Micatin) to the rash and surrounding area 3 to 4 times a day. Because the fungus can continue to live under the skin even after your symptoms disappear, you should continue to use the antifungal cream for 1 week after the rash clears.

- Apply a body powder to absorb moisture and reduce friction.
- Avoid sharing towels to prevent infecting others with the fungus.

What to do about Jock Itch

Symptom/Sign	Action
Rash in groin area; may be itchy, scaly	Self-care
Rash or itching that does not clear up in 4 to 6 weeks, or symptoms that worsen with use of antifungal cream	See doctor
Bright red, scaly, itchy rash on penis or scrotum	See doctor
Signs of infection: increased redness and swelling	See doctor

Lice

Lice feed on human blood. As they attach to the skin, their saliva causes intense itching. A female louse can lay up to 6 eggs a day and between 50 and 100 in her lifetime. Left untreated, head lice are annoying and easily spread.

Causes

Head lice can be spread by sharing bedding, hats, or combs with a person who has lice. Having lice is no longer believed to be a sign of poor hygiene.

Symptoms

A case of head lice is often mistaken for dandruff. Symptoms include itching, white nits (football-shaped eggs) on hair shafts that aren't removed with regular shampooing.

Treatment

Over-the-counter treatments for head lice are available in two forms: shampoo or creme rinse (such as Rid or Nix). Follow directions carefully to ensure successful treatment. If you see live lice within 48 hours of treatment, start over using a different over-the-counter product. Repeat application of antilice medication within 7 to 10 days of first application.

Self Care

- If nits are visible on the eyelashes, apply petroleum jelly (such as Vaseline) with a cotton swab to eyelids twice a day for 8 days.

- Machine wash recently worn clothing, bedding, and towels in very hot water or dry in a hot dryer for at least 20 minutes. Unwashable items or toys can be dry-cleaned, stored in tightly sealed plastic bags for 2 to 3 weeks, or placed outside in cold weather for 48 hours. Soak all combs, brushes, and hair accessories in antilice creme rinse or in hot, soapy water for at least 10 minutes. Vacuum floors, rugs, carpets, mattresses, and furniture, including fabric-covered car seats and headrests. Discard vacuum cleaner bags and seal tightly.

Tips for Using Antilice Creme Rinse or Shampoo

Creme Rinse

- Remove nits with a fine-tooth comb. Dip the comb into a solution of half vinegar and half rubbing alcohol and then back-comb to loosen the substance that binds the eggs to the hair shaft.
- Shampoo hair thoroughly with an abrasive shampoo, such as Prell or baby shampoo, to remove the vinegar solution.
- Towel dry hair completely to avoid diluting the medication.
- Apply 2 ounces of over-the-counter creme rinse containing 1-percent permethrin. Thoroughly massage into the scalp, where the lice live. Leave on hair for 10 minutes, then rinse well with cool water and dry. Do not wash hair for 24 hours.

Shampoo

- Apply shampoo to dry hair. Saturate completely and massage into scalp.
- Wait 10 minutes, then add water to form lather. Shampoo and rinse thoroughly with cool water.
- Hair may be difficult to comb after treatment. Use a regular shampoo and conditioner after treatment to get tangles out. (This will not reduce the effectiveness of the antilice shampoo.)
- Comb hair with a fine-tooth comb to remove lice eggs.

What to do about Lice

Symptom/Sign	Action
Itching scalp or rash on scalp, silver/white beads on hair shaft, over the age of 2, not pregnant	Self-care
Itching scalp or rash on scalp, silver/white beads on hair shaft, less than 2 years old, or pregnant	Call doctor
Symptoms that continue after using over-the-counter choices as directed	Call doctor
Repeated occurrence of head lice	Call doctor
Tender, red scalp; crusty pus-filled bites; matted or foul-smelling hair	See doctor

Mouth Sores

Mouth sores can be painful, unsightly, and slow to heal. Mouth sores that are caused by rough teeth or braces are sometimes difficult to heal and may become infected.

Self-Care

• Clean your mouth frequently. Use a soft-bristled toothbrush or rinse your mouth with a mild saltwater solution: ½ teaspoon salt and 1 cup water.

• Try popsicles, fruit slushes, or crushed ice to increase your fluid intake and numb the pain.

• Sip liquids through a straw if drinking is painful.

What to do about Mouth Sores

Symptom/Sign	Action
One or more red- or yellow-centered, craterlike sores inside the mouth, on the gums, or inside the lips and cheeks	Self-care
One or more blisters on the outside of the mouth area	Self-care
Mouth sores caused by poorly-fitting dentures or rough or broken teeth	Call dentist
Recurring mouth sores	See doctor
Possible exposure to a sexually transmitted disease	See doctor
Facial swelling and signs of infection; severe pain and inability to eat	See doctor
Watery or red eye	See doctor
Canker sore with loss of appetite or bad breath or that does not get better in 2 weeks	See doctor
Large, bleeding, painful ulcers on gums	See doctor

Prevention

Good general health practices are the best precaution against mouth sores:

- Eat a nutritious diet with lots of vitamin-rich fruits and vegetables.

- Get enough rest and exercise.
- Try to avoid getting colds and the flu.
- Wash your hands often with warm, soapy water.
- Avoid sharing glasses or utensils with someone who has a cold.
- Avoid smoking or chewing tobacco.
- Brush your teeth at least twice a day and floss daily.
- See your dentist regularly.

Cold Sores

Cold sores, also called *fever blisters*, occur outside the mouth or on or around the lips. They are caused by the herpes simplex virus and can start before or during a cold or the flu.

The virus that causes cold sores can be dangerous to newborn babies, elderly adults, and people who have a chronic disease or who are taking immunosuppresant medications. These people should avoid being near anyone who has the symptoms of a cold sore.

Causes

Cold sores are contagious. You can get them from skin-to-skin contact, such as kissing, or from sharing eating utensils or towels with someone who has a cold sore. Certain triggers may cause repeated outbreaks, including:

- Physical or emotional stress
- Menstruation
- Cold or fever
- Upset stomach
- Excessive exposure to the sun
- Use of medications that suppress the immune system

Symptoms

Cold sores are painful, clear blisters that can appear singly or in clusters of 10 or 20. Before you get a cold sore, your body often gives you a warning signal: the affected area will itch, tingle, or burn before the sore forms.

Treatment

Most cold sores will clear up on their own in 7 to 10 days. However, if you are experiencing frequent outbreaks, your doctor may prescribe an oral antiviral medication. Medications can help cold sores clear up faster, but they won't prevent new outbreaks from occurring.

Self-Care

- Apply cold compresses or ice to relieve pain.

- Apply an over-the-counter cold sore product, following the directions on the label.
- Take analgesics (such as Bayer aspirin) for pain. Use as directed.
- Wash hands frequently.
- Avoid touching the sores.
- When you're in the sun, apply zinc oxide or lip balm with sunscreen around the mouth and nostrils to prevent an outbreak.
- Apply an over-the-counter topical antibiotic (such as Neosporin) to prevent secondary infection.
- Apply 1-percent hydrocortisone cream after the blister is gone to reduce inflammation.

Canker Sores

Canker sores usually occur inside the mouth, lips, or cheeks. They can be red or yellowish-white with a red border. No one knows for sure what causes them. Unlike cold sores, canker sores are not contagious.

Treatment

There is no cure for canker sores, but if you have unusually large, persistent canker sores or frequent outbreaks, your doctor may be able to prescribe a special mouthwash or other solution to ease your symptoms.

Self-Care

- Gargle or swallow 1 tablespoon of an antacid (such as Mylanta) four times a day, ideally after meals.

- Rinse your mouth with a solution of half hydrogen peroxide, half water.

- Avoid eating acidic foods such as citrus fruits or tomatoes. Salty, spicy, or vinegary foods may irritate canker sores as well. Milk, Jell-O, yogurt, ice cream, custard, and other soft foods are often easier to tolerate.

- Avoid eating foods with sharp edges, such as potato chips.

Poison Ivy/Poison Oak/Poison Sumac

A walk in the woods or garden may become an itchy experience if you encounter poison ivy, poison oak, or poison sumac. Contact with these plants usually occurs when you're pulling weeds or cleaning up at the cabin, gardening around the edges of the lawn, or exploring in wooded areas.

Causes

The rash that occurs after contact with poison ivy, oak, or sumac is caused by *urushiol*, an almost invisible, clear-to-slightly-yellow oil that comes from any cut or crushed part of the leaves, stem, or vine crawling on the ground. The oil can be carried for up to 3 days on the paws or fur of cats and dogs. It can be carried on shoes, clothing, or on garden tools for weeks or months.

Symptoms

When urushiol touches the skin, it penetrates within minutes. In 12 to 48 hours a red, itchy rash and tiny, weeping blisters may appear.

Treatment

Usually exposure to these poisonous plants can be treated at home with self-care. If the rash covers a large area or involves your face or eyes, see your doctor. Your doctor may treat a very bad reaction with cortisone.

Self-Care

- Wash suspected areas of contact with soap and water as quickly as you can. If necessary, use water from a nearby stream, lake, or garden hose. Washing skin within 60 minutes of exposure will lessen your reaction.

- If water isn't available, wipe affected areas with rubbing alcohol (though this may cause urushiol to spread).

- Use water to rinse off pets, clothes, shoes, and camping or gardening gear if you or your pets have been in infested areas.

- *Tecnu* is a solvent specially designed to remove urushiol oil from the skin. It needs to be flushed off with water to avoid spreading the urushiol to other parts of your skin.

- Cool compresses are the best treatment for a rash. Calamine lotion or Cortaid may also be used to relieve initial itching and help dry the rash.

- Over-the-counter antihistamine pills (such as Bendadryl) may relieve itching. However, these medications may cause drowsiness.

- A soak in lukewarm water mixed with an oatmeal bath product or baking powder may soothe irritated skin and dry oozing blisters over large areas.

What to do about Poison Ivy/Poison Oak/ Poison Sumac

Symptom/Sign	Action
Mild itching; self-care effective in treating discomfort	Continue self-care
Rash covering a large area or involving the face, eyes, or genitals	Call doctor
Rash that does not improve after self care	Call doctor
Increased redness, tenderness, red streaks, or fever	See doctor
Severe swelling from rash	See doctor
Symptoms rapidly worsening	See doctor

Prevention

Your best defense against these poisonous plants is to learn to identify them by sight, and watch what you're handling when gardening, hiking, or cleaning up around the yard. Try not to break the plant, because the oil is in all parts of the plant.

Poison ivy usually grows east of the Rocky Mountains as a vine or shrub. Its leaves are in clusters of three, and it has yellowish-white berries. It grows easily and is widespread both inside and outside city limits.

Poison oak grows west of the Rockies as a shrub, small tree, or, less often, a vine. It has greenish-white berries and has leaves in clusters of three, similar to those of poison ivy.

Poison sumac is found in swampy, boggy areas in the South and northern wetlands. It's a tall shrub with 7 to 13 pointed, small leaves per branch and cream-colored berries.

If you have to work near infested areas, wear long pants, long sleeves, rubber gloves, and boots. Over-the-counter barrier products, such as Ivy Block and Stokoguard, can also offer protection.

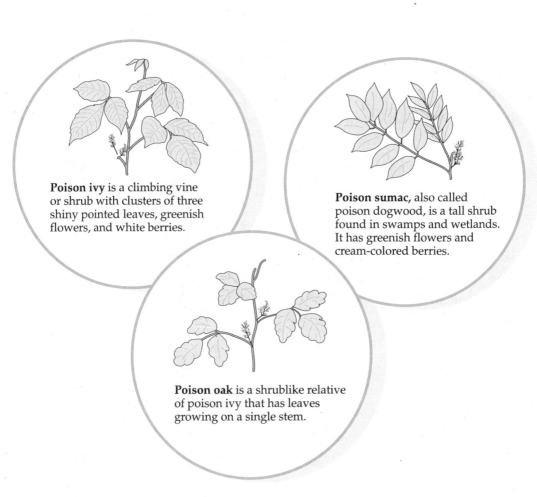

Poison ivy is a climbing vine or shrub with clusters of three shiny pointed leaves, greenish flowers, and white berries.

Poison sumac, also called poison dogwood, is a tall shrub found in swamps and wetlands. It has greenish flowers and cream-colored berries.

Poison oak is a shrublike relative of poison ivy that has leaves growing on a single stem.

Rashes

A rash, also called *dermatitis* or *eczema*, is an inflammation of the skin. Most people have had skin rashes at one time or another. Rashes can have a number of causes, including allergies, irritants, or illness.

Types of Rashes

There are several different types of rashes.

Contact dermatitis is a common form of skin rash. It results from an allergy or exposure to an irritant. When the skin touches something to which it is allergic or that it finds irritating, it may become itchy and red. Other symptoms of contact dermatitis include raised red dots; burning, red, swollen patches; and blisters that may weep. Cosmetics, deodorants, soaps, metals, and dozens of other natural and artificial substances can cause contact dermatitis. (Also see Poison Ivy/Poison Oak/Poison Sumac, p. 82, and Hives, p. 73.)

Atopic dermatitis usually develops in childhood and may last into adulthood, although an adult can develop atopic dermatitis without a previous history of it. People with atopic dermatitis have a greater chance of having hay fever or asthma. Usually the skin is extremely itchy and dry. It may also be red and flaky or scaly.

Itch-scratch-itch cycle dermatitis develops when an itchy area is scratched or rubbed repeatedly. The skin becomes harder and annoyingly itchy. Scratching makes this worse. It can be hard to break the itch-scratch-itch cycle.

Seborrheic dermatitis is red, flaky, slightly itchy skin on an adult's scalp and face. The area from the side of the nose to the corner of the mouth may be affected, as well as the scalp and eyebrows. If you have seborrheic dermatitis, you may also have dandruff, which may be treated with a variety of anti-dandruff shampoos.

Self-Care

- Bathe once a day for short periods. Pat skin dry; do not rub.
- When bathing, minimize use of soap or use moisturizing or soap-free cleanser. Avoid bath oils and bubble baths.
- Keep nails short to reduce damage done to the skin by scratching.
- Dress lightly and wear soft, non-scratchy clothes.
- Apply cold compresses for temporary relief of itching.

- Apply over-the-counter 1-percent hydrocortisone creams as often as 4 times a day to relieve itching.

- Protect your skin from contact with harsh chemicals and substances to which you are allergic; use latex gloves (if you do not have a latex allergy) and wear protective clothing if possible.

- Humidify air in winter.

What Caused my Rash?

The first step in treating a rash is to find out what may have caused it. Ask yourself these questions.

- Have I started a new medication?
- Have I changed soaps, shampoos, deodorants, cosmetics, or hair dyes lately?
- Does the rash appear on a part of the body where clothes are worn?
- Have I worn any new jewelry or used new hand cream or nail polish?
- Have I been near plants such as poison oak, poison ivy, or poison sumac?

If you suspect any of these substances may have caused your rash, try to avoid them in the future.

What to do about Rashes

Symptom/Sign	Action
Mild pain, itching, or flaking	Self-care
Sores that are crusting or weeping, or itching that is very bad	Call doctor
No response to self-care after 1 week	Call doctor
Temperature of 101°F or higher	Call doctor
Reddened, sunburned-looking skin that feels like sandpaper	Call doctor
Expanding circular rash	Call doctor
Red streaks leading away from rash	See doctor
Swollen joints, chills, dizziness, nausea	See doctor
Burning eyes and nose; weeping blisters around nose and lips	See doctor
Extensive rash with swelling around face and in throat and mouth; difficulty breathing	Call 911

Ringworm

R*ingworm* is an outdated term for a fungal skin infection. The name *ringworm*—dating back to the early fifteenth century—comes from the idea that the infection was caused by a burrowing worm. There is no such thing as a ringworm.

Causes

Ringworm, and other fungal skin infections such as athlete's foot and jock itch, are really caused by tiny organisms that can be seen only under a microscope. Fungal infections are moderately contagious among susceptible people, and some kinds can be spread to people by cats and dogs.

Symptoms

Ringworm starts as a small spot, then spreads or radiates out in a ringlike pattern. It can infect most surfaces of the body, including the nails. On the scalp it may cause itchy, red areas and hair loss. To determine if you have ringworm or another infection, your doctor can do tests by examining a piece of your nail, hair, or skin under a microscope.

Self-Care

- Over-the-counter antifungal creams work well for fungal infections. Try tolnaftates (Tinactin, Aftate), clotrimazoles (Lotrimin AF, Mycelex), or miconazoles (Micatin, Monistat) on small patches, especially for areas other than the feet. Apply twice a day at least 2 centimeters past the border of the lesion for at least 2 weeks (it may take 4 to 6 weeks). Continue using for 1 week after lesion disappears.

- Keep moist areas dry. Use powder after bathing. Try drying the affected area with a hair dryer set on cool.

- Thoroughly clean combs and hats.

- Avoid sharing towels, clothing, or other personal items during treatment.

- Launder all personal items frequently using hot water.

- If your pets develop scaly, hairless skin lesions, have them checked for fungal infections by a veterinarian.

What to do about Ringworm

Symptom/Sign	Action
Fungal infections on the feet and groin	Self-care
Fairly small affected area	Self-care
Improvement within 1 to 2 weeks with over-the-counter remedies	Continue self-care
Fungal infection of the scalp, face, or fingernails	See doctor
More than one infected area or the infection is spreading	See doctor

Prevention

If you have a pet that develops a patch of skin where fur is missing, have the pet treated by a veterinarian. Avoid touching the animal until it has been treated and all sores or bare spots are gone. Do not share shoes with someone else who has athlete's foot.

Rosacea

Rosacea is an inflammatory skin condition that causes redness, bumps, pimples, and other symptoms. It is a form of acne. Rosacea usually affects the face, though it can also affect the neck and upper chest. It may get worse over time, but in many people it occurs in cycles, getting better and worse on its own.

Rosacea most often affects people between the ages of 30 and 60. It's more common in women but often more severe in men.

Causes

Doctors aren't sure what causes rosacea, but it's believed to be a combination of genetic and environmental factors. Though the cause is unknown, there are some things that are known to make it worse:

- Drinking alcohol
- Hot foods or beverages
- Spicy foods
- Sunlight
- Strenuous exercise
- Extreme temperatures
- Emotional stress

Symptoms

- *Inflammatory rosacea* involves small red bumps and pustules that appear on the cheeks, nose, forehead, and chin.

- *Rhinophyma* is a rare complication of rosacea, in which the oil glands of the nose and the surrounding tissues enlarge, causing a buildup of tissue that can look thick and knobby. Rhinophyma is more common in men.

More than half of people with rosacea also experience ocular rosacea, a condition that affects the eyes. Symptoms include a burning, gritty sensation in the eyes, redness, and tearing.

Treatment

There's no cure for rosacea, but it can be treated and controlled. Your doctor may prescribe a topical antibiotic, such as metronidazole, which comes in a cream, lotion, or gel form that you apply directly to your skin. In many cases, doctors will also prescribe oral antibiotics such as tetracycline, minocycline, erythromycin, and doxycycline.

Enlarged blood vessels, redness, and rhinophyma sometimes become permanent. In these cases, laser surgery or electrosurgery may be used to reduce the visibility of blood vessels, remove excess tissue, reduce the size of the nose, and improve appearance.

Self-Care

In addition to following your doctor's treatment plan, there are some self-care steps you can take to prevent flare-ups.

- Keep a record of things that seem to trigger flare-ups. Try to avoid these triggers.

- Wear sunscreen with a sun protection factor (SPF) of 15 or higher.

- Avoid using facial products that contain alcohol or other ingredients that irritate your skin.

- Use products that are labeled noncomedogenic, which will not clog your pores.

- Protect your face in cold weather with a scarf or ski mask.

- Avoid irritating your skin by rubbing or touching it too much.

What to do about Rosacea

Symptom/Sign	Action
Occasional flushing or redness of the skin	Call doctor
Symptoms are becoming progressively worse	See doctor
Redness or other symptoms are not going away with treatment	See doctor

Scabies

Scabies produces small, itchy bumps that are caused by tiny mites. The mites burrow into the skin, where the females lay eggs. Within about 5 days, the eggs hatch. Itching begins several weeks after the mites have started living in the skin. Like head lice, scabies is no longer thought to be a sign of poor hygiene.

Causes

The tiny mites that cause scabies pass easily from one person to another. You can get scabies from close physical contact with someone who has scabies or from their bedding or clothing. Scabies can be spread both sexually and nonsexually (usually nonsexually).

Symptoms

Scabies most often appears in the finger webs and around the wrists, but itchy areas may occur anywhere. It often affects the male genital area. The burrowing of these mites leaves very small grooves and tunnels on the skin that may look like tiny gray, black, or white splinters.

Self-Care

When someone in your household has scabies, everyone in the household should be treated at the same time.

- Call your doctor to discuss the problem. If the symptoms are clearly from scabies—or if you know you were in contact with someone infested by scabies—your doctor can call your pharmacy with a prescription for a lotion that will kill the mites. Your doctor will also give you specific instructions to halt the infestation. You may need to repeat these procedures 1 week later.

- Apply the insecticide lotion to all members of the household according to package directions.

- Take an over-the-counter antihistamine, such as Benadryl, to help relieve itching.

- Wash all bedding and clothing used before or during treatment.

What to do about Scabies

Symptom/Sign	Action
Very itchy gray lines or red patches appearing on the body	Call doctor
Criss-crossing, itchy lines or tunnels in the skin	Call doctor
You know someone who has scabies, and you've developed a rash and itching	Call doctor
Side effects from insecticide lotion	Call doctor
Constant itching and rash of an unknown cause	See doctor

Skin Cancer

Skin cancer is the most common type of cancer in the United States. The number of people getting skin cancer is increasing, and people are getting it at younger ages. The good news is that skin cancer can be cured in 85 to 95 percent of all cases. It is also preventable.

Causes

Ultraviolet (UV) radiation from the sun is the main cause of skin cancer. Artificial sources of UV radiation, such as sunlamps and tanning booths, can also cause skin cancer.

Some people are at higher risk than others for getting skin cancer. Factors that can put you at higher risk include:

- Fair to light complexion
- Family history of skin cancer
- Chronic exposure to the sun
- History of sunburns in childhood
- Large number of moles
- Freckles

Where you live can affect your risk for developing skin cancer. In the United States, skin cancer is more common in southern states, where the sun is stronger. Age can also be a factor. Most skin cancers appear after age 50.

Symptoms

The most common warning sign of skin cancer is a change on the skin, especially a new growth or a sore that crusts or bleeds occasionally (see Know the Signs of Cancer, p. 149). Not all skin cancers look the same. It is rare for skin cancer to cause pain.

Actinic keratosis, which appears as rough, scaly, red or brown patches on the skin, is known as a *precancerous condition* because it sometimes develops into squamous cell cancer. It usually appears on sun-exposed parts of the body, especially the ears, face, scalp, and hands. The scaly areas may be easier to feel than to see.

Types of Skin Cancer

Basal cell cancer is the most common skin cancer in the United States, accounting for more than 90 percent of all cases. It is slow growing and rarely spreads to other parts of the body. Basal cell cancers may look like pearly or waxy lumps that sometimes have depressions in the middle. As the cancer grows, the center becomes more ulcerated and looks "gnawed."

Squamous cell cancer is often raised or lumpy with rough, scaly surfaces on a reddish base. Often the border is irregular. Squamous cell cancers occurring on sun-exposed skin uncommonly spread to other parts of the body, though it happens more often than with basal cell cancer.

Malignant melanoma may appear as a mole or freckle that changes size, color, surface, shape, or border. The faster these changes occur, the more suspicious it is. Look for an irregular border with different colors in the same mole and some black color. Most melanomas are not bumps. In the early stage, most resemble a very dark and larger-than-normal freckle. Melanomas are most often found on the back in men and on the back, thighs, and calves in women. If not detected early, malignant melanoma can spread to other areas of the body—mainly the lymph nodes, liver, lungs, and central nervous system—and can be lethal.

Treatment

Treatment for skin cancer usually involves some type of surgery to remove the cancer. In some cases, chemotherapy or radiation therapy may also be used to damage cancer cells and stop them from growing. If the cancer only involves the outer layer of skin, laser therapy may be used to remove or destroy cancer cells.

If a large cancer is removed, your doctor may perform a skin graft. In this procedure a piece of healthy skin from another part of your body is used to close the wound and reduce the amount of scarring.

What to do about Skin Cancer

Symptom/Sign	Action
Rough, scaly, red or brown patches on the skin	See doctor
Pearly or waxy lump; irregular mole; mole that changes color, size, or texture	See doctor
A sore that doesn't heal in 2 weeks	See doctor

Prevention

- Avoid too much sun, particularly between 10 AM and 2 PM and in midsummer.

- Use a sunscreen with an SPF of 15 or higher. Make sure you apply sunscreen thoroughly to all exposed skin, so you don't leave unprotected areas.

- Avoid sunlamps and tanning beds. They damage the skin, despite what tanning-salon owners and employees might tell you.

- Use sunscreen even on cloudy days.

- Use lip balm with the sunscreen paraaminobenzoic acid (PABA), wear UV-opaque sunglasses to protect your eyes, and be sure to apply sunscreen around eyes, ears, mouth, and any bald or thinning areas on your head.

• UV rays can penetrate through loosely woven clothing and beach umbrellas, so wear sunscreen even when using these other forms of sun protection. Also, look for the sun-protective clothing that's now available, including shirts, pants, and hats for adults and children.

How To Do a Skin Self-Exam

After your shower or bath, start by noticing where birthmarks, moles, and blemishes are and what they look like. Be sure to check your entire body, including back, scalp, buttocks, and genitals. Use a mirror to check hard-to-see areas. Check for anything new—a change in the size, texture, or color of a mole or a sore that does not heal. Do a skin self-exam once a month.

Sunburn

Sunburn results from overexposure to UV radiation from the sun. There are two types of UV rays that can damage skin. Ultraviolet A (UVA) rays don't cause sunburn, but they penetrate deep into the skin and can cause long-term damage. Ultraviolet B (UVB) rays are the rays that burn your skin.

Frequent overexposure to the sun can cause long-term damage to the skin, resulting in premature aging, wrinkling, and skin cancer.

Symptoms

In a first-degree burn, symptoms include redness, sensitivity, and pain. Long exposure can lead to the swelling and blistering of a second-degree burn.

Self-Care

Sunburn is usually uncomfortable for 24 to 48 hours. If you have sunburn, stay out of the sun until your skin recovers, and try these suggestions to relieve symptoms:

• The best treatment for sunburn is to soak the affected area in cold water (not ice water) or apply cold compresses for 15 minutes. This will reduce swelling and provide quick pain relief.

- If sunburn affects large areas of your body, soak in a cool bath. Half a cup of cornstarch, oatmeal, or baking soda in the bath will help reduce inflammation and soothe sunburned skin.

- Adults who do not have stomach problems or a history of allergy to aspirin products can take aspirin to reduce inflammation.

What to do about Sunburn

Symptom/Sign	Action
Minor sunburn	Self-care
Blistering, painful sunburn over a large area	See doctor
Sunburn and purple blotches, skin discoloration, or blisters	See doctor
Elderly person with sunburn	See doctor
Sunburned eyelids	See doctor
Sunburn with severe pain or eye pain	See doctor
Sunburn with chills, nausea, fever of 102°F or higher, faintness, dizziness, or vision problems	Go to hospital
Signs of heatstroke: hot, red, dry skin; absence of sweat; rapid pulse; fever over 104°F	Call 911

Prevention

- Sunburn can be prevented by avoiding too much sun, particularly between 10 AM and 2 PM and in midsummer. Sunscreens and sun-blocking lotions protect by filtering out the UV rays that cause sunburn. A sunscreen of at least SPF 15 is recommended. Make sure you apply sunscreen thoroughly to all exposed skin, so you don't leave unprotected areas that can burn.

- For the most protection from sunburn, apply sunscreen 45 minutes before you go outside. Apply it to dry skin, and reapply after swimming or activities that make you sweat. Reapply sunscreen often if you're outside for a long period. A waterproof sunscreen will stay on until you rub or towel it off, at which time you'll need to reapply it.

- The sun's rays are more intense at higher altitudes, nearer the equator, on the water, and in snow and can be reflected by sand, cement, water, and snow. Protect yourself with sunscreen. Thickly applied zinc oxide products block all the sun's rays and are good for protecting the nose and lips.

- Avoid sunlamps and tanning beds. They damage the skin, despite what tanning-salon owners and employees might tell you.

- Use sunscreen even on cloudy days.

- Use lip balm with the sunscreen PABA to prevent sunburned lips, wear UV-opaque sunglasses to protect your eyes, and be sure to apply sunscreen around eyes, ears, mouth, and any bald or thinning areas on your head.

- UV rays can penetrate through loosely woven clothing and beach umbrellas, so wear sunscreen even when using these other forms of sun protection. Also, look for the sun-protective clothing that's now available, including shirts, pants, and hats for adults and children.

- Some medications can make you more sensitive to the sun. These medications cause you to burn with little exposure to the sun. Before starting a medication, ask your doctor or pharmacist about the possible reactions to sunlight. Medications that react to sunlight include doxycycline and sulfa antibiotics.

Prevention for Children

- For children less than 6 months of age, exposure to sun and use of sunscreen, other than zinc oxide or titanium dioxide, is not recommended. Their skin is especially sensitive.

- Infants over 6 months of age should be kept out of the sun or have limited exposure to the sun and should wear sunscreen.

- Sunscreens with a minimum SPF of 15 are recommended for children. Avoid alcohol-based sunscreens and those with PABA, because they can cause irritation.

- Children should wear hats when in the sun.

- Be especially careful with children who have light skin and hair, because their skin burns more easily.

- Children in strollers should wear sunscreen, because stroller trays can reflect the sun's rays.

Sunscreen Facts

The SPF indicates the amount of time the sunscreen provides protection. Reapplication doesn't increase the time allowed in the sun before burning.

Sunscreen should protect against both UVA and UVB rays. Today's best products contain an ingredient called Parsol 1789.

Do not confuse sunscreen, which blocks the sun's rays, with sun lotions or oils, which mainly lubricate and can enhance the sun's rays. Self-tanning creams also do not protect against sunburn, although they are an excellent way to get a tan safely.

Warts

Warts are painless lumps on the outermost layer of the skin. They are slightly contagious. Most people have a natural immunity to warts and can't get them. However, some people seem to lose this natural immunity and become susceptible. If this happens to you, it means you can get warts. When your immunity returns, however, the warts will go away. There is no way to know when a person's immunity to warts will return.

Causes

Warts are a harmless overgrowth of skin tissue caused by a virus. Warts shed virus particles that can be "planted" in other areas of the body through scratching, friction, or unknown factors. Some types of warts can also be spread by person-to-person contact. Genital warts, for example, are usually spread through sexual contact.

From the time you are exposed to a wart, it usually takes weeks or months for a wart to become visible. Children and young adults get warts most frequently. People who take immune-suppressing medication or who have a chronic condition that suppresses their immune system tend to get warts.

Types of Warts

The six types of warts include:

- *Common warts*. These warts have a rough, raised surface and can appear anywhere on the body. They are most commonly found on the tops of hands.

- *Flat warts*. These very small, smooth, flat warts appear in clusters, most commonly on the hands, legs, and especially the face. Unlike common warts, they may go unnoticed.

- *Plantar warts*. These flat, calluslike warts appear on the bottom surface of the foot. They can be painful when pressure is applied to them, such as when you are stepping on the affected foot.

- *Filiform warts*. These tiny, long, and narrow warts occur around the eyelids, face, and neck.

- *Periungual warts*. Appearing under and around the fingernails, these warts occur in people who bite their nails and pick their cuticles. They are difficult to get rid of.

- *Genital warts*. These small warts appear on or around the genitalia or anus (see Genital Warts, p. 321).

Self-Care

Most warts disappear on their own, although it may take some time. If you have a wart that is unsightly but not serious, you may want to use an over-the-counter wart medication, available in a liquid or pad. Carefully apply the medication to the top and sides of the wart. Do not apply it to the skin around the wart.

If you have a wart that does not respond to over-the-counter medication, see your doctor. He or she may prescribe medication or remove the wart. A wart can be removed by freezing it with liquid nitrogen, by applying a local anesthesia and scraping it off, or by using an electric needle or laser.

Do not put medications on sensitive areas such as your face or on or near your genitals or anus.

What to do about Warts

Symptom/Sign	Action
Warts on hands, feet, legs, face, or neck	Self-care
Genital or anal warts	Call doctor
Over age 45 and have a new wart	Call doctor
Wart not responding to over-the-counter medication	See doctor

Head, Neck, and Nerve Problems

Your head and neck are easily affected by tension and stress. Many concerns, such as most headaches and neck pain, are simply caused by the pressures of everyday life. Although these symptoms can often be treated at home, they sometimes signal a more serious condition.

This section explains common concerns of the head and neck and of the nerves, which send signals to your brain from other parts of your body. ∷

Encephalitis

Encephalitis is an inflammation of the brain. There are many different types of encephalitis, though all are rare. Some cases are mild, short, and end with complete recovery. Other cases can be serious, resulting in permanent impairment or death. Most people recover from encephalitis. The infection is fatal in only a small percentage of people who get it.

Causes

Primary encephalitis occurs when the virus directly invades your brain and spinal cord. The herpes simplex virus, which also causes cold sores and genital herpes, can cause this type of encephalitis.

You can also get primary encephalitis if you are bitten by a mosquito carrying the virus. Mosquitoes carry the virus after biting infected birds or small animals. You cannot get the virus directly from birds, animals, or other people.

Birds living near bodies of standing water are most likely to be infected with encephalitis. People usually are only affected if certain unusual environmental conditions cause an increase in the number of infected birds and mosquitoes. The risk of encephalitis is highest during warm months, when birds and mosquitoes reproduce.

Secondary encephalitis is a form of encephalitis that occurs during or after a viral infection in another part of your body, such as chickenpox, measles, mumps, and rubella. It may be caused by an overreaction of the immune system.

Symptoms

In mild cases, there may be no symptoms other than fever and headache. In more severe infections, symptoms may include:

• Sudden fever

• Headache

• Stiff neck

• Confusion

• Drowsiness

• Nausea and vomiting

Symptoms that require emergency treatment include loss of consciousness, seizures, sudden severe dementia, and poor responsiveness.

In infants, key symptoms are a stiff neck and bulging in the soft spots of the skull. Older children may have a severe headache and sensitivity to light.

Treatment

Treatment usually focuses on resting, eating well, and getting plenty of fluids to help your immune system fight the virus. Antiviral medications may be prescribed in the early stages of the illness. Several different types of medication may be prescribed to treat symptoms, such as:

• Anticonvulsants to prevent or treat seizures

• Corticosteroids to reduce brain swelling and inflammation

• Sedatives for irritability or restlessness

Over-the-counter medications may also be used for fever and headache. In severe cases, physical and speech therapy may be needed.

What to do about Encephalitis

Symptom/Sign	Action
Sudden fever and headache following a viral infection or mosquito bite	Call doctor
Stiff neck, confusion, drowsiness, nausea, and vomiting	See doctor
Infant has bulging in the soft spots of the skull	Go to hospital
Extreme confusion, loss of consciousness, poor responsiveness, seizures	Call 911

Prevention

You can protect your family against mosquito-borne encephalitis by taking steps to reduce your chances of being bitten by mosquitoes:

- Wear long sleeves and pants if you're outside between dusk and dawn.

- Apply mosquito repellent that contains DEET to your skin and clothing.

- Eliminate standing water in your yard (such as in birdbaths, buckets, and puddles) and clean your gutters regularly.

- Repair holes in screens on windows and doors.

To prevent secondary encephalitis, make sure you and your family are immunized against the viral infections that can lead to encephalitis—chickenpox, measles, mumps, and rubella.

Headaches

Headaches are one of the most common health complaints. Although headaches are not usually a sign of serious illness, there are certain situations that need attention. If you experience what feels like the worst headache of your life, seek immediate help. If you are pregnant, talk to your doctor about what to do if you have headaches.

Types of Headaches

Nearly 90 percent of headaches can be classified into three general categories: tension, cluster, and migraine.

Tension-type headaches are often associated with the tightening of muscles of the back and shoulders. This may be caused by a reaction to emotional and physical stress, anxiety, or depression. Tension-type headaches are believed to be the most common cause of head pain. If you have chronic tension headaches (occurring 3 or more times weekly for 6 months or longer), see your doctor.

Symptoms of a tension-type headache include:

- Steady pain that doesn't pulse

- Tightness, fullness, or pressure over the top of the head, both sides of the head, or back of the neck

• Discomfort that's not made worse or only slightly made worse by everyday activities

Learning to relax by using biofeedback, meditation, music, visualization, hypnosis, or taking a stress-management class may help prevent tension-type headaches.

Cluster headaches are very painful and occur mainly in middle-aged men. The pain from a cluster headache gets worse quickly and lasts from 30 minutes to 2 hours, then recurs within a few hours. There is no signal before a cluster headache begins or any sign that it is going to end.

Symptoms of a cluster headache include:

• Steady, sharp pain in or around one eye, occurring in episodes that often begin at the same time each day

• Watering and redness of one eye, with nasal congestion on the same side of the face

• Swelling of eyelid

If you have a cluster headache, don't lie down—this usually makes the pain worse. Over-the-counter pain relievers may not work for cluster headaches, because they take effect too slowly. Your doctor may prescribe a medication or suggest oxygen therapy.

Migraine headaches may be associated with changes in the nerve system and chemicals in the brain and dilation (widening) of the blood vessels in the head. Possible triggers of migraine headaches include hunger, fatigue, bright light, alcohol or caffeine, excitement or stress, certain medications, environmental factors, and certain foods.

Symptoms of a migraine headache include:

• Throbbing, pulsating, or pounding pain

• Pain more often on one side of the head

• Pain made worse by walking or everyday activities

• Painful light sensitivity or nausea

About 20 percent of people who have migraines see bright spots, flashes of light, or areas of blindness just before the headache strikes. These symptoms are called an aura. Some people have great bursts of energy and activity just before a migraine starts.

Most migraines require professional diagnosis and treatment. See your doctor to discuss appropriate treatment. He or she may prescribe a medication to relieve your pain.

Self-Care

- Do exercises that help you relax. Ask your doctor to show you some of these exercises, or call your local hospital to see if they offer any exercise classes for relaxation.

- Over-the-counter pain relievers, such as aspirin, acetaminophen, or ibuprofen, can often control a headache. However, be careful of overuse. Taking too much pain medication for too long can result in a "rebound" effect, which causes headaches to return. Children should not take aspirin because it may be linked to a dangerous condition called Reye's syndrome.

- Relax or sleep in a dark, quiet room with your head elevated.

- Apply a cool or warm compress to your head for pain relief.

- Take a hot or cold shower.

- Massage your neck muscles.

What to do about Headaches

Symptom/Sign	Action
Occasional headaches, causing minor discomfort	Self-care
Recurring headaches	Call doctor
Headaches after head trauma in the last 18 months	Call doctor
Headaches accompanied by nausea and vomiting	See doctor
Severe headache for more than 3 days	See doctor
Sudden severe headache; disabling pain	Go to hospital
Headache with fever and stiff neck	Go to hospital
Headache accompanied by weakness or numbness in arms or legs, slurred speech, blurred vision, unsteady walking, or facial drooping	Call 911

Prevention

For many headaches, including cluster, migraine, and tension-type headaches, a headache calendar may help you to identify possible triggers. Use a headache calendar to record everything you eat, your sleep and exercise patterns, and your work or home activities. Women should also record their menstrual cycles, because hormonal changes can trigger headaches.

To prevent headaches, avoid any triggers you've identified with your headache calendar and follow these general guidelines:

- Avoid skipping or delaying meals. Eat three to six small meals a day.

- Have a regular pattern of sleep and aerobic exercise.

- Reduce stress. Headaches are often the result of fatigue, tension, and emotional upset.

- Be aware of your posture. Avoid craning forward.

- Stop smoking. It can trigger headaches or increase their intensity.

Meningitis

Meningitis is an infection of the membranes and fluid that surround your brain and spinal cord. It can be caused by bacteria or viruses. With early diagnosis and prompt treatment, most people recover from meningitis. However, the disease is fatal in about 10 percent of cases.

Causes

Meningitis can be caused by many different bacteria or viruses. It's important to know the cause, because the severity of illness and treatment differ. Seventy percent of meningitis cases occur in children under age 5. Young people between the ages of 15 and 24 and older adults may also have an increased risk.

Viral meningitis can be caused by common intestinal viruses and viruses associated with mumps, herpes infection, or other diseases. In some cases, people can get viral meningitis from drinking polluted water.

The viruses that cause meningitis are contagious. However, most people who become infected don't actually develop meningitis. Viral meningitis is usually mild and often clears up within 1 to 2 weeks.

Bacterial meningitis is usually much more serious. It can lead to brain damage, hearing loss, or learning disabilities. Some forms of bacterial meningitis are contagious. The bacteria are spread though coughing, sneezing, kissing, or sharing items such as eating utensils or toothbrushes with an infected person.

Symptoms

The symptoms of meningitis usually come on suddenly. Early symptoms can sometimes be mistaken for the flu. They may not be the same for every person, but common symptoms include:

• Fever

• Severe headache

• Stiff neck

• Drowsiness or confusion

• Nausea and vomiting

• Sensitivity to light

Babies with meningitis may seem unusually irritable or sleepy or may refuse to eat.

Early diagnosis and treatment are very important. Your doctor can diagnose meningitis by doing a spinal tap, in which he or she inserts a needle into your lower back to remove spinal fluid. The fluid can then be tested for bacteria or viruses.

Treatment

Viral meningitis usually doesn't require treatment. Doctors often recommend bed rest, fluids, and over-the-counter medications to relieve fever and headache. Most patients completely recover on their own.

Bacterial meningitis needs to be treated immediately to prevent serious complications. A number of antibiotics can be used to treat bacterial meningitis. Other medications may also be used to treat symptoms and prevent permanent damage from the disease.

What to do about Meningitis

Symptom/Sign	Action
Fever, headache, neck pain, vomiting	See doctor
Confusion, drowsiness, sensitivity to light	See doctor
Infant has bulging in the soft spots of the skull, is unusually fussy or sleepy	Go to hospital
Loss of consciousness, poor responsiveness, seizures	Call 911

Prevention

You can reduce your risk of getting meningitis by washing your hands often to prevent the spread of viruses or bacteria. Boost your immune system by eating well, exercising, and getting plenty of rest.

There are a number of vaccines available to protect against the different types of meningitis. If your child hasn't been vaccinated, talk to your doctor. Vaccines are also recommended for college students who live in dormitories and people traveling to countries where meningitis is common.

Neck Pain

The neck is the most flexible part of your spine. However, because it is not well protected by muscles, it's also easy to injure.

Causes

- *A bad night's rest.* How you sleep at night can affect your neck during the day. A soft mattress, pillows that force your neck into awkward angles, and uncomfortable sleeping positions may be to blame if you wake up with a sore neck. But the tossing and turning of a bad night's rest may be less to blame than waking suddenly from a sound sleep. A sudden jerk of the neck upon awakening can leave neck muscles tight and sore.

- *Body mechanics.* Poor sitting and standing posture—slumped shoulders, a "drooping" head, slouching or rounding of the lower back—can cause neck pain. However, bad body mechanics are more than poor posture. Repeated tasks, such as holding the phone with your shoulder or always carrying a heavy briefcase or shoulder bag on the same side of your body, can cause muscle stiffness or imbalance. Workstations can also force you into poor positions.

- *Stress.* The neck and upper-back muscles are often among the first to become tense when you are under emotional stress. Whenever these muscles remain tight for a long time, they may ache, become sore, and even cause headaches.

- *Neck sprains and strains.* The term *whiplash* is often used to refer to neck sprains and strains that result when the neck is forced suddenly forward, backward, or both—such as from a rear-end collision. Contact sports, a fall, or a sudden twist can cause similar injuries. Pain from neck sprains and strains may spread into the shoulders, upper back and arms, and sometimes as far as the legs. Pain may remain for 6 weeks or longer but generally improves with normal activity. In some cases, physical therapy or special exercises may help.

- *Degenerative joint disease (DJD).* Between each bone (vertebra) of the spine is a cartilage disk filled with a gelatin-like substance that provides cushioning. As we age, these disks become thinner, losing some of their capacity to absorb shock. The joints of the neck may also become inflamed as a result of arthritis or bone spurs, or a disk may herniate (push outward) from its normal space and place pressure on the nerves. DJD usually occurs in people over age 40. It often causes painful muscle spasms in the neck and upper back, a dull aching in one arm, or numbness and tingling in the arm or fingers. A direct blow can also make disks bulge or break, causing problems similar to those of disk degeneration. Any persistent pain, numbness, or tingling should be evaluated by a doctor.

Self-Care

Even if your neck pain is caused by an injury or a worsening condition, self-care can often provide relief.

- If your neck or upper-back muscles feel tight and sore, especially from stress, ask a friend to massage the area for a few minutes.

- Ice a sore neck for 10 to 15 minutes several times a day to relieve pain and inflammation. A bag of frozen peas or corn makes a great cold pack for the neck. Ice can be good for relieving pain even long after an injury, especially if muscle spasms are present. Switching between heat and ice may also work.

- A warm shower, heating pad, or moist warm towel can help loosen sore, tight muscles. Wait 48 hours before applying heat. Then apply heat for 20 minutes three times a day.

- Take a pain medication. If pain persists, your doctor may prescribe other medication. When pain is at its worst, rest. Lie flat on your back for an hour or so, with a fairly flat pillow supporting your head. (Extended bed rest, however, can make neck problems worse by allowing muscles to weaken from lack of use.)

- Stretch! Reduce stiffness and soreness and gain motion and strength by moving your neck often.

What to do about Neck Pain

Symptom/Sign	Action
Stiff, sore neck upon awakening	Self-care
Muscle tension and pain, especially while working or under stress	Self-care
Neck pain that is worse after 24 hours or does not improve after 7 to 10 days	Call doctor
Pain after a sudden twist of the head being thrown forward or backward	Call doctor
Burning, shooting pain; shoulder weakness; or loss of feeling in shoulder after a trauma	See doctor
Stiff, sore neck with fever and headache	Go to hospital
Any severe trauma or blow to the head or neck	Call 911

Prevention

Neck pain can often be prevented with a few adjustments to the way you work and rest:

- If you often wake up with a sore neck, consider sleeping in a different position, getting a new mattress and box spring, or putting a ¾-inch plywood board between the mattress and box spring for extra support.

- If you sleep on your side, choose a pillow that allows your head to rest comfortably centered between your shoulders. If you sleep on your back, choose a pillow that doesn't push your chin toward your chest. A special cervical-support pillow or a rolled towel pinned around your neck can also help you position your spine correctly. Avoid sleeping on your stomach.

- If daily stress makes your neck and upper-back muscles tense, take time out to relax. Your spine naturally curves in at the neck, out at the upper back, and in again at the lower back. An easy way to improve your posture is to focus on keeping the natural curve at the lower back. When you do this, the rest of the spine tends to pull into place, straightening your shoulders and head as well. However, be sure that your effort to straighten up doesn't cause your neck or abdomen to stick out.

- Improve your work area. If you spend a lot of time on the phone, use a telephone headset. Keep your briefcase or purse as light as possible, and routinely switch carrying sides. When either is packed full, try to distribute the weight evenly on each side of your body by splitting the contents into two bags or briefcases. Hold reading materials and place computer screens at eye level; don't bend over your work. Type with your elbows, hips, and knees at a 90-degree angle, and make sure you have good lower-back support.

Responding to a Neck Injury

Severe trauma to the neck may cause a fracture, creating risk for permanent paralysis. If you suspect possible neck or other spinal injuries from a severe blow or other trauma, keep the injured person still. Do not move the person without a backboard or cervical collar and the help and direction of a trained paramedic or other medical professional.

Numbness and Tingling

Almost everyone experiences numbness and tingling at one time or another. It may be a feeling of "pins and needles" or of having a hand or foot "fall asleep." Numbness and tingling is often a temporary nuisance but can sometimes indicate a more serious problem.

Causes

Having a hand or foot fall asleep is caused by a compressed nerve. This is a normal, common occurrence, and the feeling will go away on its own when the pressure is taken off the nerve.

A feeling of numbness or tingling is often caused by a pinched nerve. The term *pinched nerve* describes a type of damage or injury to a nerve or set of nerves. Pinched nerves can sometimes lead to other conditions, such as carpal tunnel syndrome (see p. 271), tennis elbow, and peripheral neuropathy.

Peripheral neuropathy is a general term for disorders of the peripheral nervous system. The peripheral nervous system is the network of nerves outside the central nervous system (the brain and spinal cord) connected to the spinal cord. Peripheral neuropathy is a common condition that can cause numbness and tingling. It can be caused by diseases of the nerves or by other illnesses. Diabetes is one of the most common causes of peripheral neuropathy. A ruptured disk in the spine can also cause the disorder. Other causes may include:

- Excessive alcohol consumption
- Nutritional deficiencies
- Infection or inflammation
- Overexposure to toxic chemicals, such as mercury or lead
- Tumors
- Rheumatoid arthritis

Numbness and tingling can also be signs of multiple sclerosis, a disease of the central nervous system, or fibromyalgia (see p. 242).

Treatment

Treatment for a pinched nerve usually involves resting the affected area. Pain medication may be prescribed. In some cases, surgery is recommended. Physical therapy and splints or collars may also be used.

Treatment for peripheral neuropathy often focuses on treating the condition that caused it—for example, controlling diabetes or repairing a ruptured disk. Physical therapy may also be recommended.

What to do about Numbness and Tingling

Symptom/Sign	Action
Unusual numbness, tingling, or pain in hands and feet	Call doctor
Numbness/tingling and double vision	See doctor
Numbness of hand, arm, face, or lips (especially one-sided)	Call 911

Prevention

You can reduce your risk of peripheral neuropathy by:

- Eating well
- Avoiding excessive use of alcohol
- Avoiding exposure to toxic chemicals
- Controlling your blood sugar if you have diabetes

Eye Problems

Many people take their vision and eye health for granted until they notice a problem. Some eye concerns can easily be treated at home, whereas others require the help of your doctor. This section explains how to handle common eye concerns to ensure a lifetime of good vision.

Many eye concerns are treated by eye specialists. Optometrists can test your eyes for nonmedical vision concerns and prescribe corrective lenses. Ophthalmologists are medical doctors who treat eye diseases and can also perform surgery on the eyes. ▪▪

Burning Eyes

Lots of different things can make your eyes burn. Smoke, pollen, or a viral infection such as a cold or the flu can cause eyes to itch, burn, water, and redden. In these cases the burning and itching usually go away when the irritant is removed.

Causes

Chronic dry or burning eyes can be caused by age, some medications, and disease. Itchy, burning eyelids can also result from infection.

Unprotected eyes can also be burned by the ultraviolet (UV) rays from the sun, tanning lamps, or arc welding equipment. Like sunburns to the skin, you won't feel pain until hours later, when the eyes and the area around them swell. UV rays can damage your retina. The risk of sunburning the eyes is very high when sunlight is reflected off water, sand, or snow.

Substances such as paint thinner, dishwashing detergent, lye, toilet cleaner, drain cleaner, and gasoline can chemically burn the eyes. Chemical burns are painful medical emergencies that can result in decreased vision (see Burns: Chemical, p. 17).

Self-Care

- If your eyes burn and water, try to trace the source of irritation, then avoid it. Smoke, cosmetics, chemical fumes, and pollen are some possibilities. Nonprescription eye drops other than artificial tears can also cause irritation.

- Apply a cool compress to sunburned eyes. Stay out of the sun until swelling is gone.

- Chemical burns to the eyes require immediate action (see Burns: Chemical, p. 17).

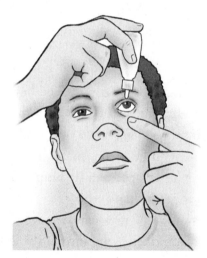

To put eyedrops into the eye, pull down the lower lid and look up.

- If you wear contact lenses, remove them until the irritation goes away.

- Use over-the-counter lubrication drops (artificial tears) two to three times a day for comfort (see illustration below).

- Call your doctor if you have sunburned eyes and the pain and swelling do not improve after 24 hours.

What to do about Burning Eyes

Symptom/Sign	Action
Irritated or sunburned eyes	Self-care
Sunburned eyes that can be closed	Self-care
Pink, red, or watery eyes	Call doctor
Sunburned eyes that cannot be closed	See doctor
Eyes that continue to be irritated after 48 hours of self-care	See doctor
Pain, swelling, or impaired vision	See doctor

Prevention

Many causes of eye burning and irritation can be prevented.

- Don't rub your eyes, which may introduce bacteria and cause infection or irritation.

- Take breaks from long periods of close work—such as crafts, reading, or computer work—to avoid eye strain.

- Work in adequate lighting.

- Wear sunglasses with UV protection when you're in the sun.

- Wear protective glasses or goggles when working with caustic chemicals.

Foreign Object in the Eye

A foreign object in your eye should be taken seriously. If you feel something in your eye, don't rub it. Rubbing can damage the cornea (the clear tissue covering the colored part of the eye).

Treatment

If the object is on your cornea, you need to see a doctor immediately. Wash your hands and look in your eye. If you find any of the following, put a patch over your eye (without putting pressure on your eyeball) and seek help right away:

- A piece of glass or metal anywhere in your eye

- An object that is stuck or embedded in your eye

- An object floating anywhere in your eye that you cannot remove

- An object on the cornea of the eye

Self-Care

If the object is on the white part of your eye, try self-care. There are several different methods you can try for removing a foreign object from the white part of your eye:

• Wash the eye with water dropped from an eyedropper or squeeze bottle. The object may loosen and flow out of the eye with the water. Use saline instead of water if it's available. It's more comfortable and less irritating to the eye.

• Fill a sink or other large, open container with lukewarm water. Hold your breath and plunge your face into the water with your eyes open. Roll your eye and move your head around until the object floats away. (Don't try this with young children who don't know how to hold their breath.)

• Roll the corner of a clean handkerchief, tissue, paper towel, or other clean cloth to a point and gently push the object out of the eye with the cloth (see illustration below left).

• If the object feels like it's stuck on the inside of the upper lid, pull the lid out and down over the lower lashes, and hold for a few seconds. This may help dislodge the object. You can remove the object with a moistened cotton swab if you take care to avoid brushing the cornea.

• The following technique works best when someone else helps you. Look up and pull the lower lid down while your helper looks under the lower lid. Then look down at your shoes and pull the upper lid up by the lashes while your helper looks under the upper lid. A cotton swab can help you grasp the upper lid (see illustration below right). Never insert a toothpick, matchstick, tweezers, or other hard object into the eye itself to remove an object.

• Don't wear contacts until the irritation goes away.

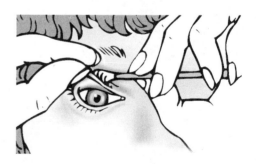

What to do about a Foreign Object in the Eye

Symptom/Sign	Action
Stinging irritants in the eye, such as soap, spice, perfume, or aftershave	Self-care (flush eye for 5 minutes)
Object on white part of the eye that can be removed	Self-care
Eye pain, discomfort, constant tearing, or increasing redness after removal of foreign object	See doctor
Object on white part of the eye that can't be removed	Go to hospital
Object on colored part of the eye	Go to hospital
A piece of metal or glass or other object related to an eye trauma is in the eye	Go to hospital
Severe eye pain or impaired vision	Call 911
Object is embedded or penetrates the eyeball	Call 911

Prevention

Most eye injuries are preventable. Use common sense and take a few precautions when there is potential for eye injury:

• Wear protective eyewear when doing work such as scraping, painting, welding, sawing, or any task that produces flying particles.

• Use caution around aerosol sprays or solvents that may spray or splash in the eye.

• Use BB guns and air rifles with caution. They shoot objects that can easily penetrate the eye.

Pinkeye

Have you ever woken up in the morning with your eyes stuck shut? That memorable experience is often caused by conjunctivitis, also known as *pinkeye*. Pinkeye is an infection of the membrane that lines the inside of the eyelids and covers the surface of the eye.

Causes

Pinkeye can be caused by viruses, bacteria, allergies, pollution, or other irritants. It can be very contagious and spreads easily from person to person.

Symptoms

Pinkeye causes red, swollen, itchy, watery eyes. Eyes may burn or feel like they have sand in them. Bacterial pinkeye usually has a yellow-green discharge throughout the day. Viral pinkeye may be crusty in the morning but have a clear discharge throughout the day.

Treatment

Treatment for pinkeye depends on what type you have. Bacterial pinkeye is treated with antibiotic ointments or drops. Viral pinkeye doesn't require medical treatment and usually clears up within 1 week. See your doctor if it lasts longer than 1 week.

Self-Care

- Apply warm, moist compresses to the eyes to relieve irritation and buildup of discharge.

- Use a cold compress to relieve itching.

- Gently wipe away the discharge or crust with a washcloth or cotton ball and warm water.

- Don't rub your eyes. It can spread the infection from one eye to the other.

- If you wear contact lenses, don't wear them until the redness and irritation are gone.

- Don't use over-the-counter eye preparations other than artificial tears.

- Wear sunglasses or avoid bright lights if your eyes are sensitive.

- Call your doctor if eyes are pink or red with watery discharge for more than 7 days.

What to do about Pinkeye

Symptom/Sign	Action
Pink or red eyes with watery discharge for less than 7 days	Self-care
Eye discharge is thick and yellow or greenish	Call doctor
Excessive tearing	See doctor
Eye pain (not irritation) or the feeling that something is in the eye	See doctor
Severe sensitivity to light	See doctor
Blurred or unclear vision	See doctor
Pinkeye with cold sores, shingles, or chickenpox	See doctor
History of recent eye injury or foreign object in the eye	See doctor
Eyelids and area around eye is red, swollen, and tender	See doctor

Prevention

If you or your child has pinkeye, there are several things you can do to prevent the spread of the infection:

- Don't share towels, washcloths, or anything else that touches the eyes. Wash these items separately in hot water.

- Wash your hands frequently and thoroughly if you have pinkeye, if you are caring for someone who does, or even if you are around someone who has the infection, especially before and after eye care.

- Keep a child with pinkeye home from school until he or she is no longer contagious. Bacterial pinkeye is contagious until 24 hours after antibiotic drops are started.

Styes

A stye is a red, tender bump on the eyelid that appears when an oil gland at the base of an eyelash becomes clogged.

Symptoms

Styes can make your eyelid swell and itch. They are normally smaller than a pebble, but the discomfort and swelling can make them feel huge.

Growths on the eyelid that are not red and painful are usually cysts, not styes. Although any unusual lump or growth should be checked by a doctor, most eyelid cysts are harmless and don't need to be removed.

Treatment

Over a few days a stye usually comes to a head—like a pimple—and drains on its own. Sometimes a stye will persist for weeks without coming to a head. In these cases a doctor may choose to open and drain the stye.

Self-Care

- Hot compresses will help a stye come to a head and drain. Place a clean washcloth in water as hot as you can stand it without burning yourself (use lukewarm water for children). Wring out the cloth and place it on your eye for 5 to 10 minutes. Repeat three or four times a day.

- If pus discharges on its own or during this process, carefully clean the entire area with warm water.

What to do about Styes

Symptom/Sign	Action
Red, swollen, itchy lump on eyelid	Self-care
Lump on eyelid that isn't painful	Call doctor
Fever, eye pain, redness/swelling over entire lid	Call doctor
Stye that persists and remains painful for 1 to 2 weeks	See doctor
Stye that returns	See doctor
Vision problems	Go to hospital

Prevention

To prevent styes, wash your face daily. This can keep oil glands from clogging and forming styes.

Vision Problems

Blurry, fuzzy, or distorted vision can be caused by a number of conditions. Most can be corrected. If your vision blurs suddenly, see your doctor right away.

Causes

The following conditions can cause blurry vision to develop slowly:

Nearsightedness (myopia) is difficulty in seeing objects that are far away. Objects close up are seen clearly. People who are nearsighted may hold reading material just a few inches from their noses.

Farsightedness (hyperopia) causes nearby objects to appear fuzzy. Objects at a distance are seen clearly. People who are farsighted often hold their reading material at arm's length.

Astigmatism can cause areas of blurry vision because the cornea of your eye is not perfectly spherical (circular) as it should be. People with astigmatism may find it hard to see vertical, horizontal, or diagonal lines clearly. Astigmatism can be accompanied by nearsightedness or farsightedness.

Presbyopia is a problem of aging. As you get older, the eye lens hardens and loses its flexibility, making it hard to focus on nearby objects. Eyeglasses with bifocal lenses can correct most cases of presbyopia.

Cataracts cloud the lens of the eye, impairing vision. They usually take several years to develop. Most cataracts are a result of aging, but they can also be caused by injuries, birth defects, too much heat or ultraviolet light, medications, and diabetes. Lenses affected by cataracts can be replaced by surgery if necessary.

Glaucoma, a major cause of blindness, is increased pressure within the eyeball. This pressure can damage the optic nerve, which controls sight. Symptoms of glaucoma include loss of vision to each side (peripheral vision), halos around lights, eye pain, blurred vision, and gradual loss of sight. Glaucoma destroys peripheral vision first, so it often is not caught until a good deal of vision is lost. Early diagnosis through routine glaucoma checks after age 40 is the key to treating this problem.

Macular degeneration causes increasingly blurred central vision and most often strikes elderly people. Reduced or distorted vision caused by macular degeneration is most noticeable when you read. If diagnosed early, laser treatment can sometimes keep it from getting worse.

Treatment

The shape of your cornea is what determines whether you are nearsighted, farsighted, or have astigmatism. LASIK surgery is a relatively new procedure that can be used to correct these vision problems. The term *LASIK* is short for *laser in-situ keratomileusis*, which is a special type of laser surgery. In this procedure a thick layer of the cornea is folded back using a special instrument. The exposed cornea is then reshaped with a laser, and the corneal flap is returned to its original position. No stitches are needed.

LASIK surgery is performed as an outpatient procedure. Most people recover in a couple of days, and the need for glasses or contacts is reduced or eliminated.

What to do about Vision Problems

Symptom/Sign	Action
Occasional blurring of vision, related to fatigue or overuse	Self-care
Occasional black spots floating across vision field	Self-care
Visual disturbances, such as jagged lines and heat waves, accompanied by dizziness and nausea	Call doctor
Vision changes possibly related to change or addition of new medication	Call doctor
Gradual decrease in vision in a person older than 50 (possible cataracts)	See doctor
Tunnel vision or loss of peripheral vision	See doctor
Seeing bright lights or sudden appearance of large numbers of "floaters"	Go to hospital
Sudden loss of vision	Go to hospital
Loss of vision related to injury to eyes or head	Go to hospital
Loss of vision with weakness or paralysis	Call 911

Prevention

- Have regular eye exams—every 3 to 5 years if you don't have vision problems, every 2 years if you wear eyeglasses or have other vision problems. Your doctor or eye specialist may recommend more frequent exams, especially if you wear contact lenses.

- Wear safety glasses or goggles whenever you use power tools, lawnmowers, or other devices that could cause objects to fly toward your eyes.

- Wear sunglasses with UV protection when you are out in bright sunlight. Be especially careful when sunlight is reflected by water or snow. Too much UV light has been linked to cataracts.

- Don't smoke. It can put you at higher risk for macular degeneration and other eye problems.

- If you have diabetes or high blood pressure, keep it under control. Both conditions are risk factors for macular degeneration, glaucoma, and other eye problems.

Vision Changes That Can Signal a Stroke

Most vision problems develop gradually. If any of the following symptoms occur suddenly, they may be signs of a stroke.

- Sudden loss of sight, especially in one eye
- Loss of part of your visual field
- Double vision
- Vision changes with paralysis or weakness

(See Stroke, p. 59.)

Ear, Nose, and Throat Problems

Ear, nose, and throat problems are among the most frequently occurring health concerns that affect Americans. This section describes common conditions related to your ears, nose, and throat and suggests ways to take care of nonurgent conditions at home.

Your doctor can also offer advice and treatment for most ear, nose, and throat concerns. In some cases you may need to see an ear, nose, and throat (ENT) specialist, also called an *otolaryngologist*. ▪▪

Bad Breath

Bad breath, also referred to as *halitosis*, is a periodic or persistent odor exhaled from the mouth. It is a common problem.

Causes

• *Poor dental hygiene.* Although there are dozens of possible causes of bad breath, the most common is poor dental hygiene. Without proper brushing and flossing, food particles and plaque build up on the teeth, gums, and tongue, as well as on dentures or other orthodontic appliances. Bacteria begin to grow and produce bad mouth odors.

• *Smoking.* Smoking is another leading cause of bad breath. Tar and nicotine residues coat the teeth, tongue, and inside of the mouth and lungs, making breath especially smelly.

• *Health conditions.* Bad breath can also be caused by tonsillitis, pneumonia, mouth sores, sinus infections, and even the common cold. Stomach problems such as heartburn can produce bad breath, and so can certain medications.

• *Diet.* Eating garlic, onions, cabbage, or hot and spicy foods and drinking alcohol can cause bad breath for a day or so after consumption. Foods high in milk and butterfat are also culprits. Hunger can also contribute to bad breath. Chewing leads to the flow of saliva, which decreases bad breath.

- *Dry mouth.* Bad breath can be caused by dry mouth related to sleeping with your mouth open (morning mouth), talking for long periods, breathing through your mouth, and some medications or medical conditions.

- *Age.* Even with good oral hygiene, the breath of older people may not be as pleasant due to changes in the glands that produce saliva.

Self-Care

Bad breath can generally be managed with self-care. However, it can be a sign of underlying health problems. If self-care is not helpful, call your dentist.

- The best way to fix a bad breath problem is to brush up on your dental hygiene. Brush your teeth twice a day and floss daily. See your dentist for an exam and cleaning twice a year.

- If your gums bleed when you floss or brush, you may have gum disease (gingivitis), which can cause bad breath. If the condition doesn't improve after 3 weeks of careful dental hygiene, see your dentist.

- Brush the top of your tongue with a soft toothbrush. The tongue, especially far in the back as it goes down your throat, can have bacteria that cause bad breath. Studies have shown that people who brush the top and back surface of their tongue, as well as their teeth, have better breath than people who brush only their teeth.

- If you smoke, stop now. It takes 2 weeks after you stop smoking before the smelly effects of tobacco are out of your system.

- Drink plenty of fluids to avoid dry mouth. Eat apples, citrus fruits, lettuce, and other raw vegetables, which cleanse the teeth. Avoid strong-smelling foods, such as onions, garlic, and cabbage, and hot and spicy foods.

- Parsley is a natural breath freshener. Mouthwashes, breath mints, and sprays may mask the odor of bad breath temporarily, but they don't get at the source of the problem. Avoid sugary breath mints, which can make bad breath worse. (Bacteria thrive on sugar and can cause dental cavities.)

- Clean dentures and removable braces every night as directed by your dentist.

- Use saliva substitutes for dry mouth caused by health conditions or medications.

- Don't skip meals. Chewing foods promotes salivary flow and a detergent action that decreases mouth odor.

What to do about Bad Breath

Symptom/Sign	Action
Most cases of bad breath	Self-care
Constant or recurring bad breath that doesn't respond to self-care	Call dentist
Bad breath from decayed teeth or gum disease	Call dentist

Earaches

There are many possible causes of earaches. The most common is an infection of the middle ear. Middle ear infections are especially common in children: Up to 70 percent of children will develop an ear infection during their first 3 years of life. Other causes of earaches can include swimmer's ear, earwax buildup, and traveling on airplanes.

Middle Ear Infections

Middle ear infections result from a buildup of fluid in the middle ear that gets infected. Fluid buildup is caused by congestion that blocks the natural channel (eustachian tube) that allows air and fluid to go in and out of your middle ear. Once the fluid is infected with bacteria, a middle ear infection develops.

Colds or allergies are almost always to blame for the congestion and fluid buildup (see Colds, p. 211). This is why ear infections often occur on the second or third day of a cold.

Symptoms

When children tug at their ears, act irritable, or have a fever after a cold, suspect an ear infection and seek medical attention.

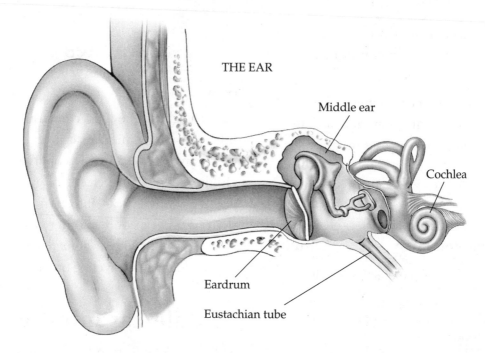

THE EAR

Middle ear

Cochlea

Eardrum

Eustachian tube

Plugging of the eustachian tube leads to fluid buildup in the middle ear. Fluid can build up in this tube from congestion caused by colds or allergies. This fluid can become infected with bacteria, resulting in a middle ear infection. Middle ear infections may require medical attention.

Treatment

Ear infections may require regular treatment with low doses of antibiotics. However, your doctor may recommend that an ear infection not be treated with antibiotics because of problems with resistant bacteria. Some ear infections will get better on their own. Your child's doctor may recommend ear tubes to drain fluids from the ears if your child has fluid that does not go away or is not responding to treatment.

Self-Care

• If your doctor has prescribed antibiotics, take as directed to reduce the risk of recurring problems. That means not skipping doses, measuring doses carefully, and taking the medication exactly the way it is prescribed. Store the antibiotic as directed; some require refrigeration.

• Follow your doctor's recommendations for follow-up exams or other measures to prevent future ear problems.

- For relief from pain or help with sleep, use acetaminophen (Tylenol or a generic) instead of aspirin.

- Ask your doctor if swimming is okay. Avoid diving, because the pressure change could cause ear pain.

Prevention

There are several steps you can take to prevent ear infections in children:

- Encourage breastfeeding.
- If using a bottle, feed child upright.
- Avoid exposure to passive smoke.
- Limit exposure to large numbers of children as much as possible.
- Wash hands carefully—both adults and children.
- Limit exposure to viral upper respiratory infections.
- Avoid pacifier use in children older than 10 months of age.

Swimmer's Ear and Earwax Buildup

Swimmer's ear is an infection of the skin in the ear canal and is often caused by water trapped in the canal. Earwax is normally protective; however, it sometimes becomes impacted. This makes it hard to remove and makes the ear feel plugged.

Symptoms

The symptoms of swimmer's ear and wax buildup are an itchy feeling, redness of the outer ear, and pain from simply wiggling the earlobe.

Self-Care

- If earwax has built up, do not probe in the ear with cotton swabs. They can push earwax farther into your ear, causing even more problems. Instead, direct a warm (never hot) shower at your ear to loosen the wax, and then wipe it out with a clean towel. Sometimes, gently squeezing warm water into the ear using a soft, rubber-nose syringe helps. Don't try to wash your ear if you think you have ruptured your eardrum or if you have ear drainage. (Symptoms of a ruptured eardrum are earache, partial hearing loss, and slight bleeding or discharge from the ear.)

- A heating pad or warm cloth on the ear may provide pain relief.

- Ask your pharmacist for over-the-counter earwax drops, which help soften the wax for easier removal.

If earwax can't be easily removed or if you still have ear stuffiness, muffled hearing, or blocked ear passages after 3 days of self-care, call your doctor.

Prevention

To prevent swimmer's ear, dry your ears after swimming. Use a clean towel or hair dryer set on low. You may also want to use drying ear drops if your doctor recommends them.

Ear Stuffiness/ Airplane Ears

The pilot says, "We will now begin our descent," but your ears have already told you there's something going on. Sound is muffled and there's a painful, uncomfortable feeling in your ears. You have barotitis, commonly called "airplane ears." As the plane descends, the air pressure inside your ears is lower than the pressure outside your ears. This creates a vacuum inside your ears, pushing your eardrums inward and making your ears feel full or stuffed up.

If you have allergies or a cold when traveling by plane, descent can cause real pain. Your doctor may advise you to postpone a trip by air if you have an upper respiratory or ear infection.

Airplane ears usually cause temporary discomfort. They may cause fluid to accumulate, which can make your ears feel like they are plugged. Airplane ears can also cause an infection.

Self-Care

- Clear your ears by swallowing, yawning, or chewing gum.

- Try the ear-clearing technique pilots use. Squeeze your nostrils shut, take a big gulp of air, and tightly close your mouth. Then try to blow the air out against your closed mouth and nose. If you're successful, you'll feel your ears pop.

Prevention

- Don't sleep during descent. You don't swallow as often when you're asleep. Ask the flight attendant to wake you.

- For children too young to chew gum, give them something to drink to make them swallow.

- If you must fly when you have an upper respiratory infection, ask your doctor about using decongestant (such as Sudafed) about 2 hours before you expect to land.

- Use a nasal decongestant spray such as oxymetazoline (Atrin or Sinex) an hour before landing and then again 5 to 10 minutes later. Don't use nasal decongestant sprays if you have high blood pressure or angina, and never use them for more than 3 days.

What to do about Earaches

Symptom/Sign	Action
Painful, itchy outer ear	See doctor
Hearing loss	See doctor
Discharge of fluids from the ear or any type of severe, constant ear pain	See doctor
Symptoms of a middle ear infection	See doctor
Redness or swelling of the outer ear or face	See doctor
Fever over 101°F	See doctor

Hoarseness/ Laryngitis

When there is not enough air passing through your vocal cords, your voice will sound hoarse or husky or may disappear altogether. Hoarseness is not a disease. It is a signal that your vocal cords are not working normally.

Causes

Hoarseness can be caused by overuse of the vocal cords. Cheering at a sporting event, shouting, singing, speaking, or whispering for long periods can all cause temporary hoarseness or loss of voice. Constantly clearing your throat can also cause hoarseness.

A cold, sore throat, or other upper respiratory infection can rob you of your voice if the infection spreads to your voice box. This is called *laryngitis*.

Smoking, alcohol, exposure to tobacco smoke, or air pollution can dry your vocal cords, leading to hoarseness. Gastroesophageal reflux disease (see Gastroesophageal Reflux Disease, p. 156) is another possible cause of this condition.

Treatment

Hoarseness that is caused by overuse or by a cold or other infection will usually go away on its own within 2 weeks. Constant or repeated hoarseness that isn't linked to overuse or infection may be something more serious. See your doctor if hoarseness doesn't go away within a month.

Self-Care

- Give your vocal cords a rest. Avoid talking and whispering as much as possible. (Whispering strains vocal cords as much as talking.) Use a pencil and paper and hand gestures to communicate.

- Drink plenty of fluids. Water is best to keep your vocal cords hydrated.

- Don't smoke or drink alcohol. Both can dry out and irritate vocal cords.

- Humidify your home.

- If you have to go out in extremely cold weather, wear a scarf or mask over your mouth.

- Suck on cough lozenges if your throat feels scratchy.

- Avoid constant clearing of your throat.

What to do about Hoarseness/Laryngitis

Symptom/Sign	Action
Hoarseness or loss of voice and other cold symptoms	Self-care
Hoarseness or loss of voice caused by overuse	Self-care
Loss of voice lasting more than 5 to 7 days	See doctor
Hoarseness that lasts longer than 1 month	See doctor
Hoarseness and exposure to poisonous gas	Go to hospital
Sudden onset of difficulty swallowing or feeling of fullness in throat	Go to hospital
Trouble breathing	Call 911

Nosebleed

Everyone has nosebleeds from time to time. The blood vessels in the nose are near the surface, so even the slightest injury can cause a nosebleed. They occur more often in the winter, when viruses are common and air is drier. Most nosebleeds can be stopped with self-care, but occasionally they can be serious.

Causes

Most nosebleeds are associated with colds, allergies, or minor injury to the nose. Other causes include violent sneezing, blowing the nose too forcefully, or a foreign object in the nose. Nosebleeds are a common side effect of isotretinoin (Accutane), a medication for acne.

Self-Care

If you have a nosebleed, follow these steps:

- Gently blow nose once to remove large clots that may interfere with applying pressure.

- Apply continuous pressure to nose for 15 minutes without checking. Pinch the nostrils below the bony part of the nose and press firmly toward the face.

- Sit up with head bent forward slightly and breathe through the mouth.

- Do not swallow blood. Spit it out through your mouth.

- Apply ice over the middle of your face to constrict blood vessels and reduce bleeding.

- Don't talk, which may trigger gagging and induce vomiting.

- Sit quietly for 15 to 30 minutes. Do not blow your nose or attempt to clean or put anything in your nostrils.

- Elevate your head when resting or sleeping for the next few days.

- Discontinue use of aspirin or other nonsteroidal anti-inflammatory drugs (NSAIDs) for 3 days unless prescribed.

- Avoid drinking alcohol and straining, bending, or lifting for the next few days.

What to do about Nosebleeds

Symptom/Sign	Action
Occasional nosebleed	Self-care
Recurrent nosebleeds	See doctor
Heavy, continuous nosebleed that doesn't stop with self-care	Go to hospital
Heavy, uncontrolled nosebleed with lightheadedness; rapid pulse; rapid, shallow breathing; and cool, clammy, pale skin	Call 911

Prevention

- Avoid picking your nose or blowing it vigorously.

- Use a humidifier to increase humidity in your home during the winter.

- Limit use of aspirin, NSAIDs, or medicated nasal sprays to short term only, unless prescribed by your doctor.

- Gently apply a thin layer of bacitracin or petroleum jelly into nose one to two times a day to relieve dryness and irritation. Using a cotton swab to apply, insert into nose ½ to 1 inch and cover the entire circle of the nasal opening.

- Put two to three drops of warm saltwater in each nostril before gently blowing a stuffy nose. Use an over-the-counter brand such as Ocean or Salinex or make a homemade solution by dissolving ¼ teaspoon salt in 1 cup of water.

Sinusitis

Sinusitis is an infection or inflammation of the sinuses, the air pockets in the front of your head above and below your eyes.

Causes

Colds, allergies, or chronic irritation from smoke or dust may cause mucus in the sinuses to thicken and the tissues to become swollen. This thickening and swelling blocks the sinus drainage passages into the nose. If this mucus is not opened up in about 1 week, bacteria can grow and become a bacterial infection.

Symptoms

A runny nose or sinus congestion by itself doesn't necessarily signal a sinus infection. However, you may have sinusitis if congestion lasts for more than a week and is accompanied by any of the following symptoms:

- Thick, yellow-green nasal discharge

- Facial or sinus pain, made worse by bending over or straining

- Runny nose with cough and sore throat

- Aching teeth
- Headache
- Fever

Treatment

Sinusitis can usually be treated with the following medications:

- Decongestants to reduce congestion
- Antibiotics to fight a bacterial infection
- Pain relievers to reduce pain

Self-Care

- Drink 6 to 10 glasses of liquids a day.
- Maintain proper humidity in your home.
- Heat your sinuses by taking a hot shower or using a hot wash cloth, hot water bottle, or gel pack for 5 to 10 minutes 3 or more times a day.
- After heating, massage your sinuses to stimulate drainage. Begin at the top and work slowly downward for 2 to 3 minutes. Search for pressure points that relieve pain.
- Use an oral decongestant such as pseudoephedrine (Sudafed or a generic), or use a decongestant nasal spray such as oxymetazoline (Afrin or Sinex) or phenylephrine (Neo-Synephrine or a

generic) up to 2 times a day for up to 3 days. Follow package directions.

- Use ibuprofen (Advil or a generic) or acetaminophen (Tylenol or a generic) according to package directions.
- Use nasal irrigation (see box below) or saltwater nasal spray (Ocean or Ayr) 4 to 6 times a day. Follow package directions.
- Do not take antihistamines unless you have allergies. They tend to thicken mucus. Sleep with the head of your bed elevated.

How To Perform Nasal Irrigation

1. Make a saline solution: Place ¼ teaspoon table salt in a small bowl. Add 1 cup lukewarm water, and stir until salt is dissolved. Make a new solution every day.
2. Fill a 2-ounce rubber-bulb ear syringe (purchased at a drugstore) with saline solution.
3. Insert tip of syringe 1 inch up nostril, then lift bulb upward so the tip is pointing straight (horizontal) into the nose. Hold in position and bend over a sink. Open your mouth and squeeze with enough force that solution comes out of your mouth and both nostrils. Use ½ cup of the solution for each nostril.
4. Very gently blow your nose.
5. Clean bowl and syringe after each use.

What to do about Sinusitis

Symptom/Sign	Action
Sinus congestion lasting less than a week	Self-care
Symptoms persist after 7 days of self-care	Call doctor
Symptoms worsen after 3 days of self-care, fever higher than 101°F, history of sinus problems	See doctor
Eyeball pain, vision problems, and swelling or redness around the eyes or on face	Go to hospital

Prevention

You can't always prevent sinusitis, but there are steps you can take to reduce your risk.

- Wash your hands often to avoid catching colds.
- Don't smoke, because tobacco irritates your sinuses.
- Don't drink alcohol, which can cause the lining of your sinuses to swell.
- Avoid polluted air, which can irritate your lungs and nasal passages.

Sore Throats

Most sore throats are caused by viruses or environmental conditions. They can be annoying, but they will usually get better with a few simple self-care steps.

Causes

Sore throats can be caused by:

- Low humidity in your home
- Not drinking enough fluids
- Winter dryness
- Smoke
- Allergies

Sore throats can also be caused by two types of infections: the more common viral infection and the less common—but more serious—bacterial infection known as *strep throat*.

Symptoms

Your symptoms may be an indication of which type of infection you have.

Viral Sore Throat

A viral infection:

- Usually causes a dry cough and light-colored mucus

- Is less likely to be accompanied by a fever

- Is often associated with a cold, flu, or hoarseness

Strep Throat

Indications that you have strep throat include:

- Very red throat with white spots

- Swollen neck glands

- Fever above 101°F

- No cough or runny nose

If you have symptoms of strep throat, you should see your doctor for a strep test. Be sure to tell your doctor if you have recently been exposed to someone with strep.

Treatment

Viral sore throats will usually go away in a few days, but up to 7 to 10 days is not uncommon. They do not need to be treated with antibiotics.

If you have strep throat, your doctor will prescribe antibiotics. You will begin to feel better after about a day of taking your medication, but you need to take all your medication exactly as pre-scribed to prevent possible complications. It's easy to spread the strep bacteria to other people, so you should stay home until you've taken the medication for 24 hours and are no longer contagious.

Self-Care

- Gargle with warm saltwater every couple of hours. Use ¼ teaspoon of table salt in an 8-ounce glass of water. This will help lessen the irritation that is causing your throat to feel sore.

- Suck on popsicles or other frozen desserts. They will feel good on your throat and help you get enough liquids. Older children and adults can also suck on throat lozenges (cough drops), hard candy, or ice and gargle with saltwater.

- Drink more liquids. Make sure you are drinking 8 to 10 glasses each day. Juice and water are best. Warm liquids are soothing to the back of your throat.

- Use acetaminophen (Tylenol or a generic) or ibuprofen for a fever or other aches. Do not use aspirin for children under 18, because it may increase their risk of Reye's syndrome. Adults may take aspirin.

- Get extra rest. It helps your body get rid of the virus or bacteria that is causing the infection.

What to do about Sore Throats

Symptom/Sign	Action
Sore throat with cough and runny nose	Self-care
Throat still feels very sore and you still have a fever after being on medication for 2 complete days	Call doctor
Sore throat continues for more than 5 to 7 days	See doctor
Throat is red with white spots, accompanied by a fever	See doctor
Severe difficulty with swallowing; unable or painful to open mouth	Go to hospital

Swollen Glands

Swollen glands could be considered a mixed blessing. The fact that they are swollen probably means they're busy fighting an infection in your body. Unfortunately, because they often become enlarged quickly, swollen glands may be painful. The glands that become swollen are called *lymph glands*. Ordinarily, they are about the size of a pea, and they produce the antibodies your body uses to fight infections.

Causes

Infections are the most common cause of swollen glands. The location of the swollen gland can tell you where the infection is (see illustration on page 137). An infection in the feet, legs, or genital area—it can be as simple as athlete's foot or an ingrown toenail—may cause glands in the groin to swell. A swollen gland in the armpit might be from an infected cut on the arm or finger. Allergies and bug bites can also cause glands to swell.

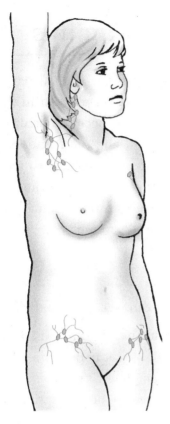

Location of lymph glands that are easy to feel.

Most people connect the term *swollen glands* with the glands between the ear and the angle of the jaw. These glands often swell during sore throats and ear infections. Swollen glands down the sides or back of the neck might be from an infection in the scalp or from mononucleosis. "Mono," as it is commonly known, is an illness that causes fever,

swollen lymph glands, sore throat, severe fatigue, and other symptoms.

If your lymph glands enlarge more slowly and continue to swell without signs of infection, call your doctor. You may have a more serious illness, such as Hodgkin's disease or lymphoma.

Treatment

Most of the time, swollen glands are caused by viral infections and no treatment is necessary. Sometimes, however, a bacterial infection will lodge in the glands themselves, making them red, hot, tender, and sore. Infected glands may require antibiotics. In some cases they need to be surgically drained.

Self-Care

If you have significant discomfort, you can take acetaminophen (Tylenol or a generic) and use warm or cold compresses to relieve pain and swelling. The soreness will get better in a few days, although the glands may remain somewhat swollen for several weeks. It takes longer for glands to return to their natural size than it does for them to enlarge.

What to do about Swollen Glands

Symptom/Sign	Action
Swollen glands without more serious symptoms	Self-care
Swollen glands with a sore throat or fever higher than 100°F	Call doctor
Swollen glands that are very tender and red	See doctor
Swelling that lasts for more than 2 weeks	See doctor
Difficulty opening your mouth or moving your neck	Go to hospital
Difficulty breathing and swallowing	Call 911

Tinnitus

T innitus is the general name given to noises people hear in their ears or head. It may occur suddenly or come on gradually, and the sound may come and go. You may be able to ignore the sound some or all of the time. In most cases, tinnitus is not an emergency and is not life threatening.

Causes

Tinnitus can be caused by the following:

- Wax in the ear canal, a stiffening of the middle ear bones, or a hole in the eardrum. These problems usually can be corrected and the tinnitus goes away.

- Exposure to loud noises. This can cause tinnitus and permanent hearing loss. Hearing loss may be sudden or gradual, depending on the volume and length of exposure to the sound. Tinnitus may occur at the same time as or after exposure to the loud sound.

- Some medications cause tinnitus as a side effect.

- Tinnitus can be a normal part of hearing loss that often comes with aging.

Less common causes of tinnitus and hearing loss include:

- Trauma to the head
- Problems with the temporomandibular (jaw) joint
- Disorders of the neck vertebrae
- Certain medications that in high doses can damage the ear

For many cases of tinnitus, the cause is unknown. Excessive caffeine, nicotine, salt, alcohol, and illegal drugs can make the symptoms of tinnitus worse. Stress and fatigue can also make tinnitus more noticeable.

Symptoms

You may experience tinnitus as a ringing sound. It can also sound like chirping, crickets, ocean noises, roaring, or hissing.

Subjective tinnitus means only you are able to hear the sound. Occasionally other people may be able to hear the same sound you hear. This is called *objective tinnitus*. Objective tinnitus occurs when there are abnormalities of the blood vessels in the outer or middle ear or because of muscle spasms in the middle ear. A clicking or crackling sound often occurs with objective tinnitus.

An ear, nose, and throat specialist can determine the cause of tinnitus. If you have tinnitus, a complete hearing evaluation can help identify any hearing loss that may be associated with the tinnitus and determine the severity of your symptoms.

Treatment

There are five different types of treatments for tinnitus. They include:

- *Amplification*. Hearing aids will not cure or eliminate tinnitus but will make other sounds louder. The tinnitus may not be as loud or may not be heard at all.

- *Masking*. Masking devices are often used to cover up the sounds a person with tinnitus is hearing. Masking devices create a different noise that is specially designed to cover up the ringing or buzzing sounds. One type of tinnitus masking device looks like a hearing aid and can be placed in the ear. Tabletop masking devices are also available. Household items such as fans, air conditioners, and radios (with the dial set between stations) can serve as masking devices.

- *Medications*. There are no medications proven to eliminate tinnitus at this time. However, some prescription medications can reduce the symptoms.

- *Acupuncture*. Acupuncture has brought some relief for tinnitus in some people.

- *Stress management*. Biofeedback, counseling, or cognitive therapy may be helpful in reducing stress that aggravates tinnitus or occurs as a result of it.

What to do about Tinnitus

Symptom/Sign	Action
Noises in your ears	See doctor
Symptoms that get worse or are accompanied by hearing loss or dizziness	See doctor

Stomach and Bowel Problems

Humans eat and digest thousands of pounds of food every year. Your body does an impressive job of digesting and excreting these foods. Still, no system is perfect. This section describes common problems of the stomach and digestive tract.

You can treat many digestive concerns at home. However, there may be times when your doctor's help is needed. If your condition is especially difficult to handle, your doctor may bring in other doctors who specialize in the diagnosis and treatment of these concerns, such as gastroenterologists. ::

Abdominal Pain

Nothing is more uncomfortable than pain in the abdominal area. It can range from dull or burning to sharp and shooting—and everything in between. Fortunately, the most common types of pain are usually not life threatening and are treatable (see Vomiting, p. 168, Constipation, p. 150, Heartburn, p. 158, and Diarrhea, p. 152).

Causes

Most abdominal pain is linked to common problems such as emotional distress, overeating, or the flu. However, it can also point to more serious illness. The type and location of the pain often gives a clue to its cause.

Appendicitis

Pain that starts at the navel and moves to the lower right side of the abdomen can signal *appendicitis*, an inflammation of the appendix. Other symptoms of appendicitis can include:

- Nausea, vomiting, or loss of appetite
- Tenderness in the lower right side of abdomen
- Inability to walk upright
- Fever ranging from 100 to 102°F

If it is detected early, mild appendicitis can sometimes be treated with antibiotics. More serious cases require sur-

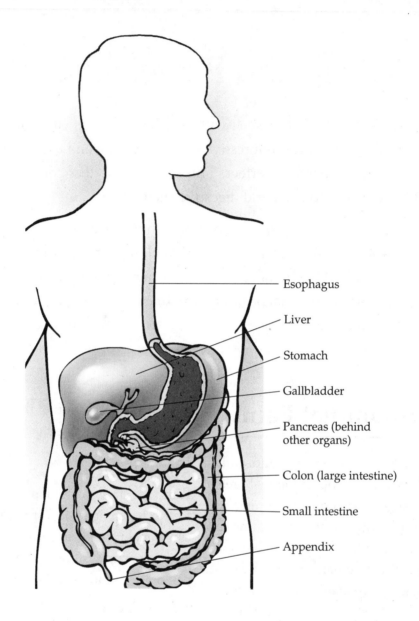

Esophagus

Liver

Stomach

Gallbladder

Pancreas (behind other organs)

Colon (large intestine)

Small intestine

Appendix

gery to remove the appendix. If left untreated, appendicitis can cause the appendix to burst. If you have any symptoms of this condition, you should talk to your doctor immediately.

Diverticulitis

Pain in the lower left-hand side of the abdomen could be a sign of diverticuli-

tis. Diverticulitis occurs when small, balloonlike sacs called *diverticula* develop in the walls of the colon and become infected and inflamed. Other symptoms of diverticulitis include fever, nausea, vomiting, chills, cramping, and constipation.

Treatment of diverticulitis usually includes clearing up the infection and inflammation, resting the colon, and preventing or minimizing complications. Your doctor may give you antibiotics and recommend a pain reliever, a diet of only liquids, and several days of bed rest. In some cases, diverticulitis may require a hospital stay. If complications develop, surgery may be needed.

The best way to prevent diverticulitis is to eat a high-fiber diet. The fiber in foods such as vegetables and whole grains aids in digestion and helps reduce pressure in the colon. As you add fiber, it is important to do it gradually (to prevent gas, bloating, and cramps) and to drink plenty of liquids. You can also help prevent diverticulitis by having bowel movements when you feel the urge to do so. Putting it off can increase pressure in the colon.

Gallbladder Disease

Sharp pain under the right rib cage that worsens after eating points to gallbladder disease. Types of gallbladder disease include gallstones and inflammation of the gallbladder.

If complications develop, gallbladder disease can cause other symptoms along with the abdominal pain. These include jaundice (yellowing of the skin and the whites of the eyes), high fever, and chills. Sometimes people with gallstones do not experience any symptoms at all.

Gallstones and attacks of gallbladder pain may be managed in a variety of ways, ranging from "watchful waiting" (watching the symptoms over time with no treatment) to medications to surgery. A person who has had gallstone pain only once may not need surgery or medications, because in some cases the condition does not recur. However, for those who have more persistent or frequent attacks, removal of the gallbladder is recommended. Reducing fat in the diet can also help reduce the symptoms caused by gallbladder disease.

Irritable Bowel Syndrome

Abdominal pain that is relieved by bowel movements and is accompanied by diarrhea or constipation may mean irritable bowel syndrome. Irritable bowel syndrome is a common disorder of the intestine that has no known cause. When irritable bowel syndrome occurs, the walls of the intestine are contracting too forcefully, too weakly, too slowly, or too rapidly. Other symptoms of irritable bowel syndrome include bloating, gas, mucus-covered stools, and a strong urge to have a bowel movement after you have already had one.

Irritable bowel syndrome cannot be treated with surgery or medication. However, you can take steps to help prevent the symptoms from getting worse.

- Drink plenty of water.

- Gradually increase your fiber intake by eating more high-fiber foods, such as fruits, vegetables, and whole grains, or by taking bulk laxatives containing psyllium.

- Keep a diary of what you eat to identify foods that make you feel worse. Avoid these foods and others that cause gas, such as onions, broccoli, cabbage, and beans. You may also want to avoid chocolate, milk products, and large amounts of alcohol because they may cause spasms and delay passage of stools.

- Limit caffeine, which can cause diarrhea.

- Get plenty of exercise. Physical activity reduces stress and aids digestion.

- Follow self-care steps to manage stress (see p. 336).

Ulcers

A sharp, burning pain in the upper middle part of your stomach (between the breastbone and the navel) could be an ulcer. An ulcer is a sore that forms in the lining of the stomach or the upper part of the small intestine. Ulcers can develop for many reasons. Smoking cigarettes and using aspirin, ibuprofen, or other nonsteroidal anti-inflammatory medication may play a role. Ulcers can also form when the stomach cannot protect itself from powerful digestive fluids. *Helicobacter pylori*, a bacteria found in the stomach, can also lead to an ulcer. Contrary to popular belief, emotional stress or spicy foods do not cause ulcers.

Heartburn alone is not a sign of an ulcer (see Heartburn, p. 158). Intense, heartburnlike pain could also be caused by a less serious condition called *gastroesophageal reflux* disease (see p. 156).

In the past, people with ulcers were told to avoid spicy, fatty, or acidic foods. However, eating a bland diet is no longer thought to be effective in treating or preventing ulcers. Today ulcers are usually treated with medications. Because smoking can prevent ulcers from healing, people with ulcers should not smoke.

Conditions of the Reproductive System

In women, abdominal discomfort may signal a problem with the reproductive system. Pelvic pain that occurs each month just before a woman's period suggests endometriosis (see p. 288). Tenderness in the lower abdominal area may mean pelvic inflammatory disease (see p. 297). For women of childbearing age, an ectopic pregnancy can produce a sudden sharp, stabbing abdominal pain along with vaginal bleeding, a history of missed or light periods, or pain radiating to the shoulder. Ovarian cysts and uterine fibroids can also cause abdominal pain in women.

Other conditions that can cause abdominal pain include urinary tract infections (see p. 177), food poisoning (see p. 154), food allergy, hernia (see p. 161), kidney stones (see p. 172), and lactose intolerance.

Treatment

Abdominal pain is difficult to diagnose because it can mean so many things. To determine the cause of your pain, your doctor may ask you these questions:

- What type of pain is it? (Is it crampy, sharp, or dull? Is it steady or is it off and on?)

- Where is the pain?

- When did it begin? How long does it last?

- How severe is the pain?

- When does it occur? (Does it occur with your period? Does it become worse after eating?)

By taking time to think about answers to these questions, you can help your doctor to diagnose the problem. The type of treatment will depend on the cause of the abdominal pain.

Self-Care

Mild abdominal pain that is not caused by ulcers, diverticulitis, or gallbladder disease can usually be treated at home. Follow these steps:

- Rest as needed.

- Use acetaminophen for pain relief. Do not use aspirin or anti-inflammatory medications, such as ibuprofen.

- Avoid things that irritate the lining of the stomach, such as alcohol, caffeine, aspirin, and ibuprofen.

- Do not use laxatives or enemas.

- Take warm baths or apply a warm water bottle to the area to ease pain.

What to do about Abdominal Pain

Symptom/Sign	Action
Mild pain that comes and goes for less than 4 weeks	Self-care
Pain that comes and goes for more than 4 weeks	Call doctor
Pain with fever, jaundice, dark urine, severe nausea or vomiting, or pale, pasty stools	See doctor
Sudden sharp, stabbing abdominal pain along with vaginal bleeding, a history of missed or light periods, or pain radiating to the shoulder	See doctor
Severe, constant abdominal pain after injury	See doctor
Sudden, very severe pain that lasts longer than 2 hours	See doctor
Abdominal pain and sudden bright red rectal bleeding, or vomiting of blood or a substance that looks like coffee grounds	Call 911
Dizziness, light-headedness, rapid pulse, or cool, clammy skin	Call 911

Black or Bloody Stools

S tools that look tarry, black, or bloody can be alarming, but they are not always a sign of serious illness. To understand what to do about this symptom, it is important to recognize which unusual-looking stools are simply bothersome and which require a visit to the doctor.

Causes

There are many reasons stools may be black, tarry, or bloody. The most common problems, along with the ways to treat them, are listed below.

- *Foods.* Large amounts of iron or iron-rich foods, such as spinach and beets, can cause stools to temporarily turn black. This change is not cause for concern. The color of the stools will return to normal after a time.

- *Medications.* Iron preparations and stomach medications that contain bismuth compounds can cause stools to darken or turn black. Stool color will return to normal when you stop taking the medication.

- *Hemorrhoids.* Swollen blood vessels in the anal canal and lower rectum are a common cause of pain, itching, and rectal bleeding, especially during bowel movements. People with hemorrhoids may notice bright red blood on the toilet tissue or on the stool itself. Hemorrhoids can be relieved through self-care steps (see Hemorrhoids, p. 160). However, you should see your doctor if they recur or persist for more than 5 days.

- *Ulcerative colitis.* Frequent, mucus-covered bloody diarrhea accompanied by fever and weight loss can be caused by an intestinal disorder called *ulcerative colitis*. This condition is serious and must be treated by a doctor.

- *Colorectal cancer.* Blood in the stool can be a symptom of colorectal cancer. This form of cancer may also cause abdominal pain and changes in bowel movements. If your stools are bloody, you should see your doctor to get screened for colorectal cancer. This cancer is often curable when it is detected and treated early.

What to do about Black or Bloody Stools

Symptom/Sign	Action
Known hemorrhoids: blood on toilet tissue or blood-tinged water in toilet bowl, or rectal pain or itching, or both (see Hemorrhoids, p. 160)	Self-care
New onset of blood on toilet tissue or blood-tinged water in toilet bowl with no history of hemorrhoids	See doctor
Black, tarry stools unrelated to intake of food or medicine	Go to hospital
Bright red rectal bleeding associated with abdominal pain or fever	Go to hospital
Bright red rectal bleeding associated with bleeding disorders, ulcers, or gastrointestinal disease or with taking blood thinners, aspirin, or nonsteroidal anti-inflammatory drugs (NSAIDs)	Go to hospital
Sudden onset of heavy, continuous, bright red rectal bleeding or black, tarry stools	Call 911

Colorectal Cancer

Colorectal cancer is one of the most common cancers in the United States today and the second-leading cause of cancer deaths in the United States. In many cases, colorectal cancer can be detected and prevented if simple steps are followed. The earlier the cancer or changes in the colon are found, the better the chance for cure.

Causes

No one knows for sure what causes colon cancer, but we do know some of the risk factors. Your chances of developing colon cancer are higher if you have any of the following:

- A personal history of ulcerative colitis, precancerous changes in the lining of the colon, or Crohn's disease

- A personal history of large polyps (growths in the colon)

- A first-degree relative—mother, father, sister, or brother—who had colon cancer before 65 years of age

- Two first-degree relatives who had colon cancer at any age

- A personal history of breast, ovarian, or endometrial cancer

Age also plays a role. Most cases occur in people over 65 years of age. Fewer than 2 percent of cases occur in those individuals under 40 years of age.

Symptoms

You may not know you have colorectal cancer because there are no warning signs in the early stages of the disease. If you have a change in your bowel habits, such as bloody or black stools, your doctor will recommend that your colon be examined. The best way to know if you have colorectal cancer—before you have symptoms—is to be screened for the disease.

Screening for Colon Cancer

Many people would rather avoid the screening tests used for colon cancer because they are embarrassed or concerned about discomfort. Don't let these worries stop you from getting the screening you need. Early detection can save lives. Discuss the following screening options with your doctor to decide the best method for you.

Fecal Occult Blood Test (FOBT). This test detects the presence of blood in the stool, which is a warning sign for colorectal cancer. Many factors can interfere with the accuracy of this screening procedure, so follow-up testing is necessary to confirm positive results. If this method of screening is chosen, it is recommended that it be done once a year for people aged 50 to 80 years.

Flexible Sigmoidoscopy. For this test a thin, lighted tube is inserted into your rectum. With this device, your doctor can see about 27 inches into your colon, which is far enough to identify about 80 percent of cancers and polyps, because they tend to accumulate toward the lower end of your bowel. If this method of screening is chosen, it is recommended that it be done every five years for people aged 50 to 80 years.

Combination Flexible Sigmoidoscopy and FOBT. You and your doctor may decide to use both flexible sigmoidoscopy and FOBT to screen for colon cancer. This approach includes an annual FOBT and a flexible sigmoidoscopy every 5 years.

Total Colon Evaluation. A total colon evaluation can be done using a colonoscopy, colon X-ray alone, or a flexible sigmoidoscopy combined with a colon X-ray. A colonoscopy is similar to a flexible sigmoidoscopy, but allows your doctor to see the entire length of your colon. A colon X-ray or a flexible sigmoidoscopy combined with a colon X-ray is usually done every 5 years. A colonoscopy is usually done every 10 years.

Prevention

- Get screened for colorectal cancer. Ask your doctor which tests are right for you.

- Watch for warning signs. Talk to your doctor if you have black, bloody, or thin stools or if you have diarrhea or constipation that persists. Keep in mind that cancer is just one of many causes of these symptoms.

- Eat less fat. Obesity and diets that are high-fat or high-calorie have been linked to cancer in both animals and humans. By cutting down on fatty foods, you can also reduce your calorie intake.

- Eat more high-fiber foods. Foods high in fiber include whole-grain cereals and breads, beans, fruits and vegetables, potatoes, and brown rice.

Know the Signs of Cancer

Cancer is a group of diseases that may cause virtually any sign or symptom. In most cases a patient's signs and symptoms do not provide enough clues to determine the cause of illness. However, you should not overlook a symptom if it occurs, particularly if it has been going on for a time. Here are some of the general signs and symptoms of cancer:

- Unexplained weight loss
- Fever
- Fatigue
- Pain
- Changes in the skin

In addition to these general symptoms, the American Cancer Society has published the following seven common symptoms that could lead to a diagnosis of cancer:

- A change in bowel habits or bladder function. These symptoms may be signs of colon, bladder, or prostate cancer.

- Sores that do not heal. Skin cancers may bleed and resemble sores that do not heal. A persistent sore in the mouth could mean oral cancer.

- Unusual bleeding or discharge. Blood in sputum is a sign of lung cancer. Blood in the stool could be a sign of colon or rectal cancer. Vaginal bleeding could indicate cancer of the uterus or cervix. Blood in the urine is a sign of possible bladder or kidney cancer. A bloody discharge from the nipple can mean breast cancer.

- Thickening or lump in the breast or other parts of the body. Cancers of the breast, testicle, lymph nodes, and soft tissues may be felt through the skin.

- Indigestion or difficulty swallowing. These symptoms may be pointing to a cancer in the esophagus, stomach, or throat.

- Recent change in a wart or mole. An increase in size, color, or shape may indicate skin cancer.

- Nagging cough. A cough that does not go away may be a sign of lung cancer.

- Hoarseness. Hoarseness can indicate cancer of the larynx or thyroid.

Constipation

Constipation is the passage of hard, dry, or infrequent stools. Some people may have a bowel movement two or three times a day; others may have one every 3 to 5 days. Unless the frequency has changed a lot, how often you have a bowel movement does not matter. It is the consistency of the stool or your own discomfort that tells you if you are constipated.

Constipation can be treated naturally using many of the self-care steps listed beginning at the bottom of this page.

Causes

In most cases your body will send a signal when it is ready to pass a stool. Constipation usually happens because that signal is ignored.

Other causes of constipation include a poor diet, decreased activity, changes in daily routines, or increased stress. Some medications, such as antacids, antidepressants, antihistamines, antihypertensives, diuretics, and narcotics, may also cause constipation.

In children, toilet training can cause stress, which can lead to constipation. Older adults, who may become less active as they age, may also become constipated.

Sometimes constipation can be a sign of a more serious problem. For example, alternating diarrhea and constipation may mean that you have irritable bowel syndrome, a common disorder of the intestine. Diverticulitis, an inflammation of small pockets in the colon wall, causes constipation, fever, and pain in the lower left abdomen. (For more information on irritable bowel syndrome and diverticulitis, see Abdominal Pain, p. 141.)

Treatment

Mild laxatives, such as Milk of Magnesia, or enemas, such as Fleets, can temporarily relieve constipation. However, these medications should not be used continually to help you have regular bowel movements because they can cause your bowel to be dependent on them. Instead, try adding high-fiber foods to your diet or use a fiber supplement, such as Metamucil.

Self-Care

• If you have no other symptoms, relax and wait it out. It is not unusual for the frequency and consistency of bowel movements to vary from time to time.

• Listen to your body. It will signal you when it's ready to have a bowel movement. When you discover the natural time during the day for you to have a bowel movement, try to set aside that time each day. Relax while you sit on the toilet.

- Change your diet. Increase your liquid intake by drinking more water. Prune juice is also helpful for relieving constipation. Add fresh fruits and vegetables and whole-grain breads to your diet.

- Be more physically active. Exercise not only helps your bowels move more freely, it also helps reduce the stress that may make you temporarily constipated.

- Use a stool softener, mild laxative, or fiber product to relieve temporary symptoms. Once your bowel movements have returned to normal, use diet modification, exercise, and stress reduction techniques to stay regular.

- Call your doctor if constipation continues after 1 week of self-care.

What to do about Constipation

Symptom/Sign	Action
Constipation, rectal pressure, gas, uncomfortable feeling of fullness	Self-care
Constipation associated with changes in bowel patterns or pencil-thin stools	See doctor
Bowel movement that becomes impacted in the rectum; only mucus and fluids can pass	See doctor
Constipation and vomiting, fever, loss of appetite, abdominal pain, cramps, or gas	See doctor
Constipation with a bloated abdomen and the inability to pass gas	Go to hospital

Prevention

Eating foods high in fiber can treat and prevent constipation. Fiber is the undigestible part of foods such as fruits, vegetables, and whole grains. Fiber helps waste pass through the intestines.

In addition to increasing the fiber in your diet, drinking extra fluids—especially water—is a good idea. Replace carbonated beverages and coffee with water. Being physically active is also helpful in preventing constipation. As a guideline, try not to sit for more than 30 minutes at a time.

Diarrhea

Diarrhea is the passage of frequent loose or watery stools. It often occurs along with abdominal cramps, vomiting, or fever. With diarrhea, stools move so quickly through the intestines that the body is unable to absorb the fluid in them.

Causes

Diarrhea can be caused by bacteria, viruses, emotional upset, stress, some chronic bowel disease, and certain medications. With bacterial infections of the colon, diarrhea is usually more severe and lasts longer than usual. Prolonged diarrhea may also be a symptom of conditions such as giardiasis (if you have been traveling), amebic dysentery, Crohn's disease, ulcerative colitis, or food allergies.

Treatment

Most diarrhea goes away on its own with self-care steps, usually within 2 days. When a diet of clear liquids does not help, your doctor may prescribe a medication that will slow down activity of the bowel, such as Lomotil or Imodium. These drugs are not recommended for children (see Diarrhea in Children, p. 369).

Self-Care

- Drink room-temperature liquids.

- Avoid alcohol, smoking, caffeine, milk, and fruit juice.

- Do not eat if your stomach feels very upset or crampy.

- Drink fluids to prevent dehydration. Throughout the day, sip a few ounces of water or diluted broths, sports drinks, soda, or rehydration solutions.

- When your appetite returns but the diarrhea remains, try eating ripe bananas, rice, applesauce, white toast, cooked cereal, potatoes, chicken, turkey, or cooked carrots.

- Until diarrhea is gone, avoid fresh fruits, green vegetables, alcohol, greasy or fatty foods, and highly seasoned or spicy foods.

- If necessary, take over-the-counter antidiarrheal medications such as Pepto-Bismol, Kaopectate, or Imodium for temporary relief. However, avoid taking these medications continually. They may prolong the length of diarrhea or cause more serious problems. (NOTE: Products that contain bismuth salicylate may temporarily darken the stools or tongue.)

- Call your doctor if you believe the diarrhea could be caused by a medication you are taking. Diarrhea is a common side effect of nonsteroidal anti-inflammatory drugs (NSAIDs), antibiotics, gold compounds, and antidepressants, such as Prozac, Zoloft, and Paxil.

- Call your doctor if diarrhea lasts longer than 72 hours.

What to do about Diarrhea in Adults

Symptom/Sign	Action
Diarrhea that lasts less than 48 hours with mild cramps that are relieved by bowel movements	Self-care
Diarrhea associated with recent international travel; ingestion of water from lakes, streams, or wells	See doctor
Blood streaking in the stool or on toilet paper and no history of hemorrhoids	See doctor
Symptoms of dehydration (dry mouth, excess thirst, decreased urination)	Go to hospital
Severe constant abdominal pain for longer than 2 hours	Go to hospital

Prevention

- To prevent the spread of organisms that can cause diarrhea, wash your hands after you use the toilet or diaper a baby and before you eat or prepare food. Remember to wash your hands in warm, soapy water if you have touched uncooked meat products.

- Handle and cook foods carefully. Unpasteurized dairy products and undercooked fish, poultry, eggs, and meat can have bacteria that can cause diarrhea and other gastrointestinal problems. Always cook foods thoroughly. Wash cutting boards and utensils in warm, soapy water. Eat only pasteurized products. Be sure to keep hot foods hot and cold foods cold. Harmful bacteria can grow in foods left at room temperature for too long.

- If you have diarrhea, avoid preparing food for others unless you wash your hands thoroughly. Do not work as a server or cook in any food-service position until your diarrhea is completely gone and you know you are not spreading your illness to others.

- If you are traveling to a foreign country, avoid drinking or cooking with unpurified water. Water can be purified by boiling it for 15 to 20 minutes, by adding iodine or chlorine drops or tablets, or by using a special water filter. It is very important to follow product directions exactly when using any water-purifying product. Travelers should also avoid fresh fruits and vegetables unless the foods have been washed thoroughly in purified water and can be peeled. Be wary of foods such as melons, which are often injected with water to increase their weight.

Foodborne Illness

Every day we are exposed to thousands of bacteria. Not all bacteria cause disease. For example, the bacteria used to make cheese and yogurt are safe and even healthy. Some bacteria, however, create problems for our digestive system. Foodborne illness develops when certain harmful bacteria get into the food supply and cause disease. Millions of cases of foodborne illness occur each year, and most cases can be prevented.

Causes

Foodborne illness is caused when harmful bacteria get on food and are eaten. The bacteria appear on the food through many different routes. They may be present on products when you purchase them. For example, plastic-wrapped chicken or other raw meats can contain bacteria. Uncooked seafood and eggs, and produce such as lettuce, tomatoes, and alfalfa sprouts, can also become contaminated.

Even if a food product is safely cooked, it can be contaminated with bacteria when it is exposed to bacteria from other sources. These sources include raw products, meat juices, or other contaminated products, as well as food handlers who may have harmful bacteria on their hands.

Symptoms

Symptoms of foodborne illness vary depending on the type of bacteria that has contaminated the food. Common symptoms include diarrhea, gas pains, abdominal cramps, nausea and vomiting, and fever or chills. Because these symptoms often resemble the flu, people often do not know that they have a foodborne illness. Some symptoms, such as double vision, droopy eyelids, or difficulty speaking, swallowing, or breathing, point to a much more serious foodborne illness called *botulism*. If you have any of these symptoms, you should see your doctor right away.

Some people may become ill after ingesting only a few harmful bacteria, while others can ingest thousands of bacteria and have no symptoms at all. People at greatest risk of having foodborne illness are those with weaker immune systems. Such groups include very young children, pregnant women, people with chronic diseases such as acquired immunodeficiency syndrome (AIDS) or diabetes, and the elderly.

Treatment

Most mild symptoms of foodborne illness go away on their own without medications. However, they can last anywhere from 24 hours to several days. In some cases, foodborne illness can be dangerous because the accompanying vomiting and diarrhea can cause severe dehydration. If the infection spreads from the intestines into the bloodstream, antibiotics may be prescribed.

Botulism, one of the most serious types of foodborne illness, requires immediate medical attention. (See Symptoms, p. 154, for information on the warning signs of botulism.) If left untreated, botulism can cause death.

Self-Care

- Rest and drink plenty of fluids. Avoid alcohol, caffeine, or milk products.

- When you begin to have an appetite, try eating semisolid and low-fiber foods, such as soda crackers and toast.

- See your doctor if your symptoms last longer than a few weeks or if you develop severe diarrhea with decreased urination, bloody stools, fever, abdominal pain, or cramps.

- Avoid taking antidiarrheal medications. They may slow the elimination of bacteria from your system.

- Call the local health department if the suspect food was served at a large gathering, if it was from a restaurant or other foodservice facility, or if you bought the product at a store.

What to do about Foodborne Illness

Symptom/Sign	Action
Mild symptoms of foodborne illness	Self-care
Mild symptoms lasting longer than a few days	Call doctor
Symptoms of dehydration: dry mouth, dizziness, dark yellow urine, or decreased urination	See doctor
Bloody diarrhea, excessive nausea and vomiting, or fever	See doctor
Foodborne illness in at-risk groups (children, pregnant women, people with chronic diseases, and the elderly)	Go to hospital
Symptoms of botulism: headache, double or blurred vision, muscle weakness	Call 911

Prevention

Bacteria multiply rapidly between 40 and 140°F. To keep food from entering this danger zone, follow these guidelines:

- Store food in the refrigerator or freezer.

- Cook food to 160°F (145°F for roasts, steaks, and chops of beef, veal, and lamb).

- Maintain hot, cooked food at 140°F or above.

- When reheating cooked food, reheat to 165°F.

Gastroesophageal Reflux Disease

Gastroesophageal reflux disease, or GERD, is a digestive disorder that causes heartburn and indigestion. *Gastroesophageal* refers to the stomach and esophagus, and *reflux* means "to return." GERD is the return of the stomach's contents back up into the esophagus.

Causes

GERD occurs when the muscle connecting the esophagus with the stomach (the lower esophageal sphincter, or LES) weakens or does not work properly. As a result, the muscle cannot keep the contents of the stomach from going up into the esophagus (see illustration).

There are many possible causes of GERD. Some doctors believe that a

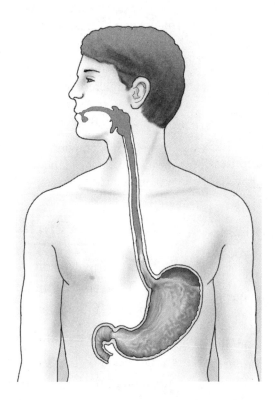

GERD begins when the lower esophageal sphincter weakens or does not work properly. As a result, stomach contents that are being digested in the stomach come back up the esophagus and cause heartburn.

hiatal hernia may weaken the LES. Foods such as chocolate, peppermint, and fried or fatty foods may also weaken the muscle, as can coffee and alcoholic beverages. Other causes include cigarette smoking, obesity, and pregnancy.

Symptoms

The main symptom of GERD is heartburn, or *acid indigestion*. Heartburn feels like a burning chest pain that begins behind the breastbone and moves upward to the neck and throat (see Heartburn, p. 158). Sometimes people who have GERD also have an acidic or bitter taste in the mouth.

Treatment

Treatment for GERD focuses on one of two things: (1) decreasing the amount of stomach contents that go back up to the esophagus or (2) reducing the damage to the lining of the esophagus.

In many cases, dietary and lifestyle changes can help reduce the symptoms of GERD. Taking antacids can also help, but they should not be used long term because they can have side effects, such as diarrhea and a buildup of magnesium in the body. For chronic GERD discomfort, medications are available to reduce the production of acid in the stomach.

Self-Care

- Avoid foods and beverages that can affect the LES or irritate the lining of the esophagus. Examples include fried or fatty foods, peppermint, chocolate, alcohol, coffee, citrus fruit and citrus fruit juices, and tomato products.

- Lose weight if you are overweight.

- Stop smoking.

- Raise the head of your bed 6 inches. Use blocks or bricks to elevate the legs of the bed rather than using pillows to prop up your head.

- Avoid large meals. Instead, eat smaller, more frequent meals.

- Avoid lying down right after eating and within 2 to 3 hours of bedtime.

- Take an antacid.

What to do about GERD

Symptom/Sign	Action
Mild symptoms that occur off and on	Self-care
Long-term GERD not relieved by self-care	Call doctor

Heartburn

Heartburn is a burning sensation in the lower chest, behind the breastbone. It may be accompanied by nausea, bloating, belching, or a sour or bitter taste in the throat and mouth. Usually heartburn occurs while you are lying down or after you eat a large meal. Heartburn may also be a symptom of gastroesophageal reflux disease (see p. 156).

Causes

When you eat, a muscle at the lower end of your esophagus (called the LES) relaxes and opens to admit food to your stomach. The LES then closes to prevent stomach acid from washing back up the esophagus. Heartburn occurs when the LES does not close completely. Acid and bile from the stomach then come back up the esophagus, causing a burning sensation.

The following things can make heartburn worse:

- Cigarette smoking
- Coffee and other drinks that have caffeine
- Alcohol
- Citrus fruits
- Tomato products
- Chocolate, mints, or peppermints
- Fatty or spicy foods
- Onions
- Being overweight
- Aspirin, ibuprofen, or naproxen
- Other medications (check with your doctor)

Treatment

Heartburn can be easily treated with changes in diet and with over-the-counter medications (see Self-Care, below). However, it can also be a sign of a more serious illness, such as ulcers or other gastrointestinal problems. Sometimes pain in the chest may be mistaken for heartburn when it's really a heart attack or heart disease.

Heartburn that is not treated properly can cause ulcers, difficulties swallowing, scarring and narrowing of the esophagus, or other serious problems. If you have heartburn that won't go away, see your doctor.

Self-Care

There are many things you can do that will reduce or relieve heartburn. Use the following self-care steps, and call your doctor if your symptoms do not improve after 2 weeks:

- Don't smoke.

- Don't overeat. Try more frequent, smaller meals, rather than large ones.

- Relax during mealtimes. Eat slowly and chew thoroughly.

- Lose weight if you are overweight.

- Avoid tight-fitting clothes and tight belts.

- Try to eat at least 2 to 3 hours before lying down or exercising. If you take naps, try sleeping in a chair.

- Eat high-protein, low-fat meals.

- Sleep with the head of your bed elevated. To do this, place 4- to 6-inch blocks under the legs at the head of the bed.

- Avoid foods and other things that can cause heartburn (see Causes, p. 158).

- Take antacids or acid controllers for temporary relief.

- Avoid chewing gum to decrease the volume of air you swallow.

Additional self-care steps can be found in Gastroesophageal Reflux Disease, p. 156.

What to do about Heartburn

Symptom/Sign	Action
Occasional heartburn relieved by self-care suggestions	Continue self-care
Heartburn in a person taking heart or asthma medications, antispasmodics, antidepressants, antihistamines, sedatives, or birth control pills	Call doctor
Heartburn with loss of appetite and fatigue	See doctor
Heartburn with black or bloody stools	Go to hospital
Heartburn and vomiting blood	Go to hospital
Signs related to heart problems: chest pain that goes into neck, jaw, back, arms, or shoulders; constant, worsening pain with sweating; shortness of breath; nausea; or vomiting	Call 911

Hemorrhoids

Hemorrhoids are swollen blood vessels in the anal canal and lower rectum. They are a common cause of itching and rectal bleeding, especially during bowel movements. People with hemorrhoids may notice bright red blood on the toilet tissue or on the stool itself.

Causes

Hemorrhoids may be caused by straining to move a stool. They can also develop for other reasons, including pregnancy, aging, chronic constipation or diarrhea, and anal intercourse.

Self-Care

- Use an over-the-counter rectal ointment such as Anusol HC or Preparation H.

- Soak in a tub of warm water for 10 to 15 minutes three times a day to help relieve pain and to clean and heal the area.

- Apply moistened wipes, such as Tucks pads, to the rectal area twice a day and after bowel movements.

- Take acetaminophen for pain relief. Do not take aspirin because it can make the bleeding worse.

What to do about Hemorrhoids

Symptom/Sign	Action
Known hemorrhoids, with blood on toilet tissue or blood-tinged water in toilet bowl and rectal pain or itching or both	Self-care
Known hemorrhoids, with symptoms lasting more than 3 to 5 days or recurring symptoms, on and off, for longer than 1 week	See doctor
New onset of blood on toilet tissue or blood-tinged water in toilet bowl with no history of hemorrhoids	See doctor
Rectal pain and fever or possible exposure to sexually transmitted diseases	See doctor
Bright red rectal bleeding associated with abdominal pain or fever	Go to hospital

Prevention

To avoid constipation that can irritate hemorrhoids:

- Take a fiber supplement, such as Metamucil or Citrucel.

- Drink plenty of fluids, especially water and fruit juices.

- Eat plenty of fresh fruits, vegetables, and foods high in fiber.

Hernia

A hernia occurs when part of the intestine bulges through the abdominal wall. There are many different types of hernias, but the most common are inguinal hernias and hiatal hernias.

Inguinal Hernias

An inguinal (groin) hernia develops when the lining of the abdominal cavity weakens and the intestines push through the weak spot in the groin area (see illustration).

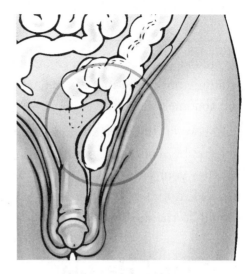

An inguinal hernia occurs when part of the intestine bulges through a weak area in the muscles in the abdomen. In this inguinal hernia the intestine has bulged through the passage where the testicle descends into the scrotum.

Causes

Causes of an inguinal hernia include obesity, pregnancy, heavy lifting, and straining to pass a stool.

Symptoms

The symptoms of an inguinal hernia may start slowly. They include the following:

• Visible bulges slightly above or within the scrotum

• Pain and tenderness in the lower abdomen and scrotum

• Feeling of pressure or weakness in the groin

• Aches and pain in the abdomen that start and stop

Treatment

Inguinal hernias are usually treated with surgery to repair the opening in the muscle wall. In some cases the hernia may become twisted (called a *strangulated hernia*) and cut off blood supply to the tissue. Rapidly increasing pain in the groin is a sign that the hernia has become strangulated. Go to the hospital if you suspect that you have a strangulated hernia.

Self-Care

- Avoid heavy lifting, which can cause straining and place more pressure on the abdomen.

- Use correct lifting techniques: Lift objects by bending your legs and keeping your back straight. Your leg muscles, not your back or abdomen, should do the most work.

Hiatal Hernias

A hiatal hernia occurs when a weak spot in the diaphragm muscle allows the stomach to push up through the diaphragm. The hernia develops at the spot where the esophagus meets the stomach.

Causes

Hiatal hernias can be caused by obesity, pregnancy, wearing tight clothing, sudden physical exertion, straining or coughing, vomiting, or injury to the abdomen.

Symptoms

Hiatal hernias cause no symptoms. However, when you have a hiatal hernia, stomach contents may pass back into the esophagus from the stomach, causing heartburn, indigestion, chest pains, and hiccupping and belching.

Treatment

Hiatal hernias usually do not require treatment unless you develop severe

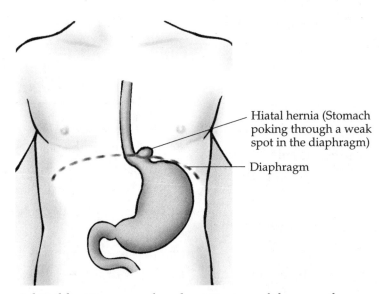

Hiatal hernia (Stomach poking through a weak spot in the diaphragm)

Diaphragm

A hiatal hernia occurs when the upper part of the stomach moves up through the chest through a small opening in the diaphragm, the muscle that separates the stomach from the chest.

heartburn or an inflammation of the esophagus. In these cases your doctor may recommend surgery to repair the problem.

Self-Care

- Take antacids.

- Avoid foods that may irritate the lining of your stomach.

- Raise the head of your bed several inches to prevent stomach contents from flowing back into the esophagus. Use 4- to 6-inch blocks under the legs at the head of the bed.

- Eat small, frequent meals.

- Avoid going to sleep or lying down right after meals.

For more information on treatment of heartburn symptoms, see Heartburn, p. 158, and Gastroesophageal Reflux Disease, p. 156.

What to do about Hernias

Symptom/Sign	Action
Mild heartburn symptoms associated with hiatal hernia	Self-care
Visible bulges slightly above or within scrotum; pain and tenderness in the lower abdomen and scrotum; feeling of pressure or weakness in the groin	Call doctor
Rapidly increasing pain in the groin	Go to hospital

Rectal Pain or Itching

Rectal pain may be accompanied by intense itching, fever, and rectal bleeding with bowel movements. Obesity, pregnancy, chronic diarrhea or constipation, and some infections may contribute to the problem.

Causes

The most common causes of rectal pain or itching are hemorrhoids (see p. 160) and fissures (cracks in the skin around the rectum).

Self-Care

If you have rectal pain or itching, several things can help you to feel better.

- Avoid straining during bowel movements.

- Cleanse the rectal area well after each bowel movement. Try moistened wipes instead of toilet paper (or use them after you use the toilet paper).

- Use a soft, white, unscented toilet tissue to reduce irritation.

- Try applying cornstarch or talcum powder to the area.

- Use zinc oxide ointment to decrease chafing and to absorb excess moisture.

Special Concerns for Children

Sometimes a child will suddenly awaken with rectal pain and itching. This often means pinworms. Seldom seen but common and harmless, these small worms are contagious and may be picked up from contaminated food. If you suspect pinworms, call your doctor for an appointment. If your child has pinworms, wash your hands (and your child's hands) thoroughly after using the bathroom and before preparing food.

- Avoid prolonged sitting.

- Raise your legs when you are sitting, especially if you are overweight or pregnant.

- Apply cold compresses (such as ice packs, moistened wipes, or witch hazel) four times a day. Follow cold compresses with a warm bath or sitz bath to soothe and cleanse the area.

- If needed, take acetaminophen or use medicated suppositories to relieve discomfort.

NOTE: Anal ointments with a local anesthetic may cause an allergic reaction. These medications will have the suffix *-caine* in the name of the product or ingredients.

What to do about Rectal Pain or Itching

Symptom/Sign	Action
History of hemorrhoids or mild rectal pain or itching or both	Self-care
Rectal itching and close contact with someone who has pinworms or visible pinworms	Call doctor
Pain lasts for more than 3 to 5 days	See doctor
Itching lasts for more than 2 weeks	See doctor
Child with rectal itching	See doctor
Rectal pain or itching and possible exposure to sexually transmitted disease	See doctor
Severe rectal pain	Go to hospital

Prevention

Rectal itching or irritation is usually not a medical emergency and in many cases can be prevented. Wearing cotton, breathable underwear and loose clothing will help. Drinking plenty of water and eating fresh fruit and high-fiber foods will help to soften stools and prevent constipation.

Viral Hepatitis

*H*epatitis means inflammation of the liver, usually caused by one of several viruses. Most forms of hepatitis clear up within a few months. However, in some cases, hepatitis can be chronic and lead to serious liver conditions.

Causes

In most cases, hepatitis is caused by one of several viruses. (The three main types of hepatitis are discussed later.) It can also result from other infectious microorganisms and exposure to alcohol, toxic chemicals, or certain medications.

Symptoms

Viral hepatitis often begins with flulike symptoms: fatigue, headache, loss of appetite, nausea or vomiting, and a low-grade fever (below 101°F). As symptoms get worse, other signs may be present, such as jaundice (yellow color to skin and whites of eyes), brown urine and pale stools, and pain or pressure on the right side below the ribs. In some cases, however, people with hepatitis may have no symptoms at all.

Types of Hepatitis

There are three main types of hepatitis: hepatitis A, B, and C.

Hepatitis A

The hepatitis A virus is spread through food, water, eating utensils, toys, and other objects that have been contaminated by feces, usually from dirty hands. Prevention of hepatitis A is one of the main reasons restaurant employees and child-care workers are required to wash their hands after using the restroom or changing babies' diapers.

After exposure to the virus, symptoms usually do not appear for 2 to 6 weeks. During this time, the virus is contagious, so a person must take care not to spread the virus to others. Most symptoms end within several days or a few weeks. However, tiredness can continue for a few months as the liver continues to heal. Complete recovery usually takes a few months. Hepatitis A usually does not permanently damage the liver, but serious and sometimes fatal complications can occur.

All close family members or close contacts of someone with hepatitis A should get a shot of gamma globulin to prevent or reduce the symptoms of hepatitis A. If you are traveling abroad or have the following risk factors for the virus, you can receive a vaccine:

- Men who have sex with men
- Travelers
- Food handlers
- Child care–center attendees

For best protection from hepatitis A, you should have two shots 6 months apart. However, travelers can be considered protected if they travel 4 weeks after the initial shot. If your trip is less than 4 weeks away, you can receive a shot of immune globulin.

Hepatitis B

Hepatitis B is a more serious form of viral hepatitis. About 10 percent of people with hepatitis B will develop chronic hepatitis, a long-term inflammation that in some cases causes worsening liver damage and even cirrhosis.

Hepatitis B spreads mainly through blood and body fluids, sexual contact, and contaminated needles used with intravenous drugs. It can also be spread if needles used for tattooing, acupuncture, or ear piercing are contaminated. In years past, another cause of hepatitis B was transfusions with contaminated blood. However, since 1972 screening of donated blood has almost wiped out the risk of getting hepatitis B from transfusions and blood products.

Risk factors for hepatitis B include being sexually active and not in a mutually monogamous relationship, being infected with the human immunodeficiency virus (HIV), being an intravenous drug user, participating in anal sex, being a health-care or dental provider, or being a recipient of dialysis.

Symptoms of hepatitis B are basically the same as those of other forms of hepatitis, but they appear later, may last longer, and may be worse. Symptoms can take up to 2 to 3 months to develop. During this time, hepatitis B is most contagious. A hepatitis B vaccination series before exposure can prevent the illness. Hepatitis B immune globulin, a special type of gamma globulin that is given shortly before possible exposure, may prevent or reduce symptoms of hepatitis B.

Children should be vaccinated routinely. It is recommended that everyone should receive a hepatitis B vaccine. Talk with your doctor about having a hepatitis B vaccination.

Hepatitis C

Hepatitis C spreads mainly through blood transfusions and through contaminated needles used for intravenous drugs. It can also be spread by sexual contact and through contaminated needles used for tattooing. Symptoms usually appear 1 to 10 weeks after exposure. Often symptoms are less severe than they are for hepatitis A and B, and jaundice may not develop. Hepatitis C leads to chronic hepatitis 80 percent of the time. Treatment is available for chronic hepatitis B and C, but it may not work for everyone.

Until recently, about 2 percent of those who received blood transfusions got hepatitis C. However, a screening test is now available to detect hepatitis C in donated blood.

Self-Care

Acute viral hepatitis has no specific treatment. However, you can do several things to get well and avoid spreading the disease to others.

- Get plenty of rest.
- Eat well. Hepatitis interferes with the liver's ability to help break down food. Therefore it is very important to eat enough easily digestible food to get enough calories. Fatty food is often poorly tolerated. Try eating mostly carbohydrates (such as grains and fruits).
- Check in with your doctor regularly. He or she may run blood tests for several months to check for recovery or continuing inflammation of the liver.
- Avoid alcohol and medications that irritate the liver, including birth-control

pills, tranquilizers, some antibiotics, antidepressants, and acetaminophen. Until you are fully recovered, do not use any medications without checking with your doctor.

- Wash your hands after using the bathroom and before handling food.
- Do not prepare food for others until 2 weeks after symptoms begin. This is especially important for those in the food-handling business.

What to do about Viral Hepatitis

Symptom/Sign	Actions
Suspected exposure to hepatitis	Call doctor
Symptoms that worsen or persist despite rest and self-care	Call doctor
Headache, low-grade fever, loss of appetite, nausea or vomiting, fatigue for more than 3 to 5 days	See doctor
Yellow color to skin or whites of eyes	See doctor
Dark urine and light, clay-colored stools	See doctor
Pain or tenderness in right upper abdomen	See doctor
Known exposure to hepatitis	See doctor

Vomiting

Vomiting is usually the result of an infection located anywhere from the stomach to the colon. More rarely, it is caused by a bacterial infection that would benefit from medical treatment. But in most cases an upset stomach is a simple virus that will disappear by itself in a few days.

Causes

Vomiting can be the body's reaction to eating spoiled food—for example, food left at room temperature for too long before being refrigerated (see Foodborne Illness, p. 154). It can be the side effect of a medication, or it may be the result of overeating or drinking too much alcohol. Nausea and vomiting may also occur during pregnancy. Certain illnesses, such as inner-ear disturbances and migraines, can lead to vomiting.

An upset stomach may occur if you are nervous, emotionally stressed, or tense. In children, an upset stomach can also be brought on by motion sickness, too much excitement, or too much sun.

Treatment

Eventually vomiting will stop on its own. Although there are no medicines that can speed recovery, there are things you can do to make yourself more comfortable (see Self-care below). Over-the-counter medications are rarely necessary.

Self-Care

Adults

- Let your stomach rest. Adults should eat nothing for 1 to 2 hours. Add liquids gradually as the nausea stops.

- Stay on clear liquids for 8 hours. Try water, cracked ice, bouillon, Popsicles, gelatin, chicken soup, or flat nondiet soda. Sip a little at a time during the day.

- Avoid caffeinated drinks, milk products, citrus juice, alcohol, aspirin, or ibuprofen.

- Add bland foods after 8 hours. Choose foods such as soup, crackers, chicken, or rice. Eat these foods in small amounts as long as you can tolerate them.

- Avoid fried, spicy foods for 1 to 2 days.

Children

- Give 1 teaspoon of room-temperature Infalyte, Pedialyte, half-strength Gatorade, or homemade rehydrating solution every 1 to 2 minutes to prevent dehydration (see box on p. 169). Increase amounts and intervals as your child can tolerate it. Children who are vomiting are not in immediate danger of dehydration if they are drinking adequately and urinating regularly.

- If your child vomits, allow the stomach to rest for a half-hour before giving fluids again.

- Fluids such as soda, apple juice, or full-strength Gatorade are not good replacement fluids for dehydration in children. The high concentration of sugar draws fluid from the cells, adding to the potential for dehydration. High salt content can have the same effect, so avoid giving your child broth and salty fluids.

- Water should not be the only fluid for dehydration. Give it in small amounts in addition to Infalyte and Pedialyte.

- Give your child liquid in small amounts to avoid further stomach irritation. Too much liquid can lead to more vomiting.

- When your child can keep liquids down, return to a regular diet. Encourage lean meats, yogurt, bananas, applesauce, vegetables, and complex carbohydrates such as rice, potatoes, bread, and cereal.

- It is not unusual for children's appetite to decrease after they have vomited. However, be sure they are drinking adequate fluids.

- Avoid over-the-counter medications to stop nausea and vomiting. Vomiting will usually stop on its own within 12 to 24 hours.

Special Concerns for Children: Rehydrating Solutions

- Pedialyte and Infalyte are fluid replacement solutions that can be given for mild to moderate dehydration. They should not be used as your child's only calorie source for more than 24 hours.

- You can make a temporary rehydrating solution at home, using half a teaspoon of salt, 2 tablespoons of sugar, and 1 quart of water. This homemade remedy does not contain the necessary potassium. Therefore you should only use it until you can purchase Infalyte, Pedialyte, or Gatorade (diluted to half strength).

- Children often don't like the taste of rehydrating solutions. Purchase flavored formulas, or improve the taste of solutions by adding a sprinkle of Kool-Aid or NutraSweet.

- Rehydrating solutions are also available as Popsicles. Make sure your child does not eat them too quickly. Like liquid rehydrating solutions, they should only be given a teaspoon at a time.

What to do about Vomiting in Adults

Symptom/Sign	Action
Vomiting caused by motion sickness, eating too much, drinking too much alcohol, or stress	Self-care
Vomiting in patient with diabetes, or patient with other chronic disease, and inability to keep medication down	Call doctor
Vomiting for more than 48 hours, or inability to keep fluids down for 24 hours	See doctor
Severe, constant abdominal pain or abdominal trauma, or vomiting more than two times following head injury	See doctor
Signs of dehydration, decreased urination, dry mouth, change in mental or functional activities in elderly person	See doctor
Vomiting with headache and stiff neck	Go to hospital
Vomiting large amounts of blood or a substance that looks like coffee grounds	Call 911

Kidney and Bladder Problems

The urinary system, or *urinary tract*, includes the kidneys, ureters, bladder, and urethra (see illustration). All four parts of the urinary system play a crucial role in removing waste material from the body and keeping our systems in balance. When any part of this waste removal system stops working properly, we usually know it. Problems in the bladder and kidney disrupt the delicate balance of fluids in our body, causing pain and discomfort.

The most common disorders of the urinary system are kidney stones, urinary incontinence, and urinary tract infections.

This chapter explains the most common concerns affecting the urinary tract. Your doctor can offer advice and

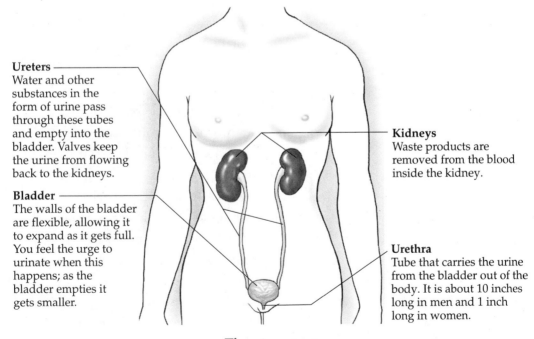

Ureters
Water and other substances in the form of urine pass through these tubes and empty into the bladder. Valves keep the urine from flowing back to the kidneys.

Bladder
The walls of the bladder are flexible, allowing it to expand as it gets full. You feel the urge to urinate when this happens; as the bladder empties it gets smaller.

Kidneys
Waste products are removed from the blood inside the kidney.

Urethra
Tube that carries the urine from the bladder out of the body. It is about 10 inches long in men and 1 inch long in women.

The urinary tract.

treatment for most of these problems. If your condition is especially difficult to handle, your doctor may recommend the help of a *urologist*, a doctor who specializes in the diagnosis and treatment of these problems.

Kidney Stones

A kidney stone is a hard, crystal-like mass. It is made of substances in your urine that build up on the inner surfaces of the kidney.

Causes

Doctors do not always know what causes a stone to form. A person with a family history of kidney stones may be more likely to develop them. Certain conditions are also linked to kidney stones, including urinary tract infections, gout, and metabolic disorders such as hyperparathyroidism. Excess intake of vitamin D and use of diuretics can cause kidney stones to form.

Symptoms

Usually the first symptom of a kidney stone is extreme pain. It begins suddenly when a stone moves in the urinary tract and blocks or irritates the area. A person may feel a sharp, cramping pain in the back (near the affected kidney) or in the lower abdomen. Nausea and vomiting may also be present. Pain may also spread to the groin.

If the stone is not passed right away, pain will continue as the muscles of the ureter try to push it out. As the stone grows, you may notice blood in your urine. When the ureters move the stone closer to the bladder, you may feel the urge to urinate more frequently or you may feel a burning sensation during urination.

If you have fever or chills with these symptoms, you may have an infection. In this case, call your doctor right away.

Treatment

In most cases, kidney stones are small enough to pass through the urine without being noticed. The best way to help a stone pass is to drink plenty of water, about 8 to 12 cups a day. If you need to, you can take a pain medication to help relieve your symptoms.

When you do urinate, catch the urine in a cup or pass it through a strainer used only for this purpose. Your doctor will probably want you to save the passed stone for testing.

Surgery may be needed to remove a kidney stone if the stone:

- Does not pass after a reasonable period and causes constant pain
- Is too large to pass on its own or is caught in a difficult place
- Blocks the flow of urine
- Causes ongoing urinary tract infections

- Damages kidney tissue or causes constant bleeding
- Has grown larger (as seen by x-ray exam)

Self-Care

- Drink plenty of water, about 12 to 16 glasses a day.
- Take a pain medication, such as acetaminophen, to relieve pain.
- Call your doctor if pain continues or if you have excessive blood in your urine or have been unable to urinate.

What to do about Kidney Stones

Symptom/Sign	Action
Symptoms of kidney stones present: back or side pain, lower abdominal pain, nausea or vomiting, pain in groin, urge to urinate, or burning sensation while urinating	Call doctor
Symptoms present, family or personal history of kidney stones	Call doctor
Symptoms present along with chronic urinary tract infections	See doctor
Symptoms present along with fever and chills	Go to hospital
Continual bleeding, inability to urinate	Go to hospital

Prevention

If you have had a kidney stone, you are likely to form another, so prevention is important.

- Drink 12 to 16 glasses of water per day.

- Follow the advice of your doctor regarding what type of dietary modification you need to make. Dietary restrictions are based on the type of kidney stone you have.

- If your doctor prescribes medication, take it as directed.

Urinary Incontinence

Urinary incontinence is the inability to control leakage of urine. It's one of those embarrassing problems people don't like to talk about—even with their doctors. But there is help for incontinence. In most cases the problem is treatable. It can usually be improved, if not completely cured.

Types of Urinary Incontinence

There are four types of incontinence. Each has its own symptoms and causes.

Stress Incontinence

Stress incontinence can occur when you cough, sneeze, laugh, lift heavy objects, exercise, or even get up from a chair. Sometimes the muscles that hold the bladder in place are weak. Then the muscle that controls the flow of urine may not be able to do its work.

Stress incontinence can occur at any age, but it is most common in women who have borne children, because childbirth can weaken pelvic-floor muscles. Often, stress incontinence occurs after menopause because the decrease in estrogen can lead to thinning and weakening of the pelvic muscles and surrounding tissues.

Treatment for mild incontinence usually includes pelvic-floor exercises (see Kegel Exercises box, p. 176). In moderate or severe cases of incontinence, other treatments may be necessary. These therapies include use of estrogen creams, collagen injections, and surgery.

Urge Incontinence

Urge incontinence is also known as *detrusor instability*. The bladder wall is a muscle called the *detrusor muscle*. This muscle may contract more often and more strongly than it should. That can cause a sudden need to urinate. The contractions may be strong enough to cause urine loss before you reach the bathroom.

Urge incontinence is often linked to bladder infections or disorders, anxiety, dementia, or strokes. Excess caffeine intake can also play a role.

Urge incontinence is treated most successfully without surgery. Nonsurgical treatment options include electrical stimulation, "timed voiding" (urinating at scheduled intervals), and reductions in caffeine. Certain medications may also be helpful. In some cases, surgery may be required. One operation for women moves the bladder, allowing the bladder neck to return to its normal, closed position.

Overflow Incontinence

Overflow incontinence occurs when the bladder does not empty all the way. With this problem, you can leak small amounts of urine all day long. You may feel the need to go to the bathroom and then urinate only a little. You may not feel completely "empty" after you finish. This may be more common at night.

In general, men seem to experience overflow incontinence more than women. Some disorders, such as diabetes, stroke, paralysis, and multiple sclerosis, may prevent people from sensing when their bladder is full. Chronic use of muscle relaxants or antidepressants can also interfere with bladder control.

To treat overflow incontinence, doctors first try to treat whatever disorder is causing the incontinence. They may also prescribe medications that relax the bladder outlet. In men, surgery may be recommended to remove part of the prostate gland that may be blocking urination.

Functional Incontinence

Functional incontinence happens in people who have physical limitations and cannot get to the bathroom before urination occurs. It is particularly common in hospitals and nursing homes and in any setting where a person may be unfamiliar with his or her surroundings. It can also be a side effect of certain medications.

Treatment for functional incontinence depends mostly on society's help. Better-staffed nursing homes and better public restrooms can help, as can adjusting doses of medications to accommodate an individual's schedule. Providing an easy or shorter route to the bathroom is another easy way to assist those with functional incontinence.

Self-Care

- Do Kegel exercises as often as you can (see box).

- If urinary incontinence is worse for you at night, don't drink anything after dinner.

- Don't drink alcohol, especially after dinner.

- Cut out drinks with caffeine, such as coffee, tea, and colas.

- Use Depends or another brand of absorbent undergarment. They are made for both men and women.

- Keep a list of your symptoms. It will help your doctor find the exact problem.

Self-Care for Urinary Incontinence: Kegel Exercises

Kegel exercises are designed to strengthen the pelvic-floor muscles, the muscles used to stop the flow of urine. There are many different ways to do Kegel exercises. All types involve tightening the pelvic floor muscles and then releasing them.

To determine which muscles you need to strengthen, try doing a Kegel exercise the first time you urinate after waking. While your bladder is full, start and stop the flow of urine. Let out only small amounts of urine at a time. Start and stop the flow of urine in this way until your bladder is empty. The muscles that you use to stop urination are the same ones that you will be tightening and releasing for Kegel exercises.

Here are two ways that you can do Kegel exercises:

Exercise 1: Contract the pelvic muscles as far as possible. Hold tightly for 3 seconds. Release and repeat 20 to 25 times. You can do these exercises anywhere—while doing the dishes, brushing your teeth, reading the paper, even driving. If you do a set of 20 to 25 exercises three to five times a day, you should notice a difference within a few months.

Exercise 2: Think of the pelvic floor as an elevator. Tighten the pelvic-floor muscles slightly to reach floor one. Hold for several seconds. Without releasing this hold, tighten the muscles again, this time moving to floor two. Pause again for several seconds. Continue to move up floor by floor until you reach floor five. At this point, the muscles should be fully contracted. Gradually release the muscles floor by floor in the same way you did to tighten them.

What to do about Urinary Incontinence

Symptom/Sign	Action
Symptoms that are occasional and manageable	Self-care
Symptoms that do not improve after using self-care	See doctor
Symptoms that are frequent and troublesome and interfere with your lifestyle	See doctor

Urinary Tract Infections

A urinary tract infection is a bacterial infection that usually begins in the urethra (see illustration, p. 171). From here, bacteria often travel to the bladder, causing a bladder infection. If the infection is not treated right away, it may move to the kidneys, causing an infection called *pyelonephritis*. Urinary tract infections can be bothersome, embarrassing, and painful. Sometimes they may point to a serious health problem. Luckily, most cases of frequent urination can be cleared up quickly—often with just a couple days of treatment.

Causes

When a urinary tract infection involves the bladder, it is often caused by *Escherichia coli* bacteria. These bacteria are common in the bowel.

Urinary tract infections are more common in women. Bacteria may enter the urinary tract during sexual intercourse or when you use a diaphragm.

Urinary tract infections can be a problem for men, too, especially those over 50 years of age. An enlarged prostate gland, common in older men, can restrict the flow of urine and lead to bacterial growth and infection.

Symptoms

- Frequent or urgent urination or both, especially at night

- A burning feeling during urination

- Blood in the urine

- Pressure in the lower abdomen

- Urine that looks cloudy or smells very bad or both

Keep in mind that sometimes a urinary tract infection will have no symptoms.

Treatment

A urinary tract infection with no other complicating factors has an excellent chance of being cured with a 3-day course of antibiotics. Advantages of using a shorter course of antibiotics include fewer side effects, fewer yeast infections, and lower cost. But the 3-day course of antibiotics is not effective for all women. You may need to be treated with a longer course if you:

- Are pregnant or breastfeeding

- Have a complicating medical condition, such as diabetes

- Have a history of frequent urinary tract infections

If antibiotics are prescribed, inform your doctor if you are pregnant, breastfeeding, or have any medication allergies. Avoid being in the sun too much, and use backup birth control if you are on the pill.

Self-Care

- Avoid caffeine, alcohol, and spicy foods, which can make symptoms worse.

- Drink eight glasses of fluid per day. Water is the best type of fluid.

- Take a warm bath to relieve discomfort.

- Call your doctor. You may be told to have your urine tested, be treated with antibiotics right away, or be scheduled for an appointment. You may be sent to an urgent care center or emergency room if your symptoms include fever and chills.

- If you are prescribed medication, take it exactly the way it is prescribed.

Testing for a Urinary Tract Infection

To determine if you have a urinary tract infection, your doctor will request a urine specimen. To do this, you first release a small amount of urine into the toilet. Then you catch some of the urine in a special sterile container that your doctor or nurse gives you. Often you can get the results of the urinalysis within an hour, but it may take 24 to 48 hours.

What to do about Urinary Tract Infections

Symptom/Sign	Action
Women with symptoms of urinary tract infection: urinary frequency, burning, and urgency for less than 7 days	Self-care
Men with symptoms of urinary tract infection: urinary frequency, burning, and urgency	See doctor
Women with symptoms of urinary tract infection for more than 7 days	See doctor
Urinary tract infection symptoms along with nausea, vomiting, fever, or pain in back, abdomen, or pelvis	See doctor
Symptoms of urinary tract infection and possible exposure to sexually transmitted diseases	See doctor
Symptoms of urinary tract infections and shaking chills	Go to hospital

Prevention

- Drink lots of water—at least six to eight glasses a day.

- Empty your bladder every 3 hours while you are awake, even if you don't feel an urge to do so.

- Urinate before and after sexual intercourse.

- Wear clean cotton underwear.

- If you are a woman, wipe from front to back after using the toilet to avoid spreading bacteria from the rectal area.

- Switch from the diaphragm to another type of birth control if urinary tract infections are a problem.

- Do not avoid the need to urinate. Holding urine for long periods may decrease the ability of the bladder to empty fully, which can increase the risk of urinary tract infections.

- Shower instead of taking a bath. Avoid using bubble bath or other perfumed bath products.

Heart and Circulation Problems

Your heart and blood vessels make up your circulatory system. The heart is a remarkable organ. It is made of muscle tissue and is about the size of your fist. It is continuously working to pump blood throughout your body and requires a constant supply of nutrients to do its job.

Your doctor can treat many heart and circulation concerns. There may be times when your doctor needs to refer you to a specialist such as a cardiologist. Managing these conditions usually requires commitment on your part to become a member of your health care team. There is much you can do when it comes to taking care of your heart. ::

Chest Pain

Feelings of pain or pressure in the chest area could signal a problem as simple as indigestion or as serious as a heart attack. Pay attention to those signals. Learn the signs of a heart attack, and call 911 if you have them!

Causes

Heart Attack
A heart attack almost always causes chest pain. This pain may be mild or se-

Know the Signs of a Heart Attack

- Crushing, squeezing, burning feeling in the chest
- Feeling of pressure in the chest
- Pain that spreads to the jaw, arms, neck, or back
- Pain lasts longer than 15 minutes
- Rest or prescribed drug doesn't relieve pain
- Nausea, vomiting, shortness of breath, sweating
- Pain while you are resting or that wakes you from sleep

vere. Pain from a heart attack does not go away quickly. Rest and medications don't completely relieve the pain.

Angina

Angina can also cause chest pain (see Angina, p. 187). Angina may feel like a heart attack, but it is different. Most angina attacks last about 15 minutes.

Heartburn

Heartburn can cause a burning pain behind your breastbone (see Heartburn, p. 158).

Muscle Pain

The muscles and other tissues in the chest wall can become quite painful from strains caused by exercise, a fall, or coughing. Called chest-wall pain, this type of chest pain usually feels worse when you press on the sore area.

Panic Attacks

Panic disorder can include chest-pain symptoms such as heart palpitations (a fast, strong, or uneven heartbeat; see p. 197) and shortness of breath. Other symptoms of panic disorder are anxiety and fear of suffocation or dying (see Anxiety, p. 332).

Ulcers and Gallbladder Disease

Ulcers (see p. 144) and gallbladder disease can cause pain that spreads to the chest.

Pulmonary Embolism

A pulmonary embolism is a clot blocking the arteries from the heart to the lungs. Risk factors for pulmonary embolism are surgery within the past 6 weeks, wearing a cast, prolonged siting during airplane and car travel, and conditions that confine you to bed. Symptoms include sudden shortness of breath, sudden chest pain that is worse when you breathe, and sometimes a bloody cough.

Self-Care

- Know the signs of a heart attack. If you think you are having a heart attack, call 911 and take an aspirin.

- To ease a muscle strain in the chest, take a pain reliever such as acetaminophen. Apply heat and get rest.

What to do about Chest Pain

Symptom/Sign	Action
Chest pain after exercise, a fall, or a coughing spell	Self-care
Chest pain after eating that requires repeated use of antacid	Call doctor
Chest pain or pressure that feels crushing or that spreads to the shoulder, back, neck, or jaw	Call 911
Chest pain that lasts longer than 15 minutes and is not relieved by rest	Call 911
Chest pain that wakes you up	Call 911
Chest pain or pressure with uneven or rapid heartbeat, shortness of breath, nausea or vomiting, sweating, lightheadedness, anxiety, or fainting	Call 911
Sudden, severe chest pain with shortness of breath or bloody cough	Call 911
Pain that feels like heartburn but is not relieved with antacids	Call 911

Coronary Artery Disease

Coronary artery disease (CAD) is a specific form of atherosclerosis, a disease characterized by the buildup of deposits, or *plaques*, in the blood vessels. The term *atherosclerosis* comes from two Greek words, *athero*, meaning "gruel" or "paste," and *sclerosis*, meaning "hardness."

Atherosclerotic plaques consist of both fatty substances called *lipids*, and also "harder" substances, such as calcium and fibrous tissue. Over time, plaques in the blood vessels can interfere with the supply of blood to various organs of the body. Conditions caused by atherosclerosis include:

- *Coronary artery disease.* This is when the coronary arteries, which feed the heart muscle, are affected. As the blood flow to the heart muscle is restricted, angina (chest pains) or heart attack can occur.

- *Stroke.* If atherosclerosis affects the blood vessels feeding the brain, the blood supply to a portion of the brain may be restricted or cut off. The result is a stroke.

- *Aneurysm.* Atherosclerosis can lead to an aneurysm—a fluid- and blood-filled sac in the wall of an artery or vein. If an aneurysm ruptures, the result is internal bleeding and lack of adequate blood supply where it is needed.

- *Claudication.* When atherosclerosis develops in the blood vessels going to the legs, it can result in leg pain during exercise, also called *claudication.*

People with atherosclerotic disease in one blood vessel are more likely to develop it in others as well. Just like high blood pressure or diabetes, atherosclerotic diseases such as CAD require lifelong treatment. With proper treatment, most patients are now living long, active lives, and the outlook for those with the disease is getting better every year.

Causes

Atherosclerosis begins early in adulthood, but it may be decades before it becomes obvious. Very early plaques have been found in young soldiers killed in battle. Atherosclerosis probably begins when the innermost layer of the artery, called the endothelium, becomes damaged, allowing cholesterol to enter. Causes of damage to the arterial wall include:

- Elevated levels of cholesterol and triglycerides (fats) in the blood

- High blood pressure

- Tobacco smoke

Once the endothelium is damaged, fats, cholesterol, fibrin, platelets, cellular debris, calcium, and other substances can catch on the damaged spot and over time become deposited in the artery wall, stimulating the development of plaques.

In some instances, atherosclerosis may weaken the blood vessel wall, causing the vessel to become wider, rather than narrower. Although the dangers of narrowed blood vessels are well known, widening can also be a serious problem. It can develop into an aneurysm. This often occurs in the aorta (the main artery in the heart), but it can also occur in the coronary arteries.

A blood vessel can also widen at the same spot where a plaque forms. If this occurs, the inside diameter of the blood vessel may change only slightly, despite the presence of the plaque. This explains why some people can have a fairly normal stress test or angiogram but can still have coronary artery disease and even heart attacks (see illustration).

The Problem with Plaque

Plaques contain a number of different substances. The most important are the fatty substances or lipids—the *athero,* or "gruel" part of the word atherosclerosis. The other contents—muscle cells, fibrous tissue, and calcium—are the *sclerosis* part. Most heart attacks occur because an atherosclerotic plaque has become unstable.

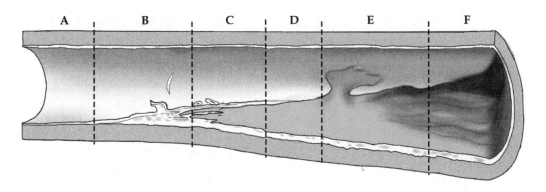

*Progression of coronary artery disease. **A,** Normal artery. **B,** Injury to endothelium allows cholesterol to enter. **C,** Inflammation causes white blood cells to enter the artery wall. **D,** Increased cholesterol deposit and inflammation causes thinning of fibrous cap. **E,** rupture of fibrous cap exposes plaque content to bloodstream. **F,** Red blood cells, platelets, and fibrin may form a clot that blocks the artery.*

Unstable Plaque

Unstable plaques contain large amounts of lipids covered by a thin coating called a *fibrous cap*. Inflammatory cells in the plaque may eat away this fibrous cap, causing the contents of the plaque to spill out into the bloodstream. There they interact with blood elements and clotting factors to cause a blood clot. If the clot is large enough to completely obstruct blood flow through a coronary artery, a heart attack occurs.

Narrowing Plaque

Plaque may narrow the blood vessel enough to limit blood flow through the vessel. This usually causes symptoms only during exercise or stress.

The likelihood that a plaque will rupture and cause a heart attack is not related to the severity of the narrowing. A plaque that narrows a vessel by only 30 percent may cause a heart attack, while a larger one that narrows a blood vessel by 90 percent may remain stable for years, perhaps causing chest pain during exercise but not resulting in a heart attack. The chance of a plaque erupting is related to its stability, not its size.

Risk Factors

Scientists continue to investigate the possible causes of coronary artery disease. Although there does not seem to be one specific cause, there are certain characteristics that have been linked to coronary artery disease and heart attacks. These are called risk factors.

Risk Factors Beyond Your Control

Although you can do much to lower your risk for CAD, some factors you can't control. These include age, gender, and a family history of heart disease:

- *Age.* Men 45 years or older or women 55 years or older are at greater risk for CAD.

- *Gender.* Middle-aged men have more heart attacks than women of the same age. This changes after menopause. After age 60, when a woman's estrogen level decreases, the rates are almost equal between both sexes.

- *Family history of heart disease.* If your mother, father, or sibling was diagnosed with coronary artery disease before age 60, you have increased risk.

Risk Factors that Can Be Changed

There are some risk factors you can control. By reducing your risks, you are taking steps to live healthier and lessen your chances of developing heart disease.

- *Tobacco use.* Tobacco use lowers your level of good cholesterol, raises your blood pressure, and promotes clotting.

- *High blood cholesterol and high triglycerides.* Most heart disease is the result of cholesterol-rich, fatty buildup that narrows the vessels that supply blood to your heart. There are two sources of cholesterol: (1) your body, which makes cholesterol to aid digestion, and (2) the foods you eat.

- *Low-density lipoprotein cholesterol (LDL, or "bad cholesterol")* accounts for most of the cholesterol in your blood and is considered most responsible for the formation of plaque. Most people with CAD require medication to achieve target LDL levels.

- *High-density lipoprotein cholesterol (HDL, or "good cholesterol").* Higher levels of HDL protect against CAD.

- *Triglycerides* are fats that are carried in the bloodstream. When triglycerides are elevated, the risk for CAD increases.

- *High blood pressure.* High blood pressure damages arteries, setting the stage for plaque formation. It also increases the stress on the heart muscle, which may cause damage to the organ.

- *Lack of exercise.* People who have had heart attacks may increase their chances of survival if they change their habits to include regular physical activity. Exercise can help control blood fats and blood glucose, maintain weight, and lower blood pressure.

- *Diabetes.* People with diabetes are very susceptible to CAD. It is especially important for people with diabetes to control their blood glucose, as well as blood pressure and cholesterol.

- *How you handle stress.* Stress is a normal part of everyone's life. It is not stress that increases your risk for CAD, but how you cope with it.

- *Excess weight or obesity.* By itself, obesity increases your risk for CAD. Obesity also contributes to other risk factors, including hypertension, high blood cholesterol, and diabetes.

Symptoms

Angina

Angina is one of the noticeable signs of coronary artery disease. It is a warning sign that the heart is temporarily not getting enough blood and oxygen to handle its workload. Angina does not cause permanent damage to the heart muscle.

Angina may feel like a heart attack, but it is different. Most angina attacks last from 2 to 15 minutes. This is because the blood supply is reduced but not cut off. The warning signs of angina include:

- Feeling of indigestion or "fullness"
- Discomfort, aching, pressure, tightness, heaviness, or burning sensation in or near the chest, back, arms, shoulders, between shoulder blades, neck, throat, or jaw

Anything that elevates blood pressure or heart rate can result in angina:

- Smoking
- Physical activity

- Heavy meals
- Hot or iced drinks
- Hot baths and saunas
- Emotional stress
- Exposure to extreme temperatures

Angina is usually treated with rest and a medication called nitroglycerin. The discomfort usually is gone within 15 minutes.

Treatment

Many people who have coronary artery disease do not realize that it is a chronic condition that cannot be cured. The good news is it can be treated and stabilized. Lifestyle changes can help treat CAD. Your doctor may ask you to do any of the following:

- Eat a diet low in fat and cholesterol.
- Be more active.
- If you use tobacco, quit.
- Lose 10 to 20 pounds.

Unfortunately, procedures such as balloon angioplasty, stents, and even bypass surgery do not decrease the chance of death or heart attacks. These therapies are very effective in reducing symptoms of chest pain and improving quality of life, but the treatments that have the best track record in prolonging life are medications such as aspirin, cholesterol-lowering drugs (statins), beta-blockers, and angiotensin-converting enzyme (ACE) inhibitors. In part these medications are successful because they provide protection 24 hours a day, 7 days a week.

Prevention

You can take steps to decrease your risk of coronary artery disease by making some lifestyle changes:

- *Check your blood cholesterol and triglycerides* (see High Blood Cholesterol, p. 189). All adults 20 years of age and older should have their cholesterol checked every 5 years.

- *Stop smoking.* This is the single most important lifestyle change to improve your overall health. Check into community resources such as the American Lung Association and the American Cancer Society for classes and support groups for help. Your doctor or employer may also be able to give you suggestions on methods to stop smoking (see Smoking, p. 413).

- *Eat a healthy diet.* Eat a variety of fruits, vegetables, and low-fat whole grains. Be careful about how much animal fat you eat—limit your intake of meat and high-fat dairy products such as cheese and ice cream (see Healthy Eating, p. 403).

- *Be active.* Find ways to be active at least 30–60 minutes every day. Take the stairs instead of the elevator, avoid sitting for longer than 30 minutes at a time, and try a variety of activities to keep exercise interesting. (See Activity, p. 399.)

- *Lose or maintain weight.* If you are overweight, losing just 10 to 20 pounds can have health benefits. If you are not overweight, take steps to prevent weight gain as you get older (see Maintaining a Healthy Weight, p. 407).

High Blood Cholesterol

High blood cholesterol is one of the major risk factors for heart attack, the leading cause of death in America. Cholesterol is a waxy substance your body produces to help it function properly. Because your liver makes all the cholesterol your body needs, you don't need to consume additional cholesterol.

About Lipids

Lipids is the scientific name for fatty substances. Cholesterol and triglycerides are two kinds of lipids carried through the blood.

In order for cholesterol to move easily throughout the body, it is packaged with a protein. These protein packages are called *lipoproteins*. Two different kinds of lipoproteins—low density and high density—are used to assess your risk of heart disease.

Low-Density Lipoproteins

Low-density lipoproteins (LDLs) contain most of the cholesterol in the blood. They carry cholesterol to body tissues, including the coronary arteries. The cholesterol found in LDL is considered most responsible for the formation of plaque, a fatty substance that builds up on the walls of the arteries. The plaque formation eventually can lead to a heart attack or hardening of the arteries. This is why the cholesterol in these particles is often called "bad" cholesterol. High levels of LDL increase the risk of heart disease.

High-Density Lipoproteins

High-density lipoproteins (HDLs) carry the same form of cholesterol as LDLs. However, the cholesterol in HDLs is not used to form plaques. HDL particles actually pick up cholesterol from other tissues in the body and are believed to be responsible for removing excess cholesterol from your blood. The cholesterol in these packages is called "good" cholesterol, because higher levels of HDL protect against heart disease.

Triglycerides

Triglyceride is another word for fat. Fat is an important source of energy and provides essential nutrients for health. Some of the triglycerides in your body come from the fat you eat. Your body also makes triglycerides when you consume more calories than you need from carbohydrates, proteins, and alcohol. The same lipoproteins that transport cholesterol also move triglycerides to cells where they are needed. High triglycerides are associated with an increased risk for heart disease, especially when HDL levels are low.

Measuring your Blood Cholesterol

Everyone age 20 or older should have their cholesterol measured at least once every 5 years. A lipoprotein profile will measure your total cholesterol, HDL, LDL, and triglycerides. You need to be fasting for these tests to be accurate.

Cholesterol levels rise with age. Women's LDL levels rise after menopause. High blood cholesterol can run in families. If you have high blood cholesterol, ask other family members if they have had their cholesterol measured.

Classification of LDL, HDL, and Total Cholesterol (in mg/dL)

LDL Cholesterol

100	Optimal*
100–129	Near optimal/above optimal
130–159	Borderline high
160–189	High
≥190	Very high

Total Cholesterol

<200	Desirable
200–239	Borderline high
≥240	High

HDL Cholesterol

<40	Low
≥60	High

Triglycerides

<150	Desirable

*Optimal LDL goal if you have heart disease, diabetes, or multiple risk factors.

Treatment

High blood cholesterol is one of the major risk factors for heart disease, but there are other factors your doctor considers when determining what your blood cholesterol goal should be and how it will be treated:

- Tobacco use
- High blood pressure (greater than 140/90 mm Hg)
- Family history of early heart disease (father or brother less than 55 years or mother or sister less than 65)
- Age (men 45 years and older, women 55 years and older)
- Low HDL level (less than 40)

Some individuals may require the added benefit of medication to help control blood lipids. Even if you do require medications to lower your cholesterol, it is important to continue to eat healthfully and be active. There are many different types of medications. Your doctor will work with you to choose the most effective medication for blood lipid control.

Self-Care

- *Eat less fat.* Reducing your total fat intake to 30 percent or less of your calories and your saturated fat intake to less than 7 percent is a major step in lowering blood cholesterol. Eliminating all fat is not necessary. The table below gives suggested limits for calorie and fat intake.

- *Eat less saturated fat.* Saturated fat raises your LDL more than anything else in your diet. All animal fats and some vegetable fats—coconut oil, palm kernel oil, palm oil, cocoa butter, and hydrogenated oils—are high in saturated fat.

- *Eat less cholesterol.* Cholesterol found in certain foods also can raise your blood cholesterol level. By eating less fat and limiting foods high in saturated fat, you can reduce your intake of dietary cholesterol.

- *Eat more dietary fiber.* Studies show soluble fiber can help lower blood cholesterol. Some good sources of soluble fiber include oats, barley, dried beans and peas, apples, pears, and carrots.

- *If you are overweight, consider losing a few pounds.* People who are overweight often have high blood cholesterol levels. A weight loss of 10 to 20 pounds can be beneficial. Use the table below to determine a safe caloric intake for weight loss (see Maintaining a Healthy Weight, p. 407).

- *Be active.* Activity plays an important role in promoting heart health. Aerobic activities, such as swimming, biking, jogging, and cross-country skiing, are especially beneficial. If you are not exercising now, try walking (see Activity, p. 399).

Daily Recommendations for Calories and Fat

To Maintain Weight			
	Calories	**Total Fat (gm)**	**Saturated Fat (gm)**
Men	2100–2400	70–80	16–19
Women	1800–2100	60–70	14–16
To Lose Weight			
	Calories	**Total Fat (gm)**	**Saturated Fat (gm)**
Men	1500–1800	50–60	12–14
Women	1200–1500	40–50	9–12

Food Choices

Fruits and Vegetables

Eat at least five servings per day. Vegetables and fruit can be fresh, frozen, or canned without added fat or sugar. Try to eat a dark green leafy or deep yellow vegetable each day.

One serving equals:

- ½ cup cooked vegetables
- 1 cup raw vegetables
- ½ cup canned or frozen fruit
- ½ cup fresh berries or cut-up pieces of larger fruit, such as melons
- 1 small piece (the size of a tennis ball) of fruit

Starches, Grains, Starchy Vegetables, and Legumes

One serving equals:

- 1 small tortilla
- 1 slice of bread, 1 dinner roll, or 4 to 5 crackers
- ½ cup cooked rice, pasta, corn, potatoes, beans, peas, or lentils
- 1 ounce of dry cereal or ½ cup cooked cereal
- ½ English muffin or small bagel
- ½ pita bread

Choose Low-Fat Starches
(containing no more than 2 grams of fat per serving)

- Low-fat baked goods, such as angel-food cake, ginger snaps, low-fat muffins, yeast breads, or bread sticks
- Low-fat snacks, such as pretzels, low-fat crackers, or baked chips

Limit High-Fat Baked Goods and Snacks

- Starches with added fat, such as granola, potato chips, tortilla chips, french fries, and onion rings
- High-fat baked goods, such as pies, cakes, doughnuts, pastries, croissants, muffins, quick breads, and high-fat cookies and crackers

Dairy Products

Eat at least three servings of nonfat or low-fat dairy products per day

One serving equals:

- 8 ounces of nonfat milk
- 8 ounces of nonfat yogurt

Choose Nonfat (Skim) or Low-Fat (1%) Dairy Products

- Skim or 1% milk
- Nonfat yogurt

Use Nonfat or Low-Fat Cheese as a Substitute for Meat

1 ounce of cheese or ¼ cup of cottage cheese can be substituted for 1 ounce of meat

- Low-fat cheese (any cheese with less than 5 grams of fat per ounce), such as low-fat cottage cheese, part-skim mozzarella, farmer's or string cheese
- Nonfat cheese (any cheese or cottage cheese with less than 1 gram of fat per ounce)

Food Choices—Continued

Limit High-Fat Dairy Products

- Regular and 2% milk and milk products, such as regular evaporated milk or yogurt
- Whole milk, processed cheese and natural cheese, such as cheddar, Swiss, Brick, Brie, Monterey Jack, Colby, American, or cream cheese
- Rich dairy desserts and condiments, such as ice cream, whipped toppings, sour cream, or half-and-half

Meats

Limit intake of cooked lean beef, pork, chicken, turkey, or fish to 6 ounces or less each day (3 ounces of cooked meat are equivalent to 4 ounces of raw meat)

A 2-ounce serving equals:

- 1 small chicken leg or thigh
- ½ cup ground or chopped meat or tuna
- 2 slices of sandwich-sized meat

A 3-ounce serving equals:

- 1 medium pork chop
- 1 quarter-pound hamburger
- 1 split chicken breast
- 1 unbreaded fish filet
- Cooked meat the size of a deck of cards

Choose Lean Meats

(containing no more than 3 grams of fat per ounce)

- Chicken, turkey, fish, and shellfish (without skin or added oil)
- Lean, trimmed cuts of beef, pork, or lamb, such as

    Beef or veal: tenderloin, sirloin tip, round steak, ground round, rump roast, flank steak

    Pork: loin chop, tenderloin, center-cut ham, Canadian bacon

    Lamb: loin or leg roasts, chops

Limit High-Fat, High-Cholesterol Meats

- High-fat, processed meats, such as bacon, bologna, salami, sausage, or hot dogs
- High-fat cuts of beef, pork, and lamb, such as prime-grade steaks, roasts, ribs, or veal cutlets
- High-cholesterol meats, such as liver, sweetbreads, kidneys, or brains

Eggs

Limit egg yolks (including those used in baked goods and cooking) to no more than three per week. One egg yolk has 5 grams of fat.

Fats and Oils

Limit all added fats, especially sources of saturated fat. Depending on your caloric intake, eat no more than three to eight servings per day. One serving contains 4 to 5 grams of fat. Added fat includes fat used in cooking and baking, and fat contained in convenience foods. Limit fat intake carefully to avoid extra calories.

One serving of fat equals:

- 1 teaspoon butter, margarine, or oil
- 2 teaspoons salad dressing or 2 tablespoons light salad dressing
- 2 teaspoons peanut butter, nuts, or seeds
- 5 large olives (black or green)
- ⅛ medium avocado

Continued

Food Choices—Continued

Choose Unsaturated Fats

When selecting dietary fat, use the following in the quantities suggested on page 193:

- Unsaturated oils, such as corn, olive, canola, safflower, sesame, soybean, or sunflower
- Margarine made with the unsaturated or partially hydrogenated oils listed above; the softer the margarine, the less hydrogenated it is

- Nuts, seeds, olives, avocados, or peanut butter
- Salad dressing or mayonnaise made with unsaturated vegetable oil. Use reduced-fat versions of these products.

Limit Saturated Fats

- Saturated fats and oils, such as butter, lard, bacon fat, coconut oil, or palm oil
- Hydrogenated oil found in shortening, some margarines, some salad dressings, and peanut butter

NOTE: These recommendations are not intended for children under age 2. Recommended limits are based on typical calorie needs for adults. Individuals with higher calorie needs can have more unsaturated oils and fats and should increase their intake of fruits, vegetables, and starches.

Park Nicollet Institute © 2002.

High Blood Pressure (Hypertension)

High blood pressure, or *hypertension*, is the most common chronic adult illness in the United States. There is no cure for high blood pressure, but it can be controlled.

High blood pressure is one of the three major controllable risk factors for cardiovascular disease (risk relates not only to how high your blood pressure is but also to how long it has been raised).

Controlling your blood pressure can also reduce your risk of kidney disease. The sooner your blood pressure is controlled, the less you risk future problems.

Causes

High blood pressure can be hereditary. It can also be caused by a number of lifestyle factors, such as being overweight, smoking, or drinking excessive amounts of alcohol. A small number of people have secondary hypertension, which is high blood pressure caused by organ problems or disease.

Treatment

Two numbers are used to measure your blood pressure: for example, 130 (systolic) over 85 (diastolic). The higher number, the *systolic pressure*, refers to the pressure inside the artery when the heart squeezes to pump blood through the body. The lower number, the *diastolic pressure*, refers to the pressure inside the artery when the heart is relaxed and filling with blood. You have hypertension if your systolic pressure is consistently 140 or greater and/or your diastolic pressure is consistently 90 or greater (see table on p. 196).

Treatment decisions are based on your blood pressure measurement, presence or absence of heart or kidney damage, and presence of other risk factors. Your doctor may give you medications right away or may try a period of lifestyle changes (such as regular exercise or change in diet) for up to 1 year. Depending on your treatment plan and medications prescribed, your doctor will tell you how often to have your blood pressure checked.

Self-Care

Reduce high blood pressure and cardio-vascular risks by:

- *Losing weight.* Being overweight increases your risk of developing high blood pressure. A weight loss of 5 to 10 pounds can lower and help control blood pressure. Weight loss can also decrease blood cholesterol, triglycerides, and blood sugar levels. Weight loss is the most effective method for controlling hypertension without medication.

- *Exercising regularly.* Regular aerobic exercise—such as walking, running, bicycling, or swimming laps—can prevent and reduce high blood pressure. More activity can also help reduce weight and stress. Experts recommend 30 to 60 minutes of aerobic exercise three to five times a week.

- *Controlling salt in your diet.* Limit sodium to less than 2400 milligrams per day by not adding salt to food, and limiting processed, convenience, and fast foods.

- *Limiting alcohol.* Drinking too much alcohol can raise blood pressure, add weight, and make blood pressure control more difficult. Avoid alcohol or limit yourself to two drinks a day for men, and one drink a day for women. A drink is defined as 12 ounces of beer, 4 ounces of wine, or 1 ounce of 100-proof liquor.

- *Increasing potassium intake.* A high intake of potassium may improve your blood pressure control. Not getting enough potassium may actually increase blood pressure. Many fruits and vegetables are good sources of potassium—try to eat at least five servings a day.

- *Quitting smoking.* Smoking cigarettes does not cause chronic high blood pressure, but smoking is a major risk factor for cardiovascular disease.

- *Eating less fat.* Evidence shows a low-fat diet may lower blood cholesterol and the risk for coronary artery disease. Eating less fat will also aid in weight loss.

- *Taking your medications.* If your doctor prescribes medication, take it as directed. Discuss any side effects or reactions you experience with your doctor. Do not stop taking medications without talking to your doctor.

What the Numbers Mean

Blood Pressure Classifications for Adults Age 18 Years and Older

Category	Systolic (Top Number)		Diastolic (Bottom Number)	What to Do
Optimal	<120		<80	Recheck in 2 years
Normal	<130		<85	Recheck in 2 years
High-normal	130–139	or	85–89	Recheck in 1 year
Hypertension				
Stage 1	140–159	or	90–99	Confirm within 2 months
Stage 2	160–179	or	100–109	See doctor within 1 month
Stage 3	≥180	or	≥110	See doctor within 1 week unless otherwise directed

• *Seeing your doctor regularly.* After your blood pressure is controlled, you should continue to have it checked regularly. There usually are not symptoms to tell you if your blood pressure is elevated. See your doctor at least once a year to make sure your blood pressure is under control.

To confirm a hypertension diagnosis, your doctor will need blood pressure readings from two or more visits. The table on p. 196 outlines blood pressure classifications and the different stages of hypertension.

Palpitations

Heart palpitations, the feeling that the heart has skipped a beat, are not usually dangerous. Most people have them from time to time. When your heart beats normally, its two upper chambers contract. Then the two lower chambers contract. That makes the two-thump heartbeat sound.

Causes

Palpitations are usually caused by alcohol, caffeine, nicotine, anxiety, (see p. 332), and stress. Some medications may cause palpitations. If you experience palpitations after starting a medication, talk to your doctor. Palpitations may be caused by a heart rhythm disorder, known as *arrhythmia*. Arrhythmias vary from feeling that the heart has skipped a beat to feeling that the heart is racing and fluttering. Arrhythmias can be serious. If you experience palpitations with a change in heart rate, dizziness, shortness of breath, or sweating, call 911.

Self-Care

- Stop using nicotine (see Smoking, p. 413).

- Avoid caffeine and alcohol.

- Increase activity. Warm up slowly and cool down at the end of your activity.

- Find ways to reduce stress and anxiety (see Stress, p. 336).

What to do about Palpitations

Symptom/Sign	Action
Occasional feeling that your heart has skipped a beat	Self-care
Persistent heart palpitations	Call doctor
Palpitations and dizziness, shortness of breath, or sweating	Call 911
Palpitations and chest pain	Call 911

Stroke

When someone has a stroke, the blood flow to part of the brain stops. Stroke is a leading cause of impairment in older adults. It is the third leading cause of death in the United States.

There are two types of strokes. An *ischemic stroke* is caused when a blood clot blocks an artery or vessel in your brain. Eighty percent of strokes are ischemic. A *hemorrhagic stroke* occurs when a blood vessel in the brain breaks and bleeds in the brain. During a stroke, cells in the brain do not get the oxygen and nutrients they need and start to die.

Symptoms

Symptoms of stroke can include:

- Sudden numbness or weakness of the face, arm, or leg, especially on one side of the body

- Sudden confusion or trouble speaking or understanding

- Sudden trouble seeing in one or both eyes

- Sudden trouble walking, dizziness, or loss of balance or coordination
- Sudden, severe headache with no known cause

Treatment

In recent years, treatments have been developed to help reduce the damage that strokes cause. Emergency room care for a stroke is very important. Early care can reduce damage to your brain and lessen the effects of stroke. Medications that dissolve blood clots that are blocking the flow of blood in the brain can be used for ischemic strokes. Recognizing the warning signs of stroke and seeking treatment can greatly reduce the chances of permanent damage.

The damage that is caused may impair your ability to function normally. What kind of impairment and how severe it is depends on what part of the brain is damaged. Brain cells that are destroyed by a stroke do not grow back; however, the brain can adapt. Physical therapy, occupational therapy, and speech and language therapy can help people relearn some of skills that are lost. The aim of these therapies is to help you care for yourself.

Prevention

There are certain factors that can increase your risk for stroke. Some factors can be controlled and some cannot. Controlling these factors can help prevent stroke:

- *High blood pressure*. Have your blood pressure measured, and if it is high, take steps to control it (see High Blood Pressure, p. 195).
- *Diabetes*. Keep your blood sugar under control (see Diabetes, p. 351).
- *Smoking*. If you use tobacco, stop (see Smoking, p. 413).
- *Coronary artery disease*. If you have CAD, manage it. Modify your diet, be active, and take your medications exactly the way they are prescribed by your doctor (see Coronary Artery Disease, p. 183).
- *Transient ischemic attacks (TIA)*. A TIA is a mini-stroke. It has the same symptoms of a stroke but lasts only a few minutes. If you experience these, do not ignore them. They can be treated with medications or surgery.

Lung Problems

Your lungs are responsible for getting oxygen to the rest of your body. They are equipped with natural defense mechanisms that keep harmful and disease-causing materials from entering your body. When these defenses are damaged by smoking, environmental pollutants, or other causes, respiratory problems or diseases can occur.

This chapter explains common lung concerns, which can range from ordinary colds to life-threatening diseases. Your doctor can offer advice and treatment for many of these problems. For some conditions, you may need the help of a pulmonologist, who specializes in dealing with lung conditions.

Allergies

An allergy is a reaction in the body to a normally harmless substance. Usually the immune system functions as the body's defense against invading bacteria and viruses. In most allergic reactions, the immune system is responding to a false alarm. When you inhale an allergen (a substance that causes allergies), your immune system releases chemical substances that inflame the linings of your nose, sinuses, eyelids, lungs and eyes. This causes itching, sneezing, runny nose, watery eyes, coughing, and wheezing.

Causes

Researchers think people may inherit the tendency to be allergic. Children are more likely to develop allergies if a parent has allergies, though they may not be allergic to the same substances. People who have allergies are often sensitive to more than one substance. Substances that cause the most allergic reactions include pollen, mold, dust mites, and pets.

Pollen

Pollen allergy, also known as *hay fever*, occurs seasonally—in the spring, summer, and fall—when trees, weeds, and grasses release tiny particles, called *pollen*, which are carried through the air. This is one of the most common chronic conditions in the United States, affecting an estimated 35 million people. In North America, most pollen comes from weeds, such as ragweed. Trees that produce allergenic pollen include oak, ash, elm, hickory, pecan, box elder, and mountain cedar. Few people are allergic to flowers. In fact, most people have little contact with the pollen of flowering plants, which is carried by insects, not the wind.

About Chemical Sensitivity

Some people report they have allergic reactions to things such as perfumes and tobacco smoke. Although the symptoms may resemble the symptoms of allergies, sensitivity to these substances is not the same as a true allergic reaction.

Mold

Molds are another cause of seasonal allergies. The mold season often peaks from June to late summer, though people who are allergic may have symptoms from spring to late fall. In the warmest parts of the United States, molds can cause year-round allergies. Molds are part of the fungus family, and their spores (reproductive particles) can produce allergic reactions when inhaled. In homes, mold is common in damp basements, bathrooms, refrigerator drip trays, houseplants, air conditioners, humidifiers, garbage pails, mattresses, and upholstered furniture. Molds can also be found in bakeries, breweries, barns, dairies, greenhouses, compost piles, and outdoor areas that are moist and shady.

Dust Mites

Dust mites are microscopic organisms in the dust found in all homes and workplaces. These mites can live in bedding, upholstered furniture, and carpets. They thrive in the summer and die in the winter, though in warm, humid homes, they can thrive year round. House dust, which is made up of a number of materials, contains dead dust mites and their waste products. It is these waste products that actually cause the allergic reaction.

Pets

Many people think that pet allergies are caused by the fur of cats and dogs. But researchers have found that the major allergens are proteins that come from the oil glands in the animals' skin and are shed in dander. Saliva, which sticks in the fur when an animal licks itself, and urine are also sources of allergy-causing proteins. Some rodents, such as guinea pigs, gerbils, mice, and rats, can also cause allergic reactions in some people.

Symptoms

Signs and symptoms of allergies to air-borne substances include:

- Sneezing, often with a runny or clogged nose

- Coughing and wheezing

- Itching eyes, nose, and throat

- Dark circles under the eyes (caused by increased blood flow near the sinuses)

- Red, swollen, or watering eyes

For people who have asthma, allergens can trigger asthma symptoms (see p. 206). Allergic reactions can also lead to sinusitis (see p. 132).

Your doctor can use skin tests to determine what allergens are causing your symptoms. In these tests, diluted extracts from different allergens are injected under the skin. If you have an allergic reaction, a small, raised, reddened area appears on the skin where you had the injection.

Treatment

Treatment for allergies often involves using self-care steps to avoid the allergen. Some people may also need medications or allergy shots.

Medications

There are several different types of medications that can help with allergic reactions:

- Antihistamines can be used to counter the effects of histamine, which is the chemical released by the body that causes allergy symptoms. Antihistamines can cause drowsiness; however, some of the newer medications available by prescription do not.

- Corticosteroid nasal sprays are very effective against allergy symptoms. It can take 3 to 10 days to get maximum relief, so you should start them as soon as you begin having symptoms.

- Decongestants can relieve symptoms caused by nasal allergies. They are available as oral medications and as nosedrops and sprays, but drops and sprays should only be used for a few days. When used for longer periods, they can make symptoms worse.

- Eyedrops containing antihistamines or decongestants can be prescribed to help relieve itchy eyes.

Allergy Shots

A series of allergy shots, also called *immunotherapy*, can be used to reduce allergy symptoms over a longer period. Allergy shots contain a small amount of the substance to which you're allergic, which helps you become desensitized to the allergen. It can take 6 months or more to feel relief. Most people need allergy shots for at least a year and probably more for best results.

Self-Care

In addition to using medications, there are steps you can take to reduce your exposure to airborne allergens and the severity of your symptoms:

- Keep your windows and doors closed and use air conditioning at home and in your car during allergy season. Avoid using window and attic fans.

- Stay indoors in the morning and on dry, hot, windy days, when outdoor pollen levels are highest.

- Be aware that pollen can be brought indoors on people and pets.

- Dry your clothes in a dryer rather than hanging them outside, where they can collect pollen.

- If you are allergic to pollen but must work outdoors, wear a facemask designed to filter pollen.

- Avoid tobacco smoke, which can aggravate allergies.

- Use a good air filter at home.

- Run a dehumidifier at home to reduce humidity, which may allow mold to grow. Clean the dehumidifier often.

- Dustproof your bedroom: avoid wall-to-wall carpets, venetian blinds, down-filled blankets, and feather pillows. Bedding should be encased in a zippered, plastic, airtight, and dustproof cover. Pets should be kept out of the bedroom.

- Use a vacuum cleaner equipped with a high-efficiency particulate air (HEPA) filter.

- Washable items should be washed often using water hotter than 130°F. Lower temperatures do not kill dust mites.

- If you must live with a pet you are allergic to, someone else should bathe the pet weekly and brush it often.

- Avoid irritants that can make symptoms worse, such as insect sprays, tobacco smoke, air pollution, and fresh tar or paint.

What to do about Allergic Reactions

Symptom/Sign	Action
Occasional allergy symptoms (itchy eyes, nose, and throat; runny nose; cough)	Self-care
Symptoms that last more than 2 weeks	Call doctor
Allergy symptoms that occur at the same time each year	See doctor
Wheezing, shortness of breath	Go to hospital

Asthma

Asthma interferes with normal breathing by narrowing the airways that are within the lungs and that lead to the lungs. This can happen when the muscles around the airways tighten, when there is inflammation and swelling of the airway's lining, or when extra mucus is produced. More than 15 million Americans have asthma, including more than 6 million children.

Causes

For most people, asthma is triggered by one or more factors. What causes an asthma episode in one person, however, may not bother another person who has asthma. Common asthma triggers include:

- *Allergens.* Some people's immune systems overreact to specific allergens that normally are not harmful to the body, such as dust mites, molds, pollen, or animal dander. The immune system's overreaction is called an *allergy* (see p. 201). For some people, the allergic reaction to a specific allergen can cause an asthma episode.

- *Infections.* Bacterial and viral infections are common asthma triggers. Viral infections, such as a cold or the flu, tend to trigger asthma episodes more often than bacterial infections, such as strep throat or sinus infections.

- *Irritants*. Asthma symptoms are also aggravated by irritants such as smoke from tobacco or wood, air pollution, and various fumes and fragrances. Some of these irritants may trigger your asthma, although others may not.

- *Exercise*. Aerobic exercise, such as jogging or cross-country skiing, sometimes causes asthma episodes—especially exercises that involves continuous movement over a long period in cold, dry air.

- *Aspirin and other NSAIDs*. Aspirin and other nonsteroidal anti-inflammatory drugs (NSAIDs) act as triggers in a small percentage of people with asthma. Because aspirin-induced asthma can be severe and come on very quickly, you should avoid taking aspirin and other NSAIDs if you have aspirin-sensitive asthma.

- *Emotions*. Excitement, stress, fear, and other emotions may trigger asthma episodes in some people. However, the emotions themselves are not the direct triggers. The asthma episodes occur as a result of rapid or heavy breathing brought on by crying, laughing, or feeling anxious.

Symptoms

Although asthma is common, its symptoms vary from person to person. Most people who have asthma develop their first symptoms while still young. About half show symptoms before age 10, and another third before age 40. But anyone can develop asthma at any time.

Asthma can range from mild and intermittent to severe and persistent. Your symptoms may range from mild shortness of breath, coughing, and wheezing to severe shortness of breath, chest tightness, difficulty speaking, and gasping for air.

Treatment

The key to managing asthma is understanding your symptoms and what triggers and relieves them. A good asthma management plan should be able to reduce the severity and frequency of asthma symptoms and prevent unscheduled visits to the clinic or emergency room.

Peak-Flow Meters

A peak-flow meter is a good tool for assessing and monitoring asthma. It measures the maximum speed at which air can be exhaled from the lungs. During an asthma episode, the peak flow slows down because the airways are constricted and partly blocked. Your breathing capacity may begin to drop up to 24 hours before asthma symptoms appear. The peak-flow meter can detect this drop so you can start taking medications before you begin to wheeze or cough.

Medications

There are many different kinds of asthma medications. The type of medication your doctor prescribes will depend on how severe your asthma is. Many people with mild, intermittent asthma do well with quick-relief medications alone. However, most people who have frequent asthma episodes or persistent asthma take at least two kinds of medications. One medication provides quick relief during an asthma episode, and one long-term control medication prevents or reduces asthma episodes.

- *Long-term control medications.* The best way to control an asthma episode is to prevent it from beginning. Several types of medications are used for long-term control of asthma. Anti-inflammatory medications, such as inhaled corticosteroids, cromolyn sodium, and nedocromil, prevent mucus production and airway swelling. Other types of long-term control medications include long-acting beta-agonists, theophylline, and leukotriene modifiers.

- *Quick-relief medications.* The common types of quick-relief medications you can use at home include beta-agonists, anticholinergics, and oral corticosteroids. Beta-agonists and anticholinergics relax the smooth muscle of the airways, making it easier to breathe. Oral corticosteroids help control the symptoms of asthma by reducing swelling, inflammation, and mucus production in the airways.

Asthma Action Plan

One way many people manage their asthma is by using an asthma action plan. An asthma action plan is something you and your doctor develop together. It can help you recognize the early warning signs of an asthma episode and outline the steps to follow for relief.

Your asthma action plan will outline a medication program based on both symptoms and peak-flow readings. Usually the first step in an action plan is to avoid asthma triggers and to take long-term control medications to prevent episodes. The second step involves the use of fast-acting medications to relieve asthma symptoms when an episode does occur.

Keep a copy of your asthma action plan in your purse or wallet and at home or at the office. Parents should provide a copy of their child's plan to the child's day care provider or teacher and to the school nurse. Although the asthma action plan can help you avoid unnecessary visits to your doctor or the emergency room, never hesitate to get care if you need it.

Self-Care

The following self-care steps assume you have seen a doctor and have the right medications for managing your asthma. If you have coughing, wheezing, or chest tightness that has not been diagnosed as asthma, see your doctor.

- Become an asthma expert. Read about asthma and attend patient information sessions and asthma support groups.

- Follow your asthma action plan. Know the warning signs of an asthma episode. Make sure you have written in-

Special Concerns for Children

Asthma causes more hospital and emergency room visits than any other chronic childhood disease. Children with well-controlled asthma, however, should be able to participate in any activity or sport they choose.

Children too young to use an inhaler are often treated with a machine called a *nebulizer*. This device uses compressed air to turn a solution of liquid medication into a fine mist, which the child breathes in through a mask or mouthpiece.

Many children outgrow asthma symptoms, although the underlying condition—extra-sensitive bronchial tube lining—remains throughout life. About half of children with asthma outgrow it by age 15. Smoking may trigger the return of the problem.

structions for what to do in an asthma emergency. Keep a record of your episodes, medications, peak-flow readings, and responses to medications.

- Manage your medications. Know the kinds of medications you should take, how much, and how often. Know the possible side effects and what you can do to minimize them. Make sure you know which medications should be taken first, and follow the instructions carefully. Learn the correct use of an inhaler with a spacer. Don't run out of your medicines. Ask your doctor or pharmacist to check all new medications for possible interactions with the asthma medications you are taking.

- Keep daily records of your symptoms and peak-flow readings, so you will be able to reduce the number and severity of asthma episodes.

- Identify and avoid triggers. Your record keeping will help you determine what triggers your asthma episodes. If inhalants such as dust and animal dander are high on your list, take steps to keep your living areas free of these triggers. Steer clear of irritants, cigarette smoke, and car exhaust fumes.

- When an episode occurs, follow your asthma action plan; stay calm, stop your activity, take a few relaxed breaths, drink extra fluids, and use your inhaler. Treat symptoms within minutes of their onset. It takes less medicine to stop an episode in its early phase.

- Stay physically fit. You should be able to control your asthma so you can exercise.

- Keep good records of your medications and dosages, and make sure someone else in your family knows where to find this information in an emergency.

- See your doctor regularly for exams.

What to do about Asthma

Symptom/Sign	Action
Mild shortness of breath, intermittent coughing, and/or wheezing	Self-care
Mild to moderate shortness of breath or wheezing; symptoms improved but not gone after 24 to 48 hours	Call doctor
Need to use inhaler more than prescribed	See doctor
Significant wheezing or coughing, persistent chest tightness, peak-flow rate less than 50 percent of personal best	Go to hospital
Severe shortness of breath, gasping for air, difficulty speaking	Call 911

Bronchitis (Acute)

A cold or flu usually lasts about a week, but after all other symptoms are gone, you may find yourself with a cough that lingers awhile longer. Such a cough is often a sign of acute bronchitis. Bronchitis occurs when the lining of the tubes leading to the lungs gets inflamed and begins making too much mucus. When this happens, your body must cough to clear out the extra mucus.

Causes

Acute bronchitis may be caused by viruses or bacteria. Airborne irritants, such as smoke, dust, chemical fumes, or even cold weather, may cause bronchitis. People who have asthma may develop bronchitis more easily when they have a respiratory infection.

Symptoms

If you have acute bronchitis, your cough may be productive, meaning you cough up mucus (usually yellow or gray instead of clear), or dry and hacking. Acute bronchitis usually lasts 1 to 2 weeks. But even after the inflammation of the bronchial tubes is gone, a dry cough, sometimes with wheezing, remains for as long as 4 to 6 weeks.

The viruses and bacteria that cause acute bronchitis can also cause pneumonia (see p. 225). If your symptoms get worse instead of better, you may have pneumonia and should see your doctor.

Treatment

In some cases, your doctor may prescribe an antibiotic. If so, you should take the medication exactly the way it is prescribed. Antibiotics are usually not helpful in shortening the time the cough lasts.

Self-Care

- Over-the-counter cough suppressants and decongestants may help relieve the nagging cough. Some cough medicines contain antihistamines or other preparations you don't need or want when you have bronchitis. Look for a cough preparation that has only the cough suppressant dextromethorphan. If you are coughing up mucus, you might also try one with the expectorant guaifenesin.
- The best treatment for bronchitis is to drink plenty of fluids. By drinking six to eight glasses of clear liquids (not milk) a day, you will help to keep the mucus from gumming up your bronchial tubes. When the mucus is thin and fluid, it's easier to clear away by coughing. When your bronchial passages are clear and the inflammation has gone away, your cough will go away too.
- Get plenty of rest. Listen to your body. You may be able to continue your daily routine while you have bronchitis, but don't overdo it. If you feel tired, rest.
- Avoid alcohol and caffeine. They can make you lose body fluid, which you need to keep the mucus thin.
- Call your doctor if your cough lasts longer than 3 weeks.

What to do about Bronchitis

Symptom/Sign	Action
Continuing cough following a cold or flu, without fever or problems breathing	Self-care
Cough without fever or problems breathing, making sleep difficult	Call doctor
Recent exposure to tuberculosis or pertussis	See doctor
Fever and shaking, chills	Go to hospital
Coughing up blood	Go to hospital
Shortness of breath, chest discomfort, and wheezing	Go to hospital

Colds (Viral Upper Respiratory Infections)

Colds are viral infections. Because they are caused by viruses, there are no medicines that will cure them or shorten their length (antibiotics are only effective for treating bacterial infections). Regardless of what you do, a cold will usually go away in 7 to 14 days.

Causes

The easiest way to catch a cold is from other people: by shaking their hands, being near their sneezes, or touching things they have touched. You can't catch a cold by walking in the rain, failing to bundle up in cold weather, or sitting by a draft.

Symptoms

The onset of symptoms is rapid. They worsen during the first 3 to 5 days and then slowly improve. Symptoms of a cold include:

- Sore or scratchy throat, mild hoarseness, cough

- Runny nose or congestion

- Fever (usually does not exceed 102°F and can last up to 3 days)

- Minor aches

Sinus congestion, colored discharge, and headaches often accompany colds and do not necessarily indicate that a serious infection is present. Some loss of appetite or difficulty sleeping is also normal with colds.

Self-Care

- Over-the-counter nasal sprays or decongestants may provide temporary relief of cold symptoms. Be sure to follow the recommended dosage and precautions, and read about potential side effects. If you have high blood pressure, diabetes, coronary artery disease, thyroid disease, or are pregnant, check with your doctor before using over-the-counter medications.

- Zinc gluconate may decrease the length of a cold if it is taken within 24 hours of the onset of symptoms. It may cause nausea and a bad taste in your mouth. Children, pregnant women, and people with chronic kidney or liver disease should not use zinc.

- Raise the humidity at home. You can sit in a bathroom with a hot shower running or use a humidifier/vaporizer (a cool mist is preferred because it is safer). If using a humidifier, empty and clean it daily following the manufacturer's instructions.

- Drink extra fluids to prevent dehydration and loosen mucus. Warm fluids, such as chicken noodle soup, are especially soothing for irritated throats.

- Sleep with your head raised on pillows to relieve nasal congestion.

- Gargle with saltwater or suck hard candy. Homemade saltwater (¼ teaspoon salt dissolved in 8 ounces warm water) will help relieve a sore throat. Hard candy is just as effective for sore throats as cough drops.

- Remain up and about. You will benefit from extra rest, but generally you'll feel better by staying moderately active.

- Try saline nosedrops or sprays, such as Ocean or Salinex.

Call your doctor if:

- Your symptoms are worse after 3 to 5 days of self-care.

- You are not feeling better after 7 days of self-care.

- You still have symptoms after 14 days of self-care.

- Your child has cold symptoms and a fever lasting longer than 72 hours or associated with symptoms of ear infections (see Earaches, p. 125).

Special Care for Children

- Over-the-counter medicine is not recommended for children without a doctor's input.

- Encourage children to drink a lot of fluids and stay active if they do not feel too tired. Do not treat cold symptoms in anyone under the age of 21 with aspirin-containing products.

- Call your doctor for advice if your child has bothersome cold symptoms and a fever lasting longer than 72 hours. It is important to assess fever in the context of other cold symptoms. For children, a fever is defined as a rectal temperature over 100.4°F or an oral temperature over 99.5°F.

- For infants younger than 3 months, call your doctor if the rectal temperature is over 100.4°F or if the infant is feeding poorly, can't be comforted, can't stay awake, or has a weak cry.

What to do about Colds

Symptom/Sign	Action
Sore or scratchy throat, mild hoarseness, cough, congestion, runny/stuffy nose, and aches lasting less than 7 days	Self-care
Fever that lasts less than 3 days	Self-care
Significant pain with breathing	Go to hospital
Continuous cough, wheezing, or difficulty swallowing	Go to hospital
Difficulty breathing or altered consciousness	Go to hospital

Prevention

To prevent the spread of viral upper respiratory infections, remember the following:

- Wash your hands often with soap and water for at least 15 to 30 seconds.

- Keep your hands away from your nose, eyes, and mouth. If cold germs get on your hands, you can infect yourself by rubbing your eyes or touching your nose or mouth.

- Wash your hands after handling objects such as doorknobs, telephones, or toys.

- Wash your hands if you have a cold to avoid infecting others.

- Keep a distance from people who are coughing and sneezing.

- Limit the time you stay in the same room with someone who is ill.

- Avoid exposure to the virus. Crowds of people may mean a lot of virus in the air. If you are sick, stay home and get the rest you need.

- Don't share your personal items, including towels, washcloths, silverware, cups, glasses, straws, razors, and toothbrushes.

- Keep up your resistance to infection with a good diet, plenty of rest, and regular exercise.

Chronic Obstructive Pulmonary Disease

Chronic obstructive pulmonary disease (COPD) is the fifth leading cause of death in the United States. Although many people think first of emphysema when they hear COPD, chronic bronchitis is actually more common and equally serious—because it can lead to emphysema and eventually cause death if it is not controlled.

Causes

Cigarette smoking is the number one cause of COPD, accounting for 82 percent of cases (see Smoking, p. 413). Other causes include repeated exposure to lots of dust (such as in coal mines, granaries, or metal molding shops), chemical vapors, and possibly air pollution.

Types of COPD

Chronic Bronchitis
Chronic bronchitis is an inflammation of the lining of the bronchial tubes, which lead to the lungs. This causes the bronchial tubes to produce too much mucus. As chronic bronchitis progresses, the tiny hairs (cilia) that sweep away

irritants from the air passages may stop working or die.

Chronic bronchitis often begins as repeated cases of acute bronchitis following colds. [See Bronchitis (Acute), p. 209]. With chronic bronchitis, however, coughing and mucus production occur more frequently and last longer after each cold. Unlike the occasional 1- to 2-week bout of acute bronchitis after a cold or flu in otherwise healthy people, those with chronic bronchitis have inflammation and coughing, with mucus, for at least 3 months each year.

Emphysema

Emphysema occurs when the tiny air sacs (alveoli) in the lungs become larger and less elastic, making the lungs less able to get oxygen into the blood. This leads to shortness of breath, eventually making even the most basic tasks, such as eating or getting dressed, difficult and tiring.

Treatment

Neither chronic bronchitis nor emphysema can be cured, but with medical treatment, the damage they cause to the lungs and heart can be slowed and their symptoms can be eased.

Because of the gradual onset of symptoms, you should see a doctor at the first signs of shortness of breath or "smoker's cough." Your doctor may prescribe some combination of bronchodilator medications (oral or inhaled), which help relax and open airways; corticosteroids, which help clear away excess mucus; antibiotics; and exercise, which helps build and support lung function.

Self-Care

In addition to taking medications prescribed by your doctor, there are several things you can do to slow further lung damage and make living with COPD easier:

- Quit smoking! Talk with your doctor about ways to stop smoking. Continuing to smoke will only speed up the progression of emphysema.

- Call your doctor at the first signs of respiratory illness, such as a cold or the flu.

- Drink plenty of fluids. Six to eight glasses of clear fluids a day, such as juice or water, will help keep air passages clear of mucus, making it easier to breathe.

- Eat a well-balanced diet. If you have emphysema, spread your meals out. By eating five or six small meals a day, you avoid having a full stomach, which interferes with your breathing.

- Strengthen your heart with aerobic exercise, and build your upper-body strength. Strengthening the muscles in your upper body will make breathing easier. Moderate aerobic exercise, such as 15 minutes of daily walking, will make your heart less susceptible to complications of COPD.

• Do breathing exercises. If you have emphysema, ask your doctor about exercises to help you breathe better. Two common exercises are "pursed-lip" breathing (inhaling through your nose and exhaling twice as long through pursed lips) and breathing from the diaphragm (expanding your diaphragm and abdomen, rather than your chest, when you inhale).

• Get a flu shot each fall and a pneumococcal pneumonia vaccination as recommended by your doctor.

Cough

Coughing is a normal reflex that helps clear the lungs. Usually it is a minor annoyance, but sometimes a cough is a sign of a more serious condition. Severe coughing episodes may cause muscle soreness or even broken ribs.

Acute cough lasts for 3 weeks or less. If a cough lasts for more than 3 weeks, it is considered chronic.

Causes

Most coughs are caused by postnasal drip, asthma, gastroesophageal reflux disease (GERD), or smoking.

Postnasal Drip

Postnasal drip is mucus that runs down your throat from the back of your nose. This may be the cause of your cough if you have allergies or sinusitis or if you have recently had a cold (see Allergies, p. 201; Sinusitis, p. 132; and Colds, p. 211).

Asthma

Asthma is a common cause of chronic cough in both children and adults. In some people with mild asthma, a cough may be the only symptom (see Asthma, p. 205).

Gastroesophageal Reflux Disease

Gastroesophageal reflux disease (GERD) is caused when acid from your stomach backs up into your throat. If you also have heartburn and your symptoms are worse at night, this may be the cause of your cough (see Gastroesophageal Reflux Disease, p. 156).

Smoking

Chronic cough is common in smokers. Twenty-five percent of people who smoke half a pack of cigarettes a day have a chronic cough, as do more than 50 percent of people who smoke more than 2 packs a day. Many smokers have chronic bronchitis, which causes a chronic cough (see Chronic Obstructive Pulmonary Disease, p. 213, and Smoking, p. 413).

Other Causes

Coughing is a side effect of some blood pressure medications. It can also be a sign of lung disease or cancer (see Lung Cancer, p. 222). See your doctor if you don't know what's causing your cough, if it's getting worse instead of better, or if it lasts for more than 3 weeks.

Treatment

Coughing can be useful because it helps clear mucus and foreign material from your airways. It should only be suppressed if it interferes with sleep or if your doctor determines it's not serving any useful purpose (such as coughing caused by medications).

Expectorants are medications used to thin cough secretions and make a cough more effective. *Suppressants* are medications intended to reduce but not eliminate coughing.

Depending on the cause of your cough, treating the underlying condition may be the most effective way to stop your coughing. For tobacco smokers, the most effective way to stop coughing is to stop smoking. Talk to your doctor if you need help.

Self-Care

- Rest with your head elevated.
- Drink plenty of clear fluids, such as juice, soup, or water, to relax the airway.
- Inhale warm, moist air. Because using steam vaporizers can cause burns, the recommended method for inhaling steam is standing in a hot shower or sitting in the bathroom with the hot water on. If you use a cool air vaporizer, it should be emptied and cleaned properly and frequently, following the manufacturer's instructions.
- Use lozenges or hard candy to soothe an irritated throat.
- Use over-the-counter cough suppressants with dextromethorphan only if

your cough interferes with sleep or other activities.

- Avoid antihistamines, which dry secretions and make them thicker. If you have chronic health problems, don't use decongestants.

- Avoid alcohol, canned aerosols, sprays, powders, and smoke from tobacco and fireplaces.

What to do about Cough

Symptom/Sign	Action
Mild cough, recent cold	Self-care
Cough that interferes with sleep or activities and doesn't respond to over-the-counter medications	Call doctor
Cough that lasts more than 3 weeks	Call doctor
Symptoms getting worse after 3 to 5 days, or not improving after 7 days	See doctor
Cough and chronic health problems or in someone over age 65	See doctor
Exposure to pertussis or tuberculosis	See doctor
Cough with fever of 101°F lasting more than 3 days	See doctor
Coughing up blood or frothy discharge; moderate chest pain; mild to moderate shortness of breath	Go to hospital
Severe shortness of breath or severe chest pain	Call 911

Fever in Adults

For good health, the body works best at a temperature of about 97 to 99°F. Although body temperature rises slightly during the day, this change is not important unless your temperature is over 100.4°F. In fact, many people have a temperature that is always a little above or below the 98.6°F that is considered normal. A fever is defined as having a temperature over 99.6°F orally, 98.6°F under the armpit, or 100.4°F rectally. (Also see Fever in Children, p. 371.)

Causes

Your body's temperature is an important indication of how well you are dealing with germs, stress, exertion, or extreme changes in weather. By itself, a high temperature is not necessarily cause for concern. It can actually be a perfectly normal way for your body to defend itself against infection. Your body shivers to help produce the heat it needs to fight germs and sweats to regulate the rise in temperature.

Symptoms

Symptoms of a fever can include:

- Shivers
- Shakes
- Sweating
- Aches

Self-Care

A fever is a special cause for concern in infants under 3 months of age, the elderly, and individuals who are taking medications that suppress the immune system. But for most people, there is no medical reason to try to reduce a fever unless it is accompanied by other symptoms of illness.

- With no other symptoms, medications are not necessary. But if fever makes you uncomfortable, take aspirin, acetaminophen (Tylenol or a generic), or ibuprofen (Advil or a generic). For children, use acetaminophen, not aspirin.

- Drink eight glasses of fluids a day. When you have a fever, you lose body fluids, so it's important to prevent dehydration.

- Call your doctor if fever lasts longer than 3 days or if you develop other symptoms.

What to do about Fever in Adults

Symptom/Sign	Action
Fever for less than 3 days without other symptoms	Self-care
Fever and sore throat, earache, back pain, abdominal pain, or painful urination	See doctor
Shaking, teeth-chattering chills	Go to hospital
Symptoms of dehydration (dry mouth, decreased urination, no energy; confusion in elderly people)	Go to hospital
Fever and stiff neck	Go to hospital
Fever and respiratory difficulty, trouble breathing, or unrelenting cough	Call 911

Influenza

Influenza is a viral respiratory infection of the nose, throat, and lungs that ranks as one of the most severe illnesses of the winter season (flu season is generally December through March). It is not the same as the "stomach flu." An estimated 10 to 20 percent of the population get influenza every year.

Usually influenza is not considered life threatening for healthy adults. However, it can lead to very serious complications, such as pneumonia and bronchitis, especially in people over age 65 and those with chronic illnesses.

Causes

Influenza is caused by a virus. It is highly contagious and is spread when an infected person touches or shakes hands with another, sneezes and coughs without covering the mouth, or touches objects, such as doorknobs, that other people may touch.

Symptoms

Influenza symptoms differ from those you have with a cold. They are usually more serious and leave you lying flat on your back. Unlike the stomach flu, influenza usually does not cause vomiting or diarrhea.

Flu symptoms include:

- Fever, often 102 to 104°F, that may last up to 7 days
- Headache
- Body aches, which may be severe
- Noticeable fatigue that can last up to 2 or 3 weeks
- Dry cough, sometimes severe
- Mild stuffy nose and sore throat

Treatment

Because influenza is a viral infection, it cannot be treated with antibiotics. However, there are antiviral medications that may reduce the severity and shorten the length of the flu if given within 48 hours of the onset of symptoms.

Two of the antiviral medications have been approved for use in preventing the flu but should not be considered replacements for the flu vaccination.

These medications are not helpful in treating the complications that may result from influenza. Each medication has a different set of side effects you should discuss with your doctor before taking the medication.

Self-Care

When you have the flu, try these steps to help you feel more comfortable:

- Stay home and get the rest you need. It is one of the best ways to deal with influenza, and it keeps you from spreading it to other people.

- Drink extra fluids. Warm fluids are soothing, especially if your throat is irritated. Drinking adequate fluids is important to prevent dehydration when you have a fever.

- To relieve nasal congestion, sleep with your head elevated. For adults, over-the-counter decongestants can be used. Be sure to follow the recommended dosage and precautions. If you have high blood pressure, diabetes, coronary artery disease, thyroid disease, or are pregnant, talk to your doctor about using decongestants.

- Treat your headache, sore muscles, and fever with aspirin, acetaminophen, or ibuprofen. Do not give aspirin to children under age 21.

Prevention

Getting a flu shot is the best way to protect yourself from influenza. However, there are other steps you can take to protect yourself and prevent the spread of the disease:

- Wash your hands often with soap and water for at least 15 to 30 seconds.

- Keep your hands away from your nose, eyes, and mouth. If flu germs get on your hands, you can infect yourself by rubbing your eyes or touching your nose or mouth.

- Wash your hands after you've handled objects such as doorknobs, telephones, and toys.

- Wash your hands if you have the flu to avoid infecting others.

- Keep a distance from people who are coughing and sneezing.

- Limit the time you stay in the same room with a sick person.

- Avoid exposure to the virus. Crowds of people may mean a lot of flu virus in the air. If you are sick, stay home and get the rest you need.

- Don't share your personal items, including towels, washcloths, silverware, cups, glasses, straws, razors, and toothbrushes.

- Keep up your resistance to infection with a good diet, plenty of rest, and regular exercise.

About Flu Shots

Influenza vaccine is effective in preventing the flu for about 70 percent of people. You need to get a flu shot every year, because the virus that causes influenza may change from year to year and protection decreases over 12 months. The vaccine does not contain live virus, so you cannot get the flu from it. The best time to get an influenza vaccination is between October and mid-November, but it can be given until the flu season (December through March) is over.

Most people have no side effects from receiving the vaccine. Redness or swelling at the injection site may occur for 1 to 2 days. Occasionally, fever and muscle aches may also be present.

People who should get a flu shot include:

- Anyone age 50 or older

- Women who will be in their second or third trimester of pregnancy during flu season

- People of all ages with heart or lung disease (including asthma), diabetes, kidney disorders, anemia, or an immune deficiency caused by cancer treatment, steroids (prednisone), or human immunodeficiency virus/acquired immunodeficiency syndrome (HIV/AIDS)

- Anyone who comes in close contact with the people listed above

- Anyone who wants to reduce the chance of catching the flu

People who should *not* get a flu shot include:

- Anyone with a serious allergy to chicken eggs

- Anyone who has had a serious reaction to a previous dose of influenza vaccine

- People who are allergic to thimerosal, a preservative used in the vaccine

- People with a history of Guillain-Barré syndrome

- Babies younger than 6 months

What to do about Influenza

Symptom/Sign	Action
Fatigue, fever, headache, muscle aches	Self-care
Symptoms worsening after 3 to 5 days	Call doctor
Persistent or worsening chest discomfort, mild wheezing	See doctor
Fever over 101°F for more than 3 days or that was gone for 24 hours and has returned	See doctor
Fever in someone who is over age 65, pregnant, has a history of chronic illness, or is immunocompromised	See doctor
Symptoms of dehydration (dry mouth, increased thirst, dizziness and no urinary output for 12 hours)	Go to hospital
Significant pain with breathing; continuous coughing or mild wheezing; fever over 101°F and stiff neck; severe headache	Go to hospital
Choking or gasping for air; inability to swallow; bluish lips or nails; severe wheezing	Call 911

Lung Cancer

Lung cancer is the uncontrolled growth of abnormal cells in the lung. Lung cancer is especially deadly because it can easily spread to other parts of the body, such as the bones, brain, or liver.

Causes

- Cigarette smoking accounts for 85 to 90 percent of all lung cancers. Harmful substances in tobacco, called *carcinogens*, damage the cells in the lungs. Over time the damaged cells may become cancerous. Your risk increases with the number of cigarettes you smoke each day, the number of years you have smoked, the earlier the age at which you started smoking, and the more deeply you inhale (see Smoking, p. 413).

- Secondhand smoke can also cause lung cancer. Daily exposure to other people's smoke may increase your chances of developing lung cancer by as much as 30 percent.

- Radon is an invisible, odorless, tasteless radioactive gas that occurs naturally in soil and rocks. It can cause damage to the lungs that may lead to lung cancer. People who work in mines may be exposed to radon. In some parts of the country, radon is found in houses.

- Asbestos is the name of a group of minerals that occur naturally as fibers and are used in certain industries, including shipbuilding, insulation, and brake repair. Asbestos fibers break easily into particles that can be inhaled and damage the lungs. Workers exposed to large amounts of asbestos have a higher risk of developing lung cancer than people who are not exposed to asbestos. The risk is even higher among asbestos workers who smoke.

- Other causes of lung cancer include cigar and pipe smoking, lung diseases such as tuberculosis, and possibly air pollution.

Symptoms

Because the lungs are so large, cancer can invade and grow in them for many years without being detected. Cancer can even spread outside the lungs without any noticeable symptoms.

The most common warning sign of lung cancer is a persistent cough. You may also have chest, back, or shoulder pain. Other symptoms include:

- Shortness of breath

- Wheezing

- Fatigue

- Repeated cases of pneumonia or bronchitis

- Coughing up blood

- Hoarseness

- Swelling of the neck and face

If a tumor is pressing on the nerves in the lung, you may have pain and weakness in your arm, shoulder, and hand.

If you have symptoms of lung cancer, your doctor will evaluate your medical history and perform a physical exam. You may have a chest x-ray examination. To confirm the presence of lung cancer, a tissue sample must be taken from your lungs, called a biopsy. If the diagnosis is lung cancer, your doctor will do more tests to determine the stage of the cancer.

Types of Lung Cancer

Lung cancer is usually divided into two types: non–small cell carcinoma and small cell carcinoma. The terms *non–small* and *small* refer to the size of the cells, not the size of the cancer growth.

Non–small cell carcinoma is more common than small cell carcinoma, and it generally grows and spreads more slowly. There are three types of non–small cell carcinoma:

- *Squamous cell carcinoma.* Also called *epidermoid carcinoma,* it forms in the cells lining your airways. It usually does not spread as rapidly as other types of cancer.

- *Adenocarcinoma.* This type of cancer usually begins near the outside surface of the lung and under the lining of the breathing tubes (bronchi). This is the most common type of lung cancer among people who do not smoke.

- *Large cell carcinoma.* This type of cancer starts growing along the outer edges of the lung. Because the tumor grows rapidly, it is usually large by the time it is found.

Small cell carcinoma accounts for about 25 percent of all cases of lung cancer. It usually starts in one of the breathing tubes and grows more rapidly and is more likely to spread to other organs that other types of lung cancer.

Treatment

Treatment for lung cancer depends on the type of cancer (small cell or non–small cell); the size, location, and extent of the tumor; and the general health of the patient. There are several different kinds of treatment, which may be used alone or in combination:

- Surgery to remove the tumor is the most common treatment for non–small cell lung cancer. Removal of a small section of the lung containing the tumor is called *wedge resection.*

When an entire lobe is removed (your right lung has three lobes and your left lung has two), the procedure is called a *lobectomy*. This is the most common type of lung cancer surgery. *Pneumonectomy* is the removal of an entire lung.

- *Chemotherapy* is the use of anticancer medications to kill cancer cells throughout the body. This is the most common treatment for small cell lung cancer and can also be used to treat non–small cell cancers. Chemotherapy may be used to control cancer growth or to relieve symptoms. It is usually given by intravenous (IV) injection into a vein or through a thin tube placed into a vein (catheter). Some anticancer medications come in the form of a pill.

- Radiation therapy kills cancer cells by exposing them to high doses of x-rays. It is directed to a limited area, and affects the cancer cells only in that area. Radiation therapy may be used before surgery to shrink a tumor or after surgery to destroy any remaining cancer cells. Doctors also use radiation therapy, often combined with chemotherapy, as the primary treatment instead of surgery.

Prevention

The most important thing you can do to reduce your risk of lung cancer is to avoid smoking and being around other people's smoke. Even people who have smoked heavily for many years can significantly reduce their risk of lung cancer by quitting smoking.

Avoid radon and asbestos by paying attention to warnings in your buildings and worksites and by following the safety rules that are in place where you work. If you are exposed to asbestos at work, wear protective equipment. If you would like to test your home for radon, you can purchase a home radon test kit, available at most hardware stores.

Pneumonia

Pneumonia is an infection of the lungs. It usually affects children younger than 2, adults age 65 or older, and people with chronic health problems. There are many different types of pneumonia, which range in seriousness from mild to life threatening.

Causes

Many cases of pneumonia are caused by bacterial infections. The most common infectious cause of pneumonia in the United States is the bacteria *Streptococcus pneumoniae*. You may develop bacterial pneumonia after you've had an upper respiratory infection such as a cold or the flu.

About 50 percent of pneumonia cases are caused by viruses. Viral pneumonia often occurs in the fall and winter and is usually not as severe as pneumonia caused by bacteria.

Mycoplasma are tiny organisms with characteristics of both bacteria and viruses. *Mycoplasma* pneumonia tends to be mild. Many people with this type of pneumonia never seek medical care.

There are a number of other causes of pneumonia, including fungi, parasites, and other diseases, but they are much less common.

Symptoms

Symptoms of pneumonia can be similar to a cold or the flu. Different types of pneumonia may have different symptoms, depending on the cause.

Bacterial Pneumonia

Symptoms of bacterial pneumonia may appear gradually or come on suddenly. They include:

- Shaking/chills
- Chattering teeth
- Severe chest pain
- Sweating
- Cough with thick, rust-colored, or greenish mucus
- Increased breathing and pulse rate
- Bluish-colored lips or nails

Viral Pneumonia

The symptoms of viral pneumonia include:

- Fever
- Dry cough
- Headache
- Muscle pain
- Weakness
- Fatigue
- Increasing breathlessness

Mycoplasma Pneumonia

Symptoms of *Mycoplasma* pneumonia are often similar to both bacterial and viral pneumonia, though they appear more gradually and are often milder.

Treatment

If you have symptoms of pneumonia, your doctor may do a chest x-ray examination. You may also have blood tests to check your white blood cell count and look for the presence of viruses, bacteria, or other organisms that cause pneumonia.

Early treatment with antibiotics can cure bacterial pneumonia and speed recovery from *Mycoplasma* pneumonia. There are no effective treatments for most types of viral pneumonia, which usually heal on their own.

Other treatments for pneumonia include rest and getting plenty of fluids. Coughing helps clear infected material from your lungs, so your doctor may not want to give you medication to completely suppress your cough.

If your pneumonia is serious, you may be hospitalized, where you can be observed closely and given antibiotics intravenously (in your vein) if necessary. In some cases you may be given supplemental oxygen or be placed on a ventilator.

What to do about Pneumonia

Symptom/Sign	Action
Persistent cough, chest pain, fever	Call doctor
Suddenly feeling worse after a cold or the flu	See doctor
Shaking chills, trouble breathing	See doctor
Pneumonia in someone who is over age 65, pregnant, has a history of chronic illness, or is immunocompromised	Go to hospital
Significant pain with breathing; continuous coughing or mild wheezing; fever over 101°F and stiff neck; severe headache	Go to hospital
Choking or gasping for air; inability to swallow; bluish lips or nails; severe wheezing	Call 911

Prevention

- A vaccine against some of the common types of *Streptococcus* pneumonia is recommended for people over age 65 and other people at high risk for pneumonia.

- A vaccine known as *Prevnar* can be used to protect young children against pneumonia. It's recommended for all children under age 2 and for children over age 2 who are at high risk for pneumonia, such as children with asthma.

- Because pneumonia often occurs as a complication of the flu, annual influenza vaccinations are also a good way to prevent pneumonia.

- Wash your hands often with soap and water for at least 15 to 30 seconds to eliminate the germs that can cause pneumonia.

- Keep up your resistance to infection with a good diet, plenty of rest, and regular exercise.

- Don't smoke. It can damage your lungs' natural defense against respiratory infections.

Shortness of Breath

Shortness of breath is an uncomfortable feeling of not getting enough air. Many causes are harmless and easily corrected; however, shortness of breath can be a symptom of a serious medical condition.

Causes

Shortness of breath has many different causes. It may occur with exercise, especially if you are not used to exercising. Other causes may include:

- Cigarette smoking
- Lung cancer (see p. 222)
- Emphysema (see Chronic Obstructive Pulmonary Disease, p. 213)
- Asthma (see p. 205)
- Pneumonia (see p. 225)
- Congestive heart failure
- Allergies (see p. 201)
- Allergic shock (see p. 4)
- Obesity
- Heart attack (see p. 43)
- Collapsed lung
- High altitude
- Neck or chest injury
- Object blocking the airway
- Anxiety

Treatment

In severe cases, hospitalization may be required. Medications to treat the cause of shortness of breath may be used. If your blood oxygen level is low, supplemental oxygen may be given.

Self-Care

If you have been diagnosed with a medical condition that causes shortness of breath, you may be able to get relief by following the treatment plan given to you by your doctor. If you have an inhaler, use it as directed. It may also help to:

- Elevate your head when resting or sleeping
- Avoid activities that aggravate symptoms
- Avoid all possible allergens or irritants

What to do about Shortness of Breath

Symptom/Sign	Action
Shortness of breath with known cause and treatment plan	Self-care
Shortness of breath after only mild exertion	Call doctor
Mild wheezing	See doctor
Swelling of legs or ankles, unable to lie down, history of congestive heart failure	Go to hospital
Coughing up blood; shaking chills	Go to hospital
Significant wheezing, persistent tight cough	Go to hospital
Chest pain; history of previous respiratory arrest; possible inhalation of foreign body; possible drug overdose; or recent exposure to fumes, smoke, or chemical inhalation	Call 911
Choking or gasping for air, difficulty speaking	Call 911

Wheezing

If you hear a whistling or high-pitched purring sound that feels as if it's coming from your chest when you breathe out, you are wheezing.

Causes

Wheezing is caused by narrowing airways in the lungs. It's a sign that there is difficulty breathing and is a common symptom of asthma (see p. 205). Wheezing can also be caused by:

- Bronchitis [see Bronchitis (Acute), p. 209]
- Smoking
- Allergies (see p. 201)
- Pneumonia (see p. 225)
- Sensitivities to chemicals or pollution
- Emphysema (see Chronic Obstructive Pulmonary Disease, p. 213)
- Lung cancer (see p. 222)
- Heart failure
- Object trapped in the airways

Treatment

If you are under a doctor's care for asthma, you don't have to see your doctor when you start to wheeze. Just follow the doctor's recommendations.

If you do not have asthma and develop wheezing, call your doctor. You will be evaluated to determine the cause. If you have already seen a doctor for wheezing and know what's causing it, you may have a plan to manage it. If the plan is working, you do not have to see your doctor every time you start to wheeze.

Self-Care

If you are wheezing, there are several things you can do to get relief:

- Stop activity if necessary.
- Use an inhaler.
- If you are in a smoky or polluted environment, leave immediately.

What to do about Wheezing

Symptom/Sign	Action
Mild bouts of wheezing associated with known asthma	Self-care
Any new wheezing	See doctor
Wheezing and persistent cough or rapid breathing	Call 911
Wheezing and severe shortness of breath or chest pain	Call 911

Muscle and Joint Problems

Your muscular and skeletal systems have remarkable jobs. From performing everyday tasks such as typing to demanding athletic activities, your muscles and bones are always at work. Although aches and pains can be uncomfortable and annoying, they serve an important purpose—letting you know you have pushed your body too hard or that something else is wrong.

This chapter describes common muscle, joint, and bone concerns. It suggests how to take care of many of these conditions at home and indicates when to get help from your doctor. For some concerns, your doctor may involve specialists, such as physiatrists, physical therapists, orthopedists, or sports medicine specialists. ::

Ankle Pain

The ankle is one of the most commonly injured joints of the body. Held together by ligaments and tendons, the ankle allows the foot a wide range of motion. Because of the ankle's crucial role in walking and standing, ankle injuries should be taken seriously and treated properly (see Fractures, p. 37).

Causes

There are several causes of ankle pain.

Strains and Sprains

Strains and sprains are the most common ankle injuries. A *strain* is the stretching or tearing of a muscle or tendon. A *sprain* is the stretching or tearing of ligaments. Ligaments connect bone to bone. Sprains occur at a joint, such as the ankle, knee, wrist, or finger.

Twisting your ankle may cause stretching or tearing of the ligaments and tendons. With a strain or sprain you may hear or feel a snap, pop, or crack at the time of injury. This most often occurs on the outside of the ankle. Mild strains or sprains may cause mild to moderate pain and little or no swelling. The ankle can support weight, but usually a limp is apparent. Moderate sprains hurt more when you move, and swelling and tenderness increase. Walking is hard, and often crutches are needed for a few days.

A sprain is generally severe when the ligament and tendons are stretched or completely torn (ruptured). Severe sprains are accompanied by intense pain, swelling and tenderness, limited motion, and inability to walk or bear weight on the ankle. Moderate and severe sprains may cause bruising in the foot and toes, around the ankle, and up the side of the leg.

Most sprains are on the outside of the ankle. Because of the strength of the ligament on the inner ankle, often bone will give way before the ligament does. Pain on the inner ankle may be a fracture and should be x-rayed in most cases.

The Rest, Ice, Compress, and Elevate (RICE) method is the right first treatment for these injuries (see RICE, p. 267). A severe injury should be seen by a doctor. Unless the ankle is obviously deformed, very painful, or unable to bear any weight, a sprained ankle can be treated safely at home for the first 24 hours using the RICE method and avoiding weight on the sprain. With a mild or moderate sprain, swelling should stop within 24 hours and the ankle should be-gin to improve (although not be healed) within 48 hours. If it doesn't, see a doctor.

Achilles Tendinitis and Bursitis

Achilles tendinitis and *bursitis* at the back of the ankle are very much alike. The Achilles tendon is a large, strong band that attaches the calf muscle to the heel. Underneath the Achilles tendon are bursas that may also become inflamed. *Bursas* are fluid-filled sacs that cushion movement within a joint.

Symptoms of Achilles tendinitis include pain in the lower calf and back of the heel that is worse when you wake up in the morning and generally gets better as the ankle is "warmed up" with use. Occasionally, with an improper warm-up or sudden movement, the Achilles tendon can tear or even rupture. Any deformity in the calf should be seen by a doctor right away. Bursitis usually causes inflammation of a bursa at the back of the ankle, along with pain similar to that of tendinitis.

Common causes of tendinitis and bursitis in the ankle include tight calf muscles, overuse, sudden stress from a quick movement, and repeated motion, such as running. But you don't have to be athletic to have either problem. Shoes are often the culprit. Switching from high heels or cowboy boots to flat shoes, or wearing shoes that fit poorly or provide inadequate support and cushioning, can also inflame tendons and bursas.

Gout

Gout often begins in the big toe, but it may move to the ankle and knee. If uric acid (a waste product) builds up in the body, it can cause gout. Symptoms of gout may show up in a joint. They include:

• Sudden pain or extreme tenderness

• Swelling

• Redness

If you have symptoms of gout, call your doctor as soon as possible. There are medications that effectively treat gout. Raise your leg and apply ice.

Self-Care

As with other joint injuries, the first step in treatment for most ankle injuries is the RICE method (see RICE, p. 267) and anti-inflammatory medications (see Medications on p. 396).

Other steps in self-care include the following:

• You can usually treat a sprain or strain at home. You should see your doctor if the injured part looks deformed. Call your doctor if the pain keeps you from using the injured part.

• Use the injured ankle as little as possible until the swelling stops.

• Use crutches if it hurts to stand or walk.

• If the swelling lasts for more than 3 days, soak the injured ankle in cold water (45 to 60°F) for 1 minute, then soak in warm water (100 to 105°F) for 2 to 3 minutes. Repeat this cycle for 15 to 20 minutes. Stop if you see more swelling.

• As the swelling and pain decrease, do gentle exercises that strengthen and stretch your ankle (see illustration below).

• If you have tendinitis or bursitis, decrease activity for 1 to 2 weeks or until fairly pain-free. Apply heat to the area before stretching and ice when you

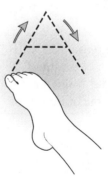

Range-of-Motion Exercise

Sit with your leg extended; keep it still while you move your foot to print the alphabet in the air with your big toe.

have finished. If there is no improvement in 10 to 14 days, call your doctor.

- If you have gout, try raising your legs and applying ice. Call your doctor for prescription medications.

What to do about Ankle Pain

Symptom/Sign	Action
Swelling, pain, and possible bruising from sudden twist or force	Self-care
Pain at back of ankle—begins slowly and may be worse when you wake up	Self-care
Ankle pain and swelling that comes on suddenly and is not related to injury; may appear discolored (reddish blue), shiny, or feel warm to the touch	See doctor
Ankle pain associated with swelling, fever, and chills	See doctor
Sudden intense pain, with rapid onset of swelling; felt or heard "snap" or "pop" at time of injury	See doctor
Unable to bear weight, stand, or walk; deformed or crooked appearance	Go to hospital
Signs of possible nerve damage—foot is numb, cold, or blue	Go to hospital

Back Pain

Backaches are one of the most common reasons people visit a doctor.

Causes

Back pain can be caused by inflammation of joints, muscles, or ligaments. Poor posture, obesity, or lifting something the wrong way can cause back pain. Pain also can develop after you sit or stand too long or when you are under physical or mental stress.

Some back pain can be caused by problems in other parts of your body. Pain in your hip or leg, for example, can make you feel back pain as well. This is called *referred pain.*

Pain in the lower back is very common. It can be caused by inflammation of structures in the back, such as the joints, muscles, or discs (see illustration, p. 235). Most often it is made worse by certain activities. It can also be affected by physical or psychological stress. Uncommonly, back pain can be caused by serious problems such as infection or other conditions your doctor can distinguish from the more common types of back pain.

Acute low back pain is also called *lumbar muscle strain* or *backache.* It is de-

THE SPINE

Cervical region (neck)
The seven top vertebrae that support the skull.

Thoracic region (chest)
The 12 middle vertebrae; each has a pair of ribs attached.

Lumbar region (low back)
The five lower vertebrae that get the most pressure when we lift.

Sacrum (pelvis)
Five fused vertebrae.

Coccyx (tailbone)
Four fused vertebrae.

Disc

View from top

Ruptured disc

Nerve root

Outer fibrous ring

View from side

Nerve root

Slipped disk ("herniated" or "prolapsed disk") – Wear and tear has caused the jelly-like center of the disc to bulge through the fibrous outer ring, putting pressure on the nerve root and causing pain.

scribed as low back pain you've had for 6 weeks or less that does not reach below the knees. Although quite painful, it usually improves after a few days of simple treatment.

Acute sciatica is known as *disc pain* or *radiating leg pain*. Acute sciatica is described as low back pain you've had for 6 weeks or less where the pain reaches below the knee. Sciatica pain is often caused by nerve irritation from discs in the lower back.

Chronic low back pain and *sciatica* are conditions of long-lasting back pain. If you have pain for more than 6 weeks, more medical evaluation is needed.

Back pain is sometimes a sign of a more serious health problem, so tell your doctor right away if you have any of these symptoms or conditions in addition to low back pain:

- Unexplained weight loss

- Constant night pain

- Fever

- Trouble urinating

- Leg weakness

Self-Care

- Moderate activity is most helpful, but avoid anything that makes the pain much worse. Staying in bed for more than 2 days can make back pain worse.

- Use ice or cold packs for 20 minutes three or four times a day during the first few days of a muscle sprain or spasm.

- A hot bath or heating pad can help reduce pain and stiffness, but don't use heat during the first few days you feel pain.

- Take a medication for pain and inflammation (see Medications on p. 396).

- Maintain good posture to keep your body's weight aligned and reduce stress on the back muscles.

- Lying on your back with a pillow under your knees or lying on your side with a pillow between your lower legs can ease pain so you can sleep.

- Weight loss is important to prevent future problems.

- Return to work or your usual daily activities within a few days, with lighter duties or limited hours. This prevents your back from becoming weak and stiff.

- Avoid lifting heavy objects and repeated bending and twisting. Change positions often during the day and use a chair with good lower back support.

- Learn to accept and deal with everyday stress. This can help your recovery from back pain. If you have particular stress in your life, discuss it with your doctor.

Treatment

- Muscle relaxers can be used during the first few days to ease muscle spasms, but they often cause drowsiness.

- Physical therapy may be prescribed by your doctor if you have severe incapacitating pain for more than 1 week, no improvement after 2 weeks of home therapy, or you are unable to return to work (limited activity) within 1 week.

- Surgery is rarely needed for back pain or sciatica. It is considered only after months of treatment.

What to do about Back Pain

Symptom/Sign	Action
Pain from tension, posture, or exercise	Self-care
Usual back or neck soreness	Self-care
No improvement in pain after 2 to 3 days of self-care	Call doctor
Back pain and temperature over 100°F for more than 48 hours	Call doctor
Back pain and nausea, vomiting, or diarrhea	Call doctor
Back pain and painful or frequent urination, menstrual bleeding, or stomachache	Call doctor
Pain traveling down leg or arm; paralysis or numbness of a lower limb	See doctor
Loss of bowel or bladder control	Go to hospital
Paralysis, confusion, inability to support body weight, or shock (see Shock, p. 55)	Call 911

Prevention

- Good posture is important for keeping the spine healthy. Stand straight. Keeping your body aligned takes stress off your back muscles (see illustration, p. 238).

- Avoid lifting heavy objects. When you do lift, bend your knees and keep your back straight (see illustration, p. 239).

- When working while seated, choose a chair that has good support for your lower back.

- Maintain a healthy weight. If you are overweight, you will put more stress on your lower back.

- Try not to reach for objects that are above your head. Use a step stool or a device that helps you reach objects on higher shelves. Store items that you use often on lower shelves.

- Avoid repeated bending or twisting.

Exercise

To help in your recovery and prevent further back problems, it is important to keep yourself in the best physical condition you can and to keep your back, abdominal muscles, and legs strong. You should plan regular daily walking as soon as you can. Adding other activities to your routine, such as swimming and biking, can also be good for the low back.

The exercises shown on p. 240 should be started at home or with the help of a physical therapist and should be started as soon as they can be performed comfortably. Don't do any exercises that make the pain significantly worse.

GOOD POSTURE
Good posture is important for keeping the spine healthy.

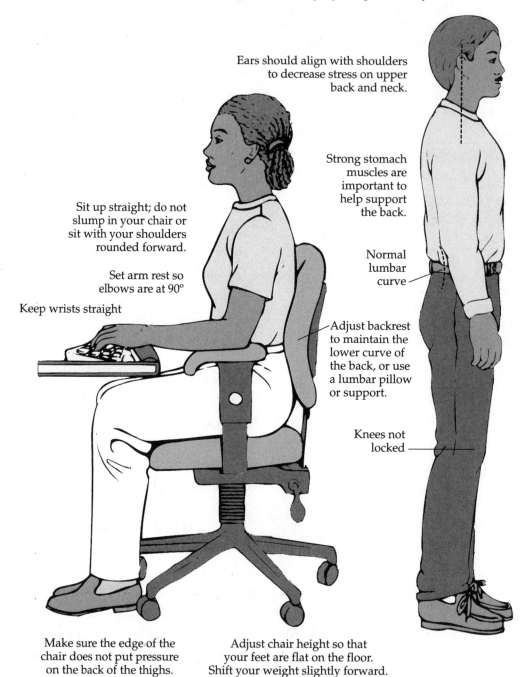

Ears should align with shoulders to decrease stress on upper back and neck.

Strong stomach muscles are important to help support the back.

Sit up straight; do not slump in your chair or sit with your shoulders rounded forward.

Normal lumbar curve

Set arm rest so elbows are at 90°

Keep wrists straight

Adjust backrest to maintain the lower curve of the back, or use a lumbar pillow or support.

Knees not locked

Make sure the edge of the chair does not put pressure on the back of the thighs.

Adjust chair height so that your feet are flat on the floor. Shift your weight slightly forward.

LIFTING SAFELY

Bend your knees with your feet shoulder width apart for balance and stability.

Tighten your stomach muscles before you start the lift. Use your leg muscles.

Keep a slight arch in your lower back. Stand up straight as you lift.

Before you lift, test the load. Ask yourself, "Is the path clear? Can I lift this alone?" Get help if the load is too heavy for you to lift. If you determine you can lift the load, follow the steps shown above.

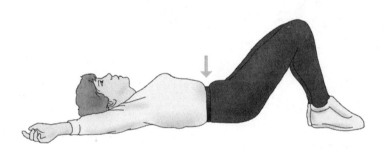

Pelvic tilt.

Pelvic Tilt. Lie flat on your back or stand with your back to a wall, knees bent, feet flat on the floor, body relaxed. Tighten abdominal muscles and tilt pelvis so that the curve of the small of the back is flat against the floor or wall. Hold 10 seconds and then relax (see illustration above).

239

Knee Raise. Lie flat on your back, knees bent, and bring one knee slowly to your chest as shown (see illustration below). Hug knee gently, then lower your bent leg. Do not straighten your legs. Repeat exercise with other leg.

Partial Press-up. First, lie face down on a soft, firm surface with your arms and head positioned as shown (see illustration below). Rest for a few minutes, relaxing completely. Second, staying in the same basic position, raise your upper body enough to lean on your elbows. Let your lower back and your legs relax as much as you can. Hold this position for 30 seconds at first, gradually working up to 5 minutes, or do slow press-ups holding for 5 seconds and repeating five or six times, whichever is most comfortable.

Knee raise.

Partial press-up. Hold this position for 30 to 60 seconds at first.

Body Aches

Some of the aches and pains you may feel throughout your body are reactions by your muscles, joints, or bones to overdoing it in work or exercise. Some come with age, and some are symptoms of injury or illness.

Arthritis

The word *arthritis* is used to describe more than 100 different conditions that cause pain, stiffness, and swelling in the joints. There are two main types of arthritis: inflammatory and noninflammatory. Each has features that set it apart from other types of joint pain. There are many types of inflammatory arthritis, including rheumatoid arthritis, gout, and arthritis caused by infections. The most common type of noninflammatory arthritis is osteoarthritis.

Causes

Osteoarthritis can be caused by various factors, including wear and tear that occurs with time. As the body ages, joints become worn down from years of movement. Osteoarthritis is very common in older adults. Rheumatoid arthritis is caused by a breakdown in the body's immune system. It is not known why this occurs.

Symptoms

The start of inflammatory arthritis varies from person to person. For some people, the pain can be sudden and intense. For others, the pain is gradual. Symptoms of inflammatory arthritis include swelling, redness, warmth, tenderness, loss of motion or function of the joint, and joint damage.

Osteoarthritis starts slowly, usually over many months or years. Symptoms may include minor swelling and changes in the joint cartilage, which can lead to joint damage, pain, and loss of function. The joints most affected are the knee, hip, and hand.

Treatment

Your doctor may prescribe medicines to help treat your arthritis. Over-the-counter medicines are often the first treatment choice for arthritic pain. Two main types of medicines are used: simple pain relievers and nonsteroidal anti-inflammatory medicines (NSAIDs). These medications reduce swelling and pain (see Medications on p. 396).

Let your doctor know about any over-the-counter products you are taking in addition to what he or she has prescribed.

Self-Care

- Over-the-counter products may be helpful. Glucosamine sulfate and chondroitin sulfate have been used to treat osteoarthritis. They may lessen pain caused by osteoarthritis of the knee and hip and are considered safe.

- Assistive devices may support painful areas or improve function in affected joints. The range of options is broad. Wrist splints, tennis elbow straps, padded arch supports, and heel pads may help reduce stress on joints and relieve some pain.

- Move your joints. Exercise reduces pain, makes you more flexible, energizes you, and increases your overall good health. The type and amount of exercise depends on which joints are involved and the degree of joint inflammation. It should be tailored to your needs. Ask your doctor about good exercises for you.

- Find ways to deal with stress such as meditation, listening to music, biofeedback, or professional counseling. Exercise is also an excellent stress reliever.

- If you still have pain after taking medication, try taking a warm shower, doing some gentle stretching exercises, using an ice pack on the sore area, or just resting the sore joint.

- Lose weight if you are overweight. Excess weight can cause pain in your knees and hips.

Prevention

The cause of rheumatoid arthritis is unknown but probably occurs for many reasons, including genetic, environmental, and hormonal factors.

There are many causes of osteoarthritis, including natural wear and tear on your body. Taking care of your body—watching your weight, participating in aerobic exercise, and avoiding repetitive stress or trauma on your joints—can delay the onset of osteoarthritis. Losing even a small amount of weight helps reduce stress on your weight-bearing joints.

Fibromyalgia

Fibromyalgia is pain in joints, ligaments, tendons, and muscles. Common areas of pain include the neck, elbows, knees, and hips. The cause of fibromyalgia is not known.

Symptoms

Pain is the main symptom of fibromyalgia. The pain can be constant, or it may seem to move around the body. Stress, activity, or even weather can make the pain worse. Fatigue, insomnia, and depression often are symptoms of fibromyalgia.

Other symptoms include:

- Numbness in parts of the body
- Sensitivity to odors, light, and noise

- Difficulty focusing
- Diarrhea, constipation, heartburn, gas, and abdominal cramps

Treatment

Your doctor may prescribe medication to reduce pain or to help you sleep.

Self-Care

- Exercise in ways that don't put stress on your joints, such as swimming or using an exercise bike.
- Reduce stress.
- Avoid alcohol and caffeine, especially close to when you go to bed.
- Take small doses of pain-reducing medication (see Medications, p. 396), such as acetaminophen (Tylenol).

Joint Pain

Joint pain, or rheumatic pain, is one of the most common reasons that people see their doctors.

Causes

Not all joint pain is caused by arthritis. Often joint or muscle pain is caused by problems with the structure around the joint, such as a tendon, bursa, ligament, or muscle.

Symptoms

Joint pain caused by arthritis usually has swelling and fluid buildup and a change in the appearance of the joint. Symptoms of joint pain not caused by arthritis include the following:

- Usually there is no swelling or joint damage.
- Joint can be moved without a lot of difficulty.
- Pain often follows activity.

Self-Care

Self-care for joint pain and osteoarthritis are similar. Over-the-counter pain medication (see Medications, p. 396), assistive devices, and movement can help ease pain (see Self-care for osteoarthritis, p. 241).

Muscle Cramps

Both activity and inactivity can lead to cramps and spasms. Muscles that have been overused may cramp. Sitting in the same position too long also may lead to cramps.

Self-Care

- Stretch out the cramped muscle. For a leg cramp, sit with your leg flat on the floor and pull your toes toward you. Walk off a foot cramp.

• Gently massage the cramp.

Muscle Imbalance

When muscles on one side of the body are much stronger than those on the other side, they can put added stress on weaker muscles and surrounding joints, often causing injury.

Self-Care

If you regularly exert the muscles on one side of your body as you work or exercise, make sure you exercise the opposing muscles in some way to keep your body balanced. Someone who lifts heavy objects all day may overdevelop the chest and arm muscles, putting strain on muscles in the back and shoulders. Workouts with weights or in a gym to strengthen the back and shoulders can help restore a good balance.

Muscle Tightness

Any time you tighten a muscle repeatedly or hold it in one position for a long time, it can become tight. Often the stiffness and pain of the tight muscle isn't felt until the next day.

The muscle that runs along the outside of the upper leg and helps the leg move to the side is a common site for muscle tightness. Other muscles, including those in the buttocks and in the inside, front, and back of the thigh, can also become tight.

Self-Care

• Take a warm bath.
• Stretch before and after an activity.

Referred Pain

Sometimes pain is felt in one part of the body, but the condition causing the pain is in a different area. Pain in the left shoulder or arm can be a sign of a heart attack. Knee pain can be caused by a hip or foot problem.

Self-Care

When there is sudden pain with no apparent cause, such as an accident or overuse, call your doctor.

Repetitive Motion Injuries

Repeating a particular motion constantly, whether it's using a computer mouse or throwing a baseball in practice, can cause damage to tendons, muscles, and joints. The injury can be a combination of an inflammation in a joint or tendon and damage to body tissues.

Self-Care

- Limit or stop the motion.
- Alternate application of heat and cold on the affected area.
- Take pain medication (see Medications, p. 396).
- Get physical therapy and exercise.
- Sit, stand, or move in ways that don't cause stress on affected joints and tendons.

What to do about Body Aches

Symptom/Sign	Action
Muscle or joint aches after exertion	Self-care
Joint pain without fever or swelling	Self-care
Joint pain with fever and sudden, significant swelling or severe pain	Call doctor
Sudden pain with no apparent cause	Call doctor
Constant pain that affects your activities	See doctor
Pain with fatigue, insomnia	See doctor

Elbow Pain

There are three bones that meet at the elbow: the humerus in the upper arm and the ulna and radius in the lower arm (see illustration).

Causes

Pain in the elbow can occur from overuse, a fall or blow to the joint, or a force that causes the elbow to bend backward.

Tendinitis in the elbow can be called many names—*tennis elbow, pitcher's elbow, golfer's elbow*. It's caused by repeated motions of the arm during work or sports. The pain of tendinitis usually is concentrated at the inside or outside of the elbow and may spread up or down the arm, depending on which tendon is inflamed. Often the pain occurs only with certain movements, such as lifting objects in certain ways, rotating your hand, or clenching or squeezing something in your fist.

Bursitis is the inflammation of a bursa, a soft, fluid-filled lump at the point of the elbow. Bursitis can be quite painful, especially at the tip of the elbow. Acute bursitis, if not treated, can lead to

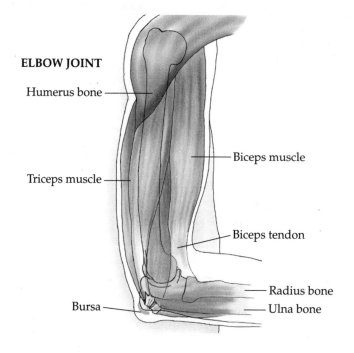

ELBOW JOINT

Humerus bone

Biceps muscle

Triceps muscle

Biceps tendon

Radius bone

Bursa

Ulna bone

chronic bursitis and small, painful lumps at the point of the elbow.

Hyperextended elbow occurs when the elbow is forced backward. It can happen in a fall or when a backhand tennis swing or similar movement goes wrong. The result is pain and swelling in the joint and in the soft tissue at the front of the elbow. A splint or sling may be needed to support the elbow until the pain stops.

Self-Care

- Use the RICE method (see p. 267) and pain medication (see Medications, p. 396) to control pain and swelling.

- Rest from the activities that caused the pain.

- Gentle stretching and strengthening exercises can help in recovery and in preventing future injury. Ask your doctor to recommend specific exercises for you.

What to do about Elbow Pain

Symptom/Sign	Action
Pain in elbow, limited to certain movements of the elbow and hand, especially after overuse	Self-care
Swelling on inner side of elbow	Self-care Call doctor
Pain, swelling, or soft lump on tip of elbow without fever, redness, or pain	Self-care Call doctor
Bruise from a fall or blow	Self-care Call doctor
Numbness or tingling in fourth and fifth fingers	See doctor
Loss of strength in hand or arm	See doctor
Elbow can't be bent or straightened	See doctor
Joint or bursa is red, swollen, or hot; fever present	See doctor
Elbow deformity after a fall	Go to hospital
Severe pain in upper arm (biceps) after sudden or violent motion	Go to hospital

Foot Pain

The foot is one of the most complex parts of the body; so complex, in fact, that a medical and surgical specialty—podiatry—is devoted solely to treating and studying foot problems.

Causes

The main source of most foot pain involves improper foot function or biomechanics. Shoes rarely cause foot deformities but may irritate them.

Flat Feet or High Arches

Flat feet or high arches can contribute to painful problems in the feet, knees, and even hips. When the arch is too high or low, other structures in the foot and leg have to work longer and harder than intended. The added stress, weight, and poor motion can cause fatigue, pain, and inflammation. Arch supports (orthotics) and exercises to stretch and strengthen the arch and lower leg help relieve many problems related to weak arches. Fortunately, many people who have flat feet or high arches never have any problems.

Plantar fasciitis is a common source of pain in the heel and arch of the foot. It involves the heel bone and the plantar fascia, a strong band of connective tissue at the bottom of the foot that runs from the heel to the base of the toes. This band of tissue helps maintain or hold the arch together and serves as a shock absorber during activity. Overstretching of this band of tissue can result in strain and inflammation where it's attached to the heel bone.

Plantar fasciitis is marked by a dull ache in the arch or pain in the heel. The pain is worse when you wake or after resting. Walking may hurt at first, but once the plantar fascia is warmed up, the pain may decrease. Plantar fasciitis most often occurs when activity suddenly increases, or it results from wearing shoes with poor support. Switching from high heels or cowboy boots to flat shoes or athletic shoes can irritate the fascia, causing pain. Gaining 10 to 20 pounds can have the same effect. Working out or standing and walking on hard surfaces, such as concrete, or wearing shoes that do not have good arch support can also lead to the problem.

Self-care and rest sometimes relieves plantar fasciitis. If symptoms continue despite these measures or if pain is severe, see your doctor. Your doctor may recommend physical therapy or steroid injections. Surgery is a last resort and used only in severe and prolonged cases.

Stress Fractures

Stress fractures of the foot occur most often in the second metatarsal. The metatarsals are the long bones that connect the ankle bones to the toes. High-impact activities such as running, basketball, or aerobics pose particular risk for stress fractures of the foot. Postmenopausal women with lower bone density, women with absent or infrequent periods, or anyone on long-term steroid or hormone therapy may be more likely to have stress fractures.

Stress fractures most often appear several weeks into a new or more intense training schedule, after changing from running on a track to running on concrete or asphalt, or after landing wrong following a jump. At first, pain may be mild enough that it can be ignored. After time, however, the mild pain gives way to sudden, intense pain. Both the top and bottom of the foot may be tender to the touch.

Treating stress fractures in the foot mostly involves time—usually at least 1 month—to allow the bone to heal. With the exception of fractures in the fifth metatarsal, a cast is usually not needed. A wooden shoe or postoperative shoe is usually worn to allow the fracture to heal. A stress fracture in the fifth metatarsal can be serious because it often resists healing. Fractures may need a cast, and crutches may have to be used for 6 weeks to several months. In some cases, surgery may be needed.

Morton's Neuroma

Morton's neuroma is a noncancerous enlargement of one of the nerves running between the metatarsal bones (long bones of the foot). The enlargement occurs when the nerve is squeezed between the bones, sometimes from narrow, tight shoes or stress from repeated motions. Most often, neuromas develop between the metatarsal bones leading to the third and fourth toes (called the third intermetatarsal space). Occasionally they may develop between the second and third metatarsals.

Morton's neuroma causes local swelling and tenderness. A person with this condition may feel as though he or she is walking on a lump, especially when barefoot. Pain may spread to the toes or toward the heel. Pressure makes the pain worse and, if constant, may cause numbness, burning, and tingling in the toes, between the toes, or at the ball of the foot.

Bunion

A bunion is a swelling on the side of the foot. Usually bunions show the foot isn't working properly, often because of flat-footedness. Instability and muscle imbalance can also cause the big toe to slant in toward the other toes. The joint where the big toe connects to the foot (the end of the first metatarsal) then pokes out on the inner side of the foot. This is caused by poor alignment and is not a growth of bone. The bunion may also become inflamed and sore, especially if rubbed by a shoe. A similar problem, called a "tailor's bunion," may develop on the opposite side of the foot, where the little toe meets the fifth metatarsal. For bunions that cause persistent pain despite self-care, steroid injections or surgery may provide relief.

Hammertoe

Hammertoe is a deformity in which the toe buckles and bends, causing the middle joint of the affected toe to poke above the other toes. The deformity may also cause the toe to become bent at the middle joint, so it turns in toward the toe next to it. Tight shoes can rub and put pressure on the raised portion of the hammertoe, often causing a corn to form. Hammertoes may cause no problems at all, or they can be a source of pain, especially if the person wears tight or ill-fitting shoes. If self-care fails to relieve the symptoms, surgery may be needed to straighten the toe or to remove the bony protrusion.

Plantar Warts

Plantar warts, like warts in other areas of the body, are caused by a virus. The weight of the body on the foot causes plantar warts to grow inward. The result is a painful lump on the bottom of the foot that feels like you are walking on a pebble. Children and teens are more likely than adults to get plantar warts. Plantar warts are often difficult to treat, but a slow approach is best. If plantar warts interfere with walking, you should see your doctor or a podiatrist to have them removed (see Warts, p. 97).

Self-Care

How you care for foot pain depends on what is causing it.

For heel spurs and plantar fasciitis:

- Rest the foot, avoiding high-impact activities, such as running, for 3 to 6 weeks.

- Switch to low-impact activities, such as walking, biking, or swimming. Walking is particularly good.

- Apply ice to the heel two to three times daily.

- Support the arches of your feet to protect them from further stretching and tearing. Place arch supports even in your slippers and put them on first thing when getting out of bed.

- See your doctor if pain is not relieved with self-care within 3 to 6 weeks.

For stress fractures:

- See your doctor if pain continues or worsens.

- Avoid high-impact activities, such as running or playing basketball. Switch to weight-bearing, low-impact, or non-impact activities, such as walking or low-impact aerobics. Weight-bearing exercises strengthen bones and prevent bone loss. Resume your regular work-out or other activities slowly after pain eases and the fracture heals.

For Morton's neuroma:

- Avoid the original activity that caused the pain, and other high-impact activities, for 3 to 6 weeks. Resume the original activity only after pain is gone.

- Try wearing shoes with a wider toe box to prevent pressure on the nerve.

For hammertoe:

- Wear shoes with a toe box large enough to accommodate the hammertoe.

For bunions:

- Choose shoes with a larger toe box (squared or rounded toe).

- Put a piece of foam or cotton between the affected toes to see if it eases the pressure.

- Place padding around the bunion to relieve pressure and rubbing from shoes. Moleskin and bunion pads are available at most drugstores.

- Try using an arch support to stop the jamming of the long bone and the big toe.

- See your doctor if pain interferes with walking, or is not relieved with self-care.

For plantar warts:

- Soak foot for 10 minutes in a solution of 2 tablespoons mild household detergent (such as dish soap) and half a gallon warm water. Cut a piece of 40-percent salicylic acid plaster (available at drugstores) the size of the wart and apply it to the wart. Cover with tape or a bandage. Remove the plaster in 2 days. Brush the wart with a toothbrush soaked in soap and water. Repeat this procedure for 2 weeks until the wart is gone.

- If warts remain despite self-care or if they interfere with walking, see your doctor.

- Do not try to cut out warts.

What to do about Foot Pain

Symptom/Sign	Action
Foot pain from overuse or injury; can bear weight	Self-care
Corns, plantar warts, bunions, or hammertoes	See doctor
Unable to move foot or bear weight after a trauma, such as a blow or fall	See doctor
Pain in heel or arch, especially upon awakening; tender points on bottom of foot between heel and ball	See doctor
Symptoms of Morton's neuroma: pain, burning, tingling, or numbness in the toes, between the toes, or at the ball of the foot; swelling at the top of the foot; symptoms get worse with pressure	See doctor
Suspected stress fracture	See doctor
Foot pain in patient with diabetes or vascular disease	See doctor

Prevention

- Have your feet measured when you buy shoes. Your feet can change size.

- Don't wear shoes that pinch your feet or toes. Don't wear shoes that are too big. Your feet should not slide around in them. Loose shoes can rub and cause blisters and other problems.

- Look for shoes that have a low heel. Heels between $\frac{1}{2}$ and $1\frac{1}{2}$ inches are the best height. Higher heels can strain the feet and legs.

- If your shoes need extra support or cushioning, buy arch supports or cushioning for soles.

- Break in new shoes. For the first few days, wear new shoes for 1 to 2 hours at a time.

- Do not walk around barefoot. Wear shoes around the house and yard to prevent injury. Even at the beach, wear sandals, thongs, or "beach socks." Broken glass, shells, hot sand, and other objects can injure your feet.

Hip and Thigh Pain

The hip is a ball-and-socket joint, surrounded by large muscles and a deep socket. The joint itself is very stable.

Causes

Most often, pain in the hip and thigh is from injury to muscles, tendons, or bursas, usually from a fall, a blow, or overuse.

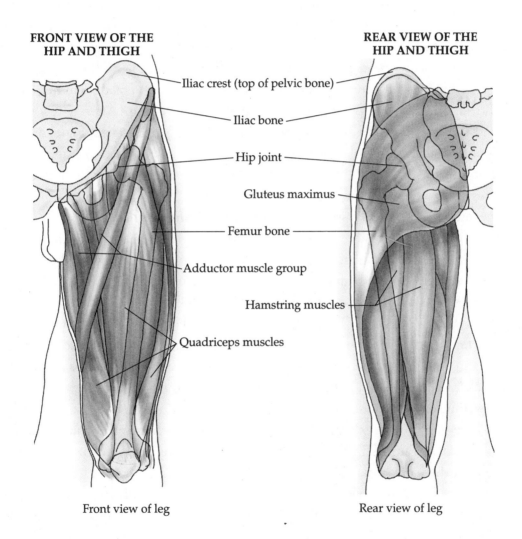

FRONT VIEW OF THE HIP AND THIGH

REAR VIEW OF THE HIP AND THIGH

Iliac crest (top of pelvic bone)

Iliac bone

Hip joint

Gluteus maximus

Femur bone

Adductor muscle group

Hamstring muscles

Quadriceps muscles

Front view of leg

Rear view of leg

Groin Pull

A groin pull can be caused by a quick change in direction while you're moving—often occurring in sports such as hockey, tennis, and basketball. A groin pull can result in pain, tenderness, and stiffness deep in the groin, making activity difficult.

Pulled Hamstring

A pulled hamstring is an injury to the group of muscles at the back of the thigh that attach at the pelvis and just behind the knee. Pulls or tears can occur from a sudden forceful move, such as sprinting to steal a base. Hamstring injuries most often occur in the center of the muscle, but the hamstring also can tear from the pelvic bone, just under the buttocks. Hamstring pulls and tears cause pain, limited motion, and sometimes bruising or a lot of swelling.

Bursitis

Bursitis in the hip usually involves the hip socket and causes tenderness, pain, and swelling on the outer part of the hip where some of the large buttock muscles attach. Bursitis in the hip can cause pain that spreads to the buttocks and down as far as the knee. Bursitis in the hip can be caused by activities such as speed-walking, aerobic dance, or carrying a baby on your hip. It also can be caused by conditions that alter the normal tilt of the pelvis, such as having one leg shorter than the other.

Charley Horse

Charley horse is a painful muscle injury caused by bruising of the thigh. The typical cramping of a charley horse can be accompanied by pain, swelling, stiffness, and skin discoloration. Use the RICE method (see p. 267) right after any significant blow to the thigh. Continue icing for several days to help with pain and swelling. After a few days, start doing gentle stretching exercises. Heat may help, but don't apply heat until at least 3 days after the injury.

Piriformis Syndrome

Piriformis syndrome is an irritation of the piriformis muscle, one of the smaller muscles lying under the large muscles of the buttocks. Irritation can occur if you sit or stand for long periods or repeat certain motions. When the piriformis muscle tightens and spasms, pressure may be placed on the sciatic nerve that serves the leg. The irritation, called *piriformis syndrome*, can cause pain, numbness, and tingling from the buttocks down the back of the leg to the foot.

The symptoms of this condition are often confused with those of disc disease in the spine. One way to tell if the problem is piriformis syndrome is to lie on your stomach with your knees together and bent, so your feet are in the air. Gently let your feet spread apart sideways. If you feel a pain in your buttocks as your feet move apart, your problem is probably piriformis syndrome.

Self-Care

For groin or hamstring pulls or tears:

- Use the RICE method (see p. 267) and pain medications (see p. 396).

- Depending on the damage to the muscle tissue, you may need crutches for a few days.

For bursitis:

- Use the RICE method (see p. 267) and pain medications (see p. 396).

- Avoid the activity that started the inflammation.

For a charley horse:

- Apply ice to the whole muscle, or as much of it as you can, right after the injury.

- Rest the area. Don't try to move it in spite of the pain.

- Use the RICE method (see p. 267) and use pain medications (see p. 396).

- See a doctor if not better in 7 to 10 days.

For piriformis syndrome:

- While sitting, cross left leg so ankle rests on top of right knee. Gently press on inside of left knee until stretch is felt deep in hip. Intensify stretch by leaning forward. Switch legs.

Special Concerns for Children

Children can have the same hip and thigh problems as adults, but there are several problems unique to children that can affect the bones of the hip and thighs. Because children are still growing, these problems require medical attention to prevent long-term problems.

Piriformis stretch.

Legg-Calvé-Perthes Disease

Legg-Calvé-Perthes disease is a breakdown of the ball of the femur, which is the long thigh bone that fits in the hip joint. Loss of blood supply to the hip causes part of the top of the bone to die and deteriorate.

Symptoms can include limping, pain in the groin area or inner thigh, and knee pain. Rest usually relieves the pain; activity makes it worse. The hip may be stiff, and the thigh may be weak.

Unless the hip is inflamed or the doctor recommends traction, a child with Legg-Calvé-Perthes disease can play normally. The deterioration caused by the disease usually heals completely and does not recur. In some cases a child with Legg-Calvé-Perthes disease may need to wear a cast or brace or require rest, traction, or even surgery to make sure the new bone on the femoral head grows properly.

Slipped Capital Femoral Epiphysis

In slipped capital femoral epiphysis, the femoral head slips out of place. This condition usually occurs in children between the ages of 9 and 12, when puberty begins. The slip can happen over several months or suddenly, following a fall or other injury to the hip. Symptoms can include limping, pain in the groin area or inner thigh, and knee pain. Rest usually relieves the pain; activity makes it worse. The hip may be stiff, and the thigh may be weak.

Treatment for slipped capital femoral epiphysis is surgery. It is usually very effective, but is needed right away. Left untreated, the condition can lead to arthritis in early adulthood.

Synovitis

Synovitis is the inflammation of any joint. The cause is unknown. In children, synovitis of the hip happens most often between the ages of 2 and 5. Children usually wake up with a limp, with or without pain. Your doctor may recommend that the child rest in bed. Symptoms usually last 3 to 14 days. You need to watch your child's temperature. If a fever develops, your child needs to see a doctor.

What to do about Hip and Thigh Pain

Symptom/Sign	Action
Overuse or injury pain that lasts less than 7 days	Self-care
Pulled or torn muscle causing tenderness to the touch, stiffness, pain, or difficulty walking, running, or climbing stairs	Call doctor
Pain on outside of hip, possibly down to the knee	Call doctor
Swelling, pain, or stiffness after a blow to the thigh	See doctor
Any of the above symptoms that do not improve within 7 to 10 days	See doctor
Dull pain in hip and groin while walking or climbing stairs	See doctor
Severe pain in buttocks with exercise; pain stops when activity stops	See doctor
Pain interrupts sleep	See doctor
Severe pain after a fall or blow	Go to hospital
Severe blow or injury to hip or thigh; unable to move or bear weight; visible deformity	Call 911

Knee Pain

The knees are regularly under stress, not only from high-impact sports but also from everyday activities such as squatting, stooping, kneeling, and climbing stairs. The knees get bent, twisted, and occasionally banged into during sports.

Causes

Most knee injuries involve a blow, a sudden twist, or a hard landing after a jump. A single strong blow in just the right place can tear cartilage and sprain several ligaments.

Sprains

Sprains are the result of a blow or sudden twist of the knee. A sprain of the ligaments of the knee causes swelling (usually within an hour), pain, and difficulty walking. The sprained side of the knee may be tender to the touch. Even mild knee sprains often take 2 to 3 weeks to fully heal. A strong blow to the inner or outer side of the knee will sprain the ligament on the opposite side as the knee is forced to bend sideways. If you feel pain on the side where the blow occurred, it's probably a bruise and not a sprain.

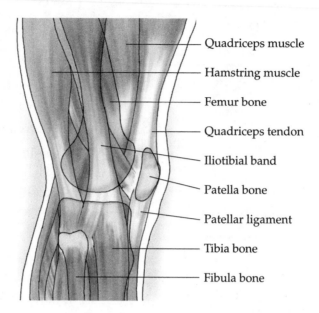

Quadriceps muscle

Hamstring muscle

Femur bone

Quadriceps tendon

Iliotibial band

Patella bone

Patellar ligament

Tibia bone

Fibula bone

Knee joint: three-quarter view of front right knee.

ACL Injuries, Torn Cartilage (Menisci), and the "Terrible Triad"

ACL injuries, torn cartilage (menisci), and the "terrible triad" are the result of damage to the ligaments or menisci (two disks of cartilage that attach to the cartilage of the knee and fit into the joint to absorb shock). The anterior cruciate ligament (ACL) can be stretched or torn. ACL injuries are common in contact sports or skiing or as the result of a twist or fall. You may hear or feel a loud pop when the injury occurs. ACL injuries often bring sudden pain, knee instability, rapid swelling, and limited movement. But in some cases, symptoms can take as long as 6 to 12 hours to occur.

The same kind of traumas that cause sprains also can tear the menisci. Repeated squatting or kneeling also can weaken menisci, increasing the risk of injury. Swelling may happen immediately or appear within 24 hours. Continuing pain and a clicking or locking with knee movement are other symptoms of torn menisci. Once the menisci are torn, the knee may buckle or lock without warning. Wearing a brace during activity can help protect the knee from further injury, but surgery may be needed to remove pieces of torn menisci.

The terrible triad is a combination of torn menisci, ACL injury, and a sprained ligament at the inner side of the knee—all from a single blow. Damage this serious usually requires surgery.

Joint Mice

Joint mice are loose bodies—often pieces of torn cartilage or bone chips—floating within the knee. A strong blow to the knee can cause a small portion of bone surface to die. Pieces of dead bone then fall away from the main bone to become "joint mice." Symptoms often take as long as a year to appear after a trauma. When the pieces of bone get trapped between moving bone, they cause sudden pain and even cause the knee to lock or buckle.

Runner's Knee

Runner's knee, also called *patellofemoral pain syndrome* or *anterior knee pain*, is the most common cause of knee pain and the most common overuse injury in the knee. Runner's knee can occur from repeated direct blows to the front of the knee or for no apparent reason. It can be brought on by a number of activities that place stress on the knee—or even by wearing shoes that don't support the foot adequately during sports. It can also develop because the kneecap doesn't fit correctly in its groove at the end of the femur. The area around the kneecap or at the back of the knee may ache or swell, especially during and after activity. Squatting or sitting with the knees bent for a long time can be painful. You may feel grinding or popping when you bend or straighten the knee. Strengthening exercises can help correct runner's knee and prevent it in the future.

Jumper's Knee

Jumper's knee, or *patellar tendinitis*, is an inflammation of the quadriceps tendon at the top of the kneecap, or of the patellar tendon at the bottom of the kneecap. Jumping or a direct blow to the knee are the common causes of inflammation and tearing of these tendons.

Housemaid's Knee/Bursitis

Housemaid's or milkmaid's knee, or *prepatellar bursitis*, is a condition common to people who work on their knees a great deal, such as carpet layers, roofers, gardeners, and people who install flooring. Symptoms include a squishy, swollen area in front of the kneecap, pain, and stiffness. In more severe cases, swelling may extend above and to the sides of the kneecap. An inflamed bursa (one of the fluid-filled sacs that cushions movement within a joint) may break internally on its own. If this happens, the body absorbs the excess fluid and the swelling and inflammation usually stop. The best prevention for housemaid's knee is wearing knee pads whenever working on your knees for a long period.

Iliotibial Band Syndrome

Iliotibial band syndrome is pain experienced during activity, such as running or an exercise routine. The iliotibial band is made up of a muscle that begins at the top rim of the pelvis and a tendon that fits into the outside of the knee. Exercise can cause the band to tighten or partially tear. The pain usually begins 10 to 20 minutes into a run or other exercise routine and stops when the activity stops. Iliotibial band syndrome often grows worse, with pain increasing and starting sooner during a workout.

Self-Care

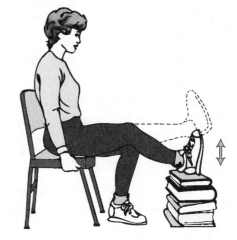

Leg extension – Rest foot on stool or pile of books with knee bent at 60-degree angle. Straighten leg; hold for a count of 6, return to rest. Repeat 8-10 times.

For mild sprains:

- Follow the RICE method (see p. 267), and take medication (see p. 396) for pain and swelling.

- Rest the knee as long as it aches.

- After the first 3 days, soak the knee in a warm whirlpool or bath.

- Use crutches if needed.

- When the pain is better, use gentle stretching exercise to strengthen the muscles around the knee. Leg extensions (see illustration) are a good strengthening exercise.

- See your doctor if symptoms don't improve in 3 to 4 days.

For severe sprains, ACL injury, and cartilage tears:

- Follow the RICE method (see p. 267), and take medication (see p. 396) for pain and swelling.

For runner's knee, tendinitis, bursitis, and joint mice:

- Follow the RICE method (see p. 267), and take medication (see p. 396) for pain and swelling.

- Check your shoes to make sure they provide proper support and wear evenly.

- When the pain is better, use gentle stretching exercise (see illustration) to strengthen the muscles around the knee.

- If swelling from bursitis lasts for more than 10 days or is very bad, a doctor may drain the fluid with a needle and then inject the bursa with cortisone.

Iliotibial band stretch – Stand and cross your right leg in front of left leg; shift weight onto left leg. Push left hip out to the side, leaning torso to the right, for a slow, controlled stretch. Hold for 5 counts, repeat 3 to 5 times on one side and then switch to your other side. Do not bounce.

For iliotibial band syndrome:

• Stretch the iliotibial band, holding the stretch for 20 to 30 seconds and repeating three to six times (see illustration). Do this three to five times a day, until you no longer feel pain when you run. To prevent it from happening again, do this stretch before and after each run.

• If symptoms aren't better in 10 to 14 days after you have begun stretching, see your doctor.

What to do about Knee Pain

Symptom/Sign	Action
Pain after sudden twist or blow to side of knee; swelling; can bear weight but may limp	Self-care
Tendon below kneecap inflamed; pain climbing stairs or jumping	Call doctor
Soft, squishy swelling beginning in front of knee; pain; stiffness	Call doctor
Pain around or under kneecap; pain increases when climbing stairs or sitting for long periods	See doctor
Bursitis symptoms do not improve within 7 to 10 days or signs of infection appear (local heat, redness, increased swelling, pain, and tenderness)	See doctor
Pain after sudden twist or blow to side of knee; swelling; cannot bear weight	Go to hospital
Pain after sudden twist or blow to side of knee; rapid swelling; limited movement	Go to hospital
Severe blow or injury to knee; severe swelling; unable to move knee; visible deformity of knee	Call 911

Lower-Leg Pain

The lower leg is made up of two bones, the tibia and the fibula.

Causes

Pain in the lower leg can be caused by overuse, overexertion, or trauma from a fall or blow. The lower leg also can be affected by heart and circulatory diseases, such as congestive heart failure, or blood clots and inflammation in the veins of the legs.

Phlebitis

Phlebitis is the inflammation of a vein, sometimes accompanied by a blood clot. The inflammation can cause aching, swelling, and redness in the lower portion of one leg. A blood clot in one of the veins of the leg can further increase swelling by blocking the flow of blood back to the heart. Phlebitis requires immediate medical attention to keep a potential clot from moving into the heart or lungs.

Narrowing of the Arteries

Narrowing of the arteries occurs when plaque builds up on the arteries in the leg. That creates an obstruction of blood flow into the leg and keeps the lower leg muscles from getting enough oxygen. The condition, called *intermit-*

tent claudication, usually occurs in older adults and heavy smokers. Activity may cause pain, because the working muscles fail to get the oxygen they need. The pain is relieved shortly after exercise or activity is stopped. If you have symptoms of intermittent claudication, see your doctor.

Shin Splint

A *shin splint* is an overuse injury that causes inflammation of the shin muscles. Shin splints are a common injury among runners and other athletes, store clerks, warehouse and factory workers, and others who are on their feet all day on hard concrete floors.

The most common causes of shin splints include:

- Muscle imbalance (the calf muscle is stronger than the shin muscles)
- A tight Achilles tendon (the tendon at the back of the heel and ankle)
- Not enough shock absorption during high-impact exercise
- Running on the balls of the feet, without allowing the heel to touch the ground
- Doing too much activity too fast

Symptoms include aching at the front or inner side of the lower leg. Generally there is no swelling, redness, or bruising. The pain may begin suddenly or build slowly.

Compartment Syndrome

Compartment syndrome is a dangerous condition that can occur after a strong blow to the leg. Sometimes, besides a painful bruise, there can be internal bleeding that causes swelling, putting pressure on the nerves and blood vessels to the muscles of the calf. Symptoms of compartment syndrome may begin with mild pain and swelling that can build to a loss of color, feeling, and pulse; severe pain; paralysis; and swelling so bad that the skin in the area of the bruise turns shiny. If the more serious symptoms appear, prompt treatment is crucial to prevent or lessen permanent nerve damage. If not treated immediately with surgery to relieve pressure, the swelling of compartment syndrome can permanently damage the nerves and muscles of the leg. When this happens, the person is left with weak or functionless muscles and a condition known as "drop foot." The person loses the ability to lift the foot, which seriously affects walking.

Stress Fracture

Stress fractures can result from repetitive or sudden movement and overuse of the lower leg. They are a common result of high-impact activities. Stress fractures are hard to detect on x-rays until 10 to 14 days after the fracture begins. You may notice a sudden spreading pain in your shin during or after exercise. In most cases, people with stress fractures can pinpoint exactly where the pain is coming from by pressing on the spot.

Depending on the bone, some stress fractures should be checked with x-rays until fully healed, usually about 6 weeks. During this time, rest the leg by avoiding high-impact activities. Generally, low-impact activities, such as walking, bicycling, or swimming, are safe to do while a stress fracture heals.

Self-Care

- For most lower-leg pain, use the RICE method (see p. 267) and pain medications (see p. 396).

- For chronic swelling in both legs without pain, try raising your legs. Call the doctor and ask if you need to be seen.

- For shin splints, rest the leg for 3 to 6 days, then do only low-impact activities (bicycling, walking, swimming) to keep up strength and prevent recurrence. When the aching has gotten better, you can return slowly to your usual activities.

- Wrap the ankle and shin with elastic wrap for support.

- Achilles tendon stretches and exercises (see illustration on p. 264) can be helpful to strengthen the front of the leg.

- An ice massage four times a day can help. Freeze water in a paper cup, tear away the cup to expose the ice, and massage the ice over the painful area for 10 to 15 minutes.

• Wear shoes with good support and cushioning. Replace your athletic shoes regularly to make sure they are not overly worn.

Achilles tendon stretch.

What to do about Lower-Leg Pain

Symptom/Sign	Action
Pain from overuse or blow; can bear weight	Self-care
Chronic swelling without pain	Self-care
Blow to shin area, bruising, no swelling	Self-care
Pain along the front or inner edge of the shin bone	Self-care
Shin splint that doesn't get better within 2 to 3 weeks	Call doctor
Gradual increase in shin or ankle pain; pain increases during or after activity	Call doctor
Painful and sudden swelling and redness in only one leg	Go to hospital
Swelling and pain after a blow to the front of the leg	Go to hospital
Numbness or tingling in foot after a blow to the shin	Go to hospital

Osteoporosis

Osteoporosis means "porous bone." It means that your bones are thinner and weaker than they should be. Osteoporosis is the leading cause of fractures in older adults and is most common in people older than 70 and in women who have gone through menopause.

Causes

Bone loss is a normal part of the aging process, but some people lose more bone than others or lose bone at a faster rate. Recognizing the risk factors for osteoporosis is important because you may be able to prevent it from occurring or slow down the loss of bone.

Risk factors that cannot be changed:

- Being female
- Thin or small frame
- Over age 65
- Family history of fracture with minor trauma in parent or sibling

Risk factors that can be changed:

- Postmenopausal and not on estrogen replacement therapy
- Diet low in calcium and vitamin D
- Use of certain medications, such as corticosteroids or some anticonvulsants
- Inactivity
- Cigarette smoking
- Excessive use of alcohol

Symptoms

Bone begins to thin without symptoms. You may not know if you have osteoporosis until a fall or an accident causes the hip or another bone to fracture. Sometimes the signs of osteoporosis are seen in the back and spine. These symptoms include pain, loss of height, a stooped posture, and spinal deformities.

Osteoporosis can be diagnosed by having your bone mass measured. Bone mineral density (BMD) tests measure bone density mass in the spine, hip, or wrist. The most common test is called dual-energy x-ray absorptiometry (DXA or DEXA). It is safe and painless. In addition to diagnosing osteoporosis, a BMD test can:

- Detect low bone density before a fracture occurs
- Estimate your chances of bone fracture in the future
- Determine your rate of bone loss
- Monitor the effects of medication

In some cases a BMD test may not be necessary. For most women, BMD tests are not needed until after menopause. Insurance usually covers the cost. Talk to your health provider about whether the test is right for you.

Self-Care

There is no cure for osteoporosis, but you can learn to live with it and to strengthen your bones. Steps for living with osteoporosis include:

- Weight-bearing activities. Walking, jogging, or dancing puts healthy stress on bones, making them stronger. Activity also can help you be steadier on your feet by improving muscle strength, coordination, and balance.

- Healthy diet with adequate calcium and vitamin D. A balanced diet, based on the food pyramid (see page 405), provides a variety of foods that are important to your overall health. It is especially important to make sure you are getting adequate calcium and vitamin D, either from the food you eat or supplements. If you have been diagnosed with osteoporosis, you should have 1500 mg of calcium per day and 400 to 800 IU of vitamin D.

Recommended Daily Calcium Intakes for Males and Females

Birth–6 months	400 mg
6 months–1 year	600 mg
1–10 years	800–1200 mg
11–24 years	1200–1500 mg
25–50 years	1000 mg
51–70 years	1200 mg
71+ years	1500 mg

- Medication. Ask your doctor about medications that can slow bone loss or help new bone to form. There are several new medications for treating osteoporosis by reducing bone loss and increasing bone density.

Prevention

Starting early is a key to preventing osteoporosis. Bone thinning happens over time. It's best to start good habits long before you become concerned about osteoporosis with the aging process.

- Make sure there is calcium in your diet, or if you can't tolerate dairy products, take calcium supplements.

- Get enough vitamin D by spending time in natural sunlight and by eating foods rich in vitamin D. If you can't get enough in your diet, or if you can't get into the sun regularly, you may take vitamin D supplements of 400 to 800 IU, the amount found in most multivitamins.

- Exercise regularly, especially weight-bearing exercises such as walking, jogging, and aerobics.

- Stop smoking. Women who smoke have lower levels of estrogen, and that increases the loss of bone density.

- Control drinking. People who drink heavily tend to have more bone loss and more fractures.

The RICE Method: Rest, Ice, Compression, Elevation

The RICE method often helps with many types of joint and muscle injuries, easing pain and helping speed recovery. The RICE method is very helpful if you use it right away after an injury.

Rest. For most injuries, rest the area until the pain decreases. For simple sore muscles, however, gentle stretching reduces stiffness more quickly. Hold the stretch for 30 to 60 seconds, then rest and repeat 5 to 10 times. Do this several times a day.

Ice. Ice is the most effective treatment for reducing inflammation, pain, and swelling of injured muscles, joints, and connective tissues, such as tendons, ligaments, and bursas. The cold helps keep blood and fluid from building up in the injured area, reducing pain and swelling. Apply ice as soon as possible after injury, even if you are going straight to the doctor. To speed recovery and ease pain, raise the injured area and apply ice for 20 minutes (10 to 15 minutes in children) every 2 to 3 hours while awake. For best results, place crushed ice in a plastic bag and wrap with a moist towel. Use an elastic bandage to hold the pack in place. During the first 48 to 72 hours, or as long as there is any swelling, do not apply heat to an injury. Heat increases blood flow to the affected area, which makes swelling and pain worse.

Compress. Between icings, wrap the injured area with an elastic bandage to help control swelling and provide support. Begin wrapping at the farthest point away from the body and wrap toward the heart. For example, to wrap an ankle you would begin at the toes and wrap to the mid-calf area. Don't sleep with the wrap on, unless told to do so by a doctor. And don't wrap too tightly! If the wrap begins to cause pain or numbness or if toes become cool or white, remove the elastic bandage and wrap it more loosely.

Elevate. Raising the injured area above your heart allows gravity to help reduce swelling by draining excess fluid. At night, place a pillow under the area to support and raise it.

Shoulder Pain

The shoulder is one of the most vulnerable joints in your body because it can move in all directions. Most of the shoulder's support comes from the rotator cuff muscles.

Causes

Pain in the shoulder may be caused by overuse or be the result of a fall, a blow, or other injury.

Referred Pain

Referred pain is a pain felt in the shoulder that is actually a symptom of injury or illness somewhere else in your body. If you feel sudden pain in your left arm, tightness in your chest, shortness of breath, or pain in your jaw with no known cause, it could be a sign of a heart attack (see p. 43). Call 911 immediately.

Tendinitis

Tendinitis can be caused by doing the same motion repeatedly. Moving quickly and moving too much can inflame tendons, leading to tendinitis. Tendinitis causes pain, swelling, and stiffness. Pain from tendinitis may be constant, or you may feel pain only when you move a certain way.

Bursitis

Bursitis is caused by an inflamed bursa. *Bursas* are the small, fluid-filled sacs in and near the joints. They cushion and lubricate areas around both the joints and the tendons. Bursitis makes a soft, fluid-filled lump in the joint, which causes pain and swelling. A sudden increase in activity can cause bursitis. Acute bursitis often heals in 7 to 10 days with self-care. Call your doctor if you don't feel better in 10 days.

Trauma to the Shoulder

Trauma to the shoulder from a sudden twist, fall, or blow can lead to a sprain, shoulder dislocation, partial dislocation, or broken bone. With any of these, you may hear or feel popping, snapping, or tearing when the injury occurs. You may be unable to move your shoulder and the shoulder may be visibly deformed

A fall or blow to the shoulder also can cause a separation of the collarbone and the front of the shoulder, called an *acromioclavicular (AC) joint separation*. The joint can be bruised, or the ligaments may be stretched or torn. With this kind of injury, a painful lump may form at the end of the collarbone, on top of the shoulder, and you may have trouble raising your arm over your head.

Rotator Cuff Injury

Rotator cuff injury is damage to the tendons or other parts of the shoulder. These injuries can come from a fall or a blow to the shoulder. They are often caused by repetitive overhead motions, such as throwing a softball, painting a ceiling, or swimming. Symptoms of rotator cuff injury include shoulder pain at night and when you raise or lower your arm between waist and shoulder. If your tendons are compressed, pain may be worst when the arm is raised with the palm down. Your arm or fingers also may tingle or feel numb.

Self-Care

- Use the RICE method (see p. 267).
- Take a medication to reduce pain and inflammation (see Medications on p. 396).
- Be less active until you feel better.
- If there is no swelling, apply heat to the affected area before activity. Do not apply heat if there is swelling.
- Ice the painful area after activity.
- If your symptoms don't improve after 10 to 14 days, call your doctor.
- Follow any instructions for physical therapy.

What to do about Shoulder Pain

Symptom/Sign	Action
Shoulder pain after activity that is limited to only certain movements	Self-care
Overuse injury that doesn't improve after 7 to 8 days of self-care	Call doctor
Inability to raise your arm	See doctor
Trauma with a sudden pain, pop, snap, cracking sound, lump or deformity, or inability to move shoulder	Go to hospital
Sudden pain in right or left shoulder with no injury and you can move arm without making pain worse	Call 911

Wrist and Hand Pain

Together the wrist and hand are composed of 29 bones: 19 in the hand and fingers, 8 in the wrist, and 2 in the forearm. The wrist, hand, and fingers are capable of a great variety of movements. But the forearm muscles are actually responsible for most of the movement and strength of the hand and fingers.

Causes

Because the wrist and hand have little protection, their bones may be more likely to fracture than other bones in the body. Falls and blows are common causes of wrist and hand injuries. But, as with other joints, overuse and repeated motions can take their toll on the hand and wrist, causing a variety of conditions, such as tendinitis and carpal tunnel syndrome.

Navicular Fracture

A navicular fracture near the wrist (the *navicular* is a small wrist bone located at the base of the thumb) can cause long-term problems, is difficult to diagnose, and takes a long time to heal. Because the bone is so small and almost all its surface touches other bones, an improperly healed fracture can cause the navicular to rub and scrape in places it shouldn't. The result is pain and loss of range of motion in the wrist. If you fall

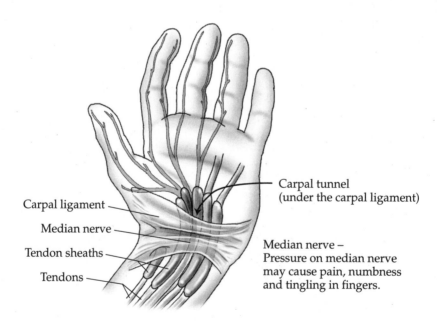

Carpal ligament

Median nerve

Tendon sheaths

Tendons

Carpal tunnel
(under the carpal ligament)

Median nerve –
Pressure on median nerve
may cause pain, numbness
and tingling in fingers.

Wrist and hand (left, palm up).

on your outstretched hand, bending your wrist back, and the pain does not get better within a day, you should see your doctor and have an x-ray. If the x-ray shows no sign of fracture but the pain is still present a week later, you will need another x-ray. Sometimes small fractures are easier to see by x-ray 7 to 10 days later.

Mallet Finger

Mallet finger occurs when something strikes the end of your finger. It can happen when you reach to catch a ball and it hits the tip of your fingers rather than your palm.

Inside the finger, a tendon is partly torn. From the outside you may see very little, but you cannot fully straighten your finger. An x-ray is recommended. Mallet fingers can heal on their own if they are properly splinted for several weeks.

Skier's Thumb

Skier's thumb is a common injury. It can happen when a skier falls and ski poles catch on the ground or snow and pull the thumb away from the fingers. Any forceful motion in the wrong direction can cause the condition, which is a tear in the ligament connecting the thumb to the metacarpal bone of the hand. In bad cases the ligament severs completely. This injury should be seen by a doctor.

Tendinitis

Tendinitis in the wrist, hand, and fingers can occur from overuse or repeated motions. Symptoms may include pain, tenderness, minor swelling, and limited motion. Tendinitis pain in the wrist may spread down to the fingers or up to the elbow. Tendinitis in the fingers may affect one or more fingers at the same time. You may feel pain constantly or only with certain movements. The area around the tendon may be tender. You may even notice a cracking sound or odd feeling when you bend or flex the finger or wrist.

Ganglions

Ganglions (soft, fluid-filled cysts near tendons or joints) are harmless, may or may not cause pain or discomfort, and may go away eventually on their own. The cause of most ganglions is unknown. If you find a ganglion bothersome, your doctor may drain it with a needle or remove it surgically.

Carpal Tunnel Syndrome

Carpal tunnel syndrome (CTS) is a condition caused by pressure on a large nerve in the wrist as it passes through a "tunnel" formed by tendons. Carpal tunnel syndrome results in pain that may spread into the hand and forearm. You may feel numbness and tingling in the fingers, especially your thumb, index, and middle finger, and loss of strength in the hand. You may find yourself dropping things often or even being awakened at night by tingling and numbness in your hand. Talk to your doctor if you have any of the symptoms of CTS. Getting proper treatment can prevent surgery.

Self-Care

Below are some general self-care guidelines for handling wrist and hand pain. However, treatment is needed for specific injuries.

- Apply ice immediately.

- Always remove rings before exercising or doing manual labor. If you are wearing rings and hurt your hand, remove them immediately before swelling has a chance to begin.

- Take aspirin or another pain reliever (see Medications, p. 396) to ease pain and swelling.

- Rest the painful hand for a few days and then begin to exercise it gently.

- Call your doctor if pain continues and is not relieved by home care after 24 hours.

What to do about Wrist and Hand Pain

Symptom/Sign	Action
Injury not affecting movement	Self-care
Numbness or tingling in fingers during day or awakened by these symptoms at night	See doctor
Fever or rapid swelling in joint, accompanied by pain	See doctor
Pain spreading up from wrist to elbow/shoulder/neck	See doctor
Difficulty holding objects	See doctor
Clicking, popping, grinding in finger or wrist	See doctor
Visible deformity or abnormal movement after a fall	Go to hospital
Tender spot on shaft of finger bones (not at joint)	Go to hospital
Pain, swelling, and bruising after thumb is accidentally bent backward	Go to hospital

Health Concerns for Men

Men, just as women, have their own unique health concerns. For example, annual death rates for men with prostate cancer are similar to the rates of breast cancer deaths for women. Many men's health concerns can be treated easily if diagnosed early, but men tend to wait to go to the doctor until there's a significant problem.

This chapter describes common health concerns for men, how to take care of nonurgent conditions at home, and when to involve your doctor. In some cases your doctor may recommend the help of other doctors who specialize in treating men's diseases. ::

Prostate Problems

The prostate is a gland the size of a walnut located between the pubic bone and the rectum in men. The prostate's main job is to make part of the fluid in which sperm travel. The urethra (the tube through which urine leaves the body) runs through the center of the prostate gland. There are many different kinds of prostate problems, and they are common in men age 50 and older.

Symptoms

Symptoms of prostate problems can include:

- Difficulty starting or stopping urination
- Frequent need to urinate
- Need to urinate in the middle of the night
- Pain with urination
- Weak or unsteady urine stream
- Urine leakage (incontinence)
- Feeling as if the bladder is not completely empty after urination
- Pain in and around the base of the penis or discomfort between the scrotum and rectum
- Pus, blood, or cloudiness in the urine
- Painful ejaculation
- Difficulty having an erection
- Pain in the lower back, hips, or upper thighs

If you have acute prostatitis, you may also have sudden fever, chills, and pain in the abdomen. Early prostate cancer often doesn't have any symptoms.

Types of Prostate Problems

Prostatitis is an inflammation of the prostate gland. There are three types of prostatitis: acute bacterial, chronic bacterial, and chronic nonbacterial. Acute prostatitis is often caused by a bacterial infection, but only about 5 percent of chronic prostatitis cases are caused by bacterial infection. Chronic prostatitis is often related to frequent urinary tract infections. Another possible cause of chronic prostatitis is an enlarged prostate.

Enlarged prostate, also called benign prostatic hypertrophy (BPH), is a noncancerous enlargement affected by the male hormone testosterone and by aging. Starting at about age 40, the prostate gland naturally begins to enlarge in most men. Almost 90 percent of men age 80 or older have an enlarged prostate.

Some men have BPH but have no problems as a result. In others, however, the enlarged prostate may begin to press inward on the urethra, partially or completely blocking the flow of urine and causing symptoms. If the bladder never completely empties, a buildup of old urine can lead to bladder or urinary tract infection. In severe cases the enlarged prostate may stop the flow of urine so much that it causes kidney problems.

Prostate cancer is the most commonly diagnosed form of cancer, other than skin cancer, among men in the United States. It is second only to lung cancer as a cause of cancer-related death among men. Although the causes of prostate cancer are not well understood, there are certain factors that can increase your risk:

- *Age.* Prostate cancer is found mainly in men over age 55.
- *Family history.* Your risk is higher if your father or brother has had the disease.
- *Race.* The disease is much more common in African American men than in Caucasian men and less common in Asian and Native American men.
- *Diet.* Some evidence suggests a diet high in animal fat may increase the risk of prostate cancer, whereas a diet high in fruits and vegetables may reduce the risk.

Treatment

If you have symptoms of prostate problems, there are several tests your doctor may perform to make a diagnosis. In a digital rectal examination (DRE), your doctor inserts a gloved finger into your rectum to feel your prostate gland and check for inflammation, enlargement, lumps, or tenderness.

In a prostate-specific antigen (PSA) test, your doctor measures the level of

PSA in a blood sample. PSA is a substance that is produced by the prostate gland and circulated through your bloodstream. Higher than normal levels of PSA can indicate a prostate problem such as prostatitis or cancer.

Urine and semen may also be tested for bacteria and white blood cells. If your doctor suspects prostate cancer, you will need to have a biopsy, in which small tissue samples are taken from your prostate for testing.

After testing, the following treatment may be recommended:

Prostatitis

- If you have a bacterial infection, your doctor will prescribe antibiotics, which need to be taken for at least 4 to 6 weeks. Hospitalization is sometimes needed so antibiotics can be given intravenously (into your vein).

- If the infection is chronic, surgery may be needed to drain pus from the prostate or to remove chronically infected or inflamed tissue.

- Treatment for chronic prostatitis that is not caused by infection often involves an alpha-blocker medication, which relaxes the muscles of the prostate.

Enlarged Prostate

- The most commonly used medications for treating an enlarged prostate are alpha-blockers and finasteride. Alpha-

blockers relax the muscles of the prostate and the opening of the bladder. Finasteride prevents testosterone from being used by the prostate, which can reduce its size.

- In balloon dilation therapy, a small balloon is inserted into the urethra and then inflated to open the passageway.

- If your bladder is not emptying completely or if you are having frequent urinary tract infections or kidney problems, you may need surgery. There are several different procedures in which part or all of the prostate may be removed.

Prostate Cancer

- Watchful waiting may be suggested if prostate cancer has been found at an early stage and appears to be growing slowly. This is often advised for older men or men with other health problems, because the side effects of treatment may outweigh the benefits.

- Surgery is a common treatment for prostate cancer. Your doctor may remove all the prostate or just part of it. A procedure called *cryosurgery* is sometimes used to kill the cancer by freezing it. If cancer has spread to the lymph nodes or other parts of the body, your doctor will usually recommend a different type of treatment.

- Radiation therapy uses high-energy x-rays to kill cancer cells and shrink tumors. Radiation may be used instead of surgery, or it may be used after surgery to destroy any cancer cells left in the area.

• Hormone therapy stops cancer cells from growing. Because the growth of prostate cancer often depends on male hormones, hormone therapy uses drugs to stop your body from producing these hormones or to block them from getting into cancer cells. This treatment is often used for prostate cancer that has spread to other parts of the body.

Self-Care

Follow these self-care steps to help reduce everyday symptoms and prevent potential problems:

• Go to the bathroom as soon as you feel the urge to urinate. Don't "hold it."

• Drink plenty of fluids to help flush away possible bacteria and old urine in the bladder, but don't drink large quantities all at one time or just before bedtime. Try drinking an 8-ounce glass of water each hour during the day.

• Avoid caffeine (coffee, tea, colas) and alcohol, which will make you urinate more.

• Soak in a hot bath to help relieve discomfort and pain.

• Avoid cold and allergy medications that contain antihistamines or decongestants.

• If your doctor prescribes an antibiotic, take your medication exactly as it is prescribed.

• Call your doctor if you have symptoms that get worse or are not relieved with self-care.

What to do about Prostate Problems

Symptom/Sign	Action
Difficulty starting or stopping urination (dribbling, frequent need to urinate or needing to urinate in the middle of the night)	See doctor
Weak or unsteady urine stream, urine leakage (incontinence), or feeling as if your bladder is not completely empty after you urinate	See doctor
Pain or burning when you urinate	See doctor
Pain or discomfort at the base of the penis or between the scrotum and the rectum	See doctor
Fever, chills, pain in the lower back or abdomen	See doctor
Cloudy urine; pus or blood in urine	See doctor
Unable to urinate or significant discomfort and urge to urinate	Go to hospital

Prevention

The three most important steps you can take to maintain prostate health are to eat well, keep physically active, and see your doctor regularly. Because prostate cancer is curable when caught early but often doesn't have symptoms, talk to your doctor about scheduling routine prostate exams.

Testicular Problems

The testicles are located inside the scrotum, a loose bag of skin underneath the penis. They produce male sex hormones and sperm cells for reproduction. Lumps, swelling, pain, or other changes in the testicles can indicate a variety of problems, ranging from minor to serious. Because these symptoms have a number of possible causes, you should see your doctor to ensure correct diagnosis and treatment.

Testicular Cancer

Cancer of the testes is fairly rare, but it is the most common form of cancer in men between the ages of 20 and 35. It accounts for 12 percent of all cancer deaths in young men. Testicular cancer usually responds well to treatment, especially when detected early.

Causes

The cause of testicular cancer is not known, but there are certain risk factors that can make you more likely to get it:

- Normally the testicles descend into the scrotum before birth. Men whose testes have not descended into the scrotum or did not descend until after age 6 are at a much higher risk for testicular cancer, even if the condition was surgically corrected.

- Testicular cancer affects younger men, especially those between the ages of 15 and 35. This type of cancer is uncommon in children and in men over age 40.

- Testicular cancer is four times more common among Caucasian men than African American men.

Symptoms

Cancer usually affects only one testicle. Symptoms may include:

- A lump or enlargement in either testicle

- Pain, swelling, or a feeling of heaviness in your scrotum or testicles

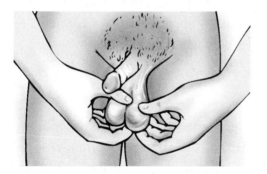

How to do a testicular self-examination

Begin by standing in front of a mirror. Look for signs of swelling in the scrotum. Next, examine each testicle with both hands. With your index and middle fingers underneath and your thumbs on top, gently roll each testicle, feeling for lumps.

- A dull ache in your lower abdomen or groin

You may have some symptoms of testicular cancer without any pain. Only a small percentage of testicular cancers are painful early on.

Examine your testicles regularly for lumps, swelling, or anything unusual. This is best done after a warm shower or bath, when the scrotal skin is relaxed (see illustration below and Know the Signs of Cancer, p. 149).

Types of Testicular Cancer

- *Seminomas* are the most common type of testicular cancer. Nearly all men recover from this type of cancer if it's found and treated early.

- *Nonseminomas* are a group of cancers that include choriocarcinoma, embryonal carcinoma, teratoma, and yolk sac tumors. These cancers tend to develop earlier in life than seminomas, usually occurring in men in their 20s.

Testicular cancers may be a combination of different types.

Treatment

Seminomas and nonseminomas grow and spread differently, and each type may need different treatment.

- Surgery to remove the testicle through an incision in the groin may be performed. Lymph nodes in the abdomen may also be removed.

- Radiation therapy uses high-energy rays to kill cancer cells and shrink tumors. Seminomas are highly sensitive to radiation therapy; nonseminomas are not.

- Chemotherapy is the use of anti-cancer medications to kill cancer cells throughout the body. Chemotherapy may be used as the initial treatment, or it may be used after surgery to kill any remaining cancer cells.

Treatments for testicular cancer have some side effects. Some treatments may affect your ability to have an erection or interfere with fertility (the ability to produce children). Talk to your doctor about possible side effects before undergoing treatment.

Testicular Pain

Testicular pain may be a sign of a serious medical condition that requires immediate attention, or it may be a less serious problem that can be treated fairly easily.

Causes

Epididymitis is the inflammation of the long, coiled tube (epididymis) that carries sperm from the testicle to the vas deferens. It is often caused by a bac-

terial or chlamydial infection traveling from the urinary duct to the sperm duct. Epididymitis is the most common cause of testicular pain and usually affects only one side. In addition to pain, there may also be swelling and a burning sensation when you urinate.

When the epididymitis spreads to involve the nearby testicle, the condition is called *epididymo-orchitis*. *Orchitis*, an infection of the testicle alone, may also occur but is much less common than epididymitis. Orchitis is usually caused by a viral infection and can be associated with the mumps. Although this condition is rare, it can cause infertility and irreversible damage to the testes.

Testicular torsion occurs when a testicle gets twisted in the spermatic cord from which it is suspended within the scrotum (see illustration). This unusual condition can occur spontaneously— even while you sleep—or after strenu-

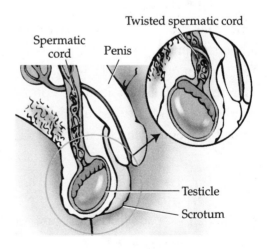

Testicular torsion.

ous activity at any age, though it is most common before age 20. It can strangle the blood supply to the testicle and without immediate treatment can cause permanent damage. Sudden pain, severe enough to cause nausea and vomiting, it the main symptom of testicular torsion.

Pain in the scrotum can also be caused by an inguinal hernia (see Hernia, p. 161).

Treatment

Epididymitis is usually treated with antibiotics. Your doctor may also recommend several days of bed rest, elevation of the scrotum, use of ice packs, and pain medication, such as acetaminophen (Tylenol). Treatment for orchitis and nonbacterial epididymitis is similar, except antibiotics won't be effective against the virus that caused the condition.

Testicular torsion is a medical emergency that needs to be treated within 6 hours to prevent permanent damage. Your doctor may be able to carefully shift the testicle back into its normal position, but surgery is usually performed to securely anchor it into place.

Self-Care

• Apply an ice pack to the scrotum for 15 to 20 minutes at a time.

• Elevate the scrotal area with a rolled-up towel.

• Wear briefs or a soft athletic supporter to provide support to the area.

• Take acetaminophen (Tylenol) as directed.

• If your doctor has prescribed antibiotics, take your medication exactly the way it is prescribed.

What to do about Testicular Problems

Symptom/Sign	Action
Mild scrotal pain or swelling after injury, lasting less than 1 hour	Self-care
Lump or feeling of heaviness in scrotum	See doctor
Mild to moderate pain with fever (101°F), scrotal area warm and tender to the touch	See doctor
Scrotal pain or swelling after injury, lasting more than 1 hour or with bruising or bleeding	Go to hospital
Sudden, painful swelling in testicles; nausea or vomiting, light-headedness, pain in lower abdomen or groin	Call 911

Health Concerns for Women

Women have many health conditions that are unique to them, such as difficult menstrual periods or hot flashes during menopause. Research into women's health is providing exciting advances, and today women have many new options available to help with these special concerns.

Your doctor can offer advice and treatment for most women's health problems. If your condition is especially hard to handle, your doctor may involve other medical providers who specialize in women's health, such as gynecologists or nurse practitioners. ▪

Bleeding between Periods

Bleeding between periods can be inconvenient and annoying. Most women have spotting (light bleeding), breakthrough bleeding (heavier bleeding), or irregular periods at some point in their lives. Spotting or breakthrough bleeding between periods usually lasts 1 or 2 days.

Causes

About 10 percent of women regularly have spotting around the time of ovulation. Bleeding between periods is also common when hormones are fluctuating (rising and falling) the most—during the first few years of menstruation and again as women approach menopause.

Spotting is very common in women with intrauterine devices (IUDs). It may also occur if the hormone levels in the birth control pills a woman is taking are not well suited to her body. In most of these cases, spotting is not cause for concern, but your doctor may be able to help end the problem by prescribing a different pill or recommending another form of birth control. Spotting and breakthrough bleeding are also very common with Depo-Provera (a birth control shot), especially during the first 3 months. Also, if you miss a dose of the pill, you may have spotting.

Bleeding between periods also can be a sign of a more serious problem, such as ectopic pregnancy or cancer.

Treatment

Your doctor may recommend an endometrial biopsy to check for cancer and other problems. A dilation and curettage (D & C), in which the uterine lining is gently scraped and cleaned away, may be suggested. For some women, a D & C will end the problem of spotting.

Self-Care

It's important to keep a menstrual diary if you begin having bleeding that is unusual for you. This diary can help your doctor or nurse practitioner find the possible cause and decide whether the between-period bleeding is anything to be concerned about. Keep a written record of the dates of your periods and any bleeding between periods. Note how long the bleeding lasted and how heavy the flow was.

Call your doctor if your menstrual pattern does not return to normal by the third month.

What to do about Bleeding between Periods

Symptom/Sign	Action
Spotting associated with use of Norplant or Depo-Provera	Self-care
Spotting associated with hormone replacement therapy	Call doctor
Spotting or breakthrough bleeding occurring more than once	See doctor
Bleeding between periods that lasts 3 or more days	See doctor
Menstrual pattern doesn't return to normal by the third month	See doctor
Vaginal bleeding in menopausal or post-menopausal women not taking hormone replacement therapy	See doctor
Painful bleeding between periods	See doctor
Soaking one or more sanitary napkins per hour for more than 4 hours or one pad or more every 15 minutes for more than 1 hour	Go to hospital

Breast Cancer

Breast cancer is the most common type of cancer in American women. Each year in the United States, more than 180,000 women learn they have this disease. Early detection increases the changes of survival. Women with small, localized breast cancers (where the cancer has not spread beyond the breast) have an excellent chance of living many years after cancer treatment.

Causes

Factors that can increase the risk of developing breast cancer include:

- *Family History.* Your risk doubles if your mother or sister has had breast cancer. It is even higher if they developed breast cancer before menopause.

- *Premalignant Cells on Biopsy.* Women who have had a previous breast biopsy that was benign but showed certain suspicious cells are at increased risk.

- *Age.* Two-thirds of all breast cancer occurs in women over age 50. As you grow older, your risk increases.

- *Alcohol Use.* Some studies have shown that alcohol consumption may be linked to breast cancer. If you drink alcohol, having more than one drink per day could put you at risk.

- *Childbirth and Menstruation.* Never having children or giving birth to your first child after age 30 increases your risk of breast cancer. Getting your first period before the age of 12 or starting menopause after the age of 55 may also add to your risk.

- *Estrogen.* Some studies suggest that the longer a woman is exposed to estrogen, the more likely she is to develop breast cancer. Beginning menstruation before the age of 12, experiencing menopause after the age of 55, never having children, or taking hormone replacement therapy for long periods are factors that increase the amount of time a woman is exposed to estrogen.

- *Other Factors.* Other factors linked to breast cancer include obesity and a history of ovarian, colon, or endometrial cancer. Even so, the most important risk factors are growing older and being a woman. About 80 percent of women who get breast cancer do not have a personal or family history of the disease.

Symptoms

Breast cancer usually does not cause pain in its early stages. There may be no symptoms when it is first developing. There are some signs to watch for (see Know the Signs of Cancer, p. 149). See your doctor if you notice any of the following:

- New lumps or changes in the size or shape of existing lumps

- Change in the shape or contour of a breast or unusual swelling

- Dimpling, puckering, crusting, or rash in the skin, especially around the nipple

- Any discharge from the nipple

Methods for Detecting Breast Cancer

Breast cancer screening includes regular breast self-exams (BSE), clinical breast exams performed by a doctor, and mammograms (see table below).

Breast Self-Examination

Many women are afraid to examine their breasts because of what they might find. Most breast lumps are not cancerous. Even if a breast lump is cancerous, your best defense is early detection. Breast self-examination (BSE) is easy and takes only about 5 minutes a month. Among women with breast cancer, 34 percent said they first discovered their breast cancer through BSE. BSE is a way to discover any change from what is "normal" for you. Your doctor can review this technique with you (see box on p. 285).

There is some disagreement in the medical community about the effectiveness of BSE. Some believe BSE is not very accurate and can create needless anxiety and expense. This is especially true for younger women who have no special risk factors. However, women who already do self-exams should not stop.

Recommendations for Breast Cancer Screening

Screening	Age 20–39	Age 40–49	Age 50–75	Age 75+
Breast self-exam	Monthly	Monthly	Monthly	Monthly
Clinical breast exam by a doctor	Every 3 years	Yearly	Yearly	Yearly
Mammogram	—	Yearly, depending on your health history or preference	Yearly	Determined by patient and doctor preference

How to Perform a Breast Self-Exam

1. While in the shower, raise your right arm, placing your hand on the back of your head. Starting at the outer edge of the right breast, use the pads of the fingertips of your left hand. Feel for lumps or changes in the breast as you firmly move your fingers in small circles, working in a spiral toward the nipple. Check the other side in the same way, then gently squeeze each nipple to check for any discharge.

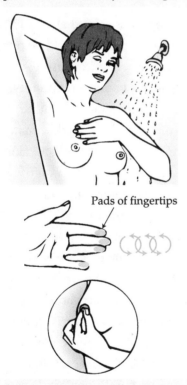

Pads of fingertips

2. After your shower, clasp your hands together and raise your arms above your head with elbows bent. In a mirror, look for changes in shape or contour, as well as any skin changes, such as dimpling or rashes.

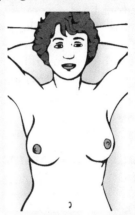

3. Still standing in front of the mirror, lower your arms. Place your hands on your hips, pull your shoulders and elbows forward, and lean slightly toward the mirror. Look again for any changes in shape or contour and for skin changes.

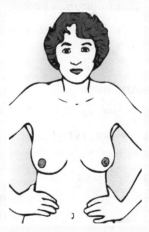

Continued

How to Perform a Breast Self-Exam—cont'd

4. Finally, lying down, place a rolled towel or pillow under one shoulder and place the hand on that same side over your head. Examine your breast again as you did in the shower, this time checking your armpit as well. Repeat this for the other breast.
5. Call your doctor if you find anything that concerns you.

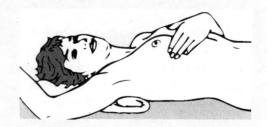

Clinical Breast Examination

Many doctors do routine breast exams for women of all ages during general physicals or pelvic exams. The doctor will check each breast using fingertips to feel for lumps and to look for other suspicious changes, such as dimpled, scaling, or puckered skin or fluid leaking from the nipple. When combined with a mammogram, a breast exam by a doctor is the best way to detect cancer in its early stages.

Mammograms

Mammograms can detect breast cancers while they are very small, sometimes 2 years earlier than they can be felt by a woman or her doctor.

A mammogram is an examination in which a low dose of radiation (an x-ray) is passed through the compressed breast. Compression of the breast tissue is necessary to ensure the highest quality image. Compression is not dangerous to your breast tissue, and any mild discomfort you experience should be temporary.

"Routine" or "screening" mammograms are for patients without symptoms. If your mammogram is routine, a radiologist may not look at the mammogram before you leave the office. Sometimes the radiologist needs to clarify findings on the mammogram, and you may be asked to return for additional views or procedures soon after your initial screening. A follow-up exam may be scheduled 3 to 6 months after your mammogram. Follow-up is common and doesn't necessarily mean that cancer is suspected.

"Nonroutine" mammograms are scheduled for patients who have known abnormalities or conditions, such as a lump, dimpling, or nipple discharge, for the first year following breast cancer diagnosis or breast surgery. If you are one of these patients, a radiologist reviews films before you leave, reducing the chance of being called back for additional views.

Cervical Cancer

An estimated 16,000 women are diagnosed with cervical cancer each year. In most cases, it's a slowly progressing disease with few, if any, clear-cut symptoms.

Causes

There are certain factors that increase your risk for cervical cancer. Research suggests that often two of the following factors are present when cervical cancer develops:

- You have had sex with many partners.
- You became sexually active before you were 18.
- You smoke.
- Your immune system is weakened, such as in women who have human immunodeficiency virus (HIV) or are on medications to suppress their immune system after a transplant.
- You or partner have human papillomavirus (HPV).

Method for Detecting Cervical Cancer

A Papanicolaou (PAP) smear is a simple procedure for women that involves swabbing a small sample of cells from the cervix during a pelvic exam. These cells are transferred to a slide and then examined and evaluated by a certified laboratory. In addition to testing for cancerous or precancerous conditions, the Pap smear is also useful for detecting some types of infections.

Women should begin having annual Pap smears at age 18 or when they become sexually active. After having three normal Pap smears in a row within 5 years, your doctor may recommend screenings less often, but you will need a Pap smear at least once every 3 years.

If you have had a hysterectomy because of cervical cancer, you should still schedule regular Pap smears.

More frequent Pap smears are recommended for women who have had an abnormal Pap smear in the past 5 years or who are HIV positive. Women with HIV infection may need more frequent Pap smears as their disease progresses.

To ensure the most accurate test results with your Pap smear, avoid using a vaginal douche or any type of lubricant for 24 hours before having a Pap smear. If you have used either, tell your doctor before the procedure.

Regular Pap smear screening makes it possible to find early evidence of cancer, when the disease is easier to cure. When diagnosed early, cervical cancer can be cured in almost all cases.

Endometriosis

Endometriosis is a disease in which tissue from the lining of the uterus moves through the fallopian tubes and attaches to the ovaries, pelvis, bladder, or other areas. Normally the lining of the uterus comes out every month when a woman has her period. With endometriosis, however, some of this tissue does not leave the body.

Causes

The cause of endometriosis is unknown. However, researchers do know of risk factors that make a woman more prone to having the disease. Women who have a mother, sister, or daughter who has endometriosis are 10 times more likely to have endometriosis than women without an affected relative. In rare cases a medical problem can prevent the normal passage of menstrual flow and cause the disease. Some studies also show that previous infections in the pelvis can damage the cells that line the pelvic area, which can lead to endometriosis.

Symptoms

Although endometriosis does not always have symptoms, the following are some common warning signs that the disease is present:

- Painful periods: Pelvic pain and cramping begins before a period and lasts several days after. Endometriosis may also involve pain in the lower abdomen and lower back.

- Heavy periods or bleeding between periods

- Pain during ovulation

- Sharp pain deep in the pelvis during intercourse

- Pain during bowel movements or urination

Endometriosis can cause fertility problems if it is not treated. In fact, for some women, endometriosis is not diagnosed until they seek treatment for infertility.

Because the cause of endometriosis is unknown, it is difficult to prevent the disease. However, evidence does suggest that women who have had children are less likely to develop the disorder.

Treatment

- *Pain medications.* Over-the-counter pain relievers (see Medication, p. 396) can relieve the menstrual pain that endometriosis causes. If you find that you are taking more than the regular dosage, you may need to try other treatment approaches.

- *Hormone therapy*. The rise and fall of hormones during a woman's menstrual cycle cause the endometrial tissue to thicken, break down, and bleed. Taking hormones can help shrink the tissue or prevent it from building up, which can help lessen the pain.

- *Surgery*. If you have endometriosis and are trying to become pregnant, your doctor can remove the misplaced tissue through surgery.

- *Hysterectomy*. In severe cases, the best treatment for endometriosis may be a hysterectomy. During this surgical procedure, some or all of a woman's reproductive organs are removed. This operation is a last resort, particularly for women in their childbearing years. A woman who has had a hysterectomy cannot get pregnant.

Self-Care

Endometriosis can be a frustrating disorder if it remains untreated. The pain that often accompanies it can cause missed school or work days. As it continues, the discomfort can cause depression, irritability, anxiety, and anger. If you are trying to have children and cannot, endometriosis can cause feelings of helplessness.

If you are dealing with the symptoms of endometriosis, consider joining a support group for women with the condition. It may help you to deal with many of the emotions you are experiencing—and help you to feel less alone.

What to do about Endometriosis

Symptom/Sign	Action
Mild symptoms of endometriosis	Self-care
Pain throughout entire menstrual cycle or pain that worsens with time	Call doctor
Pain that extends into the lungs, chest, back, or legs	See doctor
Very heavy bleeding (soaking one or more pads per hour for more than 4 hours, or one or more pads every 15 minutes for more than 1 hour)	Go to hospital

Menopause

Menopause occurs when ovulation and menstruation stop. The average age of menopause in the United States is 51, but it can occur anytime between the ages of 40 and 55. Menopause is now recognized as a normal part of aging that affects every woman in an individual way. Some women notice little difference in their bodies or moods; others find menopause very uncomfortable and disruptive. Each woman experiences the years leading up to menopause, called perimenopause, differently.

Causes

Beginning in your mid-30s, your ovaries start to change how much estrogen they produce. Estrogen is a hormone that is necessary for menstruation and pregnancy. As you get older, you produce less estrogen until menstruation stops and pregnancy can no longer occur. Changes in estrogen levels can affect many parts of the body, including your heart, bones, urinary tract, skin, and hair.

Symptoms

The hormonal changes that occur before and after menopause can cause various symptoms. Although not all women experience them, some of the symptoms of menopause are irregular periods, hot flashes, vaginal dryness, urinary problems, mood changes, and sleep disturbances.

- *Irregular periods* are often common during the years leading up to menopause. The time between periods may become shorter or longer. The flow may be lighter or heavier than you have experienced. Bleeding between periods or missed periods may also occur.

- *Hot flashes* describe a flushed feeling that usually begins around the chest and spreads to the neck, face, and arms. This sensation usually lasts 3 to 4 minutes and can occur as often as once an hour. Hot flashes are often followed by sweating and then chills. Hot flashes can occur at anytime and may wake you up at night. These are called night sweats. Three out of four women experience hot flashes. Only one out of three women have symptoms for 5 or more years.

- *Vaginal dryness* can be the result of reduced estrogen levels in the body. With much less estrogen in the body, the vaginal walls lose elasticity, become thin, and secrete less fluid. A drier, less elastic vagina can mean discomfort or pain during intercourse.

- *Loss of bladder control* can occur when reduced estrogen levels cause the muscle tone in your urinary tract to decrease. The tube that carries urine from the bladder does not have the necessary pressure and strength to prevent urine from leaking out of the body. This is called incontinence.

- *Mood changes and sleep disturbances* may occur during perimenopause and after menopause. Scientific studies suggest a relationship between lower hormone levels and depression, moodiness, irritability, fatigue, sleep problems, and psychological symptoms commonly felt during menopause. Researchers have come to believe that lack of adequate sleep as a result of nighttime hot flashes aggravates the moodiness and other psychological symptoms linked with menopause.

Health Problems That Occur at Menopause

When you reach menopause, your risk for heart disease and osteoporosis increases.

Heart disease is the number one cause of death in women. Women are protected against heart disease up until menopause because of the positive effects of estrogen, which controls the cholesterol in your blood and keeps your arteries healthy. The risk of heart disease increases dramatically after menopause, when estrogen production slows down (see Coronary Artery Disease, p. 183).

Osteoporosis risk increases at menopause, as does the risk of broken bones, because bone mass diminishes with the decrease in estrogen (see Osteoporosis, p. 265).

Treatment

Hormone replacement therapy (HRT) can be used to help manage many of the symptoms of menopause. It can relieve hot flashes, vaginal dryness, and urinary tract symptoms that occur as a result of estrogen deficiency. It can also improve symptoms of irritability and anxiety in many women and may relieve mild depressive symptoms. It is unclear whether HRT has a direct effect on mood or whether these effects are due solely to the alleviation of physical symptoms, especially hot flashes and sleep disturbances. HRT decreases skin wrinkles in some women. One of the most beneficial effects of HRT is in bone density. HRT helps decrease bone loss and prevents osteoporosis. HRT may not protect against coronary artery disease as once thought.

There are many different estrogen and progesterone preparations used for HRT. Hormone replacement therapy comes in the form of pills, patches, and creams. Your doctor will work with you to decide what type of preparation is best for you considering your current symptoms and medical history.

Risks of HRT

- *Endometrial cancer.* In the 1960s estrogen was often given alone, and some women later developed low-grade endometrial (uterine) cancer. When both estrogen and progesterone are given for hormone replacement therapy, the risk of endometrial cancer is actually less than if the woman was not taking estrogen at all. For this reason, both estrogen and progesterone are recommended for women who have a uterus. Estrogen alone is recommended as a replacement therapy for women who have had a hysterectomy.

- *Breast cancer.* There seems to be a small increase in breast cancer risk with HRT. The possibility of developing breast cancer is one of the reasons women decide not to take hormone replacement therapy. There may be a small increase in the risk of breast cancer after taking HRT for 5 to 10 years. There does not seem to be an increased risk of breast cancer in women who take HRT for less than 5 years. It's important to discuss concerns about breast cancer risk with your doctor when considering HRT.

- *Gallbladder disease.* Women taking HRT have an increased chance of developing gallbladder disease.

- *Venous thromboembolism (VTE).* The risk for developing VTE (blood clots) is increased in women who are taking HRT.

Side Effects of HRT

About 10 percent of women receiving HRT have minor side effects such as breast tenderness, nausea, headaches, fluid retention, or irregular vaginal bleeding. For most women, these side effects disappear quickly and do not interfere with continuing the hormone therapy.

Self-Care

- Eat a healthy diet. Eating well contributes to overall good health. During menopause, when your body is changing, a diet that includes a variety of fruits, vegetables, and whole grains is especially important. Select foods that are lower in fat and aim for at least three servings of dairy products a day. If you do not drink milk, take a calcium supplement (1000 milligrams) with vitamin D (400 International Units) each day. Use alcohol and caffeine in moderation.

- Exercise regularly. Try to be active at least 30 minutes of every day to help reduce hot flashes and guard against osteoporosis. Walk whenever you can, make extra trips around your yard or house, take the stairs instead of the elevator. Dress in layers so that you can remove them if you experience a hot flash.

- Use a water-soluble lubricant. Try a product such as K-Y Jelly, Astroglide, Replens, or Surgilube to relieve vaginal dryness. Don't use petroleum jelly products, such as Vaseline.

- Many women have reportedly found relief for their menopausal symptoms by using over-the-counter products that promote a holistic or natural effect. Because these "natural" hormone replacement compounds are not regulated by the Food and Drug Administration, their potency and dosage may differ among different brands of the same product. Some of the more common products claiming to help with menopause are yam extract, black cohosh, sarsaparilla, kava, licorice, dong quai root, gingko biloba, Vitex, flaxseed, DHEA, soy, red clover, and St. John's wort. There have been few, if any, clinical trials to show that these products are useful or even safe. Talk to your doctor if you have questions about any of the over-the-counter preparations that claim to help with menopausal symptoms.

What to do about Menopause

Symptom/Sign	Action
Irregular periods, hot flashes, vaginal dryness, urinary problems, mood changes, or sleep disturbances	Self-care
Fewer than 20 days from the start of one cycle to the start of the next or your cycles are longer than 90 days apart	Call doctor
Taking HRT and have breast tenderness, nausea, headaches, fluid retention, or irregular vaginal bleeding	Call doctor
Bleeding for more than 8 days	See doctor
Very heavy bleeding (soaking one or more pads per hour for more than 4 hours or one or more pads every 15 minutes for more than 1 hour)	Go to hospital

Menstrual Pain

For most women, menstruation comes and goes each month with ease. But for others, or at various times in a woman's childbearing years, periods may be complicated by pain. The medical term for menstrual pain is *dysmenorrhea*.

Causes

One type of painful period seems to run in families. Researchers in the 1970s and 1980s discovered higher than average levels of prostaglandin—fatty acids in the body that act much like hormones—in the menstrual fluid of women who suffered from cramps. Prostaglandins serve many functions in the body, but too much can cause cramplike pain from uterine irritability or contractions.

Other types of painful periods may be caused by fibroids (noncancerous growths) in the uterus, infection, or endometriosis (see p. 288). Intrauterine contraceptive devices (IUDs) may also cause pain during menstruation. If your periods become more painful or begin to last longer than they used to, see your doctor.

Symptoms

Menstrual pain usually involves a crampy feeling in the lower abdomen. It sometimes spreads to the hips, lower back, and thighs. It may be accompanied by diarrhea, nausea, and headaches. It is more common in women ages 15 to 24 and among women who have not given birth.

Self-Care

- Use aspirin, ibuprofen, or prescription pain relievers. Aspirin usually relieves mild to moderate menstrual pain. Ibuprofen (Advil, Motrin) is the medication of choice. If you do not get enough relief from these over-the-counter medications, your doctor may be able to prescribe a higher dose of ibuprofen or a prescription nonsteroidal anti-inflammatory drug (NSAID). Begin taking the medication at the first sign of symptoms, whether menstrual bleeding has actually begun or not.

- Apply heat. A heating pad or hot-water bottle placed on the lower abdomen will ease the pain. You can also take a warm bath for 20 to 30 minutes.

- Raise your hips. If you find yourself in bed because of cramps, try lying on your back with your hips elevated above the level of your shoulders. Put your feet up on the footboard of the bed or the arm of the couch and place pillows under your hips. Firm massaging of the lower back may also help.

- Maintain adequate fluid intake.
- It is always important to get adequate rest. If you are tired, you are less able to tolerate pain and cramps may seem worse.
- Call your doctor if menstrual cramps are not relieved by home care after two cycles.

What to do about Menstrual Pain

Symptom/Sign	Action
Painful periods or cramps that can be relieved	Self-care
Pain during period is worse than it used to be and possible exposure to a sexually transmitted disease (STD)	Call doctor
Very heavy bleeding (soaking one or more pads per hour for more than 4 hours, or one or more pads every 15 minutes for more than 1 hour)	Go to hospital
Pain increases and is accompanied by fever and blistery rash on your body	See doctor

Missed Periods

Periods usually begin between the ages of 11 and 14, although some girls begin earlier and others later. If a girl has not started to menstruate by age 16, she may have a type of amenorrhea (a medical term for the absence of menstruation). Hormone imbalances or problems with the ovaries, uterus, or vagina may be at fault. If menstruation hasn't begun by age 16, it is wise to see a doctor.

Causes

For most women, the first thing to come to mind when a menstrual period is missed is pregnancy. Although pregnancy is a common cause of missed periods, there are many other factors that can cause a woman not to menstruate (amenorrhea). Stress, being very overweight or underweight, birth control pills, regular hard exercise, and the approach of menopause are all possible causes of amenorrhea. Menstrual periods may not resume for several months after a woman gives birth or while she is breastfeeding. Diseases that affect the body's hormonal system can also lead to missed periods, but these are rare.

Sometimes birth control pills prescribed to regulate irregular periods can cause missed periods. If your periods stop while you are taking one type of pill, switching to another birth control pill may solve the problem. If you are on the pill and your periods stop, talk with your doctor or nurse practitioner. Going off the pill after being on it for a while also may disrupt your menstrual cycle for a few months while your body adjusts to the change in hormones.

Self-Care

- The first thing to rule out if you miss a period is pregnancy. Home pregnancy tests on the market today are considered very accurate when the directions are followed. If the test is negative, but you strongly suspect you might be pregnant, repeat the test after 1 week. It is important to avoid alcohol, tobacco, and chemicals until pregnancy is ruled out.

- If you are in your 40s or 50s, a missed period may mean you are starting menopause. Before your periods stop entirely, they may be irregular for a time. If you miss more than two periods, call your doctor.

- For some women, a bout of the flu or stress at work or home can throw their menstrual cycles off. If you are under stress, find ways to relieve it. Take time out daily to meditate, listen to soothing music, or read a book. Regular exercise and getting enough sleep each night can also reduce stress.

- Rapid weight loss or being very overweight or underweight can also cause amenorrhea. If you are trying to lose weight, make sure you are eating at least 1200 calories a day from a well-balanced variety of foods. If you are underweight, eat a well-balanced diet that provides about 2000 calories a day. Whether you are overweight, underweight, or dieting, your doctor, nurse practitioner, or dietitian may be able to help you set up a healthy diet and exercise plan.

- Very hard training and exercise are other causes of amenorrhea. If you are in training and are missing periods, easing up may return your periods to normal. If you are an endurance athlete, ask your doctor or nurse practitioner if hormone therapy or calcium supplements might be right for you to help prevent osteoporosis.

What to do about Missed Periods

Symptom/Sign	Action
Occasional missed period	Self-care
Missed one period and are pregnant	Call doctor
Missed two periods and are not pregnant	Call doctor
Missed two or more periods, not pregnant, and on birth control pills	See doctor
Age 16 or older and have never had a period	See doctor
Missed periods and have irregular spotting or pain in lower abdomen	See doctor

Pelvic Inflammatory Disease

Pelvic inflammatory disease is an infection in the lining of the uterus, the Fallopian tubes, or the ovaries.

Causes

Pelvic inflammatory disease occurs when certain bacteria enter the body. Most cases of the disease are caused by the same organisms responsible for bacterial sexually transmitted diseases, such as chlamydia and gonorrhea. However, bacteria can also enter the body during childbirth or through procedures such as insertion of an intrauterine device.

The following are risk factors for the disease:

- Sexual activity during adolescence
- Multiple sexual partners
- History of a sexually transmitted disease
- Use of nonbarrier type contraceptives, such as intrauterine devices or oral contraceptives

Symptoms

The most common symptoms of pelvic inflammatory disease include:

- Unusual vaginal discharge—abnormal in color, consistency, or odor
- Abdominal pain
- Fever

Other nonspecific symptoms may also be present, such as chills, irregular menstrual bleeding, pain during sexual intercourse or ovulation, low-back pain, fatigue, and nausea. Sometimes, pelvic inflammatory disease has no symptoms.

To find out if you have pelvic inflammatory disease, your doctor will do blood tests and a cervical exam. You may also need to have other tests, such as an ultrasound or computed tomography (CT) scan.

Treatment

If pelvic inflammatory disease is caught early and has no complications, your doctor will prescribe antibiotics to treat it. However, hospitalization or intravenous antibiotics may be needed if the infection is more serious. Surgery is usually not recommended unless complications develop or the disease continues even after you have finished taking antibiotics.

Self-Care

In addition to taking antibiotics, women who have pelvic inflammatory disease can take steps at home to relieve their symptoms.

- Get plenty of rest, particularly if you have a fever.
- Avoid sexual intercourse, and do not insert anything into the vagina, such as tampons.
- Take a hot bath or apply heat to your lower abdomen to relieve pain.

What to do about Pelvic Inflammatory Disease

Symptom/Sign	Action
Symptoms of mild pelvic inflammatory disease	Call doctor
Symptoms of pelvic inflammatory disease and possible exposure to sexually transmitted disease	See doctor
Pain that is more severe on one side than the other	See doctor
Symptoms worsen after treatment or continue with no improvement	See doctor

Prevention

The best way to prevent pelvic inflammatory disease is to keep harmful bacteria from entering the vagina.

- Avoid sexual intercourse and use of tampons when the cervix may be partially open, such as right after childbirth, a miscarriage, or an abortion.

- If you have been exposed to a sexually transmitted disease, get tested for the disease right away. The earlier you can be treated, the better chance you have of avoiding pelvic inflammatory disease.

- If you use an intrauterine device, have it checked regularly.

Premenstrual Syndrome

Premenstrual syndrome (PMS) is a disorder with a variety of emotional and physical symptoms. It's estimated that PMS affects 70 to 80 percent of women in their childbearing years; 30 to 40 percent of women have symptoms severe enough to interfere with daily activities, and 5 to 10 percent have symptoms so severe they're considered disabling. PMS usually disappears when menopause begins.

Symptoms

There are many physical symptoms of PMS; however, many of the symptoms have other possible causes. If you have any of the signs listed below, you may have PMS, but many women experience these symptoms and do not have PMS. It's the number of symptoms you have, as well as how severe they are, that helps your doctor determine if PMS is the cause.

- Bloating
- Breast tenderness
- Water retention

- Weight gain
- Swollen feet and ankles
- Headaches
- Food cravings
- Acne
- Low energy
- Backache
- Joint pain
- Insomnia
- Carbohydrate cravings/appetite changes

Hormonal fluctuations during the premenstrual phase may be associated with psychological and emotional symptoms that strongly resemble the symptoms of depression (see Depression, p. 334). If the symptoms occur only during the premenstrual phase, they may be signs of PMS. However, many women who suffer from depression mislabel their feelings as PMS. Talk to your doctor if you experience the following symptoms to determine their cause and find the most effective treatment:

- Mood swings
- Irritability
- Depression
- Aggressiveness or hostility
- Crying spells
- Difficulty concentrating
- Confusion

- Anxiety
- Decreased interest in daily activities
- Social withdrawal

Treatment

There aren't any physical tests that can confirm you have PMS. However, you should have a thorough exam to rule out other medical problems that have symptoms similar to PMS.

To accurately diagnose PMS, your doctor may ask you to keep a diary of your symptoms for about 3 months to see if they follow a pattern that points to PMS. Record your cravings and aches and pains, and keep track of your food, sleep, and exercise. This log will help your doctor with diagnosis and can also help you and your doctor determine the best treatment.

Self-Care

There is no cure for PMS, but you can reduce or prevent many symptoms through lifestyle changes. Depending on your symptoms, your doctor may also prescribe some type of medication.

- Try aspirin or ibuprofen if you have headaches, backaches, cramps, or breast tenderness.
- Nutritional supplements, including vitamin B6, calcium, and magnesium, may relieve some of your symptoms.

- If you suffer from moderate to severe anxiety, irritability, or depression, your doctor may prescribe an antidepressant or recommend you see a therapist. Antidepressants have been found to be very effective in treating the psychological and emotional symptoms of PMS.

- Oral contraceptives may decrease your symptoms by preventing hormonal fluctuations.

What to do about PMS

Symptom/Sign	Action
Mild pain, swelling, or mood swings	Self-care
More severe symptoms, such as depression, anxiety, or hostility	See doctor
Inability to function	See doctor

Prevention

Research shows that dietary changes and increased exercise have positive effects on the symptoms of PMS. Try these steps to prevent or alleviate your symptoms:

- Limit salt and drink plenty of fluids to relieve water retention and bloating.

- Avoid caffeine and alcohol to minimize irritability.

- Try eating smaller, more frequent meals to avoid cravings and reduce bloating.

- Exercise at least 30 minutes per day to improve your overall health and reduce fatigue.

- Make sure you're getting enough sleep to reduce stress.

- Look for ways to manage your stress, such as taking a bath or meditating.

Toxic Shock Syndrome

Toxic shock syndrome (TSS) is a very serious bacterial infection. Although it can affect men, women, and children, more than half the cases of TSS today occur in menstruating women.

TSS was identified during the early 1980s, when a large number of cases occurred in women who were using highly absorbent tampons. Today, TSS associated with menstruation is relatively rare—about 10 cases each year.

Causes

TSS is caused by toxins released by some *Staphylococcus aureus* bacteria. These bacteria are always in your body and normally don't hurt you, but under certain conditions they can suddenly increase and make you critically ill.

Factors that can increase the risk of TSS include:

- Use of highly absorbent tampons
- Use of diaphragms or vaginal sponges to prevent pregnancy
- Recent childbirth
- Recent surgery
- Wounds or infections

Symptoms

The symptoms of TSS can develop very quickly. If you have these symptoms—especially if you have just had a menstrual period and used tampons—see your doctor right away:

- Sudden high fever (102°F or higher)
- Sunburnlike rash, especially on the palms of your hands and soles of your feet
- Nausea, vomiting, or diarrhea
- Red eyes, mouth, and throat
- Headaches
- Dizziness, confusion
- Achy muscles

If you develop TSS you may need to be hospitalized. You will be given antibiotics.

What to do about Toxic Shock Syndrome

Symptom/Sign	Action
Sudden high fever; rash on palms and soles; headaches; nausea; severe diarrhea; and red eyes, throat, and mouth after a menstrual period, childbirth, or surgery	See doctor
Dizziness, confusion, or seizures after a menstrual period, childbirth, or surgery	Go to hospital

Prevention

- If you use tampons, avoid highly absorbent tampons and change them frequently. Do not use tampons overnight.

- If you use diaphragms or vaginal sponges for contraception, don't leave them in longer than the recommended time.

Vaginal Discharge and Irritation

Although makers of feminine hygiene sprays and douches would like you to believe otherwise, a healthy vagina cleans itself naturally. A clear or opaque vaginal discharge is part of this cleansing process.

Causes

Several conditions can cause irritation around the vagina and changes in the color, smell, amount, or consistency of the vaginal discharge. These include vaginal yeast infections, bacterial vaginosis, trichomoniasis, and sexually transmitted diseases, such as the herpes simplex virus type 2.

Yeast infections are usually marked by a thick, white discharge like cottage cheese. The vagina and labia (the lips of the vagina) may be red and swollen. Yeast infections also cause intense itching and burning in the genital area. An overgrowth of a normal fungal organism, *Candida albicans* (Monilia), is the usual culprit. This type of infection is more likely during pregnancy, after taking antibiotics, when using birth control pills, or if you have diabetes. Spreading it through sex is rare, but if your partner has genital itching and a rash, an over-the-counter antifungal cream may be used topically. Yeast infections can usually be treated safely with self-care steps.

Bacterial vaginosis is a condition that occurs when there is too much bacteria in your vagina. Symptoms include a yellow or white fishy-smelling vaginal discharge, itching, burning during urination, and pain in the vaginal area following intercourse. Bacterial vaginal infection is usually treated with specific prescription antibiotics.

Trichomoniasis is caused by a tiny organism. Symptoms include a yellow-green frothy discharge from the vagina, itching, and sometimes pain. The discharge may have a bad odor but doesn't always. Because the *Trichomonas* parasite can live in the male prostate gland, your partner should also be treated to prevent reinfection. See your doctor or nurse practitioner if you have symptoms of *Trichomonas* infection. He or she can prescribe drugs. Take your medication exactly the way it is prescribed.

Sexually transmitted diseases also may cause vaginal itching, pain, and discharge (see Sexually Transmitted Diseases, p. 319).

Self-Care

- If you think you are having your first infection, see your doctor before trying self-care. Your doctor can make sure you do not have a more serious infection.

- Use an over-the-counter antifungal vaginal cream or suppository (such as Monistat, Gyne-Lotrimin, or Mycelex). Follow the package directions and be sure to use all the medicine. Don't stop treatment just because the symptoms are gone. Medication can be used while menstruating, but you may also wait and use afterward if symptoms continue.

- Expose the area to air when possible.

- Apply cool compresses to the area between the vagina and rectum or soak in an oatmeal bath product (Aveeno bath treatment).

- Avoid bubble baths, vaginal sprays, and douching (unless prescribed). Soaking in a tub of plain, lukewarm water, however, is helpful.

- Avoid sexual intercourse until you finish the medicine. This will prevent further irritation.

- If self-care doesn't relieve your symptoms or if symptoms get worse, see your doctor. It is preferable to be off the vaginal cream for 48 hours before evaluation.

- Skin changes during perimenopause and menopause may cause thinning of the vaginal and vulvar tissue, which may result in vaginal dryness, burning, itching, painful intercourse, and urinary frequency. Estrogen creams are often helpful for these symptoms. Make an appointment to discuss treatment with your doctor.

What to do about Vaginal Discharge and Irritation

Symptom/Sign	Action
First-time itching; white, cottage cheese–like discharge; redness and swelling around vagina and labia	Call doctor
More than three yeast infections a year	See doctor
Yellow or greenish vaginal discharge with itching, burning during urination, or pain during or after intercourse	See doctor
Sores in the genital area or possible exposure to a sexually transmitted disease	See doctor
Lower abdominal pain, fever and chills, or frequent urination	See doctor

Prevention

The following are basic hygiene practices that may help prevent vaginal irritation and discharge:

- Wear cotton underwear.
- Avoid tight-fitting jeans and pantyhose.
- Avoid deodorant tampons or douches.
- Use adequate lubrication during intercourse.
- Avoid scented or deodorant soaps, laundry detergents, or fabric softeners that cause irritation.
- Thoroughly clean spermicide applicators and diaphragms after use.

Sexual Issues

Sexual issues are often complex, because they can involve both your body and emotions. Many sexual problems are linked to a physical or medical condition. Others are related to stress or other mental or emotional factors or a combination of these. Some sexual problems are long term, and some come and go suddenly.

Sexual problems are common. This chapter discusses different sexual concerns and how to deal with them. Your doctor can help with many issues. He or she may also recommend counseling or help from other experts. ::

Birth Control

Today, women and men can choose birth control (or contraception) methods that fit their lifestyles and preferences. For married couples and people in long-term relationships, the decision of when and what kind of birth control to use is one that is best made together.

The effectiveness of a birth control method is measured in terms of the number of pregnancies that can be expected if 100 couples used the method for 1 year. For example, a 2-percent failure rate means that of those 100 couples, two women could expect to become pregnant during the year while using that method. Without using any birth control, 85 of the 100 couples could be expected to conceive within the year.

Birth Control Methods

There are many ways to help you control when or if you want to have children. Birth control options range from natural means, such as the rhythm method, to surgical sterilization.

Not all birth control methods offer protection against sexually transmitted diseases (STDs). Condoms, when used correctly, provide the best protection against STDs. Using a spermacide with a condom may provide additional protection against some STDs.

Natural Methods

Natural methods (20-percent failure rate) don't use devices, pills, or other products. There are two kinds of natural birth control methods:

- To practice the rhythm method, a couple abstains from having sexual intercourse during the time a woman is ovulating (the time in the menstrual cycle when an egg is ready to be fertilized). The couple can calculate this time by counting the days during the woman's menstrual cycle (calendar method), checking for changes in vaginal mucus (ovulation method), or checking for changes in body temperature and vaginal mucus (symptothermal method). There are kits available that can help determine a woman's fertile period.

- Using the withdrawal method, the man pulls his penis from the woman's vagina before he ejaculates. This requires a great deal of control on the man's part. And even with control, sometimes sperm may be expelled before ejaculation. The failure rate of this method is very high.

Spermicides

Spermicides (18-percent failure rate) kill sperm before they can enter the uterus and fertilize the egg. They come in foams, jellies, suppositories, creams, and foaming tablets. Spermicides are inserted in the vagina before intercourse, giving protection for up to 2 hours. When used with condoms or diaphragms, spermicides give added protection against pregnancy and even some sexually transmitted diseases. Occasionally a man or woman may be allergic to spermicides.

Barrier Methods

Barrier methods (12- to 18-percent failure rate) block sperm from reaching the egg. Some, such as condoms and contraceptive sponges, can be bought over the counter and are not expensive. A diaphragm or a cervical cap must be fitted by a doctor.

- A condom is put on over the erect penis (see box on p. 311). When the man ejaculates, the fluid is collected at the end of the condom. Condoms can fail if they break or if the penis gets soft while still in the vagina and the condom slips off. When using a condom, the man should withdraw immediately after ejaculation. Condoms have a failure rate of 12 percent.

- A diaphragm is a saucer-shaped piece of rubber with a flexible metal rim. It is inserted in the vagina and then sits snugly against the cervix, or entrance to the uterus (see illustration below). Although the diaphragm is a partial physical barrier against sperm, the

Diaphragm and condom.

real protection comes from the spermicidal cream or jelly it holds against the cervix. A diaphragm must be left in place for 6 hours after intercourse. The diaphragm has a failure rate of 12 percent.

A cervical cap is smaller than a diaphragm. It provides an airtight seal over the cervix. It requires less spermicide to be effective. The cervical cap must be left in place for at least 6 hours after intercourse, but it can be left in the vagina for up to 72 hours. It has a failure rate similar to that of the diaphragm.

Intrauterine Devices

Intrauterine devices (IUDs; 2-percent failure rate) are small devices placed inside the uterus (see illustration). They may be made of plastic and may contain copper or hormones. They are thought to keep fertilized eggs from implanting in the uterine lining, although why they prevent conception is not fully known. The copper ParaGard IUD also kills sperm as they approach the IUD, preventing fertilization. A copper IUD can be worn for up to 10 years. IUDs with hormones must be replaced every year. The IUD is easier to insert and less likely to be expelled accidentally in women who have already had at least one child. In some women an IUD can cause bleeding between periods or difficult periods. A woman with an IUD is shown how to check to make sure it is still in place. Occasionally an IUD is expelled by the body.

Birth Control Pills

Birth control pills (1- to 3-percent failure rate) prevent ovulation and change cervical mucus and the lining of the uterus. Birth control pills, which are only available by prescription, contain synthetic versions of the female hormones estro-

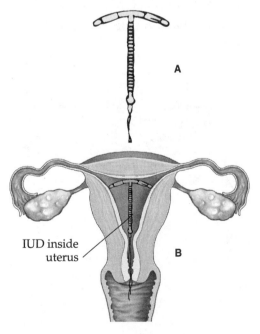

A, *Intrauterine device (IUD);* B, *IUD in place.*

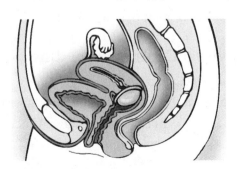

Diaphragm in place.

gen and progesterone or just progesterone. There are different formulations
of pills available, so if you have side effects with one kind of birth control pill,
your doctor can try another. The pill is
convenient and highly effective when
taken every day. Progesterone-only pills
fail 3 percent of the time; combination progesterone-estrogen pills fail only
1 percent of the time. The pill has some
risk of heart disease for women who are
older than 35 and who smoke heavily.

Implants

Implants (less than 1-percent failure rate)
can provide birth control for 5 years.
The Norplant implants look like small
sticks. A local anesthetic is used to surgically place the implants under the
skin on the inner side of the upper arm
(see illustration below). Irregular bleeding is a common side effect of contraceptive implants.

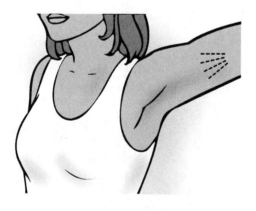

Implants.

Progesterone Injections

*Progesterone injections (less than 1-percent
failure rate)*, or Depo-Provera, prevent
ovulation and prevent implantation of
any fertilized egg by keeping the lining
of the uterus from building up. The
Depo-Provera injection is given every
3 months, but proper timing of the injections is important to provide full protection from pregnancy. When the first
injection is given within the first 5 days
of a normal menstrual cycle, protection from pregnancy is immediate. Infrequent or irregular periods are a common
side effect. Other side effects include
weight gain, bloating, and depression.

Birth Control Patch

The *birth control patch (1 percent failure
rate)* is a thin, beige square that sticks to
the skin like an adhesive bandage. It de-
livers hormones through the skin into
the bloodstream. Once a week, a new
patch is applied to the buttocks, abdomen, upper torso (but not to the breasts),
or the outside of the upper arm. Cigarette
smoking increases the risk of cardiovascular side effects with this method, especially in women over age 35.

Vaginal Contraceptive Ring

The *vaginal contraceptive ring (1 percent
failure rate)* is a soft, flexible plastic ring
about two inches in diameter. Once a

month, a new ring is inserted into the vagina, where it slowly releases estrogen and progestin hormones. As with other hormonal methods, women who smoke have an increased risk of cardiovascular side effects, especially if they are over 35.

Emergency Contraception

Emergency contraception is available when a woman has sex without using birth control or when a birth control method fails, such as a condom breaking. Generally, emergency contraception is done by giving high doses of birth control pills within 3 days of the unprotected sexual intercourse. This is not something a woman should do on her own, however; if you have had unprotected sex and are concerned about pregnancy, talk to your doctor about emergency options.

Surgical Sterilization

Surgical sterilization permanently blocks sperm from connecting with the egg. Either the sperm are blocked from leaving a man's body or the route to the egg in the woman's body is closed. It is permanent birth control and should be done only when a man or woman is sure that he or she no longer wants to be able to have children.

- In women, tubal ligation closes the fallopian tubes. It is done under a general anesthetic and the fallopian tubes are tied, cut, banded, or sealed.

- In men, a vasectomy closes the tubes that carry sperm to the penis. It is usually done in a doctor's office, under a local anesthetic.

How to Put on a Condom

Make sure the condom has space at the top to collect semen, or leave at least a half-inch extra space when it's put on.

Put the condom on when the penis is fully erect. Sit the condom on the end of the penis as if it were a cap, gently squeeze air from the top of the condom, and then roll it down over the penis until it reaches the base.

After ejaculation, hold on to the base of the condom and withdraw the penis from the vagina while it is still erect.

You can use a lubricant to help keep the condom from tearing. Be sure to use only water-based lubricants. Oil-based lubricants such as petroleum jelly or baby oil can damage condoms and cause them to break.

Use only latex condoms and follow instructions. Condoms made of other materials have tiny holes that can let sexually transmitted diseases through. Check the expiration date on the condom package. Do not use the condom if the expiration date has passed or if the package seems damaged. Store condoms in a cool, dark, dry place. Heat can harm them.

What to do about Birth Control

Symptom/Sign	Action
You need more information on birth control	Call doctor
You suspect you are pregnant or need emergency contraception	Call doctor
You wish to use a birth-control method requiring a prescription or you would like surgical sterilization	See doctor

Erection Problems

Men at any age can have problems getting or keeping an erection, making it difficult or impossible for them to have successful sexual intercourse. This is called *erectile dysfunction,* or *impotence.*

Most men have had an occasional erection problem. Physical or emotional stress, fatigue, or problems in a relationship can cause occasional erection problems. Difficulty getting and keeping an erection increases with age. But if a man of any age frequently has erection problems, it can be a sign that something is physically or emotionally wrong.

Erection problems are difficult for many men to talk about, because being able to have sexual intercourse is part of a man's self-image. Most erection problems can be successfully treated, so it's important to talk to a doctor if the problem persists for 2 months or more.

Causes

Most erection problems have a physical cause and are the result of illness, injury, or the side effect of medication or illegal drugs. Physical causes include diabetes, prostate surgery, spinal cord injury, hormonal disorders, alcoholism, drug abuse, and some heart disease. There also can be psychological causes, including stress, depression, and fatigue.

A physical cause of erection problems can lead to worry and anxiety about the problems, adding emotional stress that only increases the problems.

Treatment

Treatment for erection problems can be anything from counseling to medication to implanted devices that help create an erection. Usually your doctor will start with the least drastic treatment, which might be correcting medications you are taking for another condition. Treatment options include the following:

• Sildenafil (Viagra) allows increased blood flow in the penis, improving the chances that sexual stimulation will cause an erection. Viagra is not a miracle medication—and it can be a problem for men who have some underlying conditions that are causing erection problems—but it has allowed many men, particularly healthy older men, to return to satisfactory sexual relations. There are other medications besides Viagra that can

help increase blood flow in the penis. Some of these are injected into the penis or are in a suppository that is inserted into the tip of the penis.

• Hormone replacement therapy is an option for men whose bodies don't make enough testosterone.

• Vacuum devices actually pull blood into the penis. The device, a plastic tube, is put over the penis and then a hand pump is used to create a vacuum in the tube that forces blood into the penis. When the penis is erect, bands are placed around the base to keep blood in it so it will stay erect long enough for intercourse. Vacuum devices are available only by prescription.

• Surgery can either correct problems with the blood vessels in the penis or implant a device that allows the man to get an erection with rods or inflatable cylinders.

What to do about Erection Problems

Symptom/Sign	Action
You have problems getting or maintaining an erection	Call doctor
The problems last for more than 2 months	See doctor

Prevention

Although nothing can completely eliminate the possibility of an occasional erection problem, there are some things that help decrease problems:

- Exercise regularly.

- Drink only small amounts of alcohol or don't drink at all.

- Don't smoke.

- Try to reduce stress in your life, or find ways to cope with it without becoming anxious.

- Make sure you get enough sleep.

- Get regular medical checkups.

Loss of Sexual Desire

Sexual desire naturally varies from person to person. Some may want sex three times a day; others, three times a year. There is no "right" or "normal" level of desire. Differing levels of desire are a problem only if a couple can't find a mutually satisfying compromise.

Causes

Diminished desire is common in both men and women in times of stress, when ill or recovering from an illness, when tension exists in a relationship, or when one or both partners is just plain tired. Alcohol and certain drugs—birth control pills, antihistamines, and blood pressure medications, among others—can also cause a loss of desire. These same things can cause temporary erection problems (see p. 312) and inhibit orgasm in both men and women (see Sexual Concerns, p. 316).

Self-Care

- Relax. It is natural to have periods when one or both partners are less interested in sexual activity. If you are coping with young children, financial worries, or other life stresses, you may have little interest in sex. Don't let that lack of interest add to your stress. Accept that it's natural and that desire will return.

- Talk with your partner about your relationship and the other things in your life. Remember—and remind each other—that sex is not the only reason you care for each other.

- Review the side effects of any medications you're taking, whether they are prescribed or over-the-counter. If the medication warns that it may make you drowsy, it also may affect your interest in sex. Talk to your doctor about an alternative medication.

- Focus on your senses. This can help reduce sexual anxiety and heighten responsiveness for men and women. Agree not to have intercourse for at least a month. During that time, set aside an hour or so each day to massage each other. While naked, explore and massage all parts of each other's body, except the genitals and breasts. Once you are fully comfortable with this, begin to include the breasts and genitals, but do not have intercourse. Finally, when you are both more relaxed, start having intercourse. Continue to use whole-body sensuality in your foreplay.

What to do about Loss of Sexual Desire

Symptom/Sign	Action
Occasional loss of desire	Self-care
Loss of desire connected to medication or illness	Call doctor
Ongoing loss of desire for 2 months or more	See doctor

Sexual Concerns

The "right way" to make love and the "right" number of times to have sex are simply what work best and are most satisfying for each couple. But anxiety and physical, emotional, or relationship issues can interfere with a person's or couple's ability to enjoy or participate fully in sex.

Types of Sexual Concerns

Aging
Simply growing older brings changes in sexual function for both men and women. Most people don't have the same level of sexual desire at age 55 that they had when they were 20. Interest in sex usually declines slowly with age, although it seldom disappears totally.

As people grow older, both men and women usually need more time and more direct genital stimulation before reaching orgasm.

In older men, erections are usually not as firm as they once were and more time may be needed—days rather than hours—after ejaculation before they are able to have sex again (see Erection Problems, p. 312).

Early or Late Ejaculation
Early, or premature, ejaculation is when a man reaches climax before desired.

Delayed ejaculation is when the man cannot have an orgasm in what seems like a reasonable amount of time for himself and his partner. These problems often can be relieved by adjustments in lovemaking.

Painful Intercourse
Women may have pain during intercourse for a number of reasons.

• Vaginal dryness is the most common cause of painful intercourse for women. It can occur because of low levels of estrogen, especially after menopause, or because of illness, as a result of the side effects of medication, or for psychological reasons.

• A painful muscle spasm, called vaginismus, can occur during intercourse for some women. This can be caused by vaginal scars from childbirth or surgery, by irritation of the vagina from condoms or spermicides, or by infection.

• Pain can also be caused by emotional problems, including fear of pregnancy or reaction to earlier sexual abuse.

Failure to Have an Orgasm

Although most women can have an orgasm while having sex, some have problems. There may be physical reasons for this, but more commonly it is the result of not knowing or being able to communicate the kind of touch that will bring her to orgasm.

For most women, orgasm is more likely with oral sex or by hand stimulation by herself or her partner. Women usually need stimulation of other parts of their bodies as well to become aroused enough to have an orgasm. Stroking and touching of the breasts and nipples and other sensitive areas is important.

During sex, women are more likely to have an orgasm if they can talk to their partners about what kind of touch is arousing. Some women are shy or embarrassed to talk about their sexual needs.

Some problems in coming to orgasm can have deeper emotional roots, such as reaction to sexual abuse or fear of pregnancy.

Use of alcohol or drugs or the side effects of some medications also can affect a woman's ability to have an orgasm.

Self-Care

- Talk. Good communication is the key to good sex and a good relationship. Tell and show your partner how you like to be touched. Talk through other problems and tensions in your relationship.

- If fast ejaculation is a problem, pause, change positions, or think about something else. Doing any one of these three things at the first sensation of ejaculation can allow a man to delay ejaculation.

- Remember, good sex is possible even without intercourse. An erection is not a requirement for either person to have an orgasm.

- Avoid alcohol and drugs that warn "may cause drowsiness." If you are having sexual problems, ask your doctor if any medication you are taking could be a cause.

What to do about Sexual Concerns

Symptom/Sign	Action
Erection, ejaculation, or orgasm problems	Self-care
Sexual problems that continue or worsen despite self-care	Call doctor
Physical problem or medical condition (such as diabetes or heart disease) that may be causing sexual problems	See doctor

Sexually Transmitted Diseases

Since we first began hearing about the acquired immunodeficiency syndrome (AIDS) epidemic in the early 1980s, many people seem to have forgotten that other sexually transmitted diseases (STDs) are still common. Diseases such as syphilis, gonorrhea, genital herpes, hepatitis B, and chlamydia also pose serious health risks.

When it comes to STDs, having sex with many different partners puts you at much greater risk. It puts you at the same risk as if you had sex with all of your partners' partners. Not having sex or having sex only with a single partner who is uninfected and who has no other sexual partners are the two best ways to prevent STDs.

STDs need to be treated by your doctor. If your condition is especially difficult to handle, your doctor may bring in doctors who specialize in infectious disease. ::

Common Sexually Transmitted Diseases

STDs are some of the most common infectious diseases in the United States, affecting millions of people each year—mostly teenagers and young adults. Nearly two-thirds of all STDs occur in people younger than 25.

Women are twice as likely as men to be infected by STDs and are less likely to have symptoms. Health problems caused by untreated STDs tend to be more frequent and severe for women than for men, partly because the lack of symptoms may prevent women from seeing a doctor until serious problems have developed.

STDs are passed from person to person through sexual intercourse, genital contact, or contact with body fluids such as semen, vaginal secretions, and blood. Some STDs can also be spread by sharing intravenous drug needles or other items contaminated with the body fluids of an infected person.

Symptoms

Often, STDs have no symptoms. This is especially true for women. Symptoms that do develop vary depending on the disease and can sometimes be confused with those of other diseases.

Even when there are no symptoms, some STDs may still be passed from person to person. That is why many doctors recommend periodic testing or screening for people who have more than one trusted sex partner.

Treatment

Your doctor may make a diagnosis based on your history and a physical examination. There are also a number of laboratory tests available. Your doctor may scrape a sample of cells from the affected area to be analyzed. For some STDs, blood tests can be used to confirm a diagnosis.

When diagnosed and treated early, many STDs can be cured by antibiotics or other medications. Some people are too embarrassed to ask for help or information about STDs, but the earlier you seek treatment and warn sex partners about the disease, the less likely the disease will cause permanent physical damage or be spread to others.

Chlamydia

Chlamydia is a bacterial infection that is spread during vaginal, anal, or oral sex. In women, chlamydia infection can cause inflammation of the cervix and pelvic inflammatory disease (see Pelvic Inflammatory Disease, p. 297). In men it can cause inflammation of the urethra, the organ through which urine passes, and the epididymis, where sperm are stored.

Symptoms

You may have genital chlamydia infection without any symptoms. Experts estimate that up to 75 percent of women and 50 percent of men who have chlamydia infection have no symptoms or symptoms so mild they don't seek treatment. If you do have symptoms, they usually appear 1 to 3 weeks after exposure.

For women, symptoms may include:

- Burning or pain during urination
- Pain in the lower abdomen
- Anal discomfort
- Abnormal vaginal bleeding or discharge

For men, symptoms may include:

- Burning or pain during urination
- Watery or thin white discharge from penis

- Pain or swelling in the testicles
- Anal discomfort

Treatment

Fortunately, chlamydia infection can be treated with antibiotics. Because many people with chlamydia also have gonorrhea, antibiotics for both infections are usually given together.

Genital Herpes

Genital herpes is caused by the herpes simplex virus, which also causes cold sores around the mouth. Genital herpes infection is spread through sexual contact with someone who has the infection. Usually the virus is transmitted through the sores. It can be spread to others when sores are not present, but this is uncommon.

Symptoms

Some people, even when first infected with genital herpes, do not have any symptoms. For most people, symptoms occur within 10 days of having sex with an infected person. They include:

- Itching, burning, or pain in the genital or anal area

- Visible blisters
- Swollen glands in the genital area
- Lower back, buttock, or leg pain
- Fever
- Vaginal discharge

Symptoms can last up to 3 weeks. Even after the initial outbreak of sores heals, infected people carry the virus for the rest of their lives, with new sores erupting from time to time. It's typical to have a few outbreaks a year, although the number of outbreaks tends to decrease over time.

Treatment

There is no permanent cure for herpes. Once you become infected with the virus, it stays in your body. However, your doctor can prescribe drugs that can reduce the length and pain of herpes outbreaks.

Genital Warts

Genital warts are caused by the human papillomavirus (HPV). Some types of HPV cause common skin warts, and some are associated with cervical cancer. About one-third of HPV types are spread through sexual contact and cause warts in the genital area.

Symptoms

You may have genital warts and not be aware you are infected, because there are often no symptoms. If warts are visible, they appear as small, raised bumps that may grow larger or disappear. You may experience itching and burning on or near your sex organs or anus and may have pain with intercourse.

In women, genital warts may occur:

- On the inside or outside of the vagina
- On the cervix
- Around the anus

In men, genital warts are less common, generally occurring:

- Around the tip of the penis
- On the shaft of the penis
- On the scrotum
- Around the anus

Treatment

There is no permanent cure for HPV infection, but the warts it causes can be treated. It is important to get treatment from your doctor—do not use drugstore treatments intended for other kinds of warts. Because warts may reoccur, see your doctor regularly for checkups.

Gonorrhea

Gonorrhea is an infection caused by a bacterium that grows and multiplies in warm, moist areas of the body, including the reproductive tract, rectum, and throat. It is most commonly spread through vaginal, oral, and anal contact.

Symptoms

The symptoms of gonorrhea are so mild that you could have the disease and not know it. Even if you don't have symptoms, you are still contagious. If symptoms do develop, they usually appear within 5 days after exposure.

For women, symptoms may include:

- A painful or burning sensation during urination or bowel movements
- Abnormal vaginal discharge that is yellow or bloody
- Cramps and pain in the lower abdomen
- More pain than usual during menstrual periods

For men, symptoms may include:

- White or yellow discharge (pus) from the penis
- A burning sensation, often severe, during urination

Symptoms of rectal infection include discharge, anal itching, and, sometimes, painful bowel movements.

Treatment

Gonorrhea can be easily treated with antibiotics. It is important that partners be treated at the same time to avoid re-infecting one another or others. Because many people with gonorrhea also have chlamydia, antibiotics for both infections are usually given together. Left untreated, gonorrhea can cause pelvic inflammatory disease in women (see Pelvic Inflammatory Disease, p. 297) or urethra blockage in men.

Hepatitis B Virus

Hepatitis B virus (HBV) is a sexually transmitted disease that causes inflammation of the liver and can lead to cirrhosis, cancer of the liver, and liver failure. It is spread through contact with body fluids, so people at risk for getting HBV include anyone exposed to blood and blood products, people who share drug needles, health care workers, and anyone who has several sexual partners. However, one-third of new cases of HBV reported in the United States occur in sexually active young adults with no other risk factors.

Symptoms

Some people who have HBV don't have any symptoms. If you do have symptoms, they'll begin 45 to 180 days after exposure and may include:

- Yellow eyes or skin (jaundice)
- Loss of appetite
- Nausea and vomiting
- Fever
- Diarrhea, light-colored stools
- Stomach or joint pain
- Extreme fatigue

Treatment

There is no cure for hepatitis B. About 90 percent of adults recover from HBV in a few months, clearing the virus from their system and developing an immunity. A small percentage of adults are unable to clear the infection from their bodies, and the infection becomes chronic. Over time, chronic HBV infection may cause your liver to stop working and you may need a liver transplant. If you think you have been exposed to HBV, your doctor may be able to give you hepatitis B immune globulin to prevent hepatitis from developing (see Viral Hepatitis, p. 165).

Prevention

A very effective vaccine is available to prevent HBV infection. People who should be vaccinated include:

- All babies at birth

- All children up to 12 years of age who have not been vaccinated

- People of any age who fall into a high-risk group (people who have more than one sex partner in 6 months, men who have sex with men, and people who inject illegal drugs)

- Anyone who is exposed to human blood

Human Immunodeficiency Virus

Human immunodeficiency virus is the virus that leads to AIDS. HIV destroys CD4 cells, which help the body fight off infection and disease. When you lose CD4 cells, your immune system breaks down, allowing you to get certain infections and cancers. When you have HIV infection and your CD4 cell count is less than 200, it is called AIDS, and you are less able to fight off disease. When a person gets HIV, it can take about 10 years before AIDS actually develops.

Causes

HIV is spread through sexual contact, shared drug needles, or other situations where people are exposed to infected blood, semen, or vaginal secretions. To become infected with HIV, the blood, semen, or vaginal secretions must enter your body.

HIV is *not* spread through:

- Using public restrooms

- Coughing or sneezing

- Hugging or touching

- Food or water

- Shared work or school space

Even if an HIV-infected person is otherwise healthy and has not yet developed AIDS, he or she can spread it to other people. If you already have another sexually transmitted disease and are exposed to a person with HIV, you're at greater risk for getting HIV.

Symptoms

Early symptoms of HIV (within weeks to months after exposure) include swollen lymph glands and flulike illness. Later symptoms (years after exposure) include:

- Persistent fevers and night sweats

- Persistent fatigue

- Unexplained weight loss or loss of appetite

- Prolonged diarrhea

- Swollen lymph nodes

- Purple bumps on skin or inside mouth and nose

- Recurrent respiratory infections, shortness of breath, or dry cough

HIV is diagnosed by testing your blood for the presence of antibodies to the virus. HIV tests aren't accurate immediately after infection because it takes time for your body to develop these antibodies—usually from 6 to 12 weeks. In some cases it can take up to 6 months for an HIV antibody test to become positive.

There is no cure for HIV/AIDS, but many medications can dramatically prolong the lives of people infected with HIV by slowing damage to the immune system.

Syphilis

Syphilis is a complex disease spread through vaginal, anal, or oral sex. In its first stage, this bacterial infection can cause sores on the genitals and rectum or in the throat. Sores usually appear within 10 days to 3 months after exposure. Because they are painless, sores often go unnoticed.

Symptoms

If left untreated, the secondary stage of syphilis can produce symptoms that include:

- Rash over any area of the body, especially on the palms of the hands or soles of the feet

- Fever

- Fatigue

- Muscle aches

- Sore throat

When the secondary symptoms disappear, the latent (hidden) stage of syphilis begins. In this stage there are no symptoms, but without treatment the disease can begin to damage the internal organs. This damage may show up years later in the tertiary (late) stage of syphilis. In this stage, serious problems can occur, including paralysis, heart abnormalities, and mental illness. The damage may be serious enough to cause death.

Treatment

Syphilis can be cured with penicillin or other antibiotics. Although treatment will kill the syphilis bacterium and prevent further damage, it will not repair any damage already done. Some people need more antibiotics to cure the disease, followed by periodic blood tests to check that the infection is gone.

Trichomoniasis

Trichomoniasis is a bacterial infection that is spread through sexual activity. In women the vagina is the most common site of infection. In men, infection most often occurs in the urethra.

Symptoms

Trichomoniasis often occurs without any symptoms. When symptoms do develop, it's usually within 20 days of exposure.

For women, symptoms may include:

- Heavy yellow-green vaginal discharge
- Pain during intercourse
- Vaginal odor
- Vaginal irritation and itching
- Lower abdominal pain

For men, symptoms are rare, but may include:

- Discharge from the penis
- Painful or difficult urination

Treatment

Trichomoniasis can be treated with antibiotics. To prevent reinfection, all sexual partners should be treated at the same time, even if not all have symptoms. Avoid sexual intercourse or use a condom until treatment is completed.

Special Risks During Pregnancy

Sexually transmitted diseases pose special risks during pregnancy. Many STDs can be passed from mother to child during pregnancy, at birth, or shortly after. Often, STDs can lead to health problems for newborns. For example:

- Low birth weight and premature birth appear to be associated with STDs, including chlamydial infection and trichomoniasis.
- Chlamydial infection can cause pneumonia and eye infections.
- Gonorrhea can cause blindness or life-threatening infections.
- Syphilis can cause a baby to be stillborn or to die shortly after birth.
- Herpes simplex can cause encephalitis (see p. 99) and death.
- Babies born with HIV may not grow and develop normally and may also develop cerebral palsy. They are vulnerable to the same problems as adults with HIV, and eventually the disease is fatal.
- Children who get hepatitis at or before birth may become chronic carriers of the virus.

Women who have syphilis, gonorrhea, or chlamydia can be treated with antibiotics during pregnancy to prevent complications for themselves and their babies. Women with active genital herpes sores may need to deliver by cesarean section to keep their babies from getting the virus. Women who are HIV positive should take anti-HIV medications during pregnancy to reduce the risk of passing the virus to the baby.

What to do about Sexually Transmitted Diseases

Symptom/Sign	Action
Sore in the genital area, rectum, or throat	See doctor
Burning or pain during urination, pain in lower abdomen, or anal discomfort	See doctor
Pain or bleeding during intercourse	See doctor
For women, abnormal vaginal bleeding or discharge	See doctor
For men, discharge from the penis or pain or swelling in testicles	See doctor
Unprotected sex with someone who may have a STD or a partner who has been diagnosed with an STD	See doctor
Pregnant and think you have been exposed to an STD	See doctor

Prevention

The two best ways to prevent sexually transmitted diseases are to abstain from sex and to have a mutually monogamous sexual relationship (when you and your partner only have sex with each other) with someone who is uninfected. If neither option works for you, here are some other things you can do:

- Limit the number of sexual partners you have, and don't go back and forth between partners. The more sexual partners you have, the greater your risk for STDs.

- Always use a condom. Choose latex condoms with receptacle tips rather than natural-membrane (lambskin) condoms, which may be more likely to break or to allow viruses and bacteria to pass through. If you're sensitive to latex, choose polyurethane condoms. Never use oil-based lubricants such as petroleum jelly or baby oil, which can cause condoms to break (see How to Put on a Condom, p. 311). Keep in mind that condoms fail at a rate of 10 to 15 percent as a result of flaws or improper use.

- If a male condom cannot be used appropriately, use a female condom.

- During oral sex, use a condom, a dental dam, or plastic wrap.

- Remember that condoms don't offer complete protection against all STDs, because they don't cover the entire genital area.

- Don't share drug needles.

- If you are sexually active with multiple partners, have screening tests regularly to check for STDs.

- Avoid douching, which removes some of the normal protective bacteria in the vagina and increases the risk of getting some STDs.

Mind-Body Problems

Taking care of your mind is as important to your health as taking care of your body. People with good mind-body health are in control of their thoughts, feelings, and behaviors. Although everyone experiences stress and emotional problems from time to time, being unable to deal with them can signal a more serious problem. Many people don't recognize mental health concerns until a crisis occurs.

This chapter explains common mind-body concerns and ways they can be treated. Sometimes you can help yourself through bad feelings, but if you can't function normally, you may need the help of your doctor. Your doctor may want you to see a mental health professional, such as a psychologist or psychiatrist. ▪▪

Alcohol and Drug Abuse

People who abuse alcohol and drugs keep using them even when they know it is hurting them and those they love. This is called substance abuse.

Marijuana is the most commonly used illegal drug. Other drugs include stimulants such as cocaine, amphetamines, heroin, hallucinogens, sedatives, and inhalants. Some drugs are more likely to cause addiction—a physical need for the drug—than others, but all drugs can be abused, even those prescribed by your doctor.

Alcohol is not illegal for adults, but it can be abused. You can drink alcohol and still have a healthy lifestyle. You can enjoy a glass of wine with dinner or a drink when out with friends. But too much alcohol can lead to serious injuries and illness.

Causes

People may have an inherited tendency to alcoholism. Sometimes people are in situations where there is a lot of drinking or drug use around them, and they feel they need to participate.

Using some drugs can create a physical craving to continue that use. But it may be that the more a person uses, the less mood changes the drug causes, so the person feels a need to use more.

Individuals make the decision to take the first drink or to use drugs. But once someone is addicted to alcohol or drugs, they probably cannot quit by themselves.

Symptoms

You probably know if you or someone close to you is abusing alcohol or drugs. Drug or alcohol abuse affects a person's ability to handle normal life responsibilities. They may miss work or school, have difficulty in their personal relationships, or fail to take care of themselves properly.

Signs of possible alcohol or drug abuse include:

- Using alcohol or drugs to calm your nerves or to forget your worries

- Missing meals

- Hurting yourself or others while using alcohol or drugs

- A need for more and more alcohol or drugs

- Legal problems related to alcohol or drug use, such as arrests for driving under the influence of alcohol or drugs

- Drinking alcohol alone

- Thinking you have a problem with alcohol or drugs

Treatment

There are many ways to treat alcohol or drug abuse. Your doctor can help you decide which treatment is best for you. Options for treatment include:

- *Alcoholics Anonymous or Narcotics Anonymous.* These organizations offer support meetings with other people who have a problem with drugs or alcohol.

- *Rehabilitation programs.* You can find these programs in hospitals, outpatient centers, and private clinics. Some of these programs are inpatient. That means you stay overnight. For others, you come in each day from home.

- *Detoxification centers.* Detoxification clears your body of the harmful effects of alcohol or drugs.

Because abuse of alcohol or drugs can affect many parts of a person's life, multiple treatment approaches may be necessary. There are some medications that can help control cravings. Individual and group therapy also is helpful for many people.

Support groups, such as Alcoholics Anonymous or Narcotics Anonymous, are important for maintaining a healthy lifestyle after substance abuse has stopped.

What to do about Alcohol and Drug Abuse

Symptom/Sign	Action
Drinking or drug use is making it difficult to handle normal responsibilities	See doctor
Loss of physical control or of consciousness because of drugs or alcohol	Call 911

Prevention

Turning down the first marijuana cigarette or amphetamine a friend offers at a party is the best way to avoid drug abuse. Avoid spending time with people who use illegal drugs as part of their social life.

Alcohol is not illegal for adults and is harder to avoid. Most people can enjoy a drink now and then and still have a healthy lifestyle. Follow these guidelines:

- Cut down on the time you spend with people who drink a lot. If you avoid the time and place where you are likely to drink, you are less likely to abuse alcohol.

- Be sensible at parties. You can enjoy a glass of wine with dinner or a cocktail at a party. But have only one drink. (A *drink* is defined as 12 ounces of beer, 5 ounces of wine, or 1.5 ounces of distilled spirits.) Make your other choices nonalcoholic.

- Don't drink and drive. If you plan to drink when you are out, be sure to ask someone who isn't drinking to drive you home.

- Don't drink alone. When you drink alone, it is easy to drink too much.

- Don't drink to avoid problems. If you are having trouble at work or home, talk to a friend, a member of the clergy, or a doctor you trust.

- Feel free to say no. You don't need a reason for not drinking.

- Set an example for others. You can discourage alcohol abuse in others through your own healthy attitudes and actions.

Anxiety

Anxiety is a state of the mind and body associated with worry, tension, and nervousness.

Everyone experiences life stress and anxious moments. In fact, anxiety can help us cope with external dangers by increasing our awareness and getting our body ready to react. When anxiety becomes overwhelming and interferes with daily life, a person may be suffering from an anxiety disorder.

Anxiety disorders are among the most common mental health problems in the United States. Up to 25 percent of people in the United States will suffer from anxiety disorders sometime in their lives. Anxiety disorders usually begin in a person's late teens or early 20s. Anxiety disorders may occur with depression.

Anxiety disorders include panic disorder, social phobia, specific phobias, post-traumatic stress disorder, obsessive-compulsive disorder, and generalized anxiety disorder.

Anxiety disorders are chronic illnesses that can grow progressively worse if not treated. Effective treatments are available.

Causes

The causes of anxiety and panic are not fully understood. Life experience may trigger anxiety. Chemical imbalances in the brain can also play a role. These imbalances may run in the family.

Symptoms

Anxiety can express itself in different ways. It may be ongoing or come in bursts, lasting only a few minutes. Panic attacks are short, intense bursts of anxiety accompanied by a sense of dread and physical reactions such as heart pounding and sweating. Generalized anxiety is an ongoing condition that is not usually a direct result of a well-defined irrational fear (phobia).

The two major symptoms of generalized anxiety are uncontrollable anxiety and worry. Other symptoms may include:

• Muscle tension

• Fatigue

• Irritability or edginess

• Insomnia or sleep disturbance

• Difficulty concentrating

The symptoms of a panic attack may occur suddenly and repeatedly, including:

• Fear of losing control or "going crazy"

• Fear of dying or that something terrible is about to happen

• Fear of embarrassment or humiliation

• Chest pain or discomfort

• Rapid heartbeat

- Shortness of breath, smothering, sweating
- Chills or hot flashes
- Trembling or shaking
- Feeling of choking
- Nausea or abdominal discomfort
- Numbness or tingling

Treatment

- Share your treatment plan with people close to you. Talk to friends and relatives and explain what you are going through.
- If your doctor prescribes medication, take it exactly the way it is prescribed. You may be tempted to stop the medication when you start feeling better. However, do not stop taking your medication until your doctor tells you to.
- Tell your doctor if you experience side effects from the medication.
- Keep all follow-up appointments with your doctor.
- Keep in mind that it may take some time to start feeling better.
- Talk with your doctor before trying any natural preparations, such as St. John's Wort, Kava, or Melatonin, for the treatment of depression, insomnia, anxiety, and stress. These over-the-counter preparations can interact with other medications and cause serious side effects.

Self-Care

- Learn relaxation techniques such as deep breathing.
- Take time away from stress.
- Exercise regularly. It can improve your health and sense of well-being and increase your ability to handle stress.
- Avoid alcohol and illegal drugs.
- Limit your intake of caffeine. It can make the symptoms of anxiety worse.
- Practice confronting your fears.
- See your doctor if your symptoms aren't improving.

What to do about Anxiety

Symptom/Sign	Action
Occasional worry, tension, or nervousness	Self-care
Worry, tension, or nervousness interfering with daily life	See doctor
Chest pain, rapid heartbeat, shortness of breath	Call 911

Depression

More than 18 million people in the United States suffer from depression. About twice as many women as men suffer from this medical condition. Major depression is a whole-body illness that affects a person's body, feelings, thoughts, and behavior.

Everyone experiences bouts of the blues or periods of sadness now and then. However, if these feelings last more than a couple of weeks or interfere with daily life, a person may be suffering from clinical depression.

Depression involves a set of symptoms that can last for months and sometimes years. It is not a sign of personal weakness or a condition that can be willed or wished away. People with depression cannot merely "pull themselves together" and get better.

Causes

The causes of depression are not always known. Research shows the tendency to develop depression may be inherited and that an uneven balance of mood-influencing chemicals in the brain can play a role. People who have a poor self-image, who view themselves negatively, or who are easily overwhelmed by life challenges may be more likely than others to experience depression. A

serious loss, chronic illness, difficult relationship, or unwelcome change can trigger depression.

Symptoms

The two major symptoms of depression include a depressed mood and an inability to enjoy life. Depression may also include:

- Fatigue
- Sleep disturbances (sleeping too much or difficulty sleeping)
- Change in appetite (eating too much or too little, sometimes weight gain or weight loss)
- Poor concentration
- Feelings of guilt, worthlessness, or helplessness
- General irritability
- Thoughts of death or suicide; suicide attempt
- Vague physical aches and pains, such as stomachaches and headaches
- Excessive crying

Treatment

Treatment for depression can include counseling, medications, or both. If you take medication, you should feel better within 4 to 6 weeks. Counseling can give you support and strategies for coping. With the treatment of depression, recovery is the rule—not the exception.

- Share your treatment plan with people close to you. Talk to friends and relatives and explain what you are going through.

- Take medications exactly they way they are prescribed. You may be tempted to stop taking your medications too soon. However, it is important to keep taking them until your doctor says to stop, even if you begin feeling better. Keep in mind that it may take 2 to 4 weeks to see a noticeable change.

- Report any unusual medication side effects to your doctor, especially if the side effects interfere with your ability to function.

- Keep all follow-up appointments you have with your doctor or therapist. Do not miss an appointment, even if you are feeling better that day.

- Schedule pleasant activities into your day. People tend to feel better when they are doing activities they enjoy.

Self-Care

- Set realistic goals for yourself, and avoid taking on a great deal of responsibility.

- Divide your workload. Break large tasks into small ones, set priorities, and don't be hard on yourself if you are unable to get everything finished.

- Do activities that make you feel better, such as exercising moderately, going to a movie, or attending social events.

- Do not expect to "snap out" of your depression. Instead, help yourself as much as you can and do not blame yourself for not being up to par.

- Contact your doctor if your symptoms aren't improving. Most people begin feeling better within a couple of weeks.

What to do about Depression

Symptom/Sign	Action
Occasional feelings of "being down" lasting a few days but not interfering with daily activities	Self-care
Periods of the blues associated with the menstrual cycle	See doctor
Symptoms of depression	See doctor
Symptoms of depression leading to inability to care for dependents	Call 911
Confused about whereabouts, time, or date; unfamiliar with family or friends	Call 911
Hallucinations or violent behavior	Call 911
Threatening suicide or harm to others	Call 911

Stress

Some stress in life is necessary. If we really had no stress—no competition, no risks to take, no inspiration to try a little harder—we would be completely bored. Sometimes stress adds just the amount of challenge and motivation we need to have a happy life—even to stay alive. It's when the challenges start to pile up that we can lose our ability to effectively deal with stress.

Causes

Causes of stress fall into two categories: external and internal. External stress can be caused by major life events such as moving, changing jobs, the death of a family member, or a divorce. It can also be caused by everyday pressures such as money worries, deadlines, arguments, family concerns, and not getting enough sleep.

Internal stress comes from inside. People are often less aware of internal stress, although it can play an even greater role in the stress of daily life. Internal stressors include:

- Values and beliefs
- Faith
- Goals
- Self-image

Although all these things can be positive, they cause stress when people feel they are not living up to their own expectations in these areas.

Symptoms

When you feel stressed, your body automatically increases blood pressure, heart rate, metabolism, and blood flow to your muscles. This response helps your body react to high-pressure situations.

When you are constantly reacting to stress, it can affect your health, well-being, and relationships. Too much stress can cause symptoms such as insomnia, headaches, backaches, and constipation or diarrhea.

Chronic stress can make you more accident prone; lead to alcohol, tobacco, or drug use; and contribute to high blood pressure and heart disease.

If tension, mood swings, or other bad feelings are interfering with your daily life, it may be more than stress. Stress that depresses your mood or ruins your ability to experience joy may be the result of an anxiety disorder or depression. See your doctor if you are experiencing these symptoms (see Anxiety, p. 332, and Depression, p. 334).

Self-Care

Research has found that people who effectively manage the stress in their lives have three things in common:

- They consider life a challenge, not a series of hassles.

- They have a mission or purpose in life and are committed to fulfilling it.

- They do not feel victimized by life. They have control over their lives, even with temporary setbacks.

Steps to Manage Stress

- Identify the things in your life that cause stress. Try to avoid them, but if you can't, have a plan for dealing with them. You may have to learn to say no to things you don't want to do.

- Reduce internal stress by setting realistic goals and expectations for yourself.

- Share some of your responsibilities. A shared burden is lighter to carry—and you may develop a new friendship or learn another way of problem solving.

- Exercise regularly to relieve muscle tension and stress. Stretches and walking are especially helpful.

- Find some humor in even the worst situation—even when you have to force yourself.

- Organize your time and don't procrastinate. Focus on the individual steps for getting a job done, so you don't feel overwhelmed.

- Talk with a friend or family member. Sharing your thoughts and fears will make them less overwhelming and easier to handle.

- Get a pet to take care of and love.

- Practice deep breathing. Breathe in slowly from your diaphragm. Hold each breath for a few seconds, then exhale slowly.

- Learn progressive muscle relaxation to relieve tension. Tense and then relax every muscle in your body. Begin with your head and neck, and work your way down to your toes.

- Sit quietly and repeat to yourself a "cue" word, such as *peace*, that will make you feel calm.

- Listen to relaxation tapes or music.

- Relax in a warm bath.

- Avoid caffeine, alcohol, nicotine, and all street drugs.

- Help other people. The sense of well-being you receive will help you put life's events in better perspective.

- Balance the different areas of your life (work, relationships, play, spirituality).

- Sign up for a team sport or take up a new hobby.

- Take time to focus on the spiritual part of life, including nature or religion.

- Get a massage from a good friend, family member, or qualified massage therapist.

- Learn more about stress and how to cope with it. Contact your local clinic or community education program to find out if they offer classes on stress management or relaxation.

Holiday Stress

The holiday season can be a particularly stressful time. Busy schedules, family get-togethers, and added financial pressures can increase the stress of everyday life. Follow these tips to deal with stress during the holidays:

- Have realistic expectations. Don't expect everything to be perfect. Don't count on the holidays to make family tensions or disagreements disappear.

- Know your financial limits and budget your spending. Don't feel like you have to buy everyone an expensive gift.

- Don't try to do too much. You shouldn't have to rearrange your whole schedule to deal with the holidays. Ask others for help when you need it.

- It's okay to say no. Don't feel that you need to accept every invitation you receive.

- If you've recently experienced a breakup, death in the family, or other tragedy, holidays can be especially stressful. Ask friends and family to be understanding if you don't feel like participating in the festivities.

What to do about Stress

Symptom/Sign	Action
Occasional stress	Self-care
Signs of anxiety or depression	See doctor

Suicide

Suicide is the eleventh leading cause of death in the United States. In fact, more people kill themselves than are killed by others each year. It is a serious public health problem.

Older adults and young people are most likely to commit suicide. The rate of suicide is highest for people over age 65. For people ages 15 to 24, suicide is the third leading cause of death. Men commit suicide more often than women, but women report more attempted suicides.

There may be as many as eight suicide attempts for every person who dies in a suicide.

Causes

Most people who kill themselves are depressed, have a mental illness, or have a problem with drugs or alcohol.

Difficult life situations increase the chance of suicide, but almost always this is in combination with other factors, such as depression.

People who come from families in which there have been suicides or attempted suicides, family violence, or abuse are more likely to commit suicide themselves. Those who have made a suicide attempt are at greater risk of committing suicide at some point.

In the United States, most people who commit suicide use a gun. Having access to a gun is considered another risk factor for suicide.

Warning Signs of Suicide

When someone says he or she feels like committing suicide, take the comment seriously. Listen carefully to what the person is saying, and get the person to a doctor or counselor for treatment.

Other warning signs may be:

- A previous suicide attempt
- Threats such as "I'd be better off dead" or "You won't miss me"
- Talk about feeling hopeless
- Depression
- Changes in personality
- Dangerous or risky behavior
- Giving away things the person cares about
- A sense that there is no future

Care for Possible Suicide

- Don't leave the person alone.
- Talk to the person calmly. Don't be judgmental, no matter what the person says.
- Listen to what the person is saying. If there is a specific plan for suicide, it's

a sign that he or she may be close to attempting it.

- Don't try to be a counselor; just be a friend.
- Get the person to professional help.
- Remove anything that might be used in a suicide, such as guns or drugs.
- Keep the person away from drugs and alcohol.

What to do about Suicide

Symptom/Sign	Action
Feelings of hopelessness and difficulty doing normal daily activities	See doctor
Threats of suicide or of harming others	Call 911

Violent Behavior

Home is the place where we expect to feel the most safe, but violence in the home is a serious problem. When a parent beats a child, someone strikes his or her spouse, or a date becomes violent, it is an assault—and it's a crime.

Most people in situations of domestic violence don't think of themselves as being abused. They may be embarrassed, or they may be afraid that the person abusing them will hurt them worse if they tell someone. The abusive person may think that what he or she is doing is a normal behavior or that the abused person "deserved it."

Domestic violence can include:

- Emotional and verbal abuse
- Isolation from others
- Threats and intimidation

Causes

Domestic violence can and does happen in all kinds of homes. It's not confined to families at one economic level or to certain ethnic groups. Some stresses, such as financial problems or drug or alcohol abuse, can increase the chances of violence.

People who come from violent homes are more likely to become abusive in their own homes.

Signs of Domestic Violence

There are arguments and disagreements in every household from time to time, and people may get very angry. But domestic violence is more than just an angry exchange. Domestic abuse is an ongoing pattern of behavior. It can be immediately evident, such as physical abuse that requires medical attention, or it can be more subtle, such as vicious insults and demeaning comments. Some of the signs of domestic violence are:

- Serious physical injuries, such as broken bones or deep bruises

- Threats of serious injury, particularly with a weapon

- Physical abuse that is not life threatening but that is constant and unpleasant, such as slaps, kicks, pinches, or even unwanted tickling

- Controlling behavior, such as not allowing someone to take medications or to sleep or forcing sexual relations

- Isolating someone from other friends and relatives

- Constant belittling comments

- Unreasonable jealousy; constantly tracking where the person is and accusing him or her of being interested in others

- Destroying things that are important to someone else.

When You Suspect Abuse

If you think someone may be abused, talk to him or her.

- Say you are concerned that he or she may be harmed.

- Assure the person that he or she can talk openly to you without judgment.

- Talk about the harm domestic violence can do to children.

- Remind the person that domestic violence is a crime.

- Offer to help find social and legal services.

If you believe a child is being abused, report it to the police or the appropriate social service agency.

Sleep Problems

Sleep affects our daily functioning and our physical and mental health in ways researchers are just beginning to understand. The amount of sleep each person needs depends on many factors, but most of us don't get enough. Too little sleep impairs your memory, alertness, and productivity. It can make everyday activities, such as driving, dangerous. It may even weaken your immune system.

This chapter describes common sleep concerns and explains what you can do to get a good night's rest. Some sleep problems are serious, requiring treatment by your doctor or others who specialize in sleep disorders. ::

Fatigue

Fatigue is an overwhelming sense of tiredness that makes your body feel weak. Everyone has felt it at some time or another. It's a normal part of life. What most people refer to as fatigue is brought on by hard work or exertion and will go away with adequate sleep. When sleep and rest do not help, though, your body is sending you a signal that something else may be wrong.

Causes

Depression and anxiety are common, treatable causes of fatigue. Symptoms of these disorders may include a depressed mood, feelings of apprehension, eating or sleeping disturbances, or not being able to enjoy life (see Depression, p. 334; and Anxiety, p. 332).

Fatigue is common up to 1 month after a viral illness. People often return to their busy lifestyles after the obvious symptoms go away and do not realize their body is still recuperating.

Fatigue can be an early symptom of many types of serious illness, although usually it's not. These illnesses include cancer, diabetes, anemia, hepatitis, heart disease, obesity, hypoglycemia, hypothyroidism, mononucleosis, sleep disorders, rheumatoid arthritis, alcoholism, and urinary tract infection.

Fatigue can sometimes be caused by prescriptions or other medications you are taking. Over-the-counter medications that can rob you of energy include pain relievers, cough and cold medicines, antihistamines and allergy medicines, sleeping pills, and motion sickness pills. Prescriptions that can cause fatigue include tranquilizers, muscle relaxants, sedatives, birth control pills, and blood pressure reducers.

Self-Care

- Organize your time. Get up a few minutes earlier, so you won't have to start your day feeling rushed and tired. Learn to delegate and say no when you have enough responsibilities and activities in your life.

- Be physically active. Try to get at least 30 minutes of activity most days of the week. Avoid exercising right before you go to bed, which can disrupt your regular sleeping habits and make you tired in the morning.

- Get the right amount of sleep. Most people need 6 to 8 hours of sleep each night.

- Take a nap during the day. This may be especially helpful for teenagers who have hectic schedules and older adults who tend to sleep less soundly.

- Quit smoking. Smoking steals some of your body's oxygen supply, replacing it with deadly carbon monoxide. Nicotine is a stimulant, and going through the withdrawal symptoms that follow smoking can cause temporary tiredness.

- Drink less caffeine and alcohol. Alcohol is a depressant and will make you feel tired, not boost your energy. Caffeine will give you a temporary boost of energy, but when the effect wears off, your energy level will drop drastically.

- Find your lunch style. Some people function best after eating a lighter lunch, whereas others need to eat their largest meal of the day at lunch. In either case, avoid high-fat foods. Because fats burn off slower than carbohydrates, they will slow you down.

- Take breaks. Interrupt your work day with occasional breaks. If you haven't gone on a vacation in a while, take a trip or unplug the phone and refresh yourself at home.

- Watch less television. If you depend on television to relax, you may find yourself relaxed into a state of sluggishness. Try something more stimulating, such as reading or taking a walk.

- Find ways to calm yourself. Listen to music or relaxation tapes. Say a word, phrase, or prayer that gives you a sense of peace. Imagine yourself on a beach, at the mountains, or in your favorite spot.

Chronic Fatigue Syndrome

A pattern of extreme fatigue can be a sign of a disabling condition known as chronic fatigue syndrome (CFS). This condition affects more women than men. The onset of CFS often follows a viral illness, but the cause of CFS is unknown.

Symptoms

In addition to fatigue, symptoms of CFS may include:

- Loss of short-term memory or concentration
- Sore throat
- Tender lymph nodes in the neck and armpits
- Unexplained muscle pain
- Pain in multiple joints without swelling or redness
- Headaches of a new type, pattern, or severity
- Sleep problems
- Extreme exhaustion lasting more than 24 hours after normal exercise or activity

CFS can be difficult to diagnose because it has the same symptoms as many other diseases. First your doctor needs to rule out other possible conditions. Then you need to meet the criteria for a CFS diagnosis, which include having severe chronic fatigue for 6 months or longer with no known medical cause *and* having at least four of the eight symptoms above.

Depression often goes hand in hand with CFS. In fact, more than two-thirds of people who have CFS also have depression.

Treatment

There is no effective treatment for CFS, but treating your symptoms can help you feel better. Your doctor may prescribe medications for pain or depression if needed. A rehabilitation medicine specialist can evaluate you and teach you how to plan activities to take advantage of times when you usually feel better. Emotional support and counseling may also help you cope with CFS.

Self-Care

- Eat a balanced diet, don't smoke, and limit your caffeine intake.
- Get enough sleep.
- Pace yourself physically, emotionally, and intellectually. Too much stress can aggravate your symptoms.
- Exercise regularly, but don't overdo it. At first, physical activity may increase your fatigue, but over time it can improve your symptoms.

What to do about Fatigue

Symptom/Sign	Action
Fatigue that is better after the weekends or vacations	Self-care
Recent viral illness or fever	Self-care
Fatigue that may be caused by medication	Call doctor
Fatigue that does not improve with self-care	See doctor
Pattern of extreme fatigue	See doctor

Insomnia

Insomnia, or trouble sleeping, is an occasional problem for almost everyone, but it is a chronic problem for 15 to 20 million people in the United States. It is defined not only as a lack of sleep but the inability to get enough restful sleep. Insomnia may involve trouble falling asleep, staying asleep, or waking up too early in the morning without being able to return to sleep.

Causes

For many people, insomnia happens occasionally in response to life events. These events, exciting or stressful, can keep you awake and thinking late into the night. Other people develop poor sleep schedules, sleeping late into the morning or napping during the day. This makes sleep at night more difficult.

Insomnia may be a symptom of depression. If you are feeling down, are fatigued, and are having trouble falling asleep or are waking up early, you may be depressed (see Depression, p. 334). There are helpful treatments for depression that may cure your insomnia if the two problems are related.

Insomnia may also be a symptom of a sleep disorder or medical problem. Finding the cause of your insomnia can help your doctor determine what treatment you need.

Treatment

Insomnia sends many people to the doctor, often to get sleeping pills. Yet most doctors believe sleeping pills should be avoided whenever possible. Many over-the-counter sleep medications rely on what doctors call the placebo effect, which means they only work because you think they will. Prescription medications are likely to really knock you out, rather than producing a natural, restful sleep.

Self-Care

There are several self-care steps you can take to get a better night's sleep. It may take a few weeks to establish a new, natural sleeping routine. If you are unable to make progress after trying the following steps, call your doctor for advice:

- Avoid drinking alcohol in the evening. Although alcohol is a short-term sedative and may quickly bring on sleep, it interferes with deep sleep. You may wake up suddenly after its effects have worn off.

- Don't smoke, especially at bedtime. Nicotine is a stimulant, which can keep you awake or disrupt your sleep.

- Avoid or reduce your intake of caffeine. Caffeine stays in your system for as long as 12 to 24 hours. Remember that in addition to coffee, caffeine is present in chocolate and many colas and teas. If you suspect caffeine is contributing to your sleeplessness, don't use any caffeinated products for at least 12 hours before you go to bed.

- Be aware of other medications that may affect your sleeping patterns. Many over-the-counter decongestants (such as Sudafed) and products with pseudoephedrine can be as stimulating as caffeine. Before starting a medication, ask your pharmacist if it might keep you awake and if another product can be substituted.

- Avoid eating large meals just before going to bed. The uncomfortable feeling of having a full stomach may delay sleep. Try a light snack instead. This will satisfy your hunger without interfering with your sleep. Many people swear by the virtues of a glass of warm or cold milk. Try adding a touch of honey, cinnamon, or vanilla to this bedtime standby. A cup of herbal tea, which doesn't contain caffeine, also works for some people.

- Take a warm bath an hour or two before bedtime. This can soothe tense muscles and help make you sleepy. However, taking a bath immediately before going to bed may be too stimulating and keep you awake. Experiment with the timing to see what works best for you.

- Get regular physical activity. This will help relieve tension and clear your head. It will also tire you out, so you can sleep more soundly. Avoid strenuous physical activity for several hours before going to bed. It may stimulate you and interfere with falling asleep.

- Your bedroom should be quiet and dark. If noise is a problem, try ear plugs or "white noise." Many people like the sound of a fan or air conditioner as they drift off to sleep. A cool room temperature—between 60°F and 65°F—is best for sleeping. A firm, comfortable mattress is also important for a good night's sleep.

- Avoid long, late afternoon naps. Short "catnaps," lasting no more than 20 minutes, can be surprisingly refreshing. Longer naps and those taken later than 4 P.M. may disrupt normal sleep patterns and contribute to insomnia.

- Read in bed for a few minutes before turning out the light. This helps you relax and can increase feelings of drowsiness.

- Counting sheep is not recommended. Counting requires focusing the brain on a specific activity. Instead, try picturing yourself in a pleasant place, and use your imagination to hear relaxing sounds as you drift off to sleep.

- Reserve your bed for pleasurable, restful activities. Avoid doing activities in bed that can cause stress or anxiety, such as watching horror movies or balancing your checkbook.

What to do about Insomnia

Symptom/Sign	Action
Occasional trouble sleeping	Self-care
Insomnia related to depression	See doctor
No improvement with self-care	See doctor

Sleep Apnea

Sleep apnea is a disorder in which breathing stops and starts during sleep. More than half of all cases are diagnosed in people age 40 or older. Sleep apnea is more common in men than women. It is a major cause of daytime sleepiness and can potentially be serious.

Causes

Anyone can have sleep apnea, but you are at higher risk if you:

- Are male
- Are over age 40
- Snore loudly
- Are overweight
- Have high blood pressure
- Have a structural abnormality in your nose, throat, or other parts of your upper airway that causes blockage
- Have a family history of sleep apnea
- Use alcohol, tobacco, or sleeping pills

Symptoms

If you or someone else notices you that you stop and start breathing while sleeping, you may have sleep apnea. Other signs and symptoms include:

- Excessive daytime sleepiness
- Poor concentration
- Depression or irritability
- Early morning headaches

Types of Sleep Apnea

There are two types of sleep apnea, *obstructive* and *central*.

Obstructive sleep apnea occurs when the throat muscles and tongue relax during sleep. This can block the opening of your airway, causing breathing to become difficult or to stop altogether. When your brain senses you aren't getting enough oxygen, it briefly wakes you enough to resume breathing. This cycle can repeat itself as many as 20 or 30 times an hour. For most people with obstructive sleep apnea, each awakening is so brief they are not aware it happened. Although you may not be aware that your sleep was interrupted, this condition prevents you from reaching a deep, restful sleep. Most people with obstructive sleep apnea also snore, although not everyone who snores has sleep apnea.

Central sleep apnea is much less common than obstructive sleep apnea. This condition occurs when the brain fails to send the proper signals to the muscles that control breathing. You awake suddenly when the level of carbon dioxide in your blood rises and oxygen drops. If you have central sleep apnea, you are more likely to remember waking up than someone with obstructive sleep apnea.

Treatment

If you have symptoms of sleep apnea, you may have a test called *polysomnography*. During this test, you are hooked up to equipment that records a variety of body functions during sleep. Early diagnosis and treatment of sleep apnea is important, because the condition may be associated with irregular heartbeat, high blood pressure, heart attack, and stroke.

Treatment for sleep apnea varies, depending on your medical history, the physical examination, and the results of your polysomnography.

The most common treatment for sleep apnea is continuous positive airway pressure (CPAP). In this treatment you wear a mask over your nose during sleep, and pressure from an air blower forces air through the nasal passages. The air pressure is adjusted so it is just enough to prevent your throat from collapsing during sleep.

Some people who have sleep apnea may need surgery. Several surgical procedures can be used to increase the size of the airway. This may include the correction of structural deformities or the removal of:

- Adenoids and tonsils (especially in children)
- Nasal polyps (noncancerous tumors) or other growths
- Excess tissue in the airway

Self-Care

If you have obstructive sleep apnea, there are several steps you can take that may help your condition.

- Lose excess weight. Even a 10-percent weight loss can reduce the occurrence of sleep apnea.
- If you usually sleep on your back, try sleeping on your side. Special pillows and other devices are available to help you sleep in a side position.
- Don't use alcohol, tobacco, or sleeping pills. They can make the airway more likely to collapse during sleep and prolong the apneic periods. Sleeping pills or sedatives can prevent you from waking up enough to breathe.

What to do about Sleep Apnea

Symptom/Sign	Action
Observed episodes of sleep apnea	See doctor
Daytime sleepiness	See doctor
Choking or gasping for breath	Call 911

Endocrine Problems

Your endocrine system is a system of glands that produce hormones. These hormones regulate your metabolism, growth, development, and reproduction. Although you probably don't think about it, your endocrine system affects almost every cell, organ, and function in your body. Endocrine concerns are problems that arise when your body produces too much or too little of any hormone.

This chapter describes common endocrine concerns and explains how they are treated. In most cases your doctor will be involved in the care of these conditions. You may also have the help of a doctor who specializes in treating endocrine and hormone problems, called an *endocrinologist*. ⸬

Diabetes

Diabetes occurs when there are high levels of glucose (sugar) in the blood. All three types of diabetes involve problems with insulin, a hormone that removes glucose from the blood and allows it to enter the body's cells. (The cells use it for energy.) If your body is unable to make or use insulin properly, you have a high blood glucose level.

Causes

The risk factors for type 1 diabetes are uncertain, though family history seems to play a role. The risk factors for type 2 diabetes and gestational diabetes are:

- Over age 45
- Body mass index (BMI) greater than 30 (see Healthy Weight, p. 407)
- A family history of diabetes
- Race (diabetes is more common among American Indians, Hispanic/Latino

Americans, African Americans, Asian Americans, and Pacific Islanders)

- High blood pressure or high levels of blood fats (such as cholesterol and triglycerides)

- History of gestational diabetes

- Physical inactivity

Symptoms

Warning signs of diabetes include:

- Increased thirst

- Unusual tiredness

- Excessive appetite

- Increased urination

- Tingling or numbness in legs or feet

- Cuts and bruises that are slow to heal

- Blurred vision or any change in vision

Types of Diabetes

There are three types of diabetes: type 1 diabetes, type 2 diabetes, and gestational diabetes.

Type 1 Diabetes

Although type 1 diabetes can occur at any age, it occurs most often in children, teenagers, or young adults. Symptoms include being very thirsty, hungry, and tired and needing to urinate often. Children with type 1 diabetes rarely have these symptoms for longer than 3 weeks before the disease is diagnosed.

Type 1 diabetes occurs when the pancreas stops making enough insulin. The risk factors for type 1 diabetes are uncertain, although family history seems to play a role. Thus the main treatment for type 1 diabetes is insulin injections. Your doctor will prescribe the lowest possible insulin dosage. In addition, people with type 1 diabetes need to have a specific meal and exercise plan that fits their health, age, and lifestyle.

Type 2 Diabetes

Type 2 diabetes is the most common form of diabetes and usually develops gradually, with few, if any, warning signs. With type 2 diabetes, the pancreas keeps making insulin, but the body is not using it effectively. As a result, glucose builds up in the blood. Your doctor may diagnose diabetes by tracking a gradual increase in blood glucose levels.

The main way to treat type 2 diabetes is through lifestyle changes (see Self-care for Diabetes, p. 353). In some cases, medications or insulin may be needed to lower blood glucose levels. However, for many adults with type 2 diabetes, following self-care steps alone is all that is necessary to manage the disease.

Gestational Diabetes

In some women, the hormonal changes of pregnancy demand more insulin than the body can make, and diabetes develops. After the birth of the baby, blood glucose levels return to normal and the diabetes goes away. However, women who have had gestational diabetes are at risk for developing type 2 diabetes later in life.

Self-Care

Eat a Healthful Diet

- Watch your total carbohydrate levels. Research now shows that it is the total amount of carbohydrate eaten, not just the amount of starch or sugar, that affects the blood glucose levels after eating.

- Follow a meal plan. A meal plan tells you how much food you need and how to plan meals and snacks so you know what to eat and when. It should be suited to your lifestyle and nutritional needs.

- Maintain or attain a healthy weight. If you have type 2 diabetes and are overweight, it is important to reach a reasonable body weight. Often if you lose only 5 to 10 pounds, your blood glucose levels are easier to control. For children with type 1 diabetes, it is important to consume enough calories to provide for normal growth and development.

Monitor Your Blood Glucose Regularly

Uncontrolled, high blood glucose levels can cause serious health problems, including heart disease, kidney disease, blindness, or nerve damage. If you have diabetes, you can help prevent these problems by keeping your blood glucose levels in check. Your health care provider can teach you how to monitor your blood glucose. He or she will also recommend how often you should test your blood.

Exercise

Exercise can lower blood glucose levels, making body cells more sensitive to insulin and improving their ability to use and store glucose. In fact, exercise combined with fewer calories will often control type 2 diabetes without the need for medication. If you exercise, you can also enjoy other benefits, such as improved heart and lung efficiency, reduced body fat, improved muscle tone, and improved fitness. Your doctor can help you determine the type of program that is best for you.

Prevention

Although there are no guarantees when it comes to the prevention of diabetes, there are steps you can take to control factors that increase your risk.

- Attain or maintain a healthy weight. It is not normal to gain weight as you get older. If you are overweight, even a small amount of weight loss will be beneficial.

- Stay active. Try to get at least 30 minutes of activity most days of the week.

Hyperthyroidism

Your thyroid is a gland in your neck that produces the hormones that regulate metabolism. Hyperthyroidism is a condition caused when your thyroid produces too much thyroid hormone.

Causes

The most common cause of hyperthyroidism, especially in young people, is Graves' disease. Graves' disease is caused by antibodies in the blood that stimulate the thyroid to grow and secrete excess thyroid hormone. It tends to run in families.

In elderly people a common cause of hyperthyroidism is toxic nodular goiter, or *overactive thyroid nodules*.

Other causes of hyperthyroidism include:

- Inflammation of the thyroid gland from a viral infection
- Ingestion of excessive amounts of thyroid hormone
- Ingestion of excessive iodine

Symptoms

Symptoms of hyperthyroidism include:

- Weight loss
- Increased appetite
- Nervousness
- Irritability
- Heat intolerance
- Increased sweating
- Thinning of the skin
- Fine, brittle hair
- Shaky hands
- Racing heart
- Frequent bowel movements
- Menstrual irregularities in women
- Eyes that look enlarged
- Possible presence of goiter

To determine if you have hyperthyroidism, your doctor will do blood tests. If these tests suggest hyperthyroidism, you may also have other tests, such as a thyroid scan or a thyroid reuptake, to find out if you have Graves' disease.

Treatment

If you have hyperthyroidism, the type of treatment will depend on many things, including your age, the type of hyperthyroidism, allergies to medication, and other conditions that may affect your health. The three most common types of treatment for hyperthyroidism are medications, radioactive iodine, and surgery.

Medications
The two classes of medication that are used most often to treat hyperthy-

roidism are beta-blockers and antithyroid medications.

Beta-blockers, such as propranolol and atenolol, do not lower thyroid hormone levels. However, they can reduce some hyperthyroid symptoms, such as rapid heart rate, palpitations, hand tremors, anxiety, and nervousness. If you are taking a large dose of beta-blockers, do not stop taking it suddenly. Talk to your doctor about gradually reducing the dose.

Antithyroid medications lower thyroid hormone levels in the blood by blocking thyroid hormone production from the overactive thyroid gland. Examples of antithyroid medications include propylthiouracil or methimazole. It usually takes 2 to 4 weeks of antithyroid drug treatment before the hyperthyroid symptoms improve, and it can be several months before thyroid function becomes normal. At that time the dosage is usually reduced.

Occasionally, antithyroid medications can lower your white blood cell count or cause toxic hepatitis, both of which are serious and require medical attention. If you have a fever, sore throat, mouth sores, or other symptoms of infection or if you have nausea, vomiting, or yellowing of the eyes, stop taking your medication and call your doctor right away.

Radioactive Iodine

Radioactive iodine treats hyperthyroidism by destroying some of the cells that make the thyroid hormone. Patients swallow a capsule or drink that contains radioiodine. The radioiodine goes into the bloodstream and is absorbed by the overactive thyroid cells. Over several weeks the radioiodine destroys the overactive thyroid cells, which helps the thyroid hormone return to normal. It may take up to 6 months for the full effect to be seen.

Sometimes, hyperthyroidism continues after radioiodine treatment. In these cases, a second radioiodine treatment may be needed.

Surgery

For some patients with hyperthyroidism, doctors recommend surgery. If a single nodule or lump of thyroid tissue is overactive, the surgeon removes this part of the thyroid and the rest of the thyroid usually returns to normal.

If many nodules or the entire thyroid gland is overactive, the entire thyroid gland is removed and hyperthyroidism will never again occur. However, to prevent hypothyroidism (see p. 356), you will have to take thyroid hormone tablets for the rest of your life.

Self-Care

Because your metabolism increases with hyperthyroidism, you may have lost weight. As thyroid hormone levels become normal, your metabolism will also return to normal and you may gain weight. During this time, it may be important to watch the number of calories and types of food that you eat.

As your heart rate returns to normal, aim for 30 minutes of activity on most days of the week. If you can't do that much at once, do a little at a time. Regular activity has a lot of benefits. It can help control weight, boost your energy, and keep you physically fit.

Talk with your doctor if you have questions about maintaining a healthy weight or establishing an exercise program.

What to do about Hyperthyroidism

Symptom/Sign	Action
Symptoms of hyperthyroidism (see p. 354)	See doctor
Symptoms of hyperthyroidism that do not improve with treatment	See doctor
Rapid heart rate, palpitations, hand tremors, anxiety, and nervousness while taking beta-blockers	See doctor
Fever, sore throat, mouth sores, or other symptoms of infection while taking beta-blockers	See doctor
Nausea, vomiting, or yellowing of the eyes while taking beta-blockers	See doctor

Hypothyroidism

Hypothyroidism is a condition that occurs when your thyroid does not produce enough thyroid hormone. It is the most common thyroid disorder. One in 10 women over the age of 50 has an early stage of hypothyroidism. It is also seen in younger women and sometimes in men.

Causes

The most common cause of hypothyroidism is chronic thyroiditis, also called *Hashimoto's thyroiditis*. Chronic thyroiditis occurs when the body's immune system attacks thyroid tissue with antibodies and white blood cells—as if the tissue were foreign to the body. As a result, the thyroid produces less thyroid hormone and may become enlarged. (An enlarged thyroid is called a goiter.)

Hypothyroidism may also develop in people who have had thyroid surgery or radioactive iodine treatment for an overactive thyroid (see Hyperthyroidism, p. 354) or in people who have received high doses of radiation for head and neck cancer or Hodgkin's disease. Sometimes, infants are born without a thyroid gland or with a gland that does not function normally.

In rare cases, a condition called *secondary hypothyroidism* can also occur. Secondary hypothyroidism is caused when your pituitary gland, located at the base of your spine, does not produce enough thyroid-stimulating hormone.

Symptoms

Symptoms of hypothyroidism include:

- Fatigue
- Depression
- Feeling sluggish and cold
- Loss of interest in normal activities
- Dry and brittle hair
- Itchy, dry skin
- Constipation
- Muscle cramps
- Weight gain
- Memory problems
- Increased menstrual flow in women

Treatment

To determine if you have hypothyroidism, your doctor will take a blood sample and measure the levels of thyroid hormone and thyroid-stimulating hormone. Because hypothyroidism is an inherited condition, your family members may also develop thyroid problems and should have their thyroid function checked.

If you have hypothyroidism, your doctor will probably prescribe pure thyrox-

ine. This medication is similar to what your body makes. Doses of thyroxine are adjusted until the blood levels of thyroxine and thyroid-stimulating hormone are normal. If the dose is adjusted properly, thyroxine is essentially free of allergic reactions and side effects.

Because thyroid failure may be an ongoing process to treat, the dosage may need to be adjusted over time. When the patient is elderly or has a heart condition, it's important to start with a low dosage of thyroid hormone until the body gets used to normal thyroid hormone levels. Once the proper dosage is achieved, you should feel completely well. However, it's important to have your thyroid hormone and thyroid-stimulating hormone levels checked each year.

If you have secondary hypothyroidism, the pituitary gland itself will be treated. You may also need to take medications.

Self-Care

If you are taking medication for hypothyroidism, you should continue to be aware of any symptoms you are experiencing. If you do not take enough thyroid hormone, you may be sluggish, feel cold, or experience mental dullness or muscle cramps. You may also have an elevated cholesterol level, which could increase your risk for heart disease.

If you take too much thyroid hormone, you may have symptoms of an overactive thyroid, such as nervousness, palpitations, insomnia, shaky hands, or feeling overheated. Too much thyroid hormone may also increase your risk of osteoporosis or cause heart problems if you have underlying heart disease.

Talk to your doctor if you have any of the symptoms above or if you feel that you should be taking a different dosage of thyroid hormone.

What to do about Hypothyroidism

Symptom/Sign	Action
Symptoms of hypothyroidism (see p. 356)	See doctor
Symptoms of hypothyroidism that do not improve with treatment	See doctor
Nervousness, palpitations, insomnia, shaky hands, or feeling overheated while taking thyroid hormone	See doctor
Sluggishness, mental dullness, muscle cramps, or feeling cold while taking thyroid hormone	See doctor

Special Concerns for Children

Children may respond differently than adults to some conditions. In some cases, they bounce back more quickly. In others, they are hit harder by an illness.

While a child is growing, his or her immune system also is maturing—in part through the child's exposure to illness. The first time your child is regularly around other children, whether in day care or when going to school, you're likely to spend a lot of time taking care of influenza, colds, rashes, and other illnesses. Once the child's immune system is well established, the number of illnesses usually declines.

Many childhood illnesses are not serious, but don't take chances. If something doesn't seem quite right, call your doctor. What seems like a simple sore throat can be a strep infection and may even lead to tonsillitis. If you get treatment for it early, you can reduce the chance of serious infection. ::

Attention Deficit/ Hyperactivity Disorder

Almost all children have times when they don't seem to pay attention, can't sit still, or just have more energy than they can burn. For some children, however, difficulty concentrating or very high physical energy levels (hyperactivity) interfere with social and academic tasks appropriate for their ages.

Causes

The exact cause of attention deficit/ hyperactivity disorder (ADHD) is unknown. Popular theories that sugar, food dyes, or other food additives contribute to hyperactivity or that the condition is caused by minute levels of brain damage have not been proven.

Symptoms

A child who has true ADHD may have problems paying attention, be impulsive, be hyperactive, or have some combination of these. Such a child may talk constantly, be unable to wait his or her turn in groups, and pay little attention to details. Schoolwork may be messy or filled with careless mistakes. The child may be easily distracted, act before thinking or have trouble sitting still. The child may also have difficulty controlling anger.

In about 50 percent of cases, symptoms subside in late adolescence and early adulthood. But some teenagers and adults may continue to have feelings of restlessness or difficulty engaging in quiet, sedentary activities.

Diagnosing ADHD

In some ways, a diagnosis of ADHD is a "relative" diagnosis, meaning that a child with the disorder has far more difficulty with attention or controlling impulses or activity than do most other children. But not all children with ADHD have big problems with hyperactivity and impulsiveness. For some, inattention is the primary problem. Likewise, some children who are clearly hyperactive are able to concentrate if they can just sit still long enough.

Because there is no scientific test for ADHD, the disorder can be difficult to distinguish from age-appropriate behaviors in active children. Symptoms like those of ADHD may also be brought on by grief (over the death of a parent or a divorce); depression; posttraumatic stress (after physical or sexual abuse); or other physical, emotional, or psychological problems.

Self-Care

- Get an evaluation. A careful evaluation will look at how your child functions intellectually, socially, emotionally, physically, and academically. Ideally, the professional doing the evaluation should observe your child during normal daily activities in more than one setting (at home and at school) and at different times of the day.
- Stick to a routine and set firm limits at home and school.
- Make sure your child's schoolwork matches his or her abilities. A class that's not suited to your child's academic skills can lead to inattention, boredom, and frustration.
- Provide outlets for your child's physical energy.
- Make sure you find ways to cope. Parenting a hyperactive child can be challenging. Avoid becoming very critical, controlling, or angry with your child. Remember—and let your child know—you don't like the behavior, but you love the child.

• Use other resources. Share your concerns with your child's doctor and teacher. They will provide information on help that is available in your community. Your child's doctor may prescribe medications.

Chicken Pox

Chicken pox is a very contagious viral disease. According to the Centers for Disease Control and Prevention, every year approximately 5000 to 9000 hospitalizations and 100 deaths in the United States result from chicken pox. Normally a mild disease of childhood (it affects 4 million U.S. children each year), chicken pox may be severe in infants, adults, and people with impaired immune systems.

Chicken pox is usually spread by breathing in droplets coughed, sneezed, or exhaled by an infected person. After exposure, it can take 10 to 21 days before symptoms appear. A person usually develops the symptoms 14 to 16 days after being exposed.

A person can spread the disease to others before he or she even has any symptoms of chicken pox. The contagious period begins about 2 days before the rash appears and continues until new sores stop appearing. Once all the sores have turned to scabs, the contagious period is over.

Symptoms

The early symptoms of chicken pox are cold symptoms, fever, abdominal pain, headache, and a general feeling of illness. These can come with the rash or a day or two before it. The fever may be higher the first few days after the rash appears.

The rash appears as small, itchy, red bumps and spots on the face, scalp, shoulders, chest, and back. It is also normal for it to appear inside the mouth, on the eyelids, and in the genital area. Some people may have just a few bumps, while others are covered with them.

The early bumps are usually flat, red marks with central, clear blisters. The blisters quickly dissolve and become dry crusts or scabs, which fall off within 2 weeks. New sores continue to appear for the first 4 to 5 days, so all stages of the rash may be present at the same time.

Complications of Chicken Pox

It is rare for a person to have more than one case of chicken pox in a lifetime. Although a case of the pox brings immunity to the virus, the virus may lay quiet and later be reactivated in some adults, causing a rash. This rash, called *shingles* (or herpes zoster), is more common in people older than age 60.

Chicken pox may leave permanent scars, especially in teenagers and young adults. Temporary marks may remain for 6 months to a year before fading.

Chicken pox can cause cellulitis, viral pneumonia, or encephalitis. Cellulitis is a serious bacterial infection affecting the skin, which becomes red, swollen, and unusually warm. Viral pneumonia is an infection of the lungs caused by certain viruses and associated with symptoms of fever, cough, and shortness of breath (see Pneumonia, p. 225). Encephalitis, a viral infection of the brain, is a very rare complication of chicken pox (see Encephalitis, p. 99). Still, it's wise to be alert to its symptoms: fever, mental confusion, forgetfulness, tiredness, and a stiff neck. Take the person to the doctor's office or emergency room at once if you notice any of the symptoms associated with these three conditions.

Self-Care

- Give plenty of cold fluids.

- To reduce fever, give acetaminophen (Tylenol or Tempra). Do not use aspirin (see box on p. 363).

- To relieve mouth ulcers, prepare a soft, bland diet. Avoid salty foods and citrus fruits and juices.

- For painful or itchy pox in the genital area, apply a petroleum-based ointment or an over-the-counter local anesthetic.

- If a sore seems to be infected, wash with antibacterial soap and apply antibacterial ointment.

- Call your doctor if fever is higher than 101°F for more than 4 days.

- Children don't have to stay in bed but should be kept cool and quiet.

- Children may return to school or day care when they have no fever and all sores are crusted over.

Scratching the scabs off chicken pox sores can lead to more itching and infection. These steps will help reduce the urge to scratch:

- Take cool baths every 3 to 4 hours.

- Add an oatmeal bath product, such as Aveeno (follow directions), or baking soda (about a half cup) to tub water to reduce itchiness.

- Give nonaspirin (acetaminophen) if symptoms are very bothersome.

- Keep fingernails trimmed short and wash hands often to prevent infection.

- Wear clean cotton gloves to bed to reduce the danger of scratching while asleep.

- Apply calamine lotion or hydrocortisone products to itchy areas. Caladryl is helpful too, but on rare occasions people can develop an allergy to it.

- If you have been exposed to chicken pox and are immunocompromised, pregnant, or have had a bone marrow transplant, see your doctor.

Reye's Syndrome

Children and teenagers should not take aspirin because it may be linked to Reye's syndrome, a dangerous condition of the liver and brain. Reye's syndrome sometimes develops as a complication of viral illnesses such as influenza and chicken pox. Although it is uncommon, it is seen more often in children who have been treated with aspirin.

What to do about Chicken Pox

Symptom/Sign	Action
Normal chicken pox symptoms, including rash, fever, and itching	Self-care
Chicken pox symptoms with significant redness, watering, and burning of the eyes	Call doctor
Suspicion that several sores are infected (excessive drainage and tenderness of the sore)	Call doctor
Stiff neck and very bad headache, difficulty breathing	Call 911

Prevention

If you've been exposed to chicken pox, call your doctor. Medication or immunization may prevent the disease.

- Avoid contact with others during the contagious period (until all sores have turned to scabs). That means anyone with chicken pox should not be at work, school, or day care while contagious. If other people may have been exposed to the disease, be sure to tell them to watch out for spots about 2 weeks from the date of exposure.

- It's nearly impossible to prevent the spread of chicken pox within a household. Some studies find that 9 times out of 10, siblings of a person with chicken pox will get the disease.

- If you need to take the person to the doctor's office, call ahead and tell the staff that you suspect chicken pox, so arrangements can be made to avoid spreading the disease to other clinic patients. In most cases, people with chicken pox don't need to come to the clinic. The condition can be successfully handled at home with calls to the doctor's office for advice. Your doctor may recommend medication that can shorten the length of the disease or result in fewer sores if taken within the first few days of the onset of the rash.

The varicella vaccine for chicken pox has been approved for general use in the United States and is also used in several other countries. It is recommended for children over a year old who have not had chicken pox (see Immunizations, p. 418).

Colic

Colic may be more harmful to worried and frustrated parents than it is to babies. A colicky baby cries a great deal and seems to have some kind of abdominal pain. Many babies, about 1 in 10, will have colic at some point during their early infancy. Some babies with colic cry much of the time. Others may cry loudly for hours at around the same time every day, often in the early evening.

It's important to remember that no matter how hard it may be to cope with a colicky baby, colic is a harmless condition.

Causes

There is no known cause of colic. It occurs equally in breastfed and bottle-fed infants. Sometimes allergy to cow's milk formula may cause crying, but this is usually accompanied by loose stools and spitting up.

Symptoms

Colic is actually a collection of symptoms, rather than a disease. It usually begins within the first 2 or 3 weeks after birth and can last until the baby is 3 or 4 months old.

- The main symptom of colic is crying— hard, almost angry crying—for hours at a time. Your baby's face is likely to be red and the crying loud.
- The baby will pull its legs up, as if he or she has abdominal pain.
- Babies with colic usually eat well and gain weight normally.
- The baby may be irritable and hard to distract or comfort.

Self-Care

For generations, parents have tried different measures to calm a colicky baby. Some babies respond to some measures, some to others. You might try these suggestions to see if they help your baby:

- Many parents have discovered that riding in the car calms a colicky baby. Be sure to fasten the baby securely into a properly installed infant car seat.
- Walk or rock the baby.
- Use a pacifier, even if the baby has just eaten. Some colicky babies will spit a pacifier right out, but others may calm down a bit.
- Massage your baby gently.
- Try background noise. Some babies calm to the sounds of a hairdryer or vacuum cleaner.
- Wrap your baby tightly in a blanket.
- Sing to your baby, or play gentle music.

- There are tape recordings and toys that play the sound of a human heart beating, which sometimes calm a baby.

- Let your baby cry—for a little while. If walking, rocking, singing, massaging, and the like don't seem to make a difference, put the baby in the crib for 10 to 15 minutes and see if he or she quiets alone. Sometimes a baby needs a little time alone—and you may need time to calm yourself if you've been coping with the crying of a colicky baby for a while.

- Get a break for yourself. Ask a relative or friend to help watch the baby for a few hours during what is normally a colicky period.

What to do about Colic

Symptom/Sign	Action
Unexplained crying, eats well, and is gaining weight	Self-care
Not eating well, moaning and weak crying	Call doctor
Crying pattern changes	Call doctor
Intense crying for longer than 2 hours	Call doctor
Diarrhea, vomiting, fever with intense crying	See doctor
You feel fed up with baby's crying and want to shake the baby in order to keep him or her quiet	Call 911

Cradle Cap

Cradle cap is a condition that causes oily, yellowish scales or crusts on babies' heads—behind the ears, on the eyebrows, and along the lash line—and occasionally in the groin area.

Causes

The cause of cradle cap is not yet fully understood. Common in children less than 1 year old, cradle cap may be a mild form of dermatitis.

Self-Care

Cradle cap doesn't cause a baby discomfort and is easy to treat at home with self-care steps.

- Soften the crusty scales with baby or mineral oil and leave on for about 15 minutes.

- Use a soft brush to loosen the scales after soaking in oil.

- Gently rub difficult areas with a washcloth or gauze dipped in oil to remove scales and then wash with shampoo.

- Don't use dandruff shampoos without checking with your doctor.

- Call your doctor if cradle cap does not improve after 2 weeks of home care.

What to do about Cradle Cap

Symptom/Sign	Action
Yellowish scales or crusts on baby's head	Self-care
Spreads beyond the scalp	See doctor
Weepy, raw area on the scalp	See doctor

Croup

Croup is a viral infection that causes inflammation and swelling of the area near the vocal cords in young children. In some children, croup is a recurring problem. Children outgrow croup as their airway passages grow larger. After age 7, croup is uncommon.

Symptoms

Croup is marked by a distinctive seal-like barking cough, hoarseness, and difficult breathing. Croup lasts 3 to 5 days and may be accompanied by a cold or fever.

Croup without fever (spasmodic croup) comes on suddenly during the night. The child may have seemed perfectly healthy during the day or had a mild cold, but suddenly wakes up with a violent fit of croupy coughing.

Croup with fever (laryngotracheobronchitis) is a more serious form of croup that inflames the area around the vocal cords down to the large bronchi. It is usually accompanied by a chest cold. The child's temperature usually is above normal but lower than 102°F. The croupy cough and tight breathing usually develop slowly and are often worse at night. If your child does not respond promptly to simple home measures, see your doctor.

Epiglottitis is a bacterial infection of the respiratory tract that sometimes seems like severe croup with a fever. The child's temperature is usually higher than 102°F. The child drools and gasps for air, does not respond to the simple measures that bring relief of croup, and must receive immediate medical attention. Epiglottitis usually starts very quickly, which distinguishes it from croup. Thanks to the *Haemophilus influenza* type B (Hib) vaccine, epiglottitis is now very rare.

Self-Care

Most children with croup can be cared for at home. Three key elements in treatment are providing moist air, keeping the child sitting up or propped up, and encouraging the child to drink plenty of fluids.

- Cough medicines and antibiotics are not effective in treating croup.

- Add moisture to the air to make it easier to breathe. The simplest method to do this is to take the child into the bathroom, close the door, and turn on the hot water faucet of the shower. Sit with the child upright on your lap on the bathroom floor for 15 to 20 minutes, inhaling steam. Other options are a brief walk outdoors or a cold-mist humidifier in the child's bedroom.

- Avoid exposure to smoke from cigarettes, fireplaces, or wood-burning stoves.

- Give plenty of clear fluids, such as water or diluted juice, to prevent dehydration and help loosen the cough.

- Use a nonaspirin pain reliever (acetaminophen) to reduce fever and discomfort. Do not give a child aspirin, because use of this medication in children and teenagers has been linked to a rare but serious condition known as *Reye's syndrome* (see box on p. 363).

- Elevate the head of your child's bed.

- A child with croup is often frightened and crying, so try to reassure your child with a hug or distract him or her with a book or favorite game.

- Call your doctor if your child has croup symptoms for more than three nights.

What to do about Croup

Symptom/Sign	Action
Child wakes with a croupy cough, perhaps makes high-pitched noises when inhaling, but does not drool or have trouble swallowing	Self-care
Croup symptoms for more than three nights	See doctor
Shaking chills	Go to hospital
Continuous cough for more than 1 hour	Go to hospital
More than three episodes in one night	Go to hospital
Child cannot relax enough to sleep after 20 minutes of steam inhalation	Go to hospital
Difficulty breathing or swallowing	Call 911
Child has blue or dusky lips or skin	Call 911
Symptoms of epiglottitis	Call 911

Diarrhea

Diarrhea is common in infants and young children because their digestive systems are still developing. Diarrhea in children most often goes away on its own. A parent's job is to watch the child with diarrhea closely and to make sure that the child gets enough liquids and lots of tender loving care.

Causes

Many factors can contribute to the development of diarrhea. These include:

- Introduction of a new food or formula
- Exposure to illness
- Changes in routine, such as travel
- Teething
- Change in water
- Medications, especially antibiotics

Self-Care

Just as in adults, the major concern for children with diarrhea is dehydration. Because of their smaller body size, children can become dehydrated more rapidly than adults. Be alert to the following signs of dehydration in children:

- No urination (more than 8 hours without urinating or a wet diaper for children younger than 1 year old; more than 12 hours without urinating for children 1 year and older)

- Dry mouth
- Absence of tears
- Dizziness or disorientation
- Dry skin that does not spring back after being touched
- Dark circles around eyes
- Fever of 100.4°F or more

Make sure children drink a lot of fluids. Infants may have breast milk or formula. Electrolyte solutions such as Pedialyte and Infalyte can be used. They should not be used for more than 24 hours. Older children can have water; Popsicles; or clear, carbonated beverages that have gone flat. Avoid fruit juices. Give small amounts of fluids every half hour or so.

If the child doesn't have an appetite, do not encourage solid foods. When his or her appetite returns, offer small amounts of easily digested foods, such as:

- Rice, noodles, bread, or crackers
- Cooked carrots, peas, squash, or green beans
- Canned peaches, pears, or applesauce
- Lean meats such as turkey or chicken

Do not give products that contain aspirin or salicylates, such as Pepto-Bismol, to children or teenagers because they increase the risk of developing Reye's syndrome, a serious condition in children (see box on p. 363).

Diarrhea can be very hard on the tender skin of young children, especially those still in diapers. To protect the skin, change diapers soon after each stool. Wash your child's bottom with plain water, or sit the child in a tub with a few inches of warm water. (If you choose to use soap, use a mild one in small amounts and rinse it off well.) For cleanup, use a soft washcloth and water or a commercial diaper wipe that has been rinsed out well with water. Dry the area completely by patting it with a soft cloth or towel. Apply a generous amount of diaper ointment to protect the skin. Because cloth diapers are more gentle on the skin than disposables, consider switching to cloth diapers or lining disposable diapers with cloth ones during prolonged bouts with diarrhea.

What to do about Diarrhea in Children

Symptom/Sign	Action
Three or more stools per day lasting for more than 1 week with no other symptoms	Call doctor
Temperature greater than 100.4°F for more than 48 hours	See doctor
Eight or more stools per day over 48 hours with no improvement after changes in diet	See doctor
Intermittent abdominal pain and cramps for more than 24 hours	See doctor
Signs of dehydration (see Self-care, p. 369)	Go to hospital
Diarrhea, severe and constant abdominal pain or cramps, blood in stools, more than one stool per hour, child acting very sick	Go to hospital
Diarrhea with heavy, continuous, bright red rectal bleeding; dizziness; cool, clammy skin; or breathing difficulties	Call 911

Fever

Fever is not necessarily harmful, nor is it evidence of an illness. However, a fever is a special cause for concern in infants younger than 3 months of age, the elderly, and people who are taking medications that suppress the immune system. Parents and caregivers should be most concerned with changes in eating or sleeping habits, coughing, pain, or other marked changes in a child's behavior. Normal fever symptoms include rapid breathing and heart rate, glossy eyes, and flushed skin.

Determining If Your Child Has a Fever

An accurate temperature reading is especially important during the first 3 months of your child's life. During this time, a rectal thermometer is the most accurate way to measure your child's fever. To assure an accurate temperature, be sure the child is not overdressed or warm from activity, a hot bath, or hot weather. If your child's rectal temperature is higher than 100.4°F, call your child's doctor.

Temperatures taken orally, under the arm, or with an ear thermometer should be used for screening. If your child is mature enough and can keep his or her lips closed tightly around a thermometer, take the temperature orally. Warm food or drink can elevate an oral temperature. Wait at least 30 minutes after drinking or eating to take your child's temperature. If the temperature is more than 99.6°F, you should recheck your child's temperature rectally. Also, if the child's nose is stuffed up or if he or she has a frequent cough, then taking the child's temperature rectally is more accurate. A fever is defined as having a temperature greater than 99.6°F orally or with an ear thermometer, 98.6°F under the arm, or 100.4°F rectally.

How to Take a Child's Temperature Rectally

Because most children younger than 2 years of age cannot keep their mouths closed or remain still for an oral temperature, it is best to take their temperature rectally. Lay the baby on your lap, bottom up, with legs hanging down. Be sure to support the baby's head. If the baby is too squirmy, lay the child on a firm, flat surface. Be sure to use a rectal thermometer, which has a shorter bulb than an oral thermometer. Put petroleum jelly on the end of the thermometer to make it more comfortable, and insert the thermometer about an inch into the rectum (until you can no longer see the silver end) for about 3 minutes. Always stop at less than 1 inch if there is resistance. Be sure to

hold on to the thermometer while it is in the child's rectum, so that the child doesn't roll over or move and puncture his or her colon. A rectal temperature is normally 1° higher than an oral temperature.

Self-Care

- Give plenty of fluids—water, juice, soup, flavored gelatin, ice pops—to prevent dehydration. A desire for solids usually decreases with a fever.
- Use acetaminophen (Tylenol or Tempra) if your child's temperature is more than 102°F. Be sure to follow the package's instructions for your child's age and weight. Do not give children and teenagers aspirin or aspirin-containing products, because they have been linked to Reye's syndrome, a serious condition that can lead to coma and death (see Box on p. 363).
- Give infants and children a sponge bath in lukewarm water. Do not use cool or cold water, which may cause shivering.
- Dress the child lightly and use lighter bedclothes to avoid overheating. Cover the child with a blanket if chilled.
- When calling your child's doctor about a fever, tell him or her if you took your child's temperature rectally, orally, or with an ear thermometer.
- Children between 6 months and 5 years of age sometimes have seizures or

"fits" (called *febrile seizures*) when they have a high fever. These seizures are seldom harmful. During a seizure, protect children from hurting themselves by keeping them away from nearby objects and making sure they are breathing freely. Report the seizure to your child's doctor. If the seizures continue, go to the emergency room.

What to do about Fevers

Symptom/Sign	Action
Fever for less than 3 days without other symptoms	Self-care
Child less than 3 months of age with a rectal temperature greater than 100.4°F	Call doctor
Child with fever, acting ill, not their usual self	See doctor
Child with fever with seizure, no history of febrile seizures	See doctor
Child with fever and joint swelling or tenderness; painful rash; or dark red, purple, or bruiselike rash	See doctor
Fever and stiff neck	Go to hospital

Fifth Disease

Fifth disease is a viral infection. It starts with a rash on the cheeks and then spreads to the arms and legs.

Fifth disease is usually seen in children, from preschool through junior high school age, and it often occurs in the spring.

Causes

Fifth disease is very contagious. It spreads through saliva by coughing, sneezing, or skin-to-skin contact. Although the rash usually only lasts about 5 days, it can recur a number of times over several weeks if the child is exposed to sunlight, heat, exercise, fever, or stress.

Symptoms

- Fifth disease usually starts with a bright red rash on the cheeks that looks as if the child has been slapped. The rash then spreads to the arms, legs, and body. It fades over 1 or 2 weeks and may have a "lacy" look as it fades.

- There usually is no fever with fifth disease.

- There may be mild joint pains or mild headache.

Self-Care

- Encourage extra fluids.
- For joint pain or a headache, you may give your child acetaminophen. Do not give aspirin (see Reye's Syndrome, p. 363).

What to do about Fifth Disease

Symptom/Sign	Action
Rash starting on the cheeks and spreading to rest of the body	Self-care
Extreme itching	Call doctor

Growing Pains

Growing pains are not a myth, but a real problem in children between the ages of 6 and 12. It is common for children having growth spurts to have vague aches and pains for no apparent reason. The pains usually occur in the evening, often in the calves and thighs.

Self-Care

You can help relieve the pain for your child several ways:

- Give acetaminophen or ibuprofen.
- Use a heating pad, set on low, on the painful area.
- Have your child soak in a warm bath.

What to do about Growing Pains

Symptom/Sign	Action
Vague aches and pains with no injury	Self-care
Pain that is always in the same spot	Call doctor
Swelling, redness, tenderness to the touch, or fever	Call doctor
Your child is limping	Call doctor

Hand-Foot-and-Mouth Disease

Hand-foot-and-mouth disease is a summertime disease that afflicts mostly children. It is very contagious and is common in late summer and early fall. It is not related to hoof-and-mouth disease in cattle.

Causes

Hand-foot-and-mouth disease is caused by a virus. Although the virus is common, the disease affects mostly children between the ages of 6 months and 4 years. The virus leaves the body through the stool of the infected child and enters another person when hands, food, or objects are placed in the mouth.

Symptoms

With hand-foot-and-mouth disease, a child will have a sore throat and fever, as well as a rash. The symptoms are:

- Sore mouth, with ulcers you can see if you look into the throat
- Rash with small blisters on the soles of the feet and the palms of the hands
- Low fever
- Cough, runny nose
- Diarrhea or vomiting

Self-Care

Hand-foot-and-mouth disease is not a serious illness and usually clears up within about a week. A baby or child with the disease will be uncomfortable, but you can help relieve some of the symptoms.

- Give acetaminophen to reduce any fever and to ease some pain.
- If your child is old enough to gargle, try a saltwater rinse (½ teaspoon salt in a cup of warm water). It can help soothe the sore throat.
- Make sure the child drinks lots of fluids.

What to do about Hand-Foot-and-Mouth Disease

Symptom/Sign	Action
Mildly painful mouth, fever less than 100.4°F	Self-care
Poor fluid intake, severe mouth pain	See doctor
Symptoms of dehydration (decreased urine output, absence of tears)	Go to hospital

Prevention

Careful, thorough handwashing is the most effective way to prevent the spread of the disease. Hand-foot-and-mouth disease is contagious during the illness. Once the fever is gone, there is no need to keep your child out of day care or school.

Impetigo

Impetigo is a contagious bacterial infection most often seen at the site of broken skin. The most common location is around the mouth and nose, although it can occur on arms and legs.

Causes

Impetigo occurs more often in the summer and affects children more often than adults. Touching or picking the sores can spread the bacteria to other parts of the body or to other people.

Symptoms

Impetigo starts as a small, itchy, water-filled blister that turns into a yellow pus-filled sore. After rupturing, it appears to have a honey-colored crust.

Treatment

With quick and careful home treatment, impetigo can be brought under control in several days. If you think your child has impetigo, contact your doctor. He or she will prescribe a medication to help heal the infection.

Self-Care

- Apply Domboro solution (available without a prescription) to sores twice a day for 10 minutes.

- Remove crusts from sores with a cotton swab. Then, with a separate swab, apply Bacitracin or another topical antibiotic medication.

- Wash your hands well with antibacterial soap and water after cleaning sores and applying ointment.

- Don't cover the area with an adhesive bandage unless the sore is in an area where the scab may rub off. If needed to keep children from scratching, cover with a dry gauze pad and keep the tape as far from the sore as possible.

- Make sure everyone in the household uses separate towels, washcloths, and bath water. Wash bedding, towels, and clothes with Lysol or bleach. Dry on high heat or in the sun.

- Call your doctor if sores do not improve after 3 days of home care.

What to do about Impetigo

Symptom/Sign	Action
Mild impetigo (fewer than two sores, smaller than 1 inch)	Call doctor
Sores don't clear up after 1 week of using prescribed ointment or worsen after 48 hours	See doctor
Infant with small, pus-filled blisters that break easily and leave a raw spot behind	See doctor
More than two sores that are larger than 1 inch	See doctor
Blisters show other signs of infection, such as increased redness and swelling	See doctor
Urine turns red or cola colored; headache, fever, sore throat, or swollen eyes occur	Go to hospital

Lead Poisoning

Children can become very ill—and can have permanent damage—after being poisoned by lead.

Although you wouldn't deliberately feed your child lead, it is still present in many places. Lead once was commonly used in paints. It went onto the walls and woodwork in many homes and was even used to paint toys for many decades. If your home hasn't been painted for a while, it could have lead-based paint on its surfaces.

Infants and very young children learn about the world in part by putting things in their mouths. They may even eat or chew the bars of their crib or pieces of flaking paint. Many items in their environment may be contaminated by lead dust.

Causes

Lead is harmful to body tissues and enzymes. It gets into your body when you eat, drink, or breathe something that has lead in it. Drinking water or other liquids from a cup or bowl that has been painted with lead or that had lead in the clay that made it can give you lead poisoning.

Lead accumulates in the body. Children who regularly take in small amounts of lead can be poisoned and become extremely ill—or even die. More often, though, lead poisoning causes serious health problems, including brain damage.

Symptoms

Lead poisoning is hard to detect at first, because the symptoms are not obvious. Even children who seem to be healthy can have high levels of lead in their bodies. Usually, lead builds up in the body gradually.

Symptoms of lead poisoning can also be symptoms of other conditions. Symptoms include:

- Loss of appetite and weight loss
- Irritability
- Tired, lethargic behavior
- Vomiting
- Abdominal pain
- Constipation
- Joint pain
- Headaches
- Trouble sleeping
- Confusion

When the level of lead in the body becomes greater, more extreme symptoms may be seen, including:

- Twitching and shaking
- Convulsions
- Paralysis
- Hallucinations
- Coma

Self-Care

Lead poisoning usually happens over time, not in one incident. If you think there is a possibility that your child has lead poisoning, see your doctor as soon as possible. If the lead poisoning continues, your child may suffer permanent damage.

There is medication to help remove lead from the body, but the most important thing you can do is to stop your child's exposure to lead by following the prevention steps listed below:

Prevention

• Have your home checked by a professional to see where there may be lead hazards.

• If you have lead in your home, lead abatement experts can recommend cleaning products that will help get rid of the lead in dust.

• Make sure your child's hands are washed after he or she plays outside (there may be lead contamination in the soil), before eating, and before going to bed.

• If you have lead paint, carefully paint over it with lead-free paint.

• Be careful about canned food products from other countries. Lead is not allowed in cans made in the United States but can still be found in some cans from other countries.

• If you use older toys or cribs, make sure you have the paint on them tested for lead.

Pinworms

Pinworms are a common parasite that affect mostly children.

Cause

Pinworms are spread from person to person—usually from child to child. The pinworm eggs leave the body of an infected person through the rectum. Another person takes the eggs in unknowingly through the mouth after having touched food, bedding, or other items with eggs on them.

Once taken in through the mouth, the eggs hatch in the small intestine and then grow into worms in the large intestine. The cycle then starts again, as the female worm goes to the area around the rectum and lays eggs.

Symptoms

The main symptom of pinworms is the itching a child feels as the female worms move to the rectum to lay eggs and from the eggs themselves. Symptoms include:

• Intense itching around the rectum or, in girls, the vagina (sometimes a worm goes into the vagina instead of the rectum)

• Difficulty sleeping, usually because of the itching at night

• Irritability because of the lack of sleep and the itching

- Irritation and scabbing around the rectum because of scratching

- Visible small, white worms in the anal area, especially at night

Treatment

Pinworms can be treated successfully with prescription medication. It's an annoying condition but not a serious one. You will need a doctor's care to get rid of the infestation.

Self-Care

If one person in a household gets pinworms, the infestation easily can spread. Self-care measures can help prevent that spread. Use these measures for 3 days after taking the pinworm medication:

- Avoid scratching the area around the rectum or any other infected area.

- Everyone in the household should keep their hands and fingers away from the nose and mouth, except just after washing.

- Make sure your children wash their hands and fingernails thoroughly, especially after using the bathroom and before eating anything.

- Keep your children's fingernails short.

- Discourage thumb sucking and nail biting.

- Have your child wear shorts or panties under pajamas.

- Give your child a shower each morning and remove shorts or panties in shower. Wash immediately.

- Clean the toilet seat and bathtub after use.

- Vacuum or wet-mop your child's room. Eggs that are scattered on the floor are infectious for 1 to 3 weeks.

What to do about Pinworms

Symptom/Sign	Action
Someone in household has pinworms	Self-care
Child has itching, irritation around rectum	See doctor

Children's Rashes

Anyone can get a rash (see Rashes, p. 85), but babies and young children are particularly prone to them because their skin is still sensitive and they are likely to encounter bacteria and viruses as they begin to explore their world.

Types of Rashes in Infants and Children

There are several rashes that are seen mostly in infants and children.

Diaper rash is a red, puffy rash under and around the area covered by a diaper. It's a rash caused by the acid in urine or bowel movements or simply by moisture. Babies also can get diaper rash as a reaction to some kinds of disposable diapers or to soap used to wash cloth diapers.

Prickly heat rash is very common among infants. It's caused by perspiration when babies are overdressed and overheated. The rash appears as small red dots on an infant's head, neck, and shoulders. The baby may be overdressed if the skin is hot or moist between the shoulder blades. Once the hot, humid conditions are removed, the rash usually goes away.

Roseola is a viral disease producing a high fever, as well as a rash. It's most common in children between 9 months and 1½ years old. It begins with a fever, as high as 105°F; then the fever drops about 24 hours after the rash appears. The rash usually starts on the body and spreads to the legs, arms, and face.

Self-Care

- For diaper rash, use creams, such as Desitin, to help prevent irritation.

- Expose the area with a rash to the air whenever possible. If it must be covered, such as the diaper area, try to allow some time each day when the itchy area can be exposed to the fresh air.

- If you use cloth diapers, change laundry detergent or fabric softener if that seems to be what stimulates rashes. If you use disposable diapers, you may want to change brands.

- Keep the skin dry.

- If the rash is itchy, give cool tub baths or use a cool washcloth on the area.

- Be careful about using cornstarch or talc powders. If a baby breathes in those powders, the lungs can be injured.

What to do about Rashes

Symptom/Sign	Action
Itchy, red bumps around folds of the skin	Self-care
Rash around the diaper area	Self-care
Signs of infection in the area of the rash (increased redness and drainage)	See doctor
Rash with fever greater than 100°F	Call doctor

Tonsillitis

The tonsils are lymph nodes on each side at the back of the throat. They help fight infection from bacteria and viruses that enter through the nose and mouth, but sometimes the tonsils themselves can become inflamed and swollen. This is tonsillitis. Children ages 3 to 6 are more likely to get tonsillitis because their immune systems aren't fully developed.

Symptoms

- Very sore throat
- Trouble swallowing
- Fever and chills
- Tender, sore glands under the jaw and neck
- Headache
- Loss of voice
- Sore throat that lasts longer than 2 days

Self-Care

A child with tonsillitis needs a doctor's care; antibiotics usually are prescribed to heal the infection. But there are steps you can take to help your child feel better:

- Make sure your child has plenty of rest. Don't let him or her go back to school or day care until the fever is gone and the child is feeling better.

- If your doctor suggests it, give acetaminophen (Tylenol) to help reduce fever and pain.

- Offer warm liquids, such as tea and soup.

- Give any antibiotics exactly the way your doctor prescribed them. Don't stop giving them, even if your child seems to be better before the prescription is used up.

- If your child can gargle, have him or her gargle with warm saltwater (½ teaspoon salt in a cup of water) several times a day. Don't let your child swallow the saltwater.

Tonsillitis is quite common and not serious in itself, but if the infection isn't treated, there can be complications. If your child has symptoms of tonsillitis for more than 2 days, with a fever of 103°F or higher, has been exposed to strep throat, has had tonsillitis before, or has a sore throat that gets worse even with antibiotics, call your doctor.

Although surgery to remove tonsils was common a couple of decades ago, today surgery is generally only suggested when a child is prone to tonsillitis, with several incidences a year, or when a child has tonsillitis that doesn't respond to antibiotics.

What to do about Tonsillitis

Symptom/Sign	Action
Sore throat, fever, chills	Self-care
Sore throat and fever that last more than 24 hours	Call doctor
Fever, soreness continue, even with antibiotics	See doctor
Difficulty breathing	Go to hospital

Prevention

Because tonsillitis comes from other infections, to prevent tonsillitis you need to do what you can to prevent bacterial and viral infections. That's hard to do, because any contact with other people—especially with other children in day care or school—can spread infection.

- The best way to prevent infection is to encourage your child to wash his or her hands before eating and after using the bathroom. Teach your child to wash hands completely and vigorously with soap and running water.

- If your child is in day care, encourage the day care provider to make sure that children wash their hands often during the day, not just before meals.

- Help your children learn to cover their mouths when they cough or sneeze. Teach them to cough or sneeze into the inside of the elbow—not into their hands—to help prevent the spread of bacteria and viruses through hand contact.

- Don't smoke. Children exposed to cigarette smoke are more vulnerable to tonsillitis.

- If one of your children has tonsillitis—or any infection—make sure that no one else in your home eats or drinks from that child's dinnerware and utensils until they have been washed in hot, soapy water.

Vomiting

Vomiting in children is common and usually is not cause for concern if it occurs infrequently. It is important to give enough fluids and lots of tender loving care until your child's stomach settles down.

Causes

Vomiting in children is most commonly caused by viral or bacterial infections. A high fever may also trigger vomiting. Vomiting can be the body's reaction to eating spoiled food—for example, food left at room temperature for too long before being refrigerated. Nervousness, emotional stress, or tension can also cause an upset stomach. In addition, particularly in children, stomach upset can be brought on by:

- Motion sickness
- Too much excitement
- Too much sun
- Overeating
- Side effects of medications
- Inner ear disturbances
- Migraines

Self-Care

Fortunately, there are sensible and safe home remedies that can satisfy your child's need for fluids and provide relief. Over-the-counter medications are rarely necessary. They won't speed recovery, and your child will get well without them.

Steps To Help Your Child Feel Better

- Give 1 teaspoon room temperature Infalyte, Pedialyte, half-strength Gatorade, or homemade rehydrating solution (see About Rehydrating Solutions) every 1 to 2 minutes to prevent dehydration. Increase amounts and intervals as your child can tolerate it. Children who are vomiting are not in immediate danger of dehydration if they are drinking adequately and urinating regularly.

- If your child vomits, allow the stomach to rest for a half hour and start over with rehydration.

- Fluids such as soda, apple juice, chicken broth, or full-strength Gatorade are not good replacement fluids for dehydration. The high concentration of sugar draws fluid from the cells, adding to the potential for dehydration. High salt content can have the same effect, so broth and salty fluids should also be avoided.

- Water should not be used as the only fluid for dehydration but can be given in small amounts in addition to Infalyte and Pedialyte.

- Give your child liquid in small amounts, so it is easily absorbed by the stomach and won't cause further irritation. Too much liquid can lead to continued vomiting.

- When your child can keep liquids down, return to a regular diet. Encourage complex carbohydrates, such as rice, potatoes, bread, cereal, lean meats, yogurt, bananas, applesauce, and vegetables.

- It's not unusual for children to have a decreased appetite after vomiting, but make sure they are drinking adequate fluids. Avoid fruit juice, which may lead to diarrhea.

- Over-the-counter medications to stop nausea and vomiting aren't necessary and are not recommended. Vomiting will usually stop on its own within 12 to 24 hours.

About Rehydrating Solutions

Pedialyte and Infalyte are fluid replacement solutions that can be given for mild to moderate dehydration. They should not be used as your child's only calorie source for more than 24 hours.

You can make a temporary rehydrating solution at home, using ½ teaspoon salt, 2 tablespoons sugar, and 1 quart water. This should only be used until you can purchase Infalyte, Pedialyte, or Gatorade (use Gatorade diluted to half strength), because it doesn't contain necessary potassium.

Children often don't like the taste of rehydrating solutions. Purchase flavored formulas, or improve the taste of solutions by adding a sprinkle of Kool-Aid or NutraSweet.

Rehydrating solutions are also available as Popsicles. Be careful your child doesn't eat them too quickly. Like liquid rehydrating solutions, they should only be given a teaspoon at a time.

What to do about Vomiting

Symptom/Sign	Action
Vomiting due to motion sickness, eating too much, or stress	Self-care
Child with diabetes or other chronic disease who is unable to keep medication down	Call doctor
Vomiting for more than 48 hours or unable to keep fluids down for 24 hours	See doctor
Signs of dehydration: decreased urination, dry mouth, change in behavior, lack of tears	See doctor
Vomiting and fever in child younger than 3 months	Go to hospital
Vomiting with headache and stiff neck	Go to hospital
Vomiting with severe, constant abdominal pain, or abdominal trauma	Go to hospital
Vomiting more than three times after head injury	Go to hospital
Vomiting large amounts of blood or a substance that looks like coffee grounds	Go to hospital
Vomiting with possible poisoning	Go to hospital
Vomiting large amounts of blood or a substance that looks like coffee grounds, with dizziness, light-headedness, rapid pulse, or cool, clammy skin	Call 911

3

HEALTHY LIVING

In the long run, your health decisions and your lifestyle have more impact on your health than anything your doctor can do. By developing and maintaining healthy habits, you can prevent major health problems. Scheduling regular checkups with your doctor can help catch many concerns early, when they're easier to treat. And keeping yourself informed and organized can help you manage minor health concerns at home.

All these things are part of healthy living. If you already have health problems, it's not too late to make lifestyle changes—it may even be more important for you. Read this section to learn what you can do to take control of your health. ::

Health Care At Home

When health concerns arise, being prepared can help you respond effectively. From stocking your home with first aid supplies to keeping records of your medications, there are a number of steps you can take to make sure you're ready to deal with health concerns at home.

This chapter provides tips on what health tools to keep on hand and how to manage your medications—information you need to stay equipped, organized, and on top of your home health care. ⸬

Equipping Your Home for Self-care

The first step in handling health problems at home is to make sure you have the right tools, medication, and information on hand. Some of these basic supplies will help you treat minor health problems yourself. Others will give you the information you need to decide whether a trip to the doctor or the hospital is necessary.

Check at least once a year to make sure you have all the basic supplies and the expiration date on medications has not passed.

Near the phone, post numbers for family doctors and the local poison-control emergency numbers.

First-Aid Supplies

- Adhesive bandage strips in assorted sizes
- Butterfly-shaped bandages for closing cuts
- Elastic bandages, both 2 and 3 inches wide, for wrapping sprained ankles or wrists or for supporting and putting pressure on injured, swollen, or sore knees
- Adhesive tape (one roll)
- Sterile gauze pads, 2 and 4 inches wide, for cleaning cuts and scrapes and covering larger wounds
- Paper tape that pulls off painlessly to hold gauze pads in place
- Eye-rinse cup
- Scissors

- Two pair of tweezers: a blunt-tipped pair for such things as removing an object from a child's nose and a pair with pointed ends for removing splinters

Medications

Check expiration dates once a year.

- Antiseptic ointment
- Antihistamine tablets for allergic reactions
- Acetaminophen (Tylenol) for fever, pain, mild burns, and stings
- Syrup of ipecac to induce vomiting
- Calamine lotion for itching

Miscellaneous Items

- Antiseptic soap to clean wounds
- Ice pack, either the kind that holds ice cubes or is kept in the freezer
- Disposable gloves
- Cardiopulmonary resuscitation (CPR) mask
- Thermometer
- Penlight for examining sore throats
- Heating pad for treating sore or tense muscles

- Cold-mist vaporizer for relieving the congestion of colds and coughs

Information To Keep Handy

- Medical and self-care reference books
- List of allergies for each member of your family
- List of all prescription and non-prescription medications taken by each member of your family
- Signed medical consent forms for each member of your family, which will allow someone to authorize treatment if they are not able to give consent

Managing Your Medicine

Medication, whether it's a couple of Tylenol tablets or a prescription from your doctor, can relieve pain, fight infection, or reduce symptoms of disease. Prescribed medication and over-the-counter products need to be taken properly, however, or they can't do what they are supposed to do for your condition.

Be an Active Consumer

You can make sure you understand your medications, and have all options, if you follow a few simple steps:

- *Tell your doctor and pharmacist about all the medication you are taking.* Write down the names of the medications you take and the amount ("500 mg, three times a day," for example). Include any drugs prescribed for you, and if you see more than one doctor, make sure each one knows what the others have prescribed. List all over-the-counter medications you are taking, such as aspirin, acetaminophen (Tylenol), antacids, laxatives, cough and cold medicines, and vitamin supplements. If you take any herbal medicines or supplements, such as St. John's wort or gingko biloba, make sure you list those as well. Over-the-counter and herbal medications sometimes interact with prescribed medication in harmful ways.

- *Tell your doctor and pharmacist about any past reactions to specific medica-*

tions. If you are allergic to a certain medication or have had a bad reaction to it in the past, your doctor needs to know.

- *Ask about generic medications.* Many brand-name medications have less expensive generic equivalents. To save money, ask your doctor if a generic medication is appropriate.

- *Ask about new medications.* You may see information about new medications for your condition. Ask your doctor about any you've heard of. If you are doing fine on your current medication, you doctor probably will recommend that you stay on it.

- *Ask about nondrug options.* For many conditions, medication isn't the only solution. Ask your doctor about alternative ways of treating your condition. For example, losing weight and increasing your physical activity can help lower high blood pressure.

Choosing a Pharmacy

Whether you choose a pharmacy connected to your clinic, one near your home, or one in a store you go to often,

Personal Medication Record

Prescription Drugs

List any prescription drugs you've taken in the last 2 to 4 weeks, as well as any you have on hand to use as needed, but that you haven't taken recently. Add new drugs as they are prescribed.

Drug

(brand or generic name):
Purpose:
Dose:
Instructions:
Date Started:

Over-the-Counter Drugs

(Make a similar list for over-the-counter drugs.)
Drug:
Purpose:
Dose:
Instructions:
Date Started:

Drug Allergies and Past Reactions

List any drugs you know you are allergic to and those to which you have had a bad reaction to in the past. You may also include the names of prescription drugs that haven't worked for you.
Drug:
Purpose:
Drug:
Purpose:
What happened to make you think you are allergic to this drug?:

find one that suits you and use it consistently. That way, the pharmacist can check your records for possible drug interactions and allergies whenever a new prescription is filled. Your file will be complete if you always use the same pharmacy.

Look for a pharmacy where the pharmacists take time to answer all your questions, in person or over the phone.

If your health insurance covers prescriptions, it may require you to use only certain pharmacies. If you pay for your own prescriptions, you may want to comparison shop for a regular pharmacy, especially if you take certain medications regularly.

Some pharmacies offer special conveniences, such as 24-hour emergency service, computerized records of the medications you buy, senior citizen discounts, drive-up windows, and delivery service. Think about what services may be important to you when you decide on a regular pharmacy.

Keep Complete Records

Keep records of the medications each member of your family takes, so you can refer to them easily. Update your records whenever you get a new prescription.

The Personal Medication Record (p. 392) is a guide for listing current medications and past reactions to medication. Make your own worksheet and keep it on hand for your whole family to bring to the doctor's office or your pharmacy.

Making Your Medicine Work for You

To get the full benefit of your medications, follow these steps:

- *Understand what you're taking.* Know what the medication does, the correct dose, when and how to take it, and how long to take it. Some medications aren't effective unless you finish the entire prescription. Others, such as pain relievers, can be stopped when symptoms disappear.

- *Ask about side effects and report reactions promptly.* Some side effects are common and not dangerous. Others can signal that a medication isn't right for you. If you don't feel right, call your doctor or pharmacy and report the name of the medication you're taking and the reaction you're having. Be cautious about symptoms such as dizziness or drowsiness. They can in- terfere with driving or cause falls. Be sure to tell your doctor or pharmacist if you have a condition that might be af- fected by a medication. For example, pregnant women and nursing mothers should avoid many medications.

- *Follow instructions.* Read labels care- fully and ask your pharmacist about any special precautions. Some med- ications should be taken with food; others work best on an empty stom- ach. You may need to avoid alcohol or stay out of the sun while taking certain medications. Some medica- tions need to be shaken before being taken or must be kept in the refrig- erator. Not following these instruc- tions can make the medication less effective.

- *Be consistent.* Take your medication regularly and on time. If you miss a dose, check with your doctor or phar- macist. Sometimes you may be told to double the next dose. Other times that could be harmful. Don't make the decision on your own.

- *Remember to take your medication.* Link taking your medication with other parts of your daily routine, such as meals or bedtime or even brushing your teeth. For example:

Once a day. Take medication when you watch the evening news.

Twice a day. Take medication before brushing your teeth in the morning and evening.

Four times a day. Take medication at each meal and at bedtime. (If the medicine should be taken on an empty stomach, take it an hour before meals.)

Over-the-Counter Medications

Over-the-counter medications can cause overdoses, allergic reactions, and dangerous interactions with other medications just as prescription medications can.

Over-the-counter medications can interfere with your prescription medications. For example, a simple antacid can destroy the effectiveness of certain antibiotics. The side effects of cough or cold medicines can be serious if you're taking medicine for high blood pressure, diabetes, or glaucoma.

Some medications that once required a prescription are now sold over the counter. Ask your pharmacist for recommendations about medications. To help ask the right questions and make the right decisions, use the Over-the-Counter Medication box on p. 395 as a reminder of what to consider when choosing an over-the-counter medication.

Over-the-Counter Pain Medications

There are a number of over-the-counter options for dealing with pain. Some may work better for you than others and may have fewer side effects for you. Use the table on p. 396 to understand the differences between pain medications.

Choosing Over-the-Counter Medication

Use these steps to decide whether to take an over-the-counter medication.

Evaluate

What symptoms do you want the medication to relieve?

Can home remedies do the job?

Are you supposed to avoid certain medications for any reason (pregnancy, breastfeeding, medication interactions, allergies)?

Consult

Ask your pharmacist or doctor or check a reference book for help in choosing the proper product.

Investigate

Read the label thoroughly. What are the ingredients?

Do they conflict with any other medications you are taking?

Are you allergic to any of the ingredients?

What does the medication do?

What is the recommended dosage for you?

Do any warnings or cautions apply to you?

Confirm

Ask your pharmacist about possible interactions with food, alcohol, or your other medicines.

Decide

What is your motive for buying this medication?

Are you being influenced by recommendations, price, or advertising?

Which Pain Medication Is Right for You?

Use this table to decide what type of pain reliever is right for you. If you are not sure, talk with your pharmacist. Tell him or her what drugs you take and what medical problems you have.

	Dose	Safe for Children?	Use for Headache?	Use for Pain?
Acetaminophen (Tylenol)	Adults: Take one or two 325-milligram tablets, three to four times a day. Children: Dosage determined by weight and age. Consult with your doctor.	Consult a doctor	Yes	Yes
Ibuprofen (Advil, Motrin IB)	Adults: Take one or two 200-milligram tablets. Take with food. Don't take more than six tablets a day unless directed by a doctor. Children: Dosage determined by weight and age. Consult with your doctor.	Consult a doctor	Yes	Yes
Aspirin	Adults: Take one or two 325-milligram tablets every four hours. Take up to 12 tablets a day, unless doctor tells you not to. Children: Don't give to children.	No	Yes	Yes
Ketoprofen (Orudis)	Adults: Take one 12.5-milligram tablet every 4 to 6 hours. If you don't feel better, you may take a second tablet after 1 hour. Don't take more than six tablets in a 24-hour period. Children: Not recommended.	No	Yes	Yes
Naproxen sodium (Aleve)	Adults: Take one 220-milligram tablet every 8 to 12 hours. If you don't feel better, you may take one tablet 12 hours later. Take no more than 3 tablets in 24 hours unless directed by a doctor. Adults older than 65: Take no more than one tablet every 12 hours. Children: Not recommended.	No	Yes	Yes

Which Pain Medication Is Right for You?

Important tips:
- Don't use more than one type of pain reliever at a time.
- Be careful with products that have more than one medication. Some may have caffeine. Some may mix poorly with other medications.
- Don't take aspirin when you are taking a cold medicine.

Use for Fever?	Use for Muscle/ Joint Pain or Arthritis?	Use to Prevent Heart Attack or Stroke?	Side Effects and Other Things to Consider
Yes	Yes	No	Large doses can be harmful. If you regularly drink alcohol, talk with your doctor before taking this medication. Avoid if you have liver problems.
Yes	Yes	No	Don't take if allergic to aspirin. May cause stomach bleeding. Avoid if you have congestive heart failure, kidney problems, or ulcers. Avoid if you are taking diuretics or anticoagulants.
Yes	Yes	Yes	May cause ulcers or stomach bleeding. Use enteric-coated aspirin to reduce stomach irritation. Older adults should use with caution. High doses can cause dizziness. Dizziness may lead to falls.
Yes	Yes	No	Can irritate stomach. Avoid if you have congestive heart failure, kidney problems, or ulcers. Avoid if you are taking diuretics or anticoagulants.
Yes	Yes	No	Can irritate stomach. Avoid if you have congestive heart failure, kidney problems, or ulcers. Avoid if you are taking diuretics or anticoagulants. If you have more than three drinks per day that contain alcohol, talk with your doctor before you use this medication.

Lifestyle Choices

Many of the major causes of death—including cancer, heart disease, stroke, and lung disease—can be prevented. Although you can't control certain risk factors for health problems, such as a genetic predisposition, there are factors you *can* control.

What you eat, how often you're physically active, and whether or not you smoke are all lifestyle choices that can have a significant impact on your health. This chapter explains what you can do in these areas to maintain your health and prevent many health problems. ::

Activity

Increasing the amount of activity in our daily lives can go a long way toward improving our health and even increasing longevity. Being physically active every day is good for you.

The good news is that you can achieve some the health benefits of regular exercise even if you do not work out at the gym, attend aerobics classes, or jog three times week. The secret lies in increasing your physical activity throughout the day while doing those things you normally enjoy.

To achieve health benefits, your goal should be to accumulate at least 30 minutes of physical activity on most days of the week. The 30 minutes of activity can be 5 minutes of taking the stairs instead of the elevator or 10 minutes of walking to your car from the far end of the parking lot. Try to build up to 60 minutes a day, which can help you achieve and maintain a healthy weight.

The Benefits of Activity

It is difficult to find another health habit with as many positive benefits as physical activity. To name a few:

- Reduces the risk of heart disease, diabetes, colon cancer, and hypertension
- Reduces feelings of anxiety and depression
- Helps keep muscles, bones, and joints healthy
- Helps increase endurance

Building Your Own Activity Pyramid

The activity pyramid is a useful tool for setting goals because it helps create a realistic plan for increasing activity. The pyramid consists of four tiers, each emphasizing a different kind of activity.

Stay Active and Walk Often

The everyday activities at the base of the pyramid are key to staying active through your lifetime. The first step to becoming more active is to focus on the base. These baseline activities will help you gradually build stamina for the next level.

- Regularly park in the back row of the parking lot to walk a little farther.
- Routinely take the stairs instead of the elevator.
- Break up a long period of sitting by getting up and moving around.
- Walk around the block once.
- Look for ways to make errands more active. Take the long way around the mall.

CUT DOWN ON

Sitting
Watching TV
Working or playing
at the computer

3+ TIMES A WEEK

Stretch and strengthen your muscles

Take stretch breaks   Weight lifting
Yoga/Tai Chi   Tension bands
                             Push-ups/Curl-ups

3-5 TIMES A WEEK

Give your heart and lungs a workout

Biking/Hiking   Brisk walking
Running/Jogging   Basketball
                    In-line skating

EVERY DAY

Walk often and stay active

Walk the dog   Go bowling
Do yardwork   Park your car farther away
Play golf   Take the stairs instead
                    of the elevator

The activity pyramid.

Give Your Heart and Lungs a Workout

More vigorous forms of physical activity (aerobic exercise) help improve the efficiency of your heart, lungs, and blood vessels. Traditional aerobic exercise includes brisk walking, jogging, swimming, and biking. Consider these factors when adding aerobic activity.

- *Frequency.* Over the course of a week, aim for getting some type of aerobic exercise three to five times. Although exercising 5 days a week does benefit your heart, vigorous exercise 6 to 7 days a week does not provide additional improvement. It does increase the risk of injury.

- *Intensity.* A workout should challenge you but not exhaust you or push you to your limit. If you can hold a conversation while exercising, you're doing great. If not, slow down.

- *Duration.* You can improve your cardiovascular fitness by exercising continuously for 20 to 30 minutes. Longer periods may be necessary for weight loss.

- *Progression.* Perhaps the biggest mistake people make when starting to exercise is doing too much too fast. The discomfort and risk of injury can spoil even the best of intentions. If you are a beginner, try to increase the length of time you exercise before increasing how hard you exercise.

Stretch and Strengthen Your Muscles

Your cardiovascular fitness is probably the best indicator of your fitness level; however, flexibility, muscular strength, endurance, and body composition are also part of being fit. Yoga, stretching exercises, push-ups, and weightlifting serve to improve flexibility and strength. You will enjoy the following benefits when you engage in these activities:

- Daily activities become easier as muscles grow stronger.

- Improved flexibility and strength help reduce muscle tension in times of stress.

- Strong abdominal and lower back muscles help prevent back problems.

- Strengthening specific muscle groups improve performance in sports activities.

The Top of the Pyramid

Our ancestors never had to worry about the top of the pyramid; physical activity was part of their lives and necessary for survival. The top of the pyramid is your reminder that you need to get up and move if you find yourself sitting for longer that 30 minutes.

- When sitting at your workstation, get up and walk down the hall every half hour.
- When talking on the phone, get up and move around.
- Stretch when sitting in traffic.

Choosing the Best Time to Exercise

There is not scientific evidence that suggests exercising at a specific time of day will burn more calories or help with weight loss. Pick a time that works best for you and schedule it just like an appointment. Avoid strenuous activity right before you go to bed; it can make falling asleep more difficult.

Overcoming Obstacles

Everyone has barriers that can make it difficult to start and stick to an activity plan. Try some of these tips to overcome common obstacles.

Time

You do not have to get your 30 minutes all at once. Five minutes here and 10 minutes there will add up. Write down when you want to exercise on your calendar and do not let anything get in the way. Remember, daily activity is just as important as brushing your teeth.

Measure Your Steps

Buy a pedometer to keep track of how many steps you take in a day. Here is how to use it:

- Wear it for 2 to 3 days to see how many steps you usually take in a day.
- For 1 week, walk 1000 extra steps each day.
- The next week, add 1000 more.
- Keep adding steps until you reach 10,000 steps a day.
- Aim to walk 10,000 steps every day.

Environment

There will always be days when it is too hot or too cold to exercise. Do not let weather stop you. If you cannot go outside try mall walking. Get exercise videos from your local library. Even doing housework counts toward daily activity.

Physical Limitations

Usually there are ways you can work around physical limitations such as difficulty walking or lifting. Ask your doctor how you can be active. A physical therapist can give options that could work for you.

Boredom

Anyone gets bored with the same old routine. Keep it interesting by:

- Changing routes
- Trying something new

- Rotating activities
- Asking a friend to exercise with you

Healthy Eating

Good eating habits can do more than help you and your family stay healthy—they can even help improve your health. Studies have found that eating a diet high in fruits and vegetables—which contain fiber, vitamins, and other valuable nutrients—can help lower your risk for heart disease, diabetes, high blood pressure, and certain types of cancer.

But health is only one of the reasons why we make certain choices when it comes to food. Eating is also one of life's pleasures. And there is no reason not to enjoy all kinds of foods; just don't overdo it. The key to healthy eating is balance. Eating a balanced diet means eating a variety of foods that supply the calories and nutrients you need without excess fat, salt, sugar, or alcohol.

The Food Groups

Daily you need more than 50 nutrients from food, including those that supply calories (carbohydrates, protein, and fat) and those that help with various body functions (vitamins, minerals, and water). Despite claims to the contrary, there are no known advantages to consuming large quantities of a specific nutrient or food. Each day, you should eat a variety of foods from each food group to get the nutrients you need.

Bread, Cereal, Rice, and Pasta

Foods in the bread, cereal, rice, and pasta group have carbohydrates to give you energy, as well as B vitamins and iron. Use whole grains—100 percent whole wheat bread, barley, oats, quinoa, and brown rice—to give your meals a boost of fiber. Go easy on sugary and high-fat choices, such as cookies and cake.

Fruits and Vegetables

Fruits and vegetables provide fiber and vitamins A, C, and E. Choose deeply colored vegetables and fruits to get the most nutrients, such as cantaloupe, tomatoes, oranges, berries, and squash. Eat at least five servings from a variety of fruits and vegetables each day. Limit fruit juices, which are low in fiber and high in calories.

Milk, Yogurt, and Cheese

Dairy products are great sources of calcium and also provide protein. Choose nonfat or low-fat products such as skim milk to get nutrients without adding a lot of fat and calories.

Meat, Poultry, Fish, Dry Beans, Eggs, and Nuts

Meat, poultry, fish, dry beans, eggs, and nuts provide protein and iron. Choose lean cuts of meat. When preparing, trim the fat, remove skin from poultry, and drain any grease used in cooking.

Fats, Oils, and Sweets

Fat is an essential nutrient, but many foods in this group—including cream, butter, gravy, and salad dressing—provide a lot of calories with few nutrients. Limit the amount of foods you eat from this group, keeping your fat intake at less than 30 percent of your total calories (see High Blood Cholesterol, p. 189).

Serving Sizes

The Food Pyramid was created by the U.S. Department of Agriculture (USDA) to show how much food you should eat from each of the food groups each day (see illustration on page 405). The amount of food you need depends on your age, gender, physical condition, and activity level. Everyone should have at least the minimum number of servings from each food group daily. Many men, women, older children, and teenagers need more.

The number of servings from each food group may sound like a lot, but it's really not. One serving is not the same as one helping. Serving sizes for each food group are listed next.

Bread, Cereal, Rice, and Pasta

- 1 slice of bread
- ½ cup hot cereal
- 1 cup dry cereal
- 1 6-inch tortilla
- ½ cup rice or pasta

Fruits

- 1 medium fruit
- ½ grapefruit
- ¾ cup juice
- ½ cup cut-up fruit, berries, canned, cooked, or frozen fruit
- ¼ cup dried fruit

Vegetables

- ½ cup cooked vegetables
- 1 cup raw, leafy vegetables
- ¾ cup vegetable juice
- ½ cup chopped raw vegetables
- 1 small potato

Milk, Yogurt, and Cheese

- 1 cup (8 ounces) milk or yogurt
- 1½ ounces cheese
- 1 cup frozen yogurt
- 1 cup cottage cheese (equals half a serving)

The food pyramid
- *Build your diet from the bottom up. Grains, fruits, and vegetables should make up the bulk of your diet. These foods supply energizing carbohydrates, vitamins, minerals, and fiber.*
- *Don't count on one food group to do it all. You need more than 50 different nutrients and not one food group has them all. Have at least the minimum number of servings from each food group.*
- *Eat regularly to keep energy flowing. Do not skip meals or go more than 5 daytime hours without food.*
- *Don't feel guilty about an occasional treat. But remember, "occasional" does not mean every day.*

Meat, Poultry, Fish, Dry Beans, Eggs, and Nuts

- ½ cup tuna or ground beef
- 1 small chicken leg or thigh
- 1 medium pork chop
- 1 chicken breast
- ¼-pound hamburger patty
- 1 egg
- 2 tablespoons peanut butter
- ½ cup lentils, peas, or dry beans
- ½ cup tofu

Special Concerns

Saturated Fat and Cholesterol

Foods high in saturated fats, trans fatty acids, and cholesterol tend to raise levels of cholesterol in the blood. Limit the amount of saturated fat and cholesterol in your diet. Foods high in saturated fats include high-fat dairy products and meats, lard, palm oil, and coconut oil. Foods high in trans fatty acids include baked goods made with shortening, such as crackers and cookies. Foods high in cholesterol include liver and other organ meats, egg yolks, and dairy fats.

Calcium

Calcium requirements depend on your age, gender, and health status. Try to eat at least two or three servings of low-fat dairy products each day. If you don't like dairy products or can't tolerate them, try processed foods that have been fortified with calcium, such as orange juice and breakfast cereals.

Salt and Sodium

Most people get too much salt in their diet. Limit the amount of salt you add to your food—use herbs and spices to flavor your food instead. Limit fast, convenience, and canned foods to keep your sodium intake under control.

Alcohol

Alcoholic beverages supply calories but few nutrients. If you drink alcohol, do so in moderation. Drinking in moderation is defined as no more than one drink per day for women and no more than two drinks per day for men. (One drink equals 12 ounces of beer, 5 ounces of wine, or 1½ ounces of 80-proof liquor.) Although research has shown that drinking alcohol in moderation may have some health benefits, the evidence is not strong enough to make it worthwhile to *start* drinking if you don't. Too much alcohol can cause a number of health problems (see Alcohol and Drug Abuse, p. 329).

Dietary Supplements

Although most people don't need dietary supplements, some people with special nutrition needs can benefit from them. Some supplements can be harmful in large amounts. Talk to your doctor about whether you need dietary supplements and how much to take.

Food Safety

Eating even a small portion of food that's been contaminated by bacteria or viruses can make you sick. Follow these steps to make sure the food you eat is safe.

- Wash your hands before eating.
- Wash fruits and vegetables thoroughly.
- Use special care when handling meats. Wash all utensils, countertops, and anything else that comes in contact with raw meat.

- Cook all meat, poultry, and seafood thoroughly.

- Drink only pasteurized milk and juices.

- Store foods at low temperatures (below 40°F) to minimize bacterial growth. Thaw food in the refrigerator, not on the kitchen counter.

- In restaurants, avoid foods that may have bacterial contamination, such as salad bars, sushi and raw or undercooked meat, shellfish, poultry, and eggs.

Healthy Eating Tips

- Follow the Food Pyramid; use plant foods (fruits, vegetables, and whole grains) as the base of your diet. These foods make you full with fewer calories, promote digestion, and include protective substances that can prevent disease.

- Eat baked, grilled, and broiled foods rather than fried foods.

- Plan ahead. Know what you are going to have for supper before the day begins.

- Add fruit as the sweet treat at the end of a meal or as a snack.

- Drink water instead of soft drinks and sweetened beverages such as sports drinks and lemonade.

Maintaining a Healthy Weight

More than half of adults in the United States are overweight. Being overweight puts you at increased risk for high blood pressure, high blood cholesterol, type 2 diabetes, stroke, some forms of cancer, and many other health problems. Approximately 280,000 adult deaths in the United States each year are related to obesity.

In recent years, obesity has increased in every state of the United States. Men and women of all races, ages, and education levels weigh more than ever before.

Evaluating Your Health Risk

Because people come in a variety of shapes and sizes, weight isn't always the best predictor of whether a person will develop chronic disease. Instead, doctors look at the following information to identify those who may be at risk for health problems.

Body mass index (BMI) is a calculation that uses height and weight to measure body fat (see table on page 409). If your BMI is greater than 24, you may be at higher risk for developing weight-related health conditions.

Waist circumference indicates where fat is stored in your body. Excess fat in the abdomen may mean you're at a higher risk for health problems. To find your waist circumference, simply measure around your waist with a tape measure. A desirable waist circumference is less than 35 inches for women and less than 40 inches for men.

Inactivity, tobacco use, existing diabetes, high cholesterol, high blood pressure, and a family history of heart disease are factors that increase your risk for developing health problems from chronic conditions. If you have two or more of these other risk factors, weight management is especially important for you.

How to Achieve Your Healthy Weight

In the past, recommended weight loss goals were based on a so-called ideal body weight. Ideal body weight is determined by height and gender and can be unrealistic for many people. Fortunately, if you're overweight, even a little weight loss can improve your health, so setting a goal to lose just a few pounds can be both desirable and realistic.

For some people, simply preventing weight gain is an appropriate goal. For others, losing just 5 to 10 pounds is recommended. If you think you'd like to lose more, your chances of success are greater if you take small steps. Reach your goal of a 5- to 10-pound loss first; then reevaluate your need for further weight loss. Focus on achieving lifestyle change, not a number on the scale. If you are a numbers person, remember that weighing yourself every day might be discouraging. If you want to follow your weight loss, weigh yourself only once a week at the same time and on the same scale.

Simple Steps for Weight Management

- Eat all your vegetables, but try leaving behind one fourth of your entrée. If you clean your plate at every meal, you are probably eating too much, especially if you eat out often.

- Quench your thirst with water instead of soda pop or sweetened drinks such as Kool-Aid or sports drinks. A can of regular soda has 160 calories. If you are drinking even just one can per day, switching to water or diet soda for 6 months can eliminate 28,800 calories from your diet. That equals 8 pounds.

- Shoot for adding at least one serving of vegetables or fruits a day. In general, fruits and vegetables are low in calories, have a lot of nutrients, and can even curb your appetite for less healthy foods.

- Cut back on the number of times you eat out. Remember, eating out means restaurants, fast foods, convenience stores, and vending machines.

WEIGHT → HEIGHT ↓	100	105	110	115	120	125	130	135	140	145	150	155	160	165	170	175	180	185	190	195	200	205	210	215	220	225	230	235	240	245	250
5'0"	20	21	21	22	23	24	25	26	27	28	29	30	31	32	33	34	35	36	37	38	39	40	41	42	43	44	45	46	47	48	49
5'1"	19	20	21	22	23	24	25	26	26	27	28	29	30	31	32	33	34	35	36	37	38	39	40	41	42	43	43	44	45	46	47
5'2"	18	19	20	21	22	23	24	25	26	27	27	28	29	30	31	32	33	34	35	36	37	37	38	39	40	41	42	43	44	45	46
5'3"	18	19	19	20	21	22	23	24	25	26	27	27	28	29	30	31	32	33	34	35	35	36	37	38	39	40	41	42	43	43	44
5'4"	17	18	19	20	21	21	22	23	24	25	26	27	27	28	29	30	31	32	33	33	34	35	36	37	38	39	39	40	41	42	43
5'5"	17	17	18	19	20	21	22	22	23	24	25	26	27	27	28	29	30	31	32	32	33	34	35	36	37	37	38	39	40	41	42
5'6"	16	17	18	19	19	20	21	22	23	23	24	25	26	27	27	28	29	30	31	31	32	33	34	35	36	36	37	38	39	40	40
5'7"	16	16	17	18	19	20	20	21	22	23	23	24	25	26	27	27	28	29	30	31	31	32	33	34	34	35	36	37	38	38	39
5'8"	15	16	17	17	18	19	20	21	21	22	23	24	24	25	26	27	27	28	29	30	30	31	32	33	33	34	35	36	36	37	38
5'9"	15	16	16	17	18	18	19	20	21	21	22	23	24	24	25	26	27	27	28	29	30	30	31	32	32	33	34	35	35	36	37
5'10"	14	15	16	16	17	18	19	19	20	21	22	22	23	24	24	25	26	27	27	28	29	29	30	31	32	32	33	34	34	35	36
5'11"	14	15	15	16	17	17	18	19	20	20	21	22	22	23	24	24	25	26	27	27	28	29	29	30	31	31	32	33	33	34	35
6'0"	14	14	15	16	16	17	18	18	19	20	20	21	22	22	23	24	24	25	26	26	27	28	28	29	30	31	31	32	33	33	34
6'1"	13	14	15	15	16	16	17	18	18	19	20	20	21	22	22	23	24	24	25	26	26	27	28	28	29	30	30	31	32	32	33
6'2"	13	13	14	15	15	16	17	17	18	19	19	20	21	21	22	22	23	24	24	25	26	26	27	28	28	29	30	30	31	31	32
6'3"	12	13	14	14	15	16	16	17	17	18	19	19	20	21	21	22	22	23	24	24	25	26	26	27	27	28	29	29	30	31	31
6'4"	12	13	13	14	15	15	16	16	17	18	18	19	19	20	21	21	22	23	23	24	24	25	26	26	27	27	28	29	29	30	30

To find your BMI, simply find the intersection of the row and column for your height and weight. Your BMI is the number in the box where your row and column meet.

- Switch to food that is grilled, baked, or fresh. Frying foods and adding sauces can double the calories of a meal.

- Know how much you are eating. Get out your measuring cups and see how your portion sizes measure up.

- Keep track of what you eat for 3 days. This will help identify one or two habits that are sabotaging your weight management efforts.

Your Weight Management Plan

The best way to tackle weight management is through a combination of changed eating habits and increased activity.

What you eat is important. A healthy diet doesn't just mean eating less; it means adopting a habit of choosing healthy foods for years to come. Choosing a variety of foods using the Food Pyramid is a good way to start (see Healthy Eating, p. 403).

Physical activity burns calories and builds muscle. You can maintain your weight and even lose weight just by eating less, but weight loss comes easier when you increase your activity (see Activity, p. 399).

Slow, gradual weight loss (1 to 2 pounds a week) is healthier, easier to manage, and more likely to be permanent than rapid weight loss. One pound

of body weight equals 3500 calories. The best way to lose a pound a week is to reduce your food intake by 250 calories a day and increase your activity level by 250 calories a day.

Your Calorie Range

Your calorie needs are based on the number of calories your body burns each day. These needs are estimated based on gender, age, activity, body size, and health status. Select a calorie level within the following ranges:

Calories Per Day

Gender	Weight Maintenance	Weight Loss
Women	1800–2100	1200–1800
Men	2200–2800	1500–2000

Now, find your calorie level on the table on page 411 to see the number of servings you should have from each food group per day. Use the Food Groups worksheet on page 412 to keep track of the food group servings you eat.

About Fad Diets

When it comes to losing weight, people in the United States want fast results. We've all heard that to lose weight, we need to eat less and exercise more. But those aren't easy changes to make, and results come slowly. Most of us would rather be able to take a pill or make some simple change to our diet to lose extra pounds quickly.

Do Fad Diets Work?

Many people do lose weight on fad diets. However, experts point out that it's usually because people are eating fewer calories on the diets, not because of some magic ingredient or food combination. For example, people may lose weight on a low-carbohydrate, high-protein diet, but it's not because they cut out carbohydrates. It's because that diet limits calories. A calorie is a calorie, and whether it comes from protein, carbohydrate, or fat, you still have to eat fewer calories than you burn to lose weight.

Most fad diets promise fast results. But when you lose weight rapidly, you lose mostly water and muscle, not fat. Because fad diets don't teach you how to change your eating and activity habits, the weight comes right back as soon as you go off the diet. And diets that restrict what types of food you eat aren't easy to stick to for very long.

How to Spot A Fad Diet

Most people don't want to hear they have to change their eating habits and

Food Group Servings

Calorie Level	Grains and Starchy Veg.	Vegetables	Fruits	Milk and Dairy	Meat and Fish	Fats and Sweets
1200 calories	6	3	2	3	1	100 calories
1500 calories	7	3	3	3	1.5	150 calories
1800 calories	8	4	4	3	2	150 calories
2100 calories	10	4	4	3	2	200 calories
2400 calories	12	4	5	3	2	200 calories

Food Group Worksheet

	Grains and Starchy Veg. Servings	Vegetables Servings	Fruits Servings	Milk and Dairy Servings	Meat and Fish Servings	Fats and Sweets Servings
Breakfast						
Lunch						
Dinner						
Snacks						
Total number of servings						
Suggested number servings for your calorie level						

be more active to lose weight, and the people who promote fad diets know it. They make promises that sound so good, they convince even the most intelligent people. How do you know if it's a fad diet? Look for these clues:

- The diet suggests that certain foods can change your body chemistry or blames weight problems on specific hormones.

- It lists "good" and "bad" foods or food groups.

- It promises "rapid" results—more than 1 to 2 pounds of weight loss per week.

- A magical pill, bar, shake, or food item is involved.

- It uses words like "fat burner" or "fat blocker."

- It promises you can lose weight without exercise.

Remember this: If it sounds too good to be true, it probably is!

Medications and Surgery for Weight Loss

As in other chronic conditions, such as diabetes or high blood pressure, long-term use of prescription medications may be appropriate for some people. Although most side effects of prescription medications for obesity are mild, serious complications have been reported.

There are few studies lasting more than 2 years evaluating the safety or effectiveness of weight loss medications. Weight loss medications should be used only by patients who are at increased medical risk because of their obesity and should not be used for cosmetic weight loss.

Several surgical procedures are available to help people lose weight. Because these procedures have potential risks and complications, they are usually only done on people who have a BMI of 40 or more.

Smoking

If you have tried to quit smoking, you know how hard it can be. That's because nicotine is a very addictive drug. Just seconds after you inhale tobacco smoke, nicotine travels to the brain, telling it to release chemicals to make you want to smoke more.

Usually people try to quit several times before finally succeeding. The good news is that each time you try to quit, you will be stronger and closer to quitting for good.

Why You Should Quit Smoking

The reasons to keep trying to quit are stronger than ever. Smoking is responsible for large numbers of deaths from cancer, heart attacks, stroke, and lung disease. Low birth weight, premature delivery, respiratory distress syndrome, and sudden infant death syndrome (SIDS) are linked to smoking during pregnancy. Up to 25 percent of all deaths from home fires are from fires that were started by smoking materials.

Lung cancer (see p. 222) isn't the only cancer caused by smoking. Others include cancer of the larynx, esophagus, kidneys, pancreas, and stomach. Although many people believe smokeless (chewing) tobacco is less hazardous to your health than cigarettes, it can cause cancer of the mouth. Tobacco of all kinds can cause cancer.

The health benefits of quitting are tremendous. After 5 to 15 years of not smoking, ex-smokers' risks of developing heart and lung diseases, cancer, and lung problems drop to the same levels as if they had never smoked.

Prepare Yourself To Quit

Given the overwhelming evidence that smoking is bad for your health, most smokers want to quit. If you are one of the 47 million people in the United States who smoke, the steps below may help you quit. Remember: Anyone can quit, regardless of age, health, or lifestyle.

If you want to stop smoking, start preparing for it today. Set a quit date and stick to it. If you slip, forgive yourself, then get right back to quitting. Your success will be greatly influenced by your desire and determination to quit smoking for good.

When you decide to quit smoking, remember that you may experience symptoms of withdrawal. For heavy smokers, withdrawal may include headaches, constipation, irritability, nervousness, trouble concentrating, or insomnia. Increased coughing may also occur as the cilia (tiny hairs that sweep away irritants from the air passages) in your lungs become active again.

Identifying Your Triggers

For about a week, smoke as you normally would, doing your usual activities. Be aware of every cigarette. Even if you think you know your triggers already, try writing them down in a journal. The results may surprise you. For every cigarette you have, write down the date, time, place, who you're with, why you smoked, and how you felt. When you have enough information to identify your triggers, you can stop journaling. Be honest. Answers may repeat. Review what you've written to form a plan for avoiding the habitual traps in your life.

Steps To Quit Smoking

- Set your goal. Pick a date on which to stop smoking. Plan to quit completely and for good.

- Take it one day at a time. Focus on making it through today without a cigarette, rather than on how you will go without one for the next week. If you do slip and light up, don't give up. Forgive yourself, and work on resisting the next cigarette.

- Find support. Tell as many as 10 friends that you are quitting. Then take advantage of as much encouragement and prodding as they can give you. Also check with your doctor for support. He or she may be able to prescribe bupropion (Zyban) or suggest a nicotine substitute to help you get through withdrawal symptoms. Organizations such as the American Lung Association and the American Cancer Society offer classes and support groups for people trying to quit smoking. Many employers and health care systems also offer help.

- Find a substitute. Avoid the temptation to smoke by finding other things to keep your mouth and hands busy. Try sugarless gum, hard candy, or flavored toothpicks. Or try activities such as woodworking, needlework, or playing with fidget toys.

- Be physically active to avoid weight gain. If you're afraid of gaining weight, keep in mind that the average weight gain after quitting smoking is less than 10 pounds. While you are quitting, eat a well-balanced diet and avoid excess calories in sugary or fatty foods, drink six to eight glasses of water a day, and stay physically active (see Healthy Eating, p. 403, and Activity, p. 399). By walking at least 30 minutes a day or doing some other activity, you will ward off excess pounds and ease some of the tension of tobacco withdrawal.

- Avoid smoking situations. Go places where smoking isn't allowed, such as the nonsmoking section of a restaurant or a movie theater. Take your work breaks with nonsmoking coworkers. After eating, take a walk or do the dishes instead of lighting up a cigarette. When you can't avoid a smoking situation, plan in advance for ways to curb your desire to smoke, such as having sugarless gum or a healthy snack nearby.

- Modify your daily routines or habits if they included smoking. For instance, if your coffee break once meant having a cup of coffee and a cigarette, try walking or reading a book instead.

Maintenance

You made the commitment to quit smoking, and like any other habit, it takes time for the new habit to become a part of you. If you get the urge to smoke, remember how tough it was in the beginning and promise not to put yourself through that again. Write down each temptation and how you coped with it in your journal. This will help you build strategies for coping each time the urge comes back. Think about the joys of being a nonsmoker: better health, clearer breathing, no hacking cough, and a refreshing new sense of smell and taste.

Preventing Health Problems

Preventive care is the care you and your family receive when your doctor assesses your health risks and provides health education counseling, screening tests, and immunizations. It is different than when you visit your doctor for specific concern, such as a backache. Preventive care is aimed at keeping you and your family healthy and identifying problems while they are easier to treat.

Among the greatest achievements in modern medicine, vaccines protect children and adults from life-threatening illnesses such as mumps, measles, influenza, diphtheria, tetanus, and polio. Vaccines are necessary because many of these diseases are difficult to treat once you have them. In addition to keeping you healthy, vaccinations protect the people around you. They prevent the spread of disease.

Early detection saves lives. For diseases such as breast or colon cancer, survival rates are significantly better when treatment begins in the early stages of the disease. There are many tests available to screen for all sorts of potential health problems.

There are specific preventive care recommendations for different stages of your life. You can meet your preventive care requirements through a combination of the following:

- Complete preventive care visits
- Asking about preventive care when being seen by your doctor for other concerns
- Scheduling additional appointments as needed

The information in this chapter gives you guidelines for when to schedule preventive care. It also gives you information on how to keep up to date on immunizations. ::

Immunizations

Many people believe that immunizations are for children and people traveling abroad. Although they are important for these groups, adults who were routinely vaccinated as children may still require boosters for certain immunizations. Some adults need vaccines they have never before received.

Immunity is produced when your body is exposed to a weakened or killed virus or bacteria responsible for a particular disease. Once exposed, your body is able to recognize and produce antibodies quickly to fight off that type of infection in the future. Some vaccines give lifetime immunity, while others require periodic boosters.

There is little debate about the effectiveness of immunizations. Most doctors agree that the benefits of routine immunizations outweigh the risks. To ensure immunizations are up to date, keep a record (see Preventive Examination and Immunization Record on pp. 436–437). If you think you may be due for a booster or need a new vaccination, talk with your doctor.

Diphtheria/Tetanus/Pertussis

The diphtheria/tetanus/pertussis (DTaP) shot combines all three vaccines to protect against these life-threatening diseases. Most children should have five DTaP shots before they enter kindergarten. DTaP is a safer version of the older DTP shot. DTP is no longer used in the United States. DTaP is not given to children over the age of 7. Older children, teenagers, and adults need a booster shot called tetanus/diphtheria (Td).

Tetanus/Diphtheria

The tetanus/diphtheria booster shot is recommended at 11 to 12 years of age and then every 10 years. If you have a cut or wound that is caused by a dirty object, your doctor may recommend you have a tetanus booster even though you are up to date on your shot.

Polio

Since becoming available in the 1950s, the polio vaccine has nearly wiped out polio. However, the vaccination continues to be important, so this crippling and fatal disease does not return. Children should get this vaccine in a series of four doses. The polio vaccine can be taken orally or given by injection. In the United States the oral form is no longer available.

Haemophilus Influenza type B

Haemophilus influenza type B (Hib) is a dangerous bacterium that can cause meningitis, pneumonia, and infections in other parts of the body. The Hib vaccine protects almost all children who receive the full four doses. It is given by injection.

Measles/Mumps and Rubella

The measles/mumps and rubella (MMR) vaccine is given by injection in two doses. In most people, these two doses provide protection for life.

Hepatitis B

The hepatitis B virus (HBV) can cause inflammation to your liver (see Hepatitis B, p. 323). This vaccine is given by injection in three doses to children. The vaccine should also be offered to adults younger than 40 years of age if they have not been previously immunized.

Chicken Pox (Varicella)

The varicella vaccine is given to children between 12 and 18 months age. It can be given to anyone at any age if they have not had chicken pox.

Chicken pox is a common childhood illness that can be serious in young infants and adults. People aged 13 years and older who have not had chicken pox should receive two doses of the vaccine 4 to 8 weeks apart. It is especially important for non-pregnant women of childbearing age to be vaccinated, to reduce the risk of transmitting chicken pox to their fetus if they become pregnant.

Pneumococcal (PCV 7)

The pneumococcal (PCV 7) conjugate vaccine offers protection from *Streptococcus pneumoniae* bacteria, which can cause serious illness in children younger than 2. It is given in four doses before 15 months of age.

Influenza Vaccine

The influenza vaccine is recommended for:

- All adults 50 years and older
- Anyone who has a chronic illness
- Children aged 6 months to 2 years
- Caregivers and families of people at risk

The vaccine is updated every year because the viruses that cause influenza change from year to year. You need to get an influenza shot every year to be protected.

Pneumococcal (PPV 23)

The pneumococcal vaccine (PPV23) is recommended for all adults 65 years and older. It protects against 23 types of pneumococcal bacteria. It offers protection within 2 to 3 weeks in most healthy adults. It is given by injection. A second dose may be required for people who are at high risk. The second dose should be given 5 or more years after the first one.

Recommendations for Routine Preventive Care

Birth to 24 months

When To Schedule a Visit

Visits are usually scheduled within the first 2 weeks of birth, at 2 months, 4 months, 6 to 9 months, 12 months, and 15 months. Each visit includes a physical exam, a height and weight check, developmental assessment, head circumference measurements, vision and hearing checks, and one hemoglobin or hematocrit test within this period.

Immunizations

- Hepatitis B: series of three beginning at birth to 2 months

- Polio: 2, 4, and 6 months
- Diphtheria/pertussis/tetanus: 2, 4, 6, and 12 to 15 months
- H. *influenza* type B: 2, 4, 6, and 12 to 15 months
- Measles/mumps and rubella: 12 to 15 months
- Varicella (chicken pox): 12 to 18 months
- Pneumococcal: 2, 4, 6, and 12 to 15 months

2 to 6 years

When To Schedule a Visit

Visits usually are scheduled at 2 years, between 3 and 4 years, and at 5 years. Visits include a physical exam, height and weight check, developmental assessment, and vision, hearing, and blood pressure checks.

Immunizations

- Measles/mumps and rubella: 4 to 6 years
- Diphtheria/pertussis/tetanus: 4 to 6 years
- Polio: 4 to 6 years

7 to 11 years

When To Schedule a Visit

One visit should be scheduled between 7 and 9 years. It will include a physical exam, height and weight check, developmental assessment, and blood pressure check.

12 to 18 years

When To Schedule a Visit

Visits should include one at 12 years, then two between the ages of 13 and 18. Visits include a physical exam, height and weight check; developmental assessment; blood pressure check; counseling about tobacco, alcohol, and drug use and sexual activity; and a Papanicolaou (Pap) test for girls at age 18 (or upon becoming sexually active).

Immunizations

- Tetanus/diphthéria: 12 years (before entering seventh grade)

- Hepatitis B vaccine (series of three): before entering seventh grade if not done previously

- Varicella (chicken pox): if not done previously

- Measles/mumps and rubella vaccine: before entering seventh grade if not done previously

Birth to Age 18

Lifestyle Habits

Make sure your children receive all the recommended immunizations and that your home is a safe, smoke-free environment. Children also need to use car seats and seat belts, wear bike helmets, eat a variety of nutritious food, and be physically active.

Ages 19 to 39

When To Schedule a Visit

It is recommended that men see their doctor every 5 years for a complete preventive care visit. Women should schedule a visit every 3 to 5 years. Each visit includes a height and weight check, blood pressure check, preventive counseling, health risk assessment, and any necessary screening tests or immunizations. Blood pressure checks may need to be done more often.

Screening Tests and Immunizations

Men and Women

- Blood pressure check: every 2 years

- Hepatitis B vaccine (series of three): if not done previously

- Tetanus/diphtheria booster: every 10 years

Men

- Cholesterol check: every 5 years beginning at age 35

Women

- Clinical breast examination: every 3 years beginning at age 20

- Pap test and pelvic examination: every 3 years (after three consecutive annual normal tests)

Lifestyle Habits

The lifestyle habits you establish now can affect how you feel and what your health problems may be in the future. It is important to establish positive health habits, such as getting regular physical activity, eating a balanced diet, and avoiding tobacco products and excessive alcohol use. Remember to use your seat belt, never drink and drive, and stay within the speed limit to reduce your risk of accidental injury.

Ages 40 to 64

When To Schedule a Visit

It is recommended that men see their doctor every 5 years for a complete preventive care visit. Women should schedule a visit every 3 to 5 years. Each visit includes a height and weight check, blood pressure check, preventive counseling, health risk assessment, and any other necessary screening tests or immunizations. Blood pressure checks, influenza vaccinations, clinical breast examinations, and mammograms may need to be done more often.

Screening Tests and Immunizations
Men and Women

- Blood pressure check: every 2 years
- Cholesterol check: Men, every 5 years; women, every 5 years beginning at age 45
- Colon cancer screening beginning at age 50
- Influenza vaccine: every year beginning at age 50
- Tetanus/diphtheria booster: every 10 years

Women

- Clinical breast examination: every year
- Mammogram: every year beginning at age 50 (depending on your health history or preference, every year ages 40 to 49 also; discuss with your provider)
- Pap test and pelvic examination: every 3 years (after three consecutive annual normal tests)

Lifestyle Habits

It is never too late to eat a healthier diet, get regular physical activity, or stop using tobacco. If you have developed unhealthy habits over the years, do not give up hope. Slowly change your habits and set goals to improve the behaviors that can lead to a healthier lifestyle.

Ages 65 and Older

When To Schedule a Visit

It is recommended that men and women see their doctor every 1 to 2 years for a complete preventive care visit. Each visit includes a height and weight check, blood pressure check, preventive counseling, health risk assessment, and any necessary screening tests or immunizations.

Screening Tests and Immunizations

Men and Women

- Blood pressure check: every 1 to 2 years
- Cholesterol check: every 5 years until age 75
- Flexible sigmoidoscopy: every 5 years until age 80
- Hearing and vision screening: beginning at age 75

- Influenza vaccine: every year
- Pneumococcus vaccine: once at age 65
- Tetanus/diphtheria booster: every 10 years

Women

- Clinical breast examination: every year
- Mammogram: every year until age 75
- Pap test and pelvic examination: every 3 years (if regular screening has been done and Pap tests have been normal, screening may be deferred after age 65 if patient wishes)

Lifestyle Habits

Advice you followed or ignored about diet, physical activity, and the use of tobacco is as important now as ever. For example, regular physical activity, even for the frail or elderly, remains one of the most effective ways to stay vital. Aging should bring a renewed focus on keeping existing health problems from getting worse and maintaining the healthy habits you have developed over the years.

4 YOUR ROLE AS A HEALTH CARE CONSUMER

When you take an active role in your health, you get better health care. You have an easier time keeping control of your own life. You get to make decisions that affect the quality of your life. But to make good decisions, you need to be informed. You need to know how you can best work in your health care system. You need to know the best treatment options for you.

Becoming an active participant in your health care may require some new ways of thinking and behaving. The information in this section gives you the information and tools you need to make the most out of your next health care experience. ::

Your Role As a Health Care Consumer

Choosing a Doctor

Having a good talk with your doctor may be the best medicine around. Studies show that when patients are satisfied with how they can discuss problems with their doctors, they tend to recover from illnesses more easily. Still, for many people a trip to the doctor is stressful. And unless you are prepared to play an active role during your visit, you may forget much of what the doctor tells you, and you will be less likely to follow his or her advice.

Finding a Good Match

Finding a doctor with whom you feel comfortable can make a big difference in the quality of your health care. Doctors, like everyone else, vary widely in their communication skills and the value they place on the personal aspects of your relationship. It is very important, then, that you establish a relationship with a doctor who matches your needs and values.

Use your first meeting with your doctor as a time to explore your expectations of one another. In fact, your first meeting doesn't have to be for an examination. Many doctors are willing to meet with prospective patients for informational interviews. In addition to giving the doctor information about your medical history, the interview will help him or her understand how much of the medical decision making you wish to participate in and how much information you want about your health condition. One study showed that doctors often underestimate how much information patients want, but they overestimate their patients' desire to be in on personal health decisions.

For some people, a good relationship with a doctor is a very important part of their health care. For others, the doctor's personality and communication skills can be overlooked as long as he or she is highly skilled and knowledgeable. If you fall in the first group and are seeing a doctor who, although highly skilled, has a poor bedside manner, you may be better off changing doctors. If you are in the second group, however, you may well think this type of doctor is highly professional.

No matter what you look for in a doctor, it's important that you find one with whom you feel comfortable and confident—even if that means changing doctors. But remember that an ongoing relationship with a doctor increases your chances of getting the best possible health care.

Your Doctor as Educator

The average adult visits the doctor more than four times a year, and the most common reason for a visit is for preventive services such as physical examinations or health screenings for such diseases as colon, breast, or prostate cancer. Many find the doctor's advice about preventing health problems to be very motivating, so judge a doctor on how interested he or she is in your personal health habits. Will the doctor advise you on habits such as drinking and smoking? Is the doctor concerned about your diet or exercise practices? Finally, keep in mind that most of the health problems you will face are chronic conditions such as high blood pressure or diabetes—conditions that require long-term care involving many health professionals. So find out if your doctor works well with other health care team mem-

bers such as dietitians, physical therapists, counselors, and health educators. When it comes to handling long-term health problems, a team approach is considered the most effective. Keep in mind that an effective team approach is one in which you are at the center of the team, involved and communicating your needs clearly and consistently. Choose a doctor you want on your team, working as an expert and a concerned partner.

Deciding About Surgery

When your doctor recommends surgery, you should take an active role in deciding whether to go through with it. Your values and beliefs are often a key part of choosing surgery versus exploring other types of treatment as a road to better health. Surgery can be risky and difficult, but sometimes it's clearly the only way to go. Other times, alternatives to surgery are the wisest choice.

Learning to ask the right questions—and getting the right answers—is vital to helping you decide whether or not surgery is right for you. Being a responsible health care consumer starts with getting involved in decisions about your health. That way, you're more likely to feel calm and confident about whatever course of treatment you choose.

Deciding Which Option Is Best

When you have a health condition that may involve surgery, it is scary. That's why doctors only perform 10 to 40 percent of elective surgical procedures—those a person can choose to have or not have. (Elective surgeries relieve conditions that are basically harmless or are causing only minor symptoms.)

So how do you decide about surgery? The first step is to find out whether the surgery your doctor is recommending is nonelective or elective.

Nonelective Surgery

When surgery is needed to save a person's life (such as to remove a ruptured appendix) or must be done immediately to prevent permanent disability (such as to surgically repair a badly broken bone), it is considered nonelective. That means you have little or no choice but to have the operation. And you probably do not have time to explore other options. Fortunately, few surgical procedures are truly nonelective.

Elective Surgery

Most surgical procedures involve some degree of choice for the patient. In some cases, alternatives to surgery exist, such as medications or other ways of dealing with the problem. In other cases, surgery may be the only option for correcting a particular problem, but the symptoms don't merit the risk of surgery. For example, many people who have gallstones have no pain, discomfort, or other symptoms and do not need treatment. Surgery is appropriate when it is needed to:

- Relieve or prevent pain
- Restore or preserve normal function
- Correct a deformity
- Save or prolong your life

Even if surgery is appropriate, it may not be the only choice of treatment. It's always best to investigate all other options before choosing surgery.

Make an appointment with your doctor to discuss the Questions To Ask Before Surgery worksheet on p. 430. Write down or record the answers. If you feel anxious or nervous, take a friend or relative along for moral support. Then assess the information and decide what you want to do.

Make sure it's your own decision. Don't let yourself be pressured into having surgery you don't need or want.

Asking for a Second Opinion

Getting more information can help when you're deciding about surgery.

One way to do this is to get a second opinion (also called a "review of treatment"). Some health plans require second opinions before they will cover certain procedures. But a second opinion can also help you make a more informed decision.

Although a second opinion isn't needed in every instance, you would be wise to seek one if:

- The procedure is experimental or high risk, such as an organ transplant

- Your symptoms aren't severe and the outcome of surgery isn't clear

- The procedure has a reputation for being performed when not absolutely needed

Don't Be Timid

You might feel uncomfortable asking for a second opinion, but most doctors today are used to this and are very cooperative. A doctor who responds with anger or refuses to cooperate with such a request may not have your best interests at heart.

To find a second surgeon, ask your primary doctor, your health plan, or your local hospital for a recommendation. If you ask the first surgeon for a referral, you are less likely to get a truly objective second opinion.

Avoid the expense of repeating tests and procedures; bring your medical records and x-rays, if any, along with you. If this is not possible, you can have them sent to the second surgeon before your appointment by signing a records release form.

If the second surgeon disagrees with the first, find out why. You may find that one surgeon's philosophy and reasoning fit with your own more than the other's.

Questions To Ask Before Surgery

Name and Procedure
What's the operation called? _____
What will be done? _____
How is it performed? _____
How long will it take? _____
How serious is it? _____

Reason
Why is this surgery recommended? _____

Continued

Results
How will this procedure help my condition? _____
What are the benefits? _____

Alternatives
What other treatment options are available? _____
Is outpatient surgery an option? _____
What will happen if I don't have the surgery? _____
Is no treatment an option? _____

Timing
How soon should I have the surgery? _____
How soon must I make a decision? _____
What will happen if I postpone the operation? _____

Risks
What are the risks involved? _____
What percentage of patients die from this procedure? _____

Complications
What complications may occur? _____
Which complications are common for my age and state of health? _____

Postoperative Information
Are there any side effects of anesthesia? _____
Will I have tubes, catheters, or dressings after surgery? _____

Recovery
What's the typical recovery period? _____
How long will I be unable to care for myself? _____
When can I return to work and my normal activities? _____

Experience
How often do you perform this procedure? _____
How often is this surgery done at your hospital? _____

Cost
How much is this surgery likely to cost? _____
What are your fees? _____
What's the average hospital charge? _____
What will be covered by my health plan? _____

Family and Personal Medical History

K eeping good medical records is an important part of being an active health care consumer.

Many health problems run in families. Other health problems are easier to anticipate when you and your doctor have a complete picture of your personal medical history. That's why it's important to keep up-to-date records of your family and personal medical history. Make copies of the Family Medical History worksheet on p. 433, Your Medical History worksheet on p. 434, and Preventive Examination and Immunization Record on pp. 436–437 and complete one for yourself and for each member of your family. Keep them and a completed Medical Resources worksheet (p. 435) with your medical records, and update them as necessary.

Family Medical History

Blood Relative:	Significant Health Problem	If Deceased: Cause of Death/Age at Death
Mother	_____	_____
Father	_____	_____
Brothers & Sisters	_____	_____
	_____	_____
	_____	_____

Mother's Side:

Grandfather	_____	_____
Grandmother	_____	_____
Aunts & Uncles	_____	_____
	_____	_____

Father's Side:

Grandfather	_____	_____
Grandmother	_____	_____
Aunts & Uncles	_____	_____
	_____	_____

Have any of your blood relatives (mother, father, brothers, sisters, grandparents, aunts, uncles) had any of the following diseases or conditions?

Condition	Name/Relationship	Condition	Name/Relationship
❑ Allergies	_____	❑ High blood	_____
❑ Anemia or other	_____	pressure	
blood disorders		❑ High blood	_____
❑ Arthritis	_____	cholesterol	
❑ Asthma	_____	❑ Liver disease	_____
❑ Bowel disorder	_____	❑ Lung disease	_____
❑ Cancer	_____	❑ Nervous system	_____
❑ Cataracts	_____	disorder	
❑ Depression	_____	❑ Physical or	_____
❑ Mental illness	_____	mental abuse	
❑ Diabetes	_____	❑ Stroke	_____
❑ Eczema	_____	❑ Thyroid disorder	_____
❑ Emphysema	_____	(type:_____)	
❑ Epilepsy	_____	❑ Ulcer	
❑ Glaucoma	_____	❑ Other	_____
❑ Heart disease	_____		

Your Medical History

Name _____

Date of birth _____

Blood type _____

Acute Conditions   **Chronic Conditions**

Disease	*Date of Illness*	*Disorder*	*Date Diagnosed*	*Treatment*
❏ Chicken pox	_____	❏ Arthritis	_____	_____
❏ Ear infection	_____	❏ Asthma	_____	_____
❏ German measles	_____	❏ Blood disorder	_____	_____
(rubella)		❏ Cataracts	_____	_____
❏ Hepatitis	_____	❏ Depression	_____	_____
❏ HIV	_____	(Mental illness)		
❏ Mononucleosis		❏ Diabetes	_____	_____
❏ Measles	_____	❏ Epilepsy	_____	_____
❏ Mumps	_____	❏ Gastrointestinal	_____	_____
❏ Physical or	_____	disorder		
emotional abuse		❏ Glaucoma	_____	_____
❏ Polio	_____	❏ Heart disease	_____	_____
❏ Scarlet fever	_____	❏ High blood	_____	_____
❏ Sexually	_____	pressure		
transmitted		❏ High blood	_____	_____
disease		cholesterol		
❏ Sinus infection	_____	❏ Kidney disease	_____	_____
❏ Strep throat	_____	❏ Ulcers	_____	_____
❏ Whooping cough	_____	❏ Other	_____	_____
❏ Other	_____			

Medical Resources

Doctor _____
Clinic _____
     Telephone _____

Doctor _____
Clinic _____
     Telephone _____

Hospital _____
     Telephone _____

After-hours medical care center _____
     Telephone _____

Pharmacist _____
     Telephone _____

Poison control center _____
     Telephone _____

Preventive Examination and Immunization Record

Preventive Exams	Date	Results	Date	Results	Date	Results
Blood pressure	___	___	___	___	___	___
Cholesterol	___	___	___	___	___	___
Colon cancer screening	___	___	___	___	___	___
Mammography	___	___	___	___	___	___
Pap Smear	___	___	___	___	___	___
Other:	___	___	___	___	___	___
	___	___	___	___	___	___

Adult Immunizations	Date	Results	Date	Results	Date	Results
Influenza	___	___	___	___	___	___
Pneumococcal (PCV7)	___	___	___	___	___	___
Tetanus/ diphtheria (Td)	___	___	___	___	___	___
Other (if at risk)	___	___	___	___	___	___
	___	___	___	___	___	___

Pediatric Immunizations	Date of Immunization (Month/Year)
Diphtheria/tetanus and pertussis (DTaP)—dose 1	___ / ___
Diphtheria/tetanus and pertussis (DTaP)—dose 2	___ / ___
Diphtheria/tetanus and pertussis (DTaP)—dose 3	___ / ___
Diphtheria/tetanus and pertussis (DTaP)—dose 4	___ / ___
Diphtheria/tetanus and pertussis (DTaP)—dose 5	___ / ___
Tetanus/diphtheria (Td)—dose 6	___ / ___
H. influenza type B (Hib)—dose 1	___ / ___
H. influenza type B (Hib)—dose 2	___ / ___
H. influenza type B (Hib)—dose 3	___ / ___
H. influenza type B (Hib)—dose 4	___ / ___

Continued

Preventive Examination and Immunization Record

Pediatric Immunizations	Date of Immunization (Month/Year)
Hepatitis B—dose 1	_____ / ___
Hepatitis B—dose 2	_____ / ___
Hepatitis B—dose 3	_____ / ___
Measles/mumps/rubella (MMR)—dose 1	_____ / ___
Measles/mumps/rubella (MMR)—dose 2	_____ / ___
Pneumococcal (PCV7)—dose 1	_____ / ___
Pneumococcal (PCV7)—dose 2	_____ / ___
Pneumococcal (PCV7)—dose 3	_____ / ___
Pneumococcal (PCV7)—dose 4	_____ / ___
Polio (IPV)—dose 1	_____ / ___
Polio (IPV)—dose 2	_____ / ___
Polio (IPV)—dose 3	_____ / ___
Polio (IPV)—dose 4	_____ / ___
Varicella zoster	_____ / ___

Finding Quality Health Information on the Web

Finding health information on the World Wide Web is easy. After all, we have access to more medical data in cyberspace than we will ever need. But how do you know that what you're reading is reliable and accurate? As health care consumers, we must be aware that not all Web sites are created equal. There are no rules about what type of information can appear on the Web. Having a critical eye is our responsibility.

Here are some questions you can ask yourself as you are looking for health information on the Web:

- *Check out the source of the information.* Be wary of Web sites that (1) do not list the origin of the information, (2) are trying to sell a product or service, or (3) are promoting only one point of view. The most objective sites are government agencies such as the Centers for Disease Control and Prevention, the National Institutes of Health, the National Library of Medicine, or your local department of health. One question you could ask yourself is, Does the author have anything to gain from having only one viewpoint on the topic?

- *Know the purpose of the site.* Many sites have an About This Site or About Us link. Click on it to see what the purpose of the site is. It will help you to find out if the information is trustworthy.

- *Know who is paying for the site.* The source of funding for the site can affect what content is on it. Is the site paid for by advertising or by sponsorship from a drug company? The answer should be clearly stated or easy to find.

- *Find out when the site was last updated.* Health and medical information is constantly changing and needs to be current. If the information is old, it could be less reliable. If the Web site is rarely updated, it probably is not as accurate as a site that posts information regularly. Always know when the site was first created and when it was last revised.

- *Make sure the site is reviewed by experts.* Having this system in place will help ensure that the information is reliable.

- *Be aware of what information the site is collecting.* If you have to be a member or sign up on the site, chances are that information will be used for something other than identification. Any site that requests your name, address, credit card, or other information should tell you exactly what they will do—and not do—with this data.

- *Get a second opinion.* Compare the information with that of other sources. Ask your doctor what he or she knows about the topic or finding.

If Your Doctor Recommends Hospitalization

Many procedures that used to require hospitalization are taken care of at clinics today. In addition, surgeries and rehabilitation that used to require days and weeks in the hos- pital now are often taken care of in a matter of hours. Because procedures that required lengthy hospitalization in the past have changed so much over the past few years, it is vital that you understand all the reasons that justify the need for you to be treated at the hospital instead of at home or in a clinic. Going to the hospital is a major disruption of life for most peo- ple. When you understand why it is

---

Questions To Ask Before Hospitalization

Reason
Why is hospitalization necessary? _____

Procedure
What tests or procedures will be done? _____
Must the tests or procedures be done at the hospital? _____

Alternatives
What other choices do I have? _____
How much will I be involved in deciding about my treatment? _____

Risks
Are there any risks involved with any of the tests or procedures? _____
What are they? _____

Results
What will the tests tell us? _____

Timing and Expense
How long will I be in the hospital? _____
How much will it cost? _____

Recovery
How soon can I return to normal activities? _____
How long will I be away from work? _____

necessary, it will help you cope with the stress of hospitalization.

Because doctors are so busy, they try to be brief. But you need to know exactly why your doctor recommends hospitalization. To get your questions answered efficiently, take a copy of the Questions To Ask Before Hospitalization worksheet (p. 439) with you when you visit your doctor and jot down or record the answers. For some people, it helps to bring a friend or relative along who can help remember the details of the discussion with the doctor.

Complementary and Alternative Medicine

Complementary and alternative medicine (CAM) is a group of medical and health care practices that are not considered to be part of conventional medicine. *Conventional medicine* is a term for established and accepted methods practiced by medical doctors (MDs). Complementary and alternative practices are not part of conventional medicine because for the most part there are still questions about their safety and effectiveness.

Complementary medicine is used together with conventional medicine.

Alternative medicine is used in place of conventional medicine.

Types of CAM

There are many different types of CAM. Some of the most common types are described next.

Acupuncture is a type of traditional Chinese medicine that is based on the concept of a vital energy that flows throughout the body. It is believed that if the flow of this energy is blocked, a person can become sick or experience pain. In acupuncture, needles are inserted into key points in the body to keep the energy flowing, reducing pain and restoring health to the body and mind.

Chiropractic focuses on the relationship between the spine and overall health. Back pain is the most common reason people see a chiropractor. According to chiropractic theory, misaligned vertebrae can affect nerves that radiate out from your spine, causing pain or other health problems. Most chiropractors use spinal manipulation to realign the vertebrae. Many physical therapists and osteopathic doctors also use this technique.

Today chiropractors sometimes work with medical doctors, and their services are sometimes covered by medical insurance.

Dietary supplements can include vitamins, minerals, herbs, or other substances. They can come in many forms, including tablets, powders, or liquids, and are sold in many grocery stores, discount stores, and pharmacies. Dietary supplements are often sold as "natural" remedies. However, just because something is natural doesn't mean it is helpful or even safe. Many vitamin and herbal compounds can be toxic when taken in high doses. The Food and Drug Administration (FDA) has only limited ability to regulate supplements because they are not considered drugs.

Some recent research shows that certain herbal supplements that were thought to be safe for everyone can be harmful for some people or can interfere with conventional medical therapies.

Homeopathy is a field of alternative medicine in which small, highly diluted quantities of medicinal substances are given to cure symptoms. The belief is that when given to a healthy person in large quantities, some substances produce symptoms of disease; but when given to a sick person, much smaller doses of the same substances can relieve symptoms by stimulating the body to heal itself.

Mind-body medicine uses a variety of techniques to enhance the mind's capacity to affect bodily function and symptoms. These techniques include meditation, prayer, mental healing, and therapies involving art, music, or dance. Some techniques that were considered CAM in the past have become mainstream, such as patient support groups.

Naturopathy is a field of alternative medicine in which practitioners work with natural healing forces within the body with the goal of helping the body heal from disease. Practices may include dietary modifications, massage, acupuncture, or other alternative therapies. Practitioners often advise patients to avoid prescription drugs and surgery.

Osteopathy is a form of conventional medicine. Like traditional doctors, doctors of osteopathy go through years of training and are licensed to perform many traditional therapies, including surgery and prescribing medications. Osteopathy is different from conventional medicine in that osteopaths (doctors of osteopathy) use manipulation to treat joint, muscle, and spinal problems, much like chiropractors.

The Effectiveness of CAM

The effectiveness of many complementary and alternative therapies is based on anecdotal evidence, which means that it comes from patients who report that a certain treatment worked for them. However, there may be no scientific research to support these claims.

Many studies are being done to evaluate the safety and effectiveness of CAM therapies, often with conflicting results. Some studies may show a therapy to be effective, while other studies show it is not.

Evaluating Information About CAM

In addition to talking to your doctor, you may need to do your own research. There is a great deal of information available on the Internet, but make sure you know how to tell if the information you find is credible or not (see Finding Quality Health Information on the Web, p. 438).

When researching the results of studies, it's also important for you to know how to evaluate the quality of the studies. Look for these terms:

- *Clinical studies.* These studies involve humans, not animals.

- *Randomized, controlled trials.* Participants in these studies are randomly divided into two groups—one group receives the treatment being studied, and the other group receives a standard treatment, no treatment, or a placebo (a substance without any medical value). This gives researchers a basis for comparison.

- *Double-blind studies.* In these studies, neither the researchers nor the participants know who is receiving the actual treatment and who is receiving a placebo.

- *Prospective studies.* In these studies, researchers establish criteria ahead of time and then measure the results. This is a more reliable method than just asking people to remember past information.

- *Peer-reviewed journals.* If a study appears in a peer-reviewed journal, it means it has been reviewed by an independent panel of medical experts.

Studies using these methods usually provide better-quality information.

Before Trying CAM Therapy

- Ask your doctor before trying CAM therapies. What works for someone else won't necessarily work for you, even if you have the same condition.

- Do research to find out if there is scientific evidence about the effectiveness of the treatment. Also find out if there are any side effects. Get as much information as you can from independent sources, not just from those providing the treatment.

- Get information about the person providing the treatment. What kind of training did he or she receive? How many of these treatments has the person performed? Does the practitioner belong to an organized group of some kind?

- Find out how much the treatment will cost and whether your insurance will cover it.

Many people think their doctor won't want them to try CAM therapies, so they don't want their doctor to know. But it's important for your doctor to know about all the treatments you are receiving. Some CAM therapies can interfere with conventional treatments, with potentially negative results. For example, taking certain vitamin supplements during cancer treatment may reduce the effectiveness of chemotherapy or radiation therapy. Keeping your doctor informed will ensure you get the best total care.

Preparing for an Office Visit

When it comes to communicating well with your doctor, time is the main barrier. A typical visit lasts 15 to 20 minutes, during which evaluation, diagnosis, treatment planning, and teaching take place. To make the best use of the minutes you have, present your most pressing problem to the doctor. Avoid bringing a laundry list of other unrelated complaints.

- Write down your most important concerns. Before your visit, review (1) all your symptoms, including when they started; (2) the history of the problem, including whether you've had the problem before; and (3) any treatments you have tried. List these things in order of importance, so you will be sure to get your most pressing concerns answered.

- Bring related records. If you have information about drugs you use, allergies, or other health problems, bring these records along if you are seeing a doctor for the first time. If your appointment is with a doctor you've been with for a while, be sure to let him or her know what over-the-counter remedies you are using and whether you are taking medicine prescribed by another doctor.

- Be brief and clear. As you describe your symptoms to your doctor, avoid vague statements such as "I've been feeling sick lately." Be specific: "I've had a headache and nausea for the past week, and I don't know what's causing it."

Making the Most of Your Visit

Researchers have interviewed patients after office visits and learned that more than half the doctors' instructions are forgotten within minutes of the visit. It is difficult for you to benefit from the doctor's good advice if you can't remember the details. Here are three ways to increase your recollection of the visit:

- Take notes. Even if you can't write down everything you hear, an outline of the discussion will dramatically increase your memory of the information. Take some time immediately after the visit to fill in other details you remember about the discussion. It may also help to talk your visit over with a friend or family member soon afterward.

- Ask for information that is organized. Studies on communication show that understanding improves when information is well organized. Ask the doctor to put information into categories such as what is wrong, what tests you may need, what treatments are available, and what you must do.

- Ask for explanations. When in doubt about a term your doctor uses, ask. A good way to ensure that you understand is to restate what you believe the doctor has told you. Then if you've misunderstood something, your doctor can explain it again.

Reviewing Medical Fees and Bills

Wise consumers of goods such as cars or groceries routinely check prices before making decisions. Knowing what to expect in the way of cost is a smart idea when planning for surgery or hospitalization too. The first step is to find out what your insurance covers and whether there is anything special you need to do to qualify for coverage, such as getting preauthorization from the health plan or getting a second opinion. For care provided by a specialist, many plans also require a referral from a primary care doctor for the highest level of benefits. Most of all, find out what copayments or what percentage of the bill you will have to pay.

The next step is to find out what the total bill—for you and your health plan—is likely to be. Medical fees can vary greatly from doctor to doctor and hospital to hospital. If you have a choice of hospitals, call each one to find out what a stay for your type of surgery usually costs or at least what the daily room rate is.

Feel free to also discuss financial questions with your surgeon or the office staff. Find out if the doctor's office will fill out and submit insurance forms or if that's your responsibility. Also ask if the doctor accepts the insurance payment as the full fee (called "accepting assignment") or if you must make up the difference between the doctor's fee and insurance payment.

Reviewing Your Hospital Bill

After your surgery or hospital stay is over, review your hospital bills carefully.

Hospitals try hard to provide accurate bills, but errors do occur.

Ask the hospital billing office to explain unclear charges, terms, or tests. You can also ask for a copy of your bedside log or other medical records to use when checking your bill. If you need further help, your doctor's office might be able to help.

Just like reading the labels on the foods you buy or checking the sticker to see what options come with a car you may buy, checking your hospital bills requires some time and attention on your part to be sure you are getting value for your dollar. Look at the fine print, and ask for more information about the bill if you think things are not adding up the way you thought they would. The following questions should help you identify any special problems with a hospital bill:

- Ask for an itemized bill instead of the summary most hospitals send.

- Were you billed for a semiprivate or a private room? Which did you have?

- Does the room rate multiplied by the number of days you stayed come to the same total as on the bill? (Most hospitals do not charge for the day of discharge.)

- Did you have each of the tests and procedures listed? You may be charged for something you didn't have simply because of a clerical error or because

your doctor cancelled the orders but the billing records weren't changed.

- Do any charges seem unusually high to you, such as $3 for a dose of acetaminophen (Tylenol)?

If you find an error, call the hospital's billing department and ask that it be corrected. If necessary, ask to speak with the department supervisor. Keep a written record of all your conversations, including the names of people you speak with and what you spoke about. Once the hospital agrees to correct the mistake, ask for a revised bill and then send a copy to your health plan. If you run into problems, call your health plan for help.

Before paying your portion of the bill, make sure your questions have been answered, errors are corrected, and your health plan has already paid its portion of the bill.

Seeking Quality Health Care

Because so much is riding on your decisions, you need to make wise choices about your health care. You need information and skills to make those decisions, and you need to become an active partner with your doctors in dealing with your own health and well-being.

You can start by building a relationship with a primary care doctor, such as a family practitioner or internist. Because there are no industry standards for health care quality, a primary care doctor can ensure that diagnostic tests and treatment recommendations from other doctors are appropriate based on your history and health problems. A long-term relationship with your primary care doctor results in consistent treatment that meets your needs. Such coordinated care improves the quality of your care and lowers costs.

Finding Good Health Care

Concerned consumers of any products need accurate, up-to-date information to judge the quality of their purchases. The same is true for health care consumers. Most of us hold on to old ideas from the days when we followed the doctors' orders without question. Times have changed, and so should our attitudes about health care.

When it comes to your health, there are basically four health care providers that have the best chance to offer you successful treatment and prevent problems. Understanding how each of these contributors can influence your choices is the first step in finding quality care.

- *You.* Many people believe that the doctor's role is to manage their health care. But when it comes down to it,

you are the one who does the real managing. You decide when to seek care and whether or not to follow your doctor's advice. You also decide how to live your life—whether you will exercise, what foods you will eat, and what risks you will take with your health.

- *Your doctor.* Doctors can guide you to better health. But they can't cure everything. Our doctors are our link to medical science, but they might not always have the answers. A good doctor will admit uncertainty and seek help and advice from other health care professionals when needed. Keep in mind that more treatment, testing, or medication doesn't necessarily mean better care. And no matter how good your doctor is, all medical care involves some risk.

- *The pharmacy.* Whether it's self-care, over-the-counter remedies, or a prescription drug, your pharmacy is often the place to find the tools you need to control or relieve illness. Pharmacists can guide you through the maze of over-the-counter drugs. They can also give you clear directions on how to care for minor problems yourself or how to follow your doctor's advice on prescription drugs.

- *The hospital.* In the past, most medical tests and surgeries were performed in the hospital and often required an overnight stay. Advances in technology, changes in philosophy, and findings indicating that people tend to recover more quickly at home have led the way for many forms of minor surgery and laboratory tests to be performed on an outpatient basis. When hospitalization is needed, recovery often comes more quickly if you return home as soon as you are medically ready, rather than staying in the hospital an extra day or two.

Choosing Necessary, Appropriate Care

Wise health care consumers choose only needed and appropriate health care services. But just what is needed and appropriate when it comes to health care?

Needed care is health care required to improve or preserve your health. Getting childhood vaccinations, setting broken bones, and treating serious infections are all examples of necessary care.

Appropriate care means weighing your options and choosing procedures that are suited to your circumstances. Appropriate care is different for everyone. If you have severe headaches, appropriate care might be as simple as pain relievers and relaxation exercises. If your headaches and other symptoms make your doctor suspect a serious problem, such as a brain tumor, expensive tests and procedures such as computed tomography (CT) scans, magnetic resonance imaging (MRI), and surgery may be considered appropriate care. Appropriate care doesn't mean you can't have expensive tests when you need them. It means not having an MRI when an aspirin will do the trick.

Fortunately, health care financing has changed enough in recent years that expensive, inappropriate, or repeated procedures are seldomly recommended. Practice guidelines and managed care policies have reduced waste in past years. Consumers need to find a balance between protecting their right to receive needed care and refraining from asking for excessive treatment. In the end, we all must pay for inappropriate care through higher medical costs and insurance rates. In fact, that kind of wastefulness is a major reason why our medical costs have skyrocketed.

In part, we're paying more for health care because we're getting better, faster, or more effective medical services. We're also paying more because new technologies and procedures are overused.

What You Can Do

The best way to track down high-quality, reasonably priced medical care is by becoming an active, prudent consumer. This means:

- Staying healthy through lifestyle choices, exercise, nutrition, and preventive health care that can reduce the risk of needing treatment

- Asking questions and gathering information, so that you can actively participate in decisions about your health

- Asking health care organizations for information on how they compare with industry standards and with other health care organizations

A New Direction

Your role as an active consumer is to seek a medical group that is continually improving the quality of health care. Such a group will focus on weighing the results of patient care, using a single medical record that contains your complete medical history, and developing medical practice guidelines. The successful health practitioners of the future will not only follow standard procedures for care, they will be able to show why their approach is more effective than other approaches. Staying informed as new options in health care arise is one of the best ways to keep your own health care headed in the right direction—toward higher quality and lower cost.

RESOURCE LIST

Aging

National Institute on Aging
Building 31, Room 5C27
31 Center Drive, MSC 2292
Bethesda, MD 20892
301-496-1752
www.nia.nih.gov

Alcohol and Drugs

Alcoholics Anonymous
475 Riverside Dr.
New York, NY 10015
212-870-3400
www.alcoholicsanonymous.org

National Clearinghouse for Alcohol and Drug
Information
11426 Rockville Pike, Suite 200
Rockville, MD 20852
800-729-6686
www.health.org

National Council on Alcoholism and Drug
Dependence
20 Exchange Place, Suite 2902
New York, NY 10005
800-NCA-CALL
www.ncadd.org

National Institute on Drug Abuse
6001 Executive Blvd., Room 5213
Bethesda, MD 20892-9561
301-443-1124
www.drugabuse.gov

Alzheimer's Disease

Alzheimer's Association
919 North Michigan Ave.
Chicago, IL 60611-1676
800-272-3900
www.alz.org

Alzheimer's Disease Education and Referral Center
PO Box 8250
Silver Spring, MD 20907-8250
800-438-4380
www.alzheimers.org

Asthma and Allergies

National Institute of Allergy and Infectious
Diseases
Building 31, Room 7A-50
31 Center Drive, MSC 2520
Bethesda, MD 20892-2520
301-496-5717
www.niaid.nih.gov

National Heart, Lung and Blood Institute
PO Box 30105
Bethesda, MD 20824-0105
301-592-8573
www.nhlbi.nih.gov

Arthritis

Arthritis Foundation
PO Box 7669
Atlanta, GA 30357-0669
800-283-7800
www.arthritis.org

National Institute of Arthritis and Musculoskeletal
and Skin Diseases
Information Clearinghouse
National Institutes of Health
1 AMS Circle
Bethesda, MD 20892-3675
877-22-NIAMS
www.niams.nih.gov

Cancer

American Cancer Society
800-ACS-2345
www.cancer.org

National Cancer Institute
NCI Public Inquiries Office
Suite 3036A
6116 Executive Blvd., MSC 8322
Bethesda, MD 20892-8322
800-4-CANCER
www.nci.nih.gov

Children's Health

American Academy of Pediatrics
141 Northwest Point Blvd.
Elk Grove Village, IL 60007-1098
847-434-4000
www.aap.org

Centers for Disease Control and Prevention
1600 Clifton Rd.
Atlanta, GA 30333
800-311-3435
www.cdc.gov/health/infantsmenu.htm

Complementary Medicine

National Center for Complementary and
    Alternative Medicine
NCCAM Clearinghouse
PO Box 7923
Gaithersburg, MD 20898
888-644-6226
www.nccam.nih.gov

Diabetes

American Diabetes Association
1701 North Beauregard St.
Alexandria, VA 22311
800-342-2383
www.diabetes.org

International Diabetes Center
3800 Park Nicollet Blvd.
Minneapolis, MN 55416-2699
888-825-6315
www.idcdiabetes.org

National Diabetes Information Clearinghouse
National Institute of Diabetes and Digestive and
    Kidney Diseases
National Institutes of Health
1 Information Way
Bethesda, MD 20892-3560
800-860-8747
www.niddk.nih.gov/health/diabetes/ndic.htm

Digestive Concerns

National Digestive Diseases Information
    Clearinghouse
National Institute of Diabetes and Digestive and
    Kidney Diseases
National Institutes of Health
2 Information Way
Bethesda, MD 20892-3570
800-860-8747
www.niddk.nih.gov/health/digest/nddic.htm

Exercise

American College of Sports Medicine
PO Box 1440
Indianapolis, IN 46206-1440
317-637-9200
www.acsm.org

American Council on Exercise
4851 Paramount Dr.
San Diego, CA 92123
800-825-3636
www.acefitness.org

President's Council on Physical Fitness and Sports
200 Independence Ave., SW, Room 738-H
Washington, DC 20201-0004
202-690-9000
www.fitness.gov

Eye and Ear Concerns

National Eye Institute
2020 Vision Place
Bethesda, MD 20892-3655
301-496-5248
www.nei.nih.gov

National Institute on Deafness and Other
    Communication Disorders
31 Center Drive, MSC 2320
Bethesda, MD 20892-2320
301-496-7243
301-402-0252 (TTY)
www.nidcd.nih.gov

Self Help for Hard of Hearing People
7910 Woodmont Ave., Suite 1200
Bethesda, MD 20814
301-657-2248
301-657-2249 (TTY)
www.shhh.org

Headaches

American Council for Headache Education
19 Mantua Rd.
Mt. Royal, NJ 08061
856-423-0258
www.achenet.org

National Headache Foundation
428 West Saint James Place, 2nd Floor
Chicago, IL 60614-2750
888-NHF-5552
www.headaches.org

National Institute of Neurological Disorders and
Stroke
PO Box 5801
Bethesda, MD 20824
800-352-9424
www.ninds.nih.gov

Heart and Lung Concerns

American Heart Association
7272 Greenville Ave.
Dallas, TX 75231
800-242-8721
www.americanheart.org

American Lung Association
61 Broadway, 6th Floor
New York, NY 10006
1-800-586-4872
www.lungusa.org

National Heart, Lung and Blood Institute
PO Box 30105
Bethesda, MD 20824-0105
301-592-8573
www.nhlbi.nih.gov

Immunizations

National Immunization Hotline
800-232-0233

Kidney and Bladder Concerns

National Kidney and Urologic Diseases Information
Clearinghouse
3 Information Way
Bethesda, MD 20892-3580
800-891-5390
www.niddk.nih.gov/health/kidney/nkudic.htm

Mental Health

National Institute of Mental Health
6001 Executive Blvd., Room 8184, MSC 9663
Bethesda, MD 20892-9663
301-443-4513
www.nimh.nih.gov

National Mental Health Association
2001 N. Beauregard St., 12th Floor
Alexandria, VA 22311
800-969-6642
www.nmha.org

Muscle and Joint Concerns

National Institute of Arthritis and Musculoskeletal
and Skin Diseases
Information Clearinghouse
National Institutes of Health
1 AMS Circle
Bethesda, MD 20892-3675
877-22-NIAMS
www.niams.nih.gov

Nutrition

The American Dietetic Association
216 West Jackson Blvd.
Chicago, IL 60606-6995
800-366-1655
www.eatright.org

The Weight-control Information Network
1 WIN Way
Bethesda, MD 20892-3665
877-946-4627
www.niddk.nih.gov/health/nutrit/win.htm

Osteoporosis

National Osteoporosis Foundation
1232 22nd St. NW
Washington, DC 20037-1292
202-223-2226
www.nof.org

Parkinson's Disease

American Parkinson's Disease Association
1250 Hylan Blvd., Suite 4B
Staten Island, NY 10305-1946
800-223-2732
www.apdaparkinson.org

United Parkinson's Foundation
833 West Washington Blvd.
Chicago, IL 60607
312-733-1893

Sexually Transmitted Diseases
Centers for Disease Control and Prevention
Division of Sexually Transmitted Diseases
1600 Clifton Rd.
Atlanta, GA 30333
800-227-8922
www.cdc.gov/nchstp/dstd/dstdp.html

National Institute of Allergy and Infectious
    Diseases
Building 31, Room 7A-50
31 Center Drive, MSC 2520
Bethesda, MD 20892-2520
301-496-5717
www.niaid.nih.gov

National AIDS Hotline
800-342-2437

Skin Concerns
National Institute of Arthritis and Musculoskeletal
    and Skin Diseases
Information Clearinghouse
National Institutes of Health
1 AMS Circle
Bethesda, MD 20892-3675
877-22-NIAMS
www.niams.nih.gov

Sleep Concerns
National Center on Sleep Disorders Research
NIH/NHLBI/NCSDR
Two Rockledge Centre, Suite 10038
6701 Rockledge Drive, MSC 7920
Bethesda, MD 20892-7920
301-435-0199
www.nhlbi.nih.gov/about/ncsdr

National Sleep Foundation
1522 K Street NW, Suite 500
Washington, DC 20005
202-347-3471
www.sleepfoundation.org

Smoking
American Cancer Society
800-ACS-2345
www.cancer.org

American Heart Association
7272 Greenville Ave.
Dallas, TX 75231
800-242-8721
www.americanheart.org

Centers for Disease Control and Prevention
Office on Smoking and Health
Mail Stop K-50
4770 Buford Hwy. NE
Atlanta, GA 30341-3724
800-CDC-1311
www.cdc.gov/tobacco

Stroke
American Heart Association
7272 Greenville Ave.
Dallas, TX 75231
800-242-8721
www.americanheart.org

American Lung Association
61 Broadway, 6th Floor
New York, NY 10006
1-800-586-4872
www.lungusa.org

Courage Stroke Network
3915 Golden Valley Rd.
Golden Valley, MN 55422
800-553-6321

National Heart, Lung and Blood Institute
PO Box 30105
Bethesda, MD 20824-0105
301-592-8573
www.nhlbi.nih.gov

National Stroke Association
9707 E. Easter Lane
Englewood, CO 80112
800-787-6537
www.stroke.org

Travel

International Association for Medical Assistance to
   Travellers
417 Center St.
Lewiston, NY 14092
716-754-4883
www.iamat.org

National Center for Infectious Diseases
Centers for Disease Control and Prevention
Office of Health Communication
Mailstop C-14
1600 Clifton Rd.
Atlanta, GA 30333
877-FYI-TRIP
www.cdc.gov/travel

INDEX

A

Abdominal pain, 141–145
Abrasions, 22, 23–25
Abstention from sex, 327
Accutane
  for acne, 64
  and nosebleeds, 131
  for rosacea, 89
ACE inhibitors, 188
Acetaminophen, 396, 397
  for abdominal pain, 145
  for chest pain, 182
  for chicken pox related fever, 362
  for croup, 368
  for ear infections, 126
  for epididymitis, 280
  for fever, 218, 372
  for fibromyalgia, 243
  for fifth disease, 373
  for flu, 220
  for growing pains, 374
  for hand-foot-and-mouth disease, 375
  for headaches, 103
  for hemorrhoid pain, 160
  and hepatitis, 167
  for kidney stone pain, 173
  for rectal pain/itching, 164
  for sinusitis, 133
  for smashed fingers, 58
  for sore throat, 135
  for swollen glands, 137
  for tonsillitis, 383
Achilles tendonitis, 232
Achilles tendon stretch, 263, 264
ACL injuries, 258, 260
Acne, 63–64
Actinic keratosis, 92
Active consumerism, 391, 425
Activity pyramid, 400–402
Actron, 396, 397
Acupuncture, 440
  for tinnitus, 140
Acute bronchitis, 209–210
Acute hives, 74
Acute low back pain, 234–235
Acute sciatica, 235
Adenocarcinoma, 223
ADHD, 359–362
Adrenaline (injectable), for bee stings, 10
Advil. *See* Ibuprofen
Aerobic exercise, 401
Afrin, for sinusitis, 133
Aftate, for ringworm, 87
Aged persons. *See* Elderly

AIDS. *See also* HIV
  and flu shots, 221
  and foodborne illness susceptibility, 154
Air exposure, for rashes, 381
Air filters, 204
Airplane ears, 128–129
Air pollution
  and asthma, 206
  and chronic obstructive pulmonary disease, 213
  and laryngitis, 129
  and lung cancer, 222
  and sinusitis, 134
Alcohol
  for cleansing cuts, 23
  for cleansing scrapes, 24
Alcohol abuse, 329–331
  and erection problems, 313
  and suicide, 339
Alcoholic beverages
  and abdominal pain, 145
  and acute bronchitis, 210
  and breast cancer, 283
  in cold weather, 41
  and coughs, 217
  dietary recommendations, 406
  and erection problems, 313, 314
  and fatigue, 344
  and fibromyalgia, 243
  and heartburn, 158
  and hepatitis, 165, 167
  and high blood pressure, 195, 196
  and insomnia, 347
  and laryngitis, 129, 130
  and nosebleeds, 131
  and orgasm problems, 317
  and osteoporosis, 266
  and palpitations, 197, 198
  and premenstrual syndrome, 301
  and prostate problems, 276
  and sexual desire, 314
  and sinusitis, 134
  and sleep apnea, 350
  and tinnitus, 139
  and ulcers, 144
  and urinary incontinence, 176
  and urinary tract infections, 178
  and vomiting, 168
Alcoholics Anonymous, 330, 331
Aleve. *See* Naproxen
Allergens, 201
  and asthma, 205
  and breath, shortness of, 228
Allergic shock, 4–5
Allergies, 201–205

Allergies—cont'd
  and blisters, 66
  chemical sensitivity, 202
  dust mites, 202
  food, 144, 152
  and hives, 73
  to medications, 4, 5
  and middle ear infections, 125
  mold, 202
  and nosebleeds, 131
  pets, 202–203, 204
  pollen, 202
  and sinusitis, 132, 203
  and swollen glands, 136
Allergy shots, 204
Alopecia areata, 72
Alpha-blockers, for prostate problems, 275
Alternative medicine. *See* Complementary and alternative medicine
Amebic dysentery, 152
Amenorrhea, 295, 296
Amplification, for tinnitus, 139
Analgesics. *See* Aspirin
Anal ointments, 164
Anal sex
  and hemorrhoids, 160
  and hepatitis, 166
  STDs. *See* Sexually transmitted diseases
Anaphylaxis, 4–5
Anemia, and flu shots, 221
Aneurysms, 183–184
Angina, 182, 187
Angioplasty, 187
Animals
  allergic shock from, 4
  bites, 6–7
Ankle bursitis, 232
Ankle pain, 231–234
Antacids
  for canker sores, 82
  for gastroesophageal reflux disease, 157
  for heartburn, 159
  for hiatal hernia, 163
Antibiotic ointment
  bacitracin. *See* Bacitracin
  for bites, 6
  for ingrown toenails, 75
  for scrapes, 6
Anticholinergics, for asthma, 207
Anticonvulsants, for encephalitis, 100
Antidandruff shampoos, 70–71
Antihistamines
  for allergies, 203
  Benadryl. *See* Benadryl
  for coughs, 217
  and prostate problems, 276
  and sexual desire, 314
  for sinusitis, 133
Antilice creme rinse, 78
Antilice shampoos, 78
Antithyroid drugs, 354, 355
Anusol HC, 160
Anxiety
  disorders, 332–333

and erection problems, 313
  natural remedies for, 333
  and palpitations, 197, 198
  stress. *See* Stress
  and urge incontinence, 175
Appendicitis, 141–142
Appropriate care, 447
Arches, high, 248
Arch supports, 248, 251, 272
Arrhythmias, 197
Arthritis, 241–242
Artificial tears, 112, 116
Asbestos, and lung cancer, 222, 224
Aspirin, 396, 397
  for abdominal pain, 145
  and asthma, 206
  and bruising, 69
  and children, 103, 135
  for cold sore pain, 81
  for ear infections, 126
  for fever, 218
  for flu, 220
  for hand/wrist pain, 272
  for headaches, 103
  and heartburn, 158
  for heart disease, 187
  for menstrual pain, 294
  and nosebleeds, 131, 132
  for premenstrual syndrome, 300
Asthma, 205–209
  and allergies, 203, 205
  coughs, 215
  and flu shots, 221
Asthma action plan, 207, 208
Astigmatism, 119, 120
Astroglide, for vaginal dryness, 293
Atherosclerosis, 183
  and aneurysms, 183–184
  causes of, 184
  and claudication, 184
  coronary artery disease. *See* Coronary artery disease
  plaques, 184–185
  stroke. *See* Stroke
Athlete's foot, 65, 136
Atopic dermatitis, 85
Attention deficit/hyperactivity disorder, 359–362
Aura, before migraine onset, 102
Automobile exhausts, and carbon monoxide poisoning, 19, 20
Aveeno bath treatment. *See* Oatmeal bath treatment

B
Babies. *See* Infants
Bacitracin
  for bites, 6
  for cuts, 23
  for nails, torn, 58
  for nosebleeds, 132
Back injuries
  first aid for, 42, 56
  shock victims, 56
Back pain, 234–240
Bacterial meningitis, 104, 105
Bacterial pinkeye, 116, 117

Bacterial pneumonia, 225
Bacterial vaginosis, 304
Bad breath, 123–125
Baking soda and water
   for hives, 74
   for insect ot spider bites/stings, 8
   for marine-life stings, 50
   for poison ivy/oak/sumac, 83
   for sunburn, 94, 95
Balance problems, 28
Balding, 71–73
Balloon angioplasty, 187
Balloon dilation therapy, 275
Bandaging cuts, 23
Barotitis, 128–129
Basal cell cancer, 92
Baths. *See also* Heat or warmth
   oatmeal. *See* Oatmeal bath treatment
   sitz bath. *See* Sitz bath
Bed rest. *See* Sleep or rest
Bee-sting kits, 10
Bee stings, 7
   hives from, 74
Benadryl
   for allergic shock, 4
   for hives, 74
   for insect bites/stings, 8
   for poison ivy/oak/sumac, 83
   for scabies itching, 91
   for spider bites/stings, 8
Benign positional vertigo, 29
Benign prostatic hypertrophy, 177, 274, 275
Benzoyl peroxide, for acne, 64
Beta-agonists, for asthma, 207
Beta-blockers
   for heart disease, 187–188
   for hyperthyroidism, 354, 355
Biopsy
   of breast, 283
   of lung, 223
   of prostate, 275
Birds, encephalitis in, 99
Birth control, 307
   barrier methods, 308–309
   cervical caps, 309
   condoms, 308, 311
   diaphragms. *See* Diaphragms
   emergency contraception, 311
   implants, 310
   intrauterine devices. *See* IUDs
   natural methods, 308
   patch, 310
   pills. *See* Birth control pills
   progesterone injections, 310
   rhythm method, 308
   shots. *See* Depo-Provera
   spermicides, 308
   sterilization, surgical, 311
   tubal ligation, 311
   vaginal contraceptive ring, 310–311
   vasectomy, 311
   withdrawal method, 308
Birth control patch, 310
Birth control pills, 309–310

   and hair loss, 71–72
   and hepatitis, 167
   and missed periods, 295–296
   and premenstrual syndrome, 301
   and urinary tract infections, 178
Bismuth salicylate, 152
Bites
   animals, 6–7
   human, 6–7
   insects, 7–10, 136
   snake, 10–12
   tick, 7, 12–15
Black cohosh, for menopause, 293
Blackheads, 63
Black stools, 146–147
Bladder, 171
   urinary tract infections, 177–179
Bleeding
   from bites, 6, 7
   from cuts, 23
   from head injuries, 41, 42
   between periods, 281–282
   rectal, 160
   shock victims, 56
Blindness, and glaucoma, 119
Blisters, 66–67
   cold sores, 80–81
   from frostbite, 39, 40
Blood cholesterol. *See* Cholesterol
Blood glucose levels
   exercising to reduce, 353
   monitoring, 353
Blood pressure
   adults 18 years or older, 196
   high. *See* High blood pressure
   measurement of, 195
   and stress, 336
Blood transfusions, and hepatitis B, C, 166, 167
Bloody stools, 146–147
BMD, 265
BMI, 408, 409
Body aches, 241
   arthritis, 241–242
   fibromyalgia, 242–243
   joint pain, 243
   muscle cramps, 243–244
   muscle imbalance, 244
   muscle tightness, 244
   referred pain, 234, 244
   repetitive motion injuries, 244–245
Body mass index, 408, 409
Body mechanics, and neck pain, 106, 108–109
Body powder
   to prevent jock itch, 77
   for ringworm, 87
Body temperature, 217. *See also* Fever
Boils, 67–68
Bone fractures. *See* Fractures
Bone loss, 265–266
Bone mineral density, 265
Botulism, 154, 155
Bowel movements. *See* Stools
BPH, 177, 274, 275
Braces, and bad breath, 124

Brain
 chemical imbalances in, 332, 334
 encephalitis, 99–101
 meningitis, 104–106
Breakthrough bleeding between periods, 281
Breast cancer, 283–284
 clinical examinations, 286
 and HRT, 292
 mammograms, 286
 self-examinations, 284–286
 signs of, 284
Breastfeeding, and urinary tract infections, 178
Breast self-examinations, 284–286
Breath, shortness of, 227–228
Breath fresheners, 124
Breathing exercises, 215
Breath mints, 124
Breath sprays, 124
Bright spots, before migraine onset, 102
Broken tooth, 60
Bronchitis
 acute, 209–210
 chronic, 213–214
 croup with fever, 367
 from influenza, 219
Bronchodilator medications, 214
Bruises, 69
BSEs, 284–286
"Buddy system," 41
"Bull's-eye"rash, 12, 13, 14, 15
Bunion pads, 251
Bunions, 250, 251
Burning eyes, 111–113
Burns, 15–17
 blisters from, 66
 chemical, 17–18
 electrical, 34
 eyes, 17–18, 111, 112, 113
Bursitis
 ankle, 232
 elbow, 246–247
 hip, 254
 knee, 259, 260
 prepatellar, 259
 shoulder(s), 268
"Butterfly bandages," 23
Buzzing in ears, 33
Bypass surgery, 187

C
CAD. *See* Coronary artery disease
Caffeine
 and abdominal pain, 145
 and acute bronchitis, 210
 and chronic fatigue syndrome, 345
 and diarrhea, 144
 and fatigue, 344
 and fibromyalgia, 243
 and heartburn, 158
 and insomnia, 347
 and palpitations, 197, 198
 and premenstrual syndrome, 301
 and prostate problems, 276
 and tinnitus, 139

 and ulcers, 144
 and urge incontinence, 175
 and urinary incontinence, 176
 and urinary tract infections, 178
Caladryl, for chicken pox, 362
Calamine lotion
 for chicken pox, 362
 for insect or spider bites/stings, 8
 for poison ivy/oak/sumac, 83
Calcium
 for osteoporosis, 266
 for premenstrual syndrome, 300
Calorie needs, 410
CAM. *See* Complementary and alternative medicine
Cancer. *See also* Biopsy
 breast, 283–286, 292
 cervical, 287
 chemotherapy. *See* Chemotherapy
 colorectal, 147–149
 endometrial, and HRT, 292
 lung, 222–224
 prostate, 274, 275–276, 277
 radiation therapy. *See* Radiation therapy
 signs of, 149
 skin, 92–94
 squamous cell carcinoma, 92, 223
 testicular, 277–279
Candida albicans, 303
Canker sores, 81–82
Capital femoral epiphysis, slipped, 256
Carbon monoxide detectors, 20
Carbon monoxide poisoning, 19–20
Carbuncles, 67
Cardiopulmonary resuscitation. *See* CPR
Carpal tunnel syndrome, 271–272
 and pinched nerves, 109
Cataracts, 119
Cat bites, 6, 7
"Catnaps," 344, 348
Cat scratch, 7
Cellulitis, 361
Central sleep apnea, 349
Cervical cancer, 287
Cervical caps, 309
CFS, 345–346
Charcoal grilling indoors, 20
Charley horse, 254
Chemical imbalances in brain, 332, 334
Chemicals
 allergic shock from, 4
 blisters from, 66
 and bronchitis, 209
 burns, 17–18
 and chronic obstructive pulmonary disease, 213
 eye burns, 17–18, 111, 112, 113
 and hepatitis, 165
 sensitivity to, 202
Chemotherapy
 and hair loss, 71
 for lung cancer, 224
 for skin cancer, 93
 for testicular cancer, 279
Chest pain, 181–183
Chewing tobacco, and mouth sores, 80

Chicken pox, 361–364
  blisters from, 66
  vaccine, 364, 419
Chigger bites, 7
Childbirth
  and breast cancer, 283
  hair loss after, 72
Child care workers, and hepatitis A, 165
Children, 359
  abuse of, 340–341
  acne, 63–64
  and airplane ears, 128
  and allergies, 201
  and antifungal creams, 65
  and aspirin, 103, 135, 363
  and asthma, 205, 207, 208
  attention deficit/hyperactivity disorder, 359–362
  bites from, 6
  capital femoral epiphysis, slipped, 256
  chicken pox, 361–364
  and colds, 212
  and constipation, 150
  croup, 367–368
  and DEET, 14
  and dehydration, 26
  and diabetes, 352
  diarrhea, 369–370
  doctor visits, 420–421
  ear emergencies, 33
  and ear infections, 125, 126
  encephalitis in, 100
  fever in, 218, 371–372
  fifth disease, 373
  and foodborne illness susceptibility, 154
  growing pains, 374
  hand-foot-and-mouth disease, 374–375
  HBV vaccinations, 324
  with head injuries, 41
  healthy lifestyle, 421
  hepatitis B vaccinations, 166
  and hip and thigh problems, 255–256
  and hyperthyroidism, 354
  immune system, 359
  immunizations, 420, 421
  impetigo, 376–377
  with insect bites, 8
  lead poisoning, 377–379
  Legg-Calvé-Perthes disease, 256
  and meningitis, 104
  with pinkeye, 117
  pinworms, 379–380
  and plantar warts, 250
  and pneumonia, 225
  pneumonia vaccine for, 227
  preventive care, 420–421
  rashes, 381–382
  with rectal pain/itching, 164
  rehydrating after vomiting, 168–169
  roseola, 381
  and smashed fingers, 58
  and sore throats, 135
  and suicide, 339
  sunburn prevention, 96
  synovitis, 256
    temperature of, 371–372
    tonsillitis, 382–384
    and vomiting, 168–169, 384–386
    and warts, 97
Chiropractic medicine, 440
Chlamydia, 320–321
    and pelvic inflammatory disease, 297, 320
    during pregnancy, 326, 327
Chlorine, for water purification, 153
Chlor-Trimeton, for hives, 74
Choking, 21–22
Cholesterol
    dietary recommendations, 191–194, 406
    HDLs, 186, 189, 190
    and heart disease, 186, 188
    LDLs, 186, 189, 190
    measuring, 190
    self-care, 190–191
    treating high cholesterol, 190
    triglycerides, 186, 188, 189
Chondroitin sulfate, for osteoarthritis, 241
Chondromalacia patella, 259, 260
Choriocarcinoma, 278
Chronic bronchitis, 213–214
Chronic fatigue syndrome, 345–346
Chronic hives, 74
Chronic low back pain, 235
Chronic obstructive pulmonary disease, 213–215
Chronic thyroiditis, 356
Circulatory system, 181
Cirrhosis of the liver, 166
Citronella, 9
Citrucel, 160
Claudication, 184
    intermittent, 262
Cleansing cuts, 23
Cleansing scrapes, 24
Clinical depression, 334
Closed fractures, 37
Clothing
    for cold weather, 41, 49
    for fever in children, 372
    for hot weather, 46
    for insect protection, 9, 101
    and rectal pain/itching, 164
    for tick protection, 14
    and vaginal discharge/irritation, 305
Clotrimazole(s)
    for athlete's foot, 65
    for jock itch, 76
    for ringworm, 87
Cluster headaches, 102
Codeine, hives from, 73
Coffee. *See* Caffeine
Cold compresses. *See* Cool/cold compresses; Ice
    bags/packs
Cold lozenges, 216
Colds, 211–213
    and bad breath, 123
    and hoarseness, 130
    and laryngitis, 129
    and nosebleeds, 131
    and sinusitis, 132
Cold sores, 80–81

Cold weather
   activities in, 49
   and bronchitis, 209
   and catching a cold, 211
   clothing for, 41, 49
   frostbite, 39–41
   hypothermia, 47–49
   vocal cord protection, 130
Colic, 364–365
Collagen injections, for stress incontinence, 175
Collars, for pinched nerves, 110
Colorado tick fever, 12
Colorectal cancer, 147–149
   and black or bloody stools, 146
Common cold. *See* Colds
Common warts, 97
Compartment syndrome, 263
Complementary and alternative medicine, 440
   considerations before trying, 442–443
   effectiveness of, 441–442
   types of, 440–441
Compress. *See* RICE method (Rest, Ice, Compress, Elevate)
Compresses
   cool. *See* Cool/cold compresses
   warm. *See* Warm compresses
Computed tomography, for pelvic inflammatory disease, 298
Condoms, 308, 311
   putting on, 311
   STD prevention, 327–328
Conjunctivitis, 116–117
Constipation, 150–151
   and hemorrhoids, 160
   and rectal pain/itching, 163
Contact dermatitis, 85
Contaminated food, 144, 154–155
   lead poisoning, 379
   and vomiting, 168, 384
Contaminated needles. *See also* Intravenous drug users
   and hepatitis B, C, 166
Continuous positive airway pressure treatment, 350
Contraception. *See* Birth control
Cool air vaporizers, 216, 367
Cool/cold compresses
   for back pain, 236
   for burns, 16
   for chemical burns, 17
   for cold sore pain, 81
   for headaches, 103
   for insect or spider bites/stings, 8
   for marine-life stings, 50
   for pinkeye, 116
   for poison ivy/oak/sumac, 83
   for rash itches, 85
   for rectal pain/itching, 164
   for sunburn, 94
   for sunburned eyes, 112
   for vaginal discharge/irritation, 304
Co-payments for emergency room care, 3
COPD, 213–215
Copperhead, 10
Copper IUDs, 309
Coral snakes, 10

bites from, 11–12
Corn pads, 69
Corns, 69–70
Cornstarch
   for rashes, 381
   for rectal pain/itching, 163
   and water, for sunburn, 94
Coronary artery disease, 183, 184. *See also* Atherosclerosis
   and HRT, 292
   and menopause, 291
   prevention of, 188
   risk factors beyond your control, 185–186
   risk factors within your control, 186–187
   and strokes, 199
   treatment of, 187–188
Cortaid, for poison ivy/oak/sumac, 83
Corticosteroids
   for asthma, 207
   for chronic bronchitis, 214
   for encephalitis, 100
   nasal sprays, for allergies, 203
Cosmetics, and burning eyes, 112
Cottonmouth, 10
Cotton swabs
   and ear damage, 33, 127
   for nosebleeds, 132
   to remove foreign objects in eyes, 114
Cough, 215–217
   and acute bronchitis, 209
   in chronic bronchitis, 214
   and lung cancer, 222
   as pneumonia treatment, 226
Cough expectorants, 216
   for acute bronchitis, 210
Cough suppressants, 216–217
   for acute bronchitis, 210
   and croup, 367
Counting sheep to fall asleep, 348
CPAP treatment, 350
CPR
   for near-drowning victims, 32
   why you should learn, 43
Cradle cap, 366
Cramps
   heat, 44, 45
   menstrual, 294
   muscle, 243–244
Creme rinse, antilice, 78
Crohn's disease, 152
Cromolyn sodium, for asthma, 207
Croup, 367–368
Crutches
   for ankle sprains/strains, 233
   for foot stress fractures, 249
   for groin pulls, 255
   for hamstring pulls, 255
   for knee sprains, 260
CTS, 271–272
CT scans, for pelvic inflammatory disease, 298
Cuticles
   ingrown toenails, 75–76, 136
   smashed fingers, 58
   torn, first aid for, 58

Cuts, 22–23, 25
Cysts, 64
　ovarian, 144

D
Dandruff, 70–71
D & C, 282
Decongestants
　to prevent airplane ears, 129
　for allergies, 203
　for colds, 211
　for coughs, 210
　for flu, 220
　and prostate problems, 276
　for sinusitis, 133
Deep breathing
　for dizziness, 30
　for hyperventilation, 47
Deer tick, 13
　and Lyme disease, 14
DEET, 9, 14, 101
Degenerative joint disease, 107
Dehydration, 25–26
　rehydrating after vomiting, 168–169, 385–386
Delayed ejaculation, 316
Dementia, and urge incontinence, 175
Dental hygiene, and bad breath, 123, 124
Dentures, and bad breath, 124
Depends undergarments, 176
Depo-Provera, 310
　and bleeding between periods, 281
Depression, 334–335
　and ADHD, 360
　and erection problems, 313
　and insomnia, 346
　natural remedies for, 333
　and suicide, 339
Dermatitis, 85–86. *See* Rashes
　poison ivy/oak/sumac, 82–84
Designated drivers, use of, 331
Desitin, for diaper rash, 381
Detoxification centers, 330
Detrusor instability, 175
DEXA, 265
DHEA, for menopause, 293
Diabetes, 351–353
　and flu shots, 221
　and foodborne illness susceptibility, 154
　gestational, 352–353
　and heart disease, 186
　and overflow incontinence, 175
　and peripheral neuropathy, 110
　and strokes, 199
　type 1, 352
　type 2, 352
　and urinary tract infections, 178
　and vision problems, 121
Dialysis, and hepatitis B, 166
Diaper rash, 381
Diaphragms, 308–309
　and toxic shock syndrome, 303
　and urinary tract infections, 179
　and vaginal discharge/irritation, 305
Diarrhea, 152–153

　and caffeine, 144
　in children, 369–370
　dehydration from, 24
　and hand-foot-and-mouth disease, 375
　and hemorrhoids, 160
　and rectal pain/itching, 163
Diet
　and angina, 187
　and bad breath, 123
　calorie needs, 410
　for canker sores, 82
　for chicken pox, 362
　and chronic fatigue syndrome, 345
　for chronic obstructive pulmonary disease, 214
　and colds, 213
　and colorectal cancer, 149
　and constipation, 150, 151
　and diabetes, 353
　for diarrhea, 152, 369
　for diverticulitis, 143
　fad diets, 411–412
　and fatigue, 344
　for foodborne illness, 155
　and headaches, 104
　and heart disease, 186, 188
　for hemorrhoids, 160
　and hepatitis, 167
　and high blood cholesterol, 190–191
　and high blood pressure, 196
　and insomnia, 347
　for irritable bowl syndrome, 143–144
　and kidney stones, 174
　for menopause, 292–293
　and mouth sores, 80
　and osteoporosis, 266
　for osteoporosis, 266
　and pneumonia, 227
　and premenstrual syndrome, 301
　and prostate cancer, 274
　recommendations, 191–194
　and rectal pain/itching, 164
　and urinary tract infections, 178
　and vomiting, 168
　weight management, 407–413
Dietary supplements, 406, 440–441
Digestive tract, 142
Digital rectal exam, 148, 274
Dilation and curettage, 282
Diphtheria/tetanus/pertussis vaccine, 418
Disc pain, 235
Dislocations, 27
Diuretics, and kidney stones, 172
Diverticulitis, 142–143
　and constipation, 150
Diving accidents, 32
Dizziness, 28–30
　balance problems, 28
　benign positional vertigo, 29
　fainting, 29–30
　and hyperventilation, 46
　labyrinthitis, 29
　lightheadedness, 28
　Meniere's disease, 29
　and stroke, 30, 199

Dizziness—cont'd
    vertigo, 28–29
DJD, 107
Doctors
    choosing, 427–428, 446
    as educators, 428
    fees and bills, 443–444
    a good match, 427–428
    visits. *See* Doctor visits
Doctor visits
    birth to 23 months, 420
    7 to 11 years of age, 420
    12 to 18 years of age, 420–421
    19 to 39 years of age, 421
    40 to 64 years of age, 422
    65 years of age and older, 422–423
    preparing for, 443–444
Dog bites, 6
Domboro solution, for impetigo, 376
Domestic violence, 340–341
    and suicide, 339
Dong quai root, for menopause, 293
Douching, and sexually transmitted diseases, 328
Doxycycline, for rosacea, 89
DRE, 148, 274
"Drop foot," 263
Drowning/near drowning, 31–32
Drug abuse, 329–331. *See also* Intravenous drug users
    and erection problems, 313
    and suicide, 339
Drugs
    and hepatitis B, C, 166
    and orgasm problems, 317
    and sexual desire, 314
    and tinnitus, 139
Dryers, and carbon monoxide poisoning, 20
Dry eyes, 111–113
Dry mouth, and bad breath, 124, 125
DTaP vaccine, 418
Dual-energy x-ray absorptiometry, 265
Dust
    and bronchitis, 209
    and chronic obstructive pulmonary disease, 213
    and sinusitis, 132
Dust mites, 202
DXA, 265
Dysentery, 152

E
Earaches, 125–129
    children's colds and, 212
Eardrum ruptures, 33, 34, 127–128
Early ejaculation, 316, 317
Earplugs, 34, 348
Ears
    dizziness and, 29, 33
    emergencies, 33–34
    foreign objects in, 33
    labyrinthitis, 29
    tinnitus, 138–140
Ear stuffiness, 128–129
Earwax buildup, 127–128
Earwax drops, 128
Eating habits, 403–407

food groups, 403–405
    healthy eating tips, 407
    serving sizes, 404–405
    special concerns, 406
Ectopic pregnancy, 144
Eczema, 85–86. *See* Rashes
    poison ivy/oak/sumac, 82–84
Ejaculation problems, 316
Elbow joint, 246
Elbow pain, 246–247
Elderly
    and bad breath, 124
    and breast cancer, 283
    and carbon monoxide poisoning, 19
    and cataracts, 119
    and cold sores, 80
    and colorectal cancer, 147–148
    and constipation, 150
    and dehydration, 26
    and diabetes, 351
    erection problems, 316
    fever in, 218
    flu concerns, 219
    and flu shots, 221, 419
    and foodborne illness susceptibility, 154
    and heart disease, 186
    and heat-related problems, 46
    and hemorrhoids, 160
    and high blood cholesterol, 190
    and hyperthyroidism, 354
    and macular degeneration, 119–120
    and narrowing of the arteries, in lower leg, 262
    and osteoporosis, 265
    and pneumonia, 225
    and presbyopia, 119
    preventive care, 421–423
    and prostate problems, 273, 274
    sexual concerns, 316
    and sleep apnea, 349
    and stroke, 59
    and suicide, 339
    and tinnitus, 138
Elective surgery, 429
Electrical shock, 34–35
Electrical stimulation, for urge incontinence, 175
Electrolyte solutions
    Infalyte®, 168, 169, 369, 385–386
    Pedialyte, 26, 168, 169, 369, 385–386
    sports drink, 45
Elevate. *See* RICE method (Rest, Ice, Compress, Elevate)
Embryonal carcinoma, 278
Emergency care
    CPR. *See* CPR
    emergency room. *See* Emergency room care
    first aid. *See* First aid
Emergency contraception, 311
Emergency room care, 3
    for stroke, 199
Emotional health concerns, 329–341
Emphysema, 214
Encephalitis, 99–101
    from chicken pox, 361, 362
Endocrine system, 351

diabetes. *See* Diabetes
  hyperthyroidism, 354–356
  hypothyroidism, 356–358
  problems with, 351–358
Endometrial cancer, and HRT, 292
Endometriosis, 144, 288–289
Enemas, 145
  for constipation, 150
Enlarged prostate, 177, 274, 275
Epidermoid carcinoma, 223
Epididymitis, 279, 280
Epididymo-orchitis, 279, 280
Epiglottitis, 367
Epileptic seizures, 53, 55
Epinephrine, for bee stings, 10
EPIPEN, for allergic shock, 4
Epsom salts and warm water, for corns, 69
Erectile dysfunction, 312
Erection problems, 312–314
Erythromycin
  for Lyme disease, 15
  for rosacea, 89
Escherichia coli, 177
Estrogen, and breast cancer, 283
Estrogen creams, for stress incontinence, 175
Estrogen replacement therapy. *See* Hormone replacement therapy
Eustachian tube, plugging of, 125, 126
Exercise
  Achilles tendon stretch, 263, 264
  aerobic, 401
  allergic shock from, 4
  and amenorrhea, 296
  and angina, 187
  ankle, range-of-motion exercise for, 233
  for arthritis, 272
  and asthma, 206, 209
  for back pain, 236, 237, 239–240
  blood glucose levels, reduction of, 353
  boredom and, 402–403
  and breath, shortness of, 228
  breathing exercises, 215
  and chronic fatigue syndrome, 345
  for chronic obstructive pulmonary disease, 214–215
  and colds, 213
  and constipation, 150, 151
  dehydration from, 24
  for diverticulitis, 143
  for elbow pain, 247
  environment, 402
  and erection problems, 314
  for fibromyalgia, 243
  and foot stress fractures, 251
  frequency and duration, 399, 401, 402
  and hand/wrist pain, 272
  for headaches, 103
  and heart disease, 186, 188
  and heel spurs, 250
  and high blood cholesterol, 191
  and high blood pressure, 196
  iliotibial band stretch, 261
  and insomnia, 348
  for irritable bowl syndrome, 144
  Kegel exercises, 176

  knee raise, 239, 240
  leg extension, 260
  and lower leg stress fractures, 263
  for menopause, 293
  and Morton's neuroma, 251
  for muscle imbalance, 244
  muscle strengthening and stretching, 401
  for osteoporosis, 266
  overcoming obstacles, 402
  and palpitations, 198
  partial press-up, 240
  pelvic tilt, 237, 239
  physical limitations, 402
  piriformis stretch, 255
  and plantar fasciitis, 250
  and pneumonia, 227
  and premenstrual syndrome, 301
  for repetitive motion injuries, 245
  for runner's knee, 259
  time for, 402–403
  walking, 400–401, 402
Exposure, 47
External stress, 336
Eyedrops, for allergies, 203
Eye exams, 121
Eyelids
  scrub, 112
  styes, 118
Eye lubrication drops
  for burning eyes, 112
  to remove foreign objects, 114
Eyes
  burning, 111–113
  chemical burns, 17–18, 111, 112, 113
  foreign object in, 113–115
  pinkeye, 116–117
  vision problems, 119–121

F
Fad diets, 411–412
Fainting, 29–30
Family history
  of breast cancer, 283
  of diabetes, 351
  of heart disease, 186, 190
  of prostate cancer, 274
Family violence, 340–341
  and suicide, 339
Farsightedness, 119, 120
Fatigue, 343–344
  chronic fatigue syndrome, 345–346
  and erection problems, 313
  and tinnitus, 139
Fats, 189. *See also* Cholesterol
  and heart disease, 186, 188
  saturated, 406
Fecal occult blood test, 148
Feces. *See* Stools
Fees and bills, 443–444
Feet
  athlete's foot, 65, 136
  blisters on, 66, 67
  bunions, 250, 251
  "drop foot," 263

Feet—cont'd
  flat, 248
  heel spurs, 248, 249, 250–251
  high arches, 248
  Morton's neuroma, 249–250, 251
  pain, 248–252
  plantar fasciitis, 248–249, 250–251
  plantar warts, 97, 250, 251
  stress fractures, 249, 251
  toes. *See* Toes
Fever
  in adults, 217–218
  in chicken pox, 362
  in children, 218, 371–372
  in colds, 212
  croup with, 367
  dehydration from, 24
  of infants, 212
Fever blisters, 80–81
Fibromyalgia, 242–243
Fifth disease, 373
Filiform warts, 97
Finasteride, for enlarged prostate, 275
Fingers
  mallet finger, 271
  smashed, 58–59
  tendinitis, 271
Fireplaces, and carbon monoxide poisoning, 20
First aid
  for allergic shock, 4
  for animal bites, 6
  for back injury, 42
  for burns, 16–17
  for carbon monoxide poisoning, 19–20
  for chemical burns, 17–18
  for choking, 21
  for cuts, 23
  for dehydration, 26
  for dislocations, 27
  for dizziness, 30
  for ear emergencies, 33–34
  for electrical shock, 34–35
  for fingers, smashed, 58
  for fishhook wounds, 36–37
  for fractures, 37–38
  for frostbite, 40
  for heart attacks, 44
  for heat cramps, 45
  for heat exhaustion, 45
  for heat stroke, 45
  for human bites, 6
  for hyperventilation, 47
  for hypothermia, 48
  for inhaled poisoning, 52
  for insect bites/stings, 8
  for marine-life stings, 50
  for nails, torn, 58
  for near-drowning victims, 32
  for neck injury, 42, 109
  for poisoning, 52
  for scrapes, 24
  for seizures, 54–55
  for shock, 56
  for slivers/splinters, 57

  for smashed fingers or toes, 58
  for snakebites, 11
  for spider bites, 8
  supplies, 389–390
  teeth, knocked-out or broken, 60
  for tick bites, 13
First-degree burns, 15
Fishhook wounds, 36–37
Fishline method for removing fishhooks, 36–37
Fissures, rectal, 163
Fitness. *See* Healthy lifestyle
Fits
  in children with high fever, 372
  seizures. *See* Seizures
Flashes, before migraine onset, 102
Flat feet, 248
Flat warts, 97
Flaxseed, for menopause, 293
Fleets, 150
Flexible sigmoidoscopy, 148
Flu, 219–221
Fluid intake
  burn victims, 17
  for chicken pox, 362
  for chronic obstructive pulmonary disease, 214
  for colds, 211–212
  for constipation, 151
  for coughs, 216
  for dehydration, 26
  for diarrhea, 152, 369
  to avoid dry mouth, 124
  for fever, 218, 372
  for flu, 220
  for foodborne illness, 155
  for frostbite, 40
  for hand-foot-and-mouth disease, 375
  for heat-related problems, 45
  for hypothermia, 48
  to help prevent kidney stones, 173, 174
  and menstrual pain, 295
  for pneumonia, 226
  and premenstrual syndrome, 301
  for prostate problems, 276
  for sinusitis, 133
  for sore throats, 135
  for tonsillitis, 383
  and urinary tract infections, 179
  for vocal cord hydration, 130
  after vomiting, 168–169, 385–386
Flu season, 219
Flushing out eyes, 17–18
  to remove foreign objects, 114
Flu shots, 215, 220–221, 419
  as preventative of pneumonia, 227
Fly bites, 7
Focal seizures, 54
Food. *See also* Diet
  allergic shock from, 4
  allergies, 144, 152
  and black or bloody stools, 146
  contamination. *See* Contaminated food
  and gastroesophageal reflux disease, 157
  and heartburn, 158, 159
  and hepatitis A, 165, 166

and hiatal hernias, 163
hives from, 73
illnesses from, 154–155, 168
safety, 155, 406–407
Food groups, 403–404
servings, 404–405, 411
worksheet, 412
Food preparation
and diarrhea, 153
and hepatitis, 165, 167
Food pyramid, 405
Foot. *See* Feet; Toes
Foot powder, to prevent blisters, 67
Foreign objects
in ears, 33
in eyes, 113–115
slivers/splinters, 57
Fractures, 37–39
foot stress fractures, 249, 251
lower leg stress fractures, 263
navicular, 270–271
and osteoporosis, 265
smashed fingers, 58
smashed fingers or toes, 58–59
Freezing and removal of warts, 98
Frostbite, 39–41
Frostnip, 39
Frozen treats, for sore throats, 135
Fumes
burning eyes, 112
carbon monoxide poisoning, 19–20
inhaled poisoning, 52
Functional incontinence, 175–176
Furnaces, and carbon monoxide poisoning, 19, 20

G
Gallbladder disease, 143
and chest pain, 182
Gallstones, 143
Gamma globulin, for hepatitis A, 165, 166
Ganglions, in hand or wrist, 271
Gargling
for colds, 212
for sore throats, 135
for tonsillitis, 383
Gastroesophageal reflux disease, 156–157
coughing and, 215
and laryngitis, 129
and ulcers, 144
Gender
and heart disease, 186
men. *See* Men
women. *See* Women
Generalized anxiety disorder, 332
Genital herpes, 321
and blisters, 66
during pregnancy, 327
Genital warts, 97, 321–322
GERD. *See* Gastroesophageal reflux disease
Gestational diabetes, 352–353
Giardiasis, 152
Gingivitis, 124
Ginkgo biloba, for menopause, 293
Glass splinters, 57

Glaucoma, 119
Glucosamine sulfate, for osteoarthritis, 241
Gnat bites, 7
Golfer's elbow, 246
Gonorrhea, 322–323
and pelvic inflammatory disease, 297
during pregnancy, 326, 327
Gout
and ankle pain, 232–233
and kidney stones, 172
Grand mal seizures, 54
Graves' disease, 354
Groin hernias, 161–162
Groin pulls, 254, 255
Growing pains, 374
Guillain-Barré syndrome, flu shots and, 221
Gum disease, 124
Gyne-Lotrimin, for vaginal discharge/irritation, 304

H
Haemophilus influenza type B vaccine, 419
Hair loss, 71–73
Hairpieces, 72
Hair transplants, 72
Halitosis, 123–125
Hammertoe, 250
Hamstring pulls, 254, 255
Hand and wrist, 270
carpal tunnel syndrome, 271–272
fingers. *See* Fingers
ganglions, 271
navicular fracture, 270–271
pain in, 270–272
skier's thumb, 271
splints, 272
tendinitis, 271
Hand-foot-and-mouth disease, 374–375
Hashimoto's thyroiditis, 356
Hay fever. *See* Pollen
HDLs, 189
and heart disease, 186
levels of, 190
Headache calendar, 104
Headaches, 101–104
and colds, 211
Head injuries, 41–42
from diving accidents, 32
Head lice, 77–79
Healthy lifestyle, 387, 399
adults 19 to 39 years of age, 421–422
adults 40 to 64 years of age, 422
adults 65 years of age and older, 423
children, 421
eating habits, 403–407
physical activity, 399–403
quitting smoking, 413–415
weight management, 407–413
Hearing loss, and tinnitus, 138
Heart, 181
Heart attacks, 43–44
and chest pain, 181–182
warning signs, 181
Heartburn, 158–159
and bad breath, 123

Heartburn—cont'd
  and chest pain, 182
  and gastroesophageal reflux disease, 157, 158
  and ulcers, 144
Heart disease. *See* Coronary artery disease
Heart palpitations, 197–198
  and hyperventilation, 46
Heart rhythm disorder, 197
Heat cramps, 44, 45
Heat exhaustion, 44, 45
Heat or warmth. *See also* Warm compresses
  for abdominal pain, 145
  for back pain, 236
  for charley horses, 254
  for chest pain, 182
  for earaches, 128
  for fever, 372
  for frostbite, 40
  for growing pains, 374
  and insomnia, 347–348
  for knee injuries, 260
  for menstrual pain, 294
  for muscle tightness, 244
  for neck pain, 107
  for pelvic inflammatory disease, 298
  for shock victims, 56
  for shoulder pain, 269
Heat-related problems, 44–46
Heat stroke, 44, 45
Heavy lifting
  and back pain, 236
  and inguinal hernias, 161, 162
  and muscle imbalance, 244
Heel pads, 272
Heel spurs, 248, 249, 250–251
Heimlich maneuver, use of, 21
Helicobacter pylori, 144
Hemorrhagic stroke, 198
Hemorrhoids, 160
  and black or bloody stools, 146
  and rectal pain/itching, 163
HEPA air filter, 204
Hepatitis, 165–167
Hepatitis A, 165–166
Hepatitis B
  infants with, 326
  vaccine, 166, 323, 324, 419
  virus, 166, 323–324
Hepatitis C, 166–167
Hernia, 144, 161–163
Herpes simplex virus
  and blisters, 66
  and cold sores, 80
  encephalitis, as cause of, 99
  genital herpes. *See* Genital herpes
  during pregnancy, 326
Herpes zoster. *See* Shingles
Hiatal hernia, 162–163
  and gastroesophageal reflux disease, 157
Hib vaccine, 419
High arches, 248
High blood pressure, 195–197
  coughing and, 215
  and diabetes, 351

  and heart disease, 186
  and stress, 336
  and strokes, 199
  and vision problems, 121
High-density lipoproteins. *See* HDLs
Hip and thigh, 253
  bursitis, 254
  capital femoral epiphysis, slipped, 256
  charley horse, 254
  groin pulls, 254, 255
  hamstring pulls, 254, 255
  Legg-Calvé-Perthes disease, 256
  pain in, 253–257
  piriformis syndrome, 254–255
  synovitis, 256
HIV, 324–325
  and cervical cancer, 287
  and flu shots, 221
  and hepatitis B, 166
  from human bites, 7
  infants with, 326
  during pregnancy, 326, 327
Hives, 73–74
Hoarseness, 129–130
Hodgkin's disease, 137
Holiday stress, 338
Homeopathy, 441
Home pregnancy tests, 296
Home supplies, 389–390
Hormone replacement therapy
  for endometriosis, 289
  for erection problems, 313
  for menopause, 291–292
  for osteoporosis, 266
  for prostate cancer, 276
Hormones and hair loss, 72
Hornet stings, 7
Hospitalization, 439–440
  questions to ask before, 439
Hospitals
  fees and bills, 443–444
  finding a good hospital, 446–447
Hot compresses. *See* Warm compresses
Hot flashes, 290
Hot-water heaters, and carbon monoxide poisoning, 19, 20
Housemaid's knee, 259
HPV, 321–322
HRT. *See* Hormone replacement therapy
Human bites, 6–7
Human immunodeficiency virus. *See* HIV
Human papillomavirus, 321–322
Humidity
  and allergies, 204
  for colds, 211–212
  for coughs, 216
  and nosebleeds, 132
  and rashes, 86
  vocal cord protection, 130
Hydrocortisone cream
  for chicken pox, 362
  for cold sores, 81
  for insect ot spider bites/stings, 8
  for rashes, 86

Hydrogen peroxide solutions
    for canker sores, 82
    for cleansing cuts, 23
    for cleansing scrapes, 24
Hyperactivity disorder, 359–362
Hyperextended elbow, 247
Hyperopia, 119
Hyperparathyroidism, and kidney stones, 172
Hypertension. *See* High blood pressure
Hyperthyroidism, 354–356
Hyperventilation, 46–47
Hypothermia, 32, 47–49
Hypothyroidism, 356–358
Hysterectomy, for endometriosis, 289

I
IBS, 143–144
Ibuprofen, 396, 397
    for abdominal pain, 145
    for fever, 218
    for flu, 220
    for growing pains, 374
    for headaches, 103
    and heartburn, 158
    for menstrual pain, 294
    for premenstrual syndrome, 300
    for sinusitis, 133
    for sore throat, 135
Ice bags/packs. *See also* RICE method (Rest, Ice, Compress, Elevate)
    for back pain, 236
    for bruises, 69
    for charley horses, 255
    for cold sore pain, 81
    for dislocation pain, 27
    for epididymitis, 280
    for fractures, 37
    for hand/wrist pain, 272
    for head injuries, 41
    for heel spurs, 251
    for hives, 74
    for insect or spider bites/stings, 8
    for lower leg pain, 263–264
    for marine-life stings, 50
    for plantar fasciitis, 251
    for rectal pain/itching, 164
    for scrapes, 24
    for shoulder pain, 269
    for smashed fingers, 58
    for sore necks, 107
Iliotibial band stretch, 261
Iliotibial band syndrome, 259–260, 261
Immersion, 47
Immobilizing fractures, 37–38
Immunization record, 436–437
Immunizations. *See* Vaccines
Immunotherapy, 204
Imodium, 152
Implants, 310
Impotence, 312
Incontinence. *See* Urinary incontinence
Inducing vomiting, 52
Infalyte®, 168, 169, 369, 385–386

Infants
    and carbon monoxide poisoning, 19
    and cold sores, 80
    colic, 364–365
    cradle cap, 366
    and dehydration, 26
    diaper rash, 381
    diarrhea, 369–370
    doctor visits, 420
    encephalitis in, 100
    fever in, 212, 218
    and flu shots, 221
    hand-foot-and-mouth disease, 374–375
    HBV vaccinations, 324
    and hypothyroidism, 356
    immunizations, 420
    lead poisoning, 377–379
    with meningitis, 105
    preventive care, 420
    prickly heat rash, 381
    rashes, 381–382
    and sexually transmitted diseases, 326–327
    sunburn prevention, 96
Inflammatory rosacea, 89
Influenza, 219–221
Influenza vaccine. *See* Flu shots
Information to keep handy, 390, 435
Ingrown toenails, 75–76, 136
Inguinal hernia, 161–162
Inhaled poisoning
    carbon monoxide poisoning, 19–20
    first aid for, 52
Inhalers, 208, 209, 229
Insect repellents, 9
    DEET, 9, 14, 101
    Skin-So-Soft, 9
    Skintastic, 9
Insects
    allergic shock from, 4
    bites, 7–10, 136
    hives from bites, 74
    repellents. *See* Insect repellents
    stings, 4, 7–10
Insomnia, 346–348
    natural remedies for, 333
Insulin, and diabetes, 351, 352
Insurance coverage of ER care, 3
Intermittent claudication, 262
Internal stress, 336
Internet sites. *See* Web sites
Intrauterine devices. *See* IUDs
Intravenous drug users
    and hepatitis B, C, 166, 323
    and sexually transmitted diseases, 319, 328
Iodine
    for cleansing cuts, 23
    for cleansing scrapes, 24
    radioiodine, 355
    for water purification, 153
Ipecac, 52
Irregular periods, 290
Irritable bowel syndrome, 143–144
    and constipation, 150
    and diarrhea, 150

Ischemic stroke, 198
Isotretinoin
    for acne, 64
    and nosebleeds, 131
    for rosacea, 89
Itch-scratch-itch cycle dermatitis, 85
Itchy, burning eyes, 111–113
IUDs, 309
    and bleeding between periods, 281
    and menstrual pain, 284
    and pelvic inflammatory disease, 299

J
Jellyfish stings, 49–50
Jock itch, 76–77
Joint disease, degenerative, 107
Joint dislocations, 27
Joint mice, 259, 260
Joint pain, 243
Jumper's knee, 259

K
Kaopectate, 152
Kava, 333
    for menopause, 293
Kegel exercises, 176
Ketoprofen, 396, 397
Kidney disease
    and flu shots, 221
    and high blood pressure, 195
Kidneys, 171
    urinary tract infections, 177–179
Kidney stones, 144, 172–174
Knee joint, 258
Knee pads, 259
Knee raise exercise, 239, 240
Knees, 257
    ACL injuries, 258, 260
    housemaid's knee, 259
    iliotibial band syndrome, 259–260, 261
    joint mice, 259, 260
    jumper's knee, 259
    pain in, 257–261
    runner's knee, 259, 260
    sprains, 257, 260
    "terrible triad," 258
    torn cartilage (menisci), 258, 260
Knocked-out tooth, 60
K-Y Jelly, for vaginal dryness, 293

L
Labyrinthitis, 29
Lactose intolerance, 144
Lancing boils, 68
Language therapy, for stroke patients, 199
Large cell carcinoma, 223
Laryngitis, 129–130
Laryngotracheobronchitis, 367
LASIK surgery, 120
Latex, and allergic shock, 4
Laxatives
    for abdominal pain, 145
    for constipation, 150

LDLs, 189
    and heart disease, 186
    levels of, 190
Lead-based paint, 377
Lead poisoning, 377–379
Leg extension exercise, 260
Legg-Calvé-Perthes disease, 256
Legs
    lower leg. *See* Lower leg
    radiating leg pain, 235
LES, 156, 157, 158
Leukotriene, for asthma, 207
Lice, 77–79
Licorice, for menopause, 293
Lifestyle. *See* Healthy lifestyle
Lifting
    heavy. *See* Heavy lifting
    safely, 237, 239
Lightening victims, 34, 35
Lightheadedness, 28
    and hyperventilation, 46
Lip balm
    for cold sores, 81
    with PABA for skin cancer prevention, 93
    with PABA for sunburn prevention, 96
Lipids. *See* Fats
Lipoproteins, 189
Liquid intake. *See* Fluid intake
Lomotil, 152
Long underwear, 49
Lotrimin
    for athlete's foot, 65
    for jock itch, 76
Lotrimin AF, for ringworm, 87
Loud noises, and tinnitus, 138
Low-density lipoproteins. *See* HDLs
Lower back pain, 234–235
Lower esophageal sphincter, 156, 157, 158
Lower leg, 262
    compartment syndrome, 263
    narrowing of the arteries, 262
    pain in, 262–264
    phlebitis, 262
    shin splints, 262, 263, 264
    stress fractures, 263
Lozenges, 216
Lumbar muscle strain, 234
Lung cancer, 222–224
    coughing and, 215
Lungs, 201
Lyme disease, 12, 14–15
Lymph glands
    location of, 137
    swollen, 136–138
Lymphoma, 137

M
Macular degeneration, 119–120
Magnesium, for premenstrual syndrome, 300
Major depression, 334
Malignant melanoma, 93
Mallet finger, 271
Mammograms, 286
Marijuana, 329

Marine-life stings, 49–51
Masking devices, for tinnitus, 139
Massage
  for colicky babies, 365
  for cramped muscles, 244
  for headaches, 103
  heat cramps, 45
  for lower leg pain, 263–264
  for menstrual pain, 295
  for neck pain, 107
  sinuses, for sinusitis, 133
Measles/mumps/rubella vaccine, 419
Medical alert bracelets
  allergies, 5
  bee sting reactions, 10
  seizure victims, 54
  shock victims, 56
Medical fees and bills, 443–444
Medical history
  family, 432, 433
  yours, 432, 434
Medical resources, 390, 435
  Web sites. *See* Web sites
Medical visits. *See* Doctor visits
Medications. *See also specific medication*
  allergies to, 4, 5
  asking about, 391
  for asthma, 207, 208
  and black or bloody stools, 146
  bronchodilator, 214
  and constipation, 150
  and diarrhea, 152–153
  and fatigue, 344
  and hair loss, 71–72
  and heartburn, 158
  and hepatitis, 165, 167
  at home, 390
  and insomnia, 347
  managing, 390–391
  over-the-counter, 394, 395
  pain, 394, 396–397. *See also specific pain medication*
  pharmacies, 391–392
  record keeping, 392–393
  and sexual desire, 315
  for stroke, 199
  taking, 393–394
  telling your doctor and pharmacist about, 391
  and tinnitus, 138
  for tinnitus, 140
  understanding, 393
  and vomiting, 168
Melatonin, 333
Men, 273
  19 to 39 years of age, 421
  40 to 64 years of age, 422
  65 years of age and older, 422
  erection problems, 312–314, 316
  preventive care, 421–423
  prostate problems. *See* Prostate
  screening tests and immunizations, 421, 422, 423
  testicular cancer, 277–279
  testicular pain, 279–280
Meniere's disease, 29
Meningitis, 104–106

Menisci, torn, 258
Menopause, 290–293
  hair loss after, 72
  and missed periods, 296
Menstrual diary, 282
Menstruation
  bleeding between periods, 281–282
  and breast cancer, 283
  irregular periods, 290
  menopause. *See* Menopause
  missed periods, 295–297
  pain during, 294–295
  premenstrual syndrome, 299–301
  and toxic shock syndrome, 302
Mental health concerns, 329–341
Mental illness, and suicide, 339
Mercurochrome
  for cleansing cuts, 23
  for cleansing scrapes, 24
Merthiolate
  for cleansing cuts, 23
  for cleansing scrapes, 23
Metal splinters, 57
Metamucil, 160
Methimazole, for hyperthyroidism, 355
Metronidazole, for rosacea, 89
Micatin
  for jock itch, 76
  for ringworm, 87
Miconazoles, for ringworm, 87
Middle ear infections, 125–127
Migraine headaches, 102
  and vomiting, 168
Milkmaid's knee, 259
Milk of Magnesia, 150
Mind-body medicine, 441
Mini-strokes, 199
Minocycline, for rosacea, 89
Minoxidil, for hair loss, 72
Missed periods, 295–297
Mites
  allergies from dust mites, 202
  scabies, 90–91
MMR vaccine, 419
Mold, 202
Moleskin, 67, 251
Monilia, 303
Monistat
  for ringworm, 87
  for vaginal discharge/irritation, 304
"Mono," 137
Morton's neuroma, 249–250, 251
Mosquito bites, 7
  encephalitis, transmission of, 99
Motrin IB. *See* Ibuprofen
Mousse, for hair volume, 72
Mouth sores, 79–80
  bad breath, 123
  canker sores, 81–82
  cold sores, 80–81
Mouthwash, for canker sores, 82
Mouthwashes, 124
Multiple sclerosis, and overflow incontinence, 175
Muscle cramps, 243–244

Muscle imbalance, 244
Muscle pain, in chest, 182
Muscle relaxers, for back pain, 236
Muscle strengthening, 401. *See also* Exercise
Muscle stretching. *See* Stretching
Muscle tightness, 244
Muscular system, 231
Mycelex
    for ringworm, 87
    for vaginal discharge/irritation, 304
Mycoplasma pneumonia, 225, 226
Mylanta, for canker sores, 82
Myopia, 119

N
Nails
    ingrown toenails, 75–76, 136
    smashed fingers, 58
    torn, first aid for, 58
Naproxen, 396, 397
    and heartburn, 158
Naps, 344, 348
Narcotics Anonymous, 330, 331
Narrowing of the arteries, in lower leg, 262
Nasal irrigation, 133
Nasal sprays
    to prevent airplane ears, 129
    for allergies, 203
    for colds, 211, 212
    for nosebleeds, 132
    Ocean. *See* Ocean
    Salinex. *See* Salinex
    for sinusitis, 133
Naturopathy, 441
Navicular fracture, 270–271
Near-drowning victims, 31–32
Nearsightedness, 119, 120
Nebulizers, 208
Neck injuries
    first aid for, 42, 56, 109
    shock victims, 56
Neck pain, 106–109
Neck sprains, 107
Neck strains, 107
Nedocromil, for asthma, 207
Needed care, 447
Needle contamination. *See also* Intravenous drug users
    and hepatitis B, C, 166
Neosporin, for cold sores, 81
Neo-Synephrine, for sinusitis, 133
Nicotine. *See also* Smoking; Tobacco use
    in cold weather, 41
    and palpitations, 197, 198
    and tinnitus, 139
Nitroglycerin, for angina, 187
Nix, for lice, 77
Nonseminomas, 278
Non-small cell carcinoma, 223
"Normal" body temperature, 217
Norplant implants, 310
Nosebleeds, 131–132
Nosedrops, for colds, 212
Nose sprays. *See* Nasal sprays
Numbness, 109–110

    as stroke symptom, 198
Nuprin. *See* Ibuprofen

O
Oatmeal bath treatment
    for chicken pox, 362
    for hives, 74
    for poison ivy/oak/sumac, 83
    for sunburn, 94
    for vaginal discharge/irritation, 304
Obesity and weight management, 407–413
    and amenorrhea, 296
    and arthritis, 272
    and back pain, 236
    and breast cancer, 283
    and colorectal cancer, 149
    and gastroesophageal reflux disease, 157
    and heartburn, 158, 159
    and heart disease, 187, 188
    and heat-related problems, 46
    and hiatal hernias, 162
    and high blood cholesterol, 191
    and high blood pressure, 195
    and inguinal hernias, 161
    and rectal pain/itching, 163, 164
    and sleep apnea, 350
Objective tinnitus, 139
Obsessive-compulsive disorder, 332
Obstructive sleep apnea, 349, 350
Occupational therapy, for stroke patients, 199
Ocean
    for colds, 212
    for nosebleeds, 132
Office visits. *See* Doctor visits
Older persons. *See* Elderly
Open fractures, 37
Oral contraceptives. *See* Birth control pills
Oral sex
    and female orgasms, 317
    STD prevention during, 327
Orgasm problems, 316–317
Orthostatic hypotension, 28
Orthotics, 248, 272
Orudis, 396, 397
Osteoarthritis, 241–242
Osteopathy, 441
Osteoporosis, 265–266
    and HRT, 292
    and menopause, 291
Ovarian cysts, 144
Ovens, and carbon monoxide poisoning, 19
Overflow incontinence, 175
Over-the-counter medications, 394, 395
Oxygen supplements, 228
Oxymetazoline, for sinusitis, 133

P
Pain medications. *See also specific pain medication*
    choosing, 396–397
    over-the-counter, 394
Palpitations, 197–198
    and hyperventilation, 46
Panic attacks, 332–333

and chest pain, 182
and hyperventilation, 46
Pap smears, 287
ParaGard IUD, 309
Paralysis, and overflow incontinence, 175
Parsley, as breath freshener, 124
Partial press-up exercise, 240
Partial seizures, 54
Patch, 310
Patellar tendinitis, 259
Paxil, and diarrhea, 153
PCV 7 vaccine, 227, 419
Peak-flow meters, 206, 208
Pedialyte, 26, 168, 169, 369, 385–386
Pedometers, 402
Pelvic-floor exercises, 176
Pelvic inflammatory disease, 144, 297–299
Pelvic tilt exercise, 237, 239
Penicillin
    hives from, 73
    for Lyme disease, 15
Penile implants, 313
Pepto-Bismol, 152, 369
Periods. *See* Menstruation
Peripheral neuropathy, 109–110
Periungual warts, 97
Pertussis vaccine, 418
Petit mal seizures, 54
Petroleum jelly
    for eyelid nits, 78
    for nosebleeds, 132
    for scrapes, 24
    for vaginal dryness, 293
Pets
    allergies, 202–203, 204
    and ringworm, 87, 88
Pharmacies, 391–392
    finding a good pharmacy, 446
Phenylephrine, for sinusitis, 133
Phlebitis, in lower leg, 262
Phobias, 332
Physical activity
    exercise. *See* Exercise
    and a healthy lifestyle, 399–403
Physical therapy
    for back pain, 236
    for pinched nerves, 110
    for repetitive motion injuries, 245
    for shoulder pain, 269
    for stroke patients, 199
Pimples, 63–64
Pinched nerves, 109
Pinkeye, 116–117
Pinworms, 164, 379–380
Piriformis stretch, 255
Piriformis syndrome, 254–255
Pitcher's elbow, 246
Pit vipers, 10
    bites from, 11–12
Plantar fasciitis, 248–249, 250–251
Plantar warts, 97, 250, 251
Plaques, 184–185
Pliers method for removing fishhooks, 36
PMS, 299–301

Pneumococcal pneumonia, 215, 419
Pneumonia, 225–227
    and acute bronchitis, 210
    and bad breath, 123
    from chicken pox, 361–362
    from influenza, 219
Poisoning, 51–53
    carbon monoxide, 19–20
    food, 144
    lead, 377–379
Poison ivy, 82–83
    identification of, 83–84
Poison oak, 82–83
    identification of, 84
Poison sumac, 82–83
    identification of, 84
Polio vaccines, 418
Pollen
    allergic shock from, 4
    allergy, 202
    avoidance of, 204
    and burning eyes, 111, 112
Polysomnography test, 350
Pool heaters, and carbon monoxide poisoning, 20
Popsicle rehydration solutions, 386
Popsicles, for sore throats, 135
Portuguese man-of-war stings, 49–50
Post-nasal drip, 215
Postoperative shoes, for foot stress fractures, 249
Post-traumatic stress disorder, 332
Posture
    and back pain, 236
    and headaches, 104
    for healthy spine, 237, 238
    and hypotension, 28
    and neck pain, 106, 108–109
Potassium, and high blood pressure, 196
Powder
    body. *See* Body powder
    foot powder, to prevent blisters, 67
    talcum powder, for rectal pain/itching, 163
PPV23 vaccine, 215, 419
Pregnancy
    and chicken pox, 363
    and diabetes, 352–353
    ectopic, 144
    and flu shots, 221
    and foodborne illness susceptibility, 154
    and gastroesophageal reflux disease, 157
    headaches in, 101
    and hemorrhoids, 160
    and hiatal hernias, 162
    home pregnancy tests, 296
    and inguinal hernias, 161
    and missed periods, 295, 296
    and rectal pain/itching, 163, 164
    sexually transmitted diseases during, 326–327
    and urinary tract infections, 178
    and vomiting, 168
Premature ejaculation, 316, 317
Premenstrual syndrome, 299–301
Preparation H, 160
Prepatellar bursitis, 259
Prerosacea, 89

Presbyopia, 119
Preventive care, 417
  birth to 23 months, 420
  2 to 6 years of age, 420
  7 to 11 years of age, 420
  12 to 18 years of age, 420–421
  19 to 39 years of age, 421–422
  40 to 64 years of age, 422
  65 years of age and older, 422–423
  record of, 436–437
  immunizations. *See* Vaccines
Prevnar, 227
Prickly heat rash, 381
Primary encephalitis, 99
Primary generalized seizures, 54
Progesterone injections, 310
Propylthiouracil, for hyperthyroidism, 355
Prostate, 273
  cancer, 274, 275–276, 277
  enlarged, 177, 274, 275
  problems with, 273–277
  prostatitis, 273, 274, 275
Prostate-specific antigen test, 274–275
Prozac, and diarrhea, 153
PSA test, 274–275
Pseudoephedrine, for sinusitis, 133
Pulmonary disease, chronic obstructive, 213–215
Pulmonary embolism, 182
"Pursed-lip" breathing, 215
Pustules, 63–64
Pyelonephritis, 177

Q
Quality health care, finding, 445–448

R
Rabies, 6
Radiating leg pain, 235
Radiation, and hair loss, 71
Radiation therapy
  for lung cancer, 224
  for prostate cancer, 275–276
  for skin cancer, 93
  for testicular cancer, 279
Radioiodine, 355
Radon gas, and lung cancer, 222, 224
Range-of-motion ankle exercise, 233
Rashes, 85–86
  in chicken pox, 361
  in children, 381–382
  in fifth disease, 373
  in hand-foot-and-mouth disease, 375
  poison ivy/oak/sumac, 82–84
Rattlesnakes, 10
Reading in bed, 348
Records
  family medical history, 432, 433
  medical resources, 390, 435
  of medications, 392–393
  preventive examination and immunization record, 436–437
  your medical history, 432, 434

Rectal bleeding, 160
Rectal fissures, 163
Rectal itching, 163–164
Rectal pain, 163–164
Rectal temperature, 371–372
Recurring seizures, 53, 55
Red clover, for menopause, 293
Red ring, 12, 13, 14
Referred pain, 244
  backaches, 234
  shoulder(s), 268
Rehabilitation programs, 330
Rehydrating after vomiting, 168–169
  children, 385–386
Rehydration solutions
  homemade, 386
  Infalyte®, 168, 169, 369, 385–386
  Pedialyte, 26, 168, 169, 369, 385–386
Relaxation techniques
  for dizziness, 30
  for fatigue, 344
  for missed periods, 296
  for tension-type headaches, 102
Repetitive motion injuries, 244–245
  carpal tunnel syndrome, 271–272
Replens, for vaginal dryness, 293
Reproductive system, and abdominal pain, 144
Resorcinol, for acne, 64
Rest
  RICE method. *See* RICE method (Rest, Ice, Compress, Elevate)
  sleep or. *See* Sleep or rest
Retin-A, 64
Reye's syndrome, 103, 135, 363
Rheumatic pain, 243
Rheumatoid arthritis, 241–242
Rhinophyma rosacea, 89
Rhythm method, 308
RICE method (Rest, Ice, Compress, Elevate), 267
  for ankle sprains/strains, 232, 233
  for charley horses, 254, 255
  for elbow pain, 247
  for groin pulls, 255
  for hamstring pulls, 255
  for hip and thigh bursitis, 255
  for knee injuries, 260
  for lower leg pain, 263
  for shoulder pain, 269
Rid, for lice, 77
Ringing in the ears, 138–140
Ringworm, 87–88
Rocky Mountain spotted fever, 12
Rogaine, for hair loss, 72
Rosacea, 88–90
Roseola, 381
Rotator cuff injury, 269
Runner's knee, 259, 260

S
Safety goggles, use of, 115, 121
St. John's wort, 333
  for menopause, 293

Salicylic acid, for acne, 64
Salinex
  for colds, 212
  for nosebleeds, 132
Salt
  in diet, 406
  and high blood pressure, 196
  and tinnitus, 139
Sarsaparilla, for menopause, 293
Saturated fat, 406
Scabies, 90–91
Schoolwork, and ADHD, 360
Sciatica, 235
Scrapes, 22, 23–25
Screening tests
  adults 19 to 39 years of age, 421
  adults 40 to 64 years of age, 422
  adults 65 years of age and older, 423
Seborrheic dermatitis, 85
Sebum, 63
Secondary encephalitis, 100
Secondary hypothyroidism, 356–357
Second-degree burns, 15–16
Secondhand smoke, and lung cancer, 222
"Second opinions" about surgery, 429–430
Sedatives, for restlessness in encephalitis, 100
Seizures, 53–55
  in children with high fever, 372
Self-image
  and acne, 63
  negative, 334
  and stress, 336
Self-tanning creams, 96
Seminomas, 278
Severe burns, 16–17
Sexual concerns
  among elderly, 316
  ejaculation problems, 316
  orgasm problems, 316–317
  painful sexual intercourse, 316
Sexual desire, loss of, 314–315
Sexual intercourse
  painful, 316
  and pelvic inflammatory disease, 298, 299
  STDs. *See* Sexually transmitted diseases
  and urinary tract infections, 179
  and vaginal discharge/irritation, 304
Sexually transmitted diseases, 319–320
  AIDS. *See* AIDS
  and birth control methods, 307
  chlamydia. *See* Chlamydia
  genital herpes. *See* Genital herpes
  genital warts, 97, 321–322
  gonorrhea. *See* Gonorrhea
  hepatitis, 166
  hepatitis B virus, 166, 323–324
  HIV. *See* HIV
  and pelvic inflammatory disease, 297, 299
  pregnancy risks, 326–327
  syphilis. *See* Syphilis
  transmission of, 320
  trichomoniasis. *See* Trichomoniasis
  and vaginal discharge and irritation, 304

Shampoos
  antidandruff, 70–71
  antilice, 78
Shingles, 361
  blisters from, 66
Shin splints, 262, 263, 264
Shock, 55–56
  allergic, 4–5
  electrical, 34–35
  from hives, 73
  toxic shock syndrome, 302–303
Shoes, and foot pain prevention, 252
Shoulder(s), 268
  bursitis, 268
  pain in, 268–269
  referred pain, 268
  rotator cuff injury, 269
  tendinitis, 268
  trauma to, 268
Sildenafil, for erection problems, 313
Sinex, 133
Sinus infections, and bad breath, 123
Sinusitis, 132–134
Sitz bath
  for hemorrhoids, 160
  for rectal pain/itching, 164
Skeletal system, 231
Skier's thumb, 271
Skin, 63
Skin cancer, 92–94
Skin self-exam, 94
Skin-So-Soft, 9
Skintastic, 9
Sleep apnea, 349–350
Sleeping pills, 347, 350
Sleep or rest. *See also* Fatigue
  for acute bronchitis, 210
  for breath, shortness of, 228
  for chest pain, 182
  for chronic fatigue syndrome, 345
  and colds, 212, 213
  for croup, 368
  for elbow pain, 247
  for epididymitis, 280
  for erection problems, 314
  for fatigue, 344
  for flu, 220
  and gastroesophageal reflux disease, 157
  and headaches, 103, 104
  and heartburn, 159
  for hepatitis, 167
  and hiatal hernias, 163
  insomnia, 333, 346–348
  and menopause, 291
  for menstrual pain, 295
  and neck pain, 106, 108–109
  for pelvic inflammatory disease, 298
  and pneumonia, 227
  and premenstrual syndrome, 301
  problems, 343–350
  for sinusitis, 133
  for sore throats, 135
  for tonsillitis, 382

Slipped capital femoral epiphysis, 256
Slivers, 57
Small cell carcinoma, 223
Smashed fingers or toes, 58–59
Smoke
    and asthma, 206
    and bronchitis, 209
    and burning eyes, 111, 112
    and carbon monoxide poisoning, 19
    coughing and, 217
    and croup, 368
    and sinusitis, 132
Smoking
    and allergies, 204
    and angina, 187
    and asthma, 206, 208
    and bad breath, 123, 124
    and chronic fatigue syndrome, 345
    and chronic obstructive pulmonary disease, 213, 214
    coughing and, 215, 217
    and croup, 368
    and erection problems, 314
    and fatigue, 344
    and gastroesophageal reflux disease, 157
    and heartburn, 158, 159
    and heart disease, 186, 188
    and high blood pressure, 195, 196
    and insomnia, 347
    and laryngitis, 129, 130
    and lung cancer, 222, 224
    and macular degeneration, 121
    and mouth sores, 80
    and narrowing of the arteries, in lower leg, 262
    and osteoporosis, 266
    and palpitations, 198
    and pneumonia, 227
    quitting, 413–415
    and sinusitis, 134
    and strokes, 199
    and tonsillitis, 384
    and ulcers, 144
Snakebite kits, 11
Snakes
    bites from, 10, 11–12
    poisonous snake identification, 10
Social phobia, 332
Sodium. *See* Salt
Sores
    canker, 81–82
    cold, 80–81
    mouth, 79–80
Sore throats, 134–136
    and laryngitis, 129
Soy, for menopause, 293
Space heaters, and carbon monoxide poisoning, 20
Spasmodic croup, 367
Speech therapy, for stroke patients, 199
Spermicides, 308
Spider bites, 7–10
Spinal injuries
    from diving accidents, 32
    shock victims, first aid for, 56
Spinal meningitis, 104–106
Spinal tap, for diagnosis of meningitis, 105

Spine, 235
Splinters, 57
Splinting, 38
Splints
    for mallet finger, 271
    for pinched nerves, 110
    for smashed fingers, 58
    wrist, 272
Sponge baths, for fever, 372
Spotting between periods, 281
Spousal abuse. *See* Family violence
Sprains, 231, 257, 260
    ankle, 231–232
    neck, 107
Squamous cell carcinoma, 92, 223
Staphylococcus aureus, 302
Statins, for heart disease, 187
STDs. *See* Sexually transmitted diseases
Steam vaporizers, 216, 367
Stents, 187
Sterilization, surgical, 311
Steroid injections
    for bunions, 250
    for heel spurs, 249
Stings
    insect, 4, 7–10
    marine-life, 49–51
    spider, 7–10
Stitches, need for, 22–23
Stomach flu, 219
Stools
    black or bloody, 146–147
    constipation, 150–151
    diarrhea. *See* Diarrhea
    and hepatitis A, 165
Stool softeners, 151
Strains, 231
    ankle, 231–232
    neck, 107
Strangulated hernias, 161
Strengthening muscles, 401. *See also* Exercise
Strep throat, 134, 135
Streptococcus pneumoniae, 225
    vaccine for, 227, 419
Stress, 336–338
    and angina, 187
    and asthma, 206
    and back pain, 234
    and constipation, 150
    and diarrhea, 152
    and erection problems, 313
    and headaches, 101, 103
    and heart disease, 187
    holiday, 338
    management of. *See* Stress management
    and missed periods, 296
    natural remedies for, 333
    and neck pain, 107
    and palpitations, 197
    and tinnitus, 139
Stress fractures
    feet, 249, 251
    lower leg, 263
Stress incontinence, 174–175

Stress management, 337–338
    for arthritis, 272
    for back pain, 236
    for erection problems, 314
    for fibromyalgia, 243
    for headaches, 104
    for irritable bowl syndrome, 144
    and palpitations, 198
    for premenstrual syndrome, 301
    for tinnitus, 140
Stretching, 401
    Achilles tendon stretch, 263, 264
    for charley horses, 254
    cramped muscles, 244
    for elbow pain, 247
    iliotibial band stretch, 261
    for knee sprains, 260
    for neck pain, 108
    piriformis stretch, 255
    tight muscles, 244
    at the workplace, 402
Stroke, 59–60, 198–199
    and atherosclerosis, 183
    and dizziness, 30, 199
    and overflow incontinence, 175
    and urge incontinence, 175
    vision changes signaling, 121, 198
Styes, 118
Sudafed
    to prevent airplane ears, 129
    and insomnia, 347
    for sinusitis, 133
Suicide, 339–340
Sulfa antibiotics, hives from, 73
Sulfur, for acne, 64
Sunburn, 94–97
Sunglasses
    for pinkeye, 116
    use of, 121
Sunlamps, 93, 95
Sunscreen, 95–96
    to prevent rosacea, 89
    to prevent skin cancer, 93
Supplements
    dietary, 406, 440–441
    oxygen, 228
Suppositories
    for rectal pain/itching, 164
    vaginal, 304
Surgery. *See also* Biopsy
    for back pain, 236
    for bunions, 250
    for compartment syndrome, 263
    deciding about, 428–431
    elective, 429
    for endometriosis, 289
    for enlarged prostate, 275
    for erection problems, 313
    for ganglions in hand and wrist, 271
    for heel spurs, 249
    for hyperthyroidism, 355
    for knee injury, 258
    for Legg-Calvé-Perthes disease, 256
    for lung cancer, 223–224

nonelective, 429
    options, 429
    for pelvic inflammatory disease, 298
    for prostate cancer, 275
    for prostatitis, 275
    questions to ask before, 430–431
    "second opinions" about, 429–430
    for skin cancer, 93
    for slipped capital femoral epiphysis, 256
    for stress incontinence, 175
    for testicular cancer, 278–279
    for testicular torsion, 280
    for tonsillitis, 383
Surgilube, for vaginal dryness, 293
Sutures, need for, 22–23
Sweating
    dehydration from, 24
    and hyperventilation, 46
Swimmer's ear, 127–128
Swollen glands, 136–138
Synovitis, 256
Syphilis, 325–326
    during pregnancy, 326, 327

T
"Tailor's bunion," 250
Talcum powder
    for rashes, 381
    for rectal pain/itching, 163
Tampons
    and toxic shock syndrome, 302, 303
    and vaginal discharge/irritation, 305
Tanning beds, 93, 95
Tecnu, for poison ivy/oak/sumac, 83
Teeth, knocked-out or broken, 60
Temperature, 217. *See also* Fever
    child's oral temperature, 371
    child's rectal temperature, 371–372
Tempra. *See* Acetaminophen
Tendinitis
    Achilles tendonitis, 232
    elbow, 246
    fingers, 271
    hand and wrist, 271
    knee, 259, 260
    patellar, 259
    shoulder(s), 268
Tennis elbow, 246
    and pinched nerves, 109
Tennis elbow straps, 272
Tension-type headaches, 101–102
Teratoma, 278
"Terrible triad," 258
Testicles, 277
Testicular cancer, 277–279
Testicular pain, 279–280
Testicular self-examination, 278
Testicular torsion, 279–280
Tetanus, 6
Tetanus boosters, 6
    for frostbite, 40
Tetanus vaccines, 418
Tetracycline
    for Lyme disease, 15

Tetracycline—cont'd
  for rosacea, 89
Theophylline, for asthma, 207
Thigh. *See* Hip and thigh
Thinning of hair, 71
Third-degree burns, 16
Thorn splinters, 57
Thumb, skier's, 271
Thunderstorm protection, 35
Thyroid gland
  hyperthyroidism, 354–356
  hypothyroidism, 356–358
Thyroid hormone, excess of, 358
Thyroxine, 357
TIAs, 199
Tick bites, 7, 12–15
Tick removal, 13
"Timed voiding," for urge incontinence, 175
Tinactin
  for athlete's foot, 65
  for ringworm, 87
Tingling, 109–110
Tinnitus, 138–140
Tobacco use
  and heart disease, 186, 187
  and high blood cholesterol, 190
  and sleep apnea, 350
  smoking. *See* Smoking
Toes
  athlete's foot, 65
  corns on, 69–70
  hammertoe, 250
  ingrown toenails, 75–76, 136
  smashed, 58–59
Toilet training, and constipation, 150
Tolnaftates
  for athlete's foot, 65
  for ringworm, 87
Tonsillitis, 382–384
  and bad breath, 123
Tooth, knocked-out or broken, 60
Torn cartilage (menisci), 258, 260
Toupees, 72
Toxic shock syndrome, 302–303
Tranquilizers, and hepatitis, 167
Transient ischemic attacks, 199
Travelers' diarrhea, 153
Tretinoin, for acne, 64
Trichomoniasis, 304, 326
  during pregnancy, 326
Triglycerides, 189
  and heart disease, 186, 188
TSS, 302–303
Tubal ligation, 311
Tuberculosis, and lung cancer, 222
Tucks pads, 160
Twisting an ankle, 231–232
Tylenol. *See* Acetaminophen
Type 1 diabetes, 352
Type 2 diabetes, 352

U
Ulcerative colitis, 152
  and black or bloody stools, 146

Ulcers, 144
  and chest pain, 182
  and heartburn, 158
Ultrasound, for pelvic inflammatory disease, 298
Unconsciousness, from seizures, 53, 54
Ureters, 171
Urethra, 171
Urge incontinence, 175
Urgent care
  CPR. *See* CPR
  emergency room. *See* Emergency room care
  first aid. *See* First aid
Urgent care centers, use of, 3
Uric acid build-up, 232–233
Urinary incontinence, 174–177
  and menopause, 290–291
Urinary tract, 171–172
Urinary tract infections, 144, 177–179
  and enlarged prostate, 177, 274
  and kidney stones, 172
  and urge incontinence, 175
Urine output, dehydration from, 24
Urine specimens, providing, 178
Urushiol, 82
Uterine fibroids, 144
UV radiation
  eye burns, 111, 113
  and skin cancer, 92, 94
  and sunburn, 94
  sunglasses, use of, 121

V
Vaccines, 417, 418–419
  birth to 23 months, 420
  2 to 6 years of age, 420
  12 to 18 years of age, 420
  19 to 39 years of age, 421
  40 to 64 years of age, 422
  65 years of age and older, 423
  diphtheria/tetanus/pertussis, 418
  haemophilus influenza type B, 419
  hepatitis B, 166, 323, 324, 419
  influenza. *See* Flu shots
  Lyme disease, 15
  measles/mumps/rubella, 419
  meningitis, 106
  pneumococcal pneumonia, 215, 419
  pneumonia, 227
  polio, 418
  record of, 436–437
  varicella, 364, 419
Vacuum devices, for erection problems, 313
Vaginal contraceptive ring, 310–311
Vaginal creams or suppositories, 304
Vaginal discharge and irritation, 303–305
Vaginal dryness, 290
  lubricants for, 293
  and painful sexual intercourse, 316
Vaginismus, 316
Vaporizers, 216
Varicella. *See* Chicken pox
Vascular rosacea, 89
Vasectomy, 311
Vaseline. *See* Petroleum jelly

Venom desensitization, for bee stings, 10
Vertigo, 28–29
    benign positional, 29
Viagra, 313
Vinegar and water, for marine-life stings, 50
Violent behavior, 340–341. *See also* Family violence
Viral hepatitis, 165–167
Viral meningitis, 104, 105
Viral pinkeye, 116
Viral pneumonia, 225, 226
Viral sore throat, 134, 135
Vision problems, 119–121
Visits to the doctor. *See* Doctor visits
Vitamin B6, for premenstrual syndrome, 300
Vitamin D
    and kidney stones, 172
    and osteoporosis, 266
Vitex, for menopause, 293
Vocal chord problems, 129–130
    croup, 367–368
Vomiting, 168–170
    in children, 384–386
    dehydration from, 24
    and hand-foot-and-mouth disease, 375
    inducing, 52

W
Waist circumference, 408
Walking for fitness, 400–401
    pedometers, 402
Warm compresses
    for abdominal pain, 145
    for boils, 68
    for headaches, 103
    for neck pain, 107
    for pinkeye, 116
    for sinusitis, 133
    for styes, 118
    for swimmer's ear, 128
Warmth. *See* Heat or warmth
Warts
    common, 97–98
    genital, 97, 321–322
    plantar, 97, 250, 251
Wasp stings, 7
Water moccasins, 10
Web sites
    complementary and alternative medicine, 442
    finding quality health information on, 438
Weight management. *See* Obesity and weight management
Wet gauze, for scrapes, 24
Wheezing, 229
Whispering, 130
Whiteheads, 63

"White noise," 348
Wigs, 72
Wild-animal bites, 6
Withdrawal method, 308
Women, 281
    19 to 39 years of age, 421
    40 to 64 years of age, 422
    65 years of age and older, 422
    and abdominal pain, 144
    bleeding between periods, 281–282
    breast cancer, 283–286
    cervical cancer, 287
    and depression, 334
    endometriosis, 288–289
    and hair loss, 71–72
    and headaches, 104
    and hypothyroidism, 356
    menopause. *See* Menopause
    menstrual pain, 294–295
    missed periods, 295–297
    orgasm problems, 316–317
    and osteoporosis, 265
    painful sexual intercourse, 316
    pelvic inflammatory disease, 144, 297–299
    pregnancy. *See* Pregnancy
    premenstrual syndrome, 299–301
    preventive care, 421–423
    screening tests and immunizations, 421, 422, 423
    and sexually transmitted diseases, 319
    and stress incontinence, 174–175
    toxic shock syndrome, 302–303
    and urinary tract infections, 177
    vaginal discharge and irritation, 303–305
    yeast infections, 303–304
Wooden shoes, for foot stress fractures, 249
Wood splinters, 57
Wood tick, 13
Workplace
    ergonomics, and neck pain, 106, 109
    exercise at, 402
Wrist. *See* Hand and wrist
Wrist splints, 272

Y
Yam extract, for menopause, 293
Yeast infections, 303–304
Yellow jacket stings, 7
Yolk sac tumors, 278

Z
Zinc gluconate, for colds, 211
Zinc oxide ointment
    for cold sores, 81
    for rectal pain/itching, 163
Zoloft, and diarrhea, 153